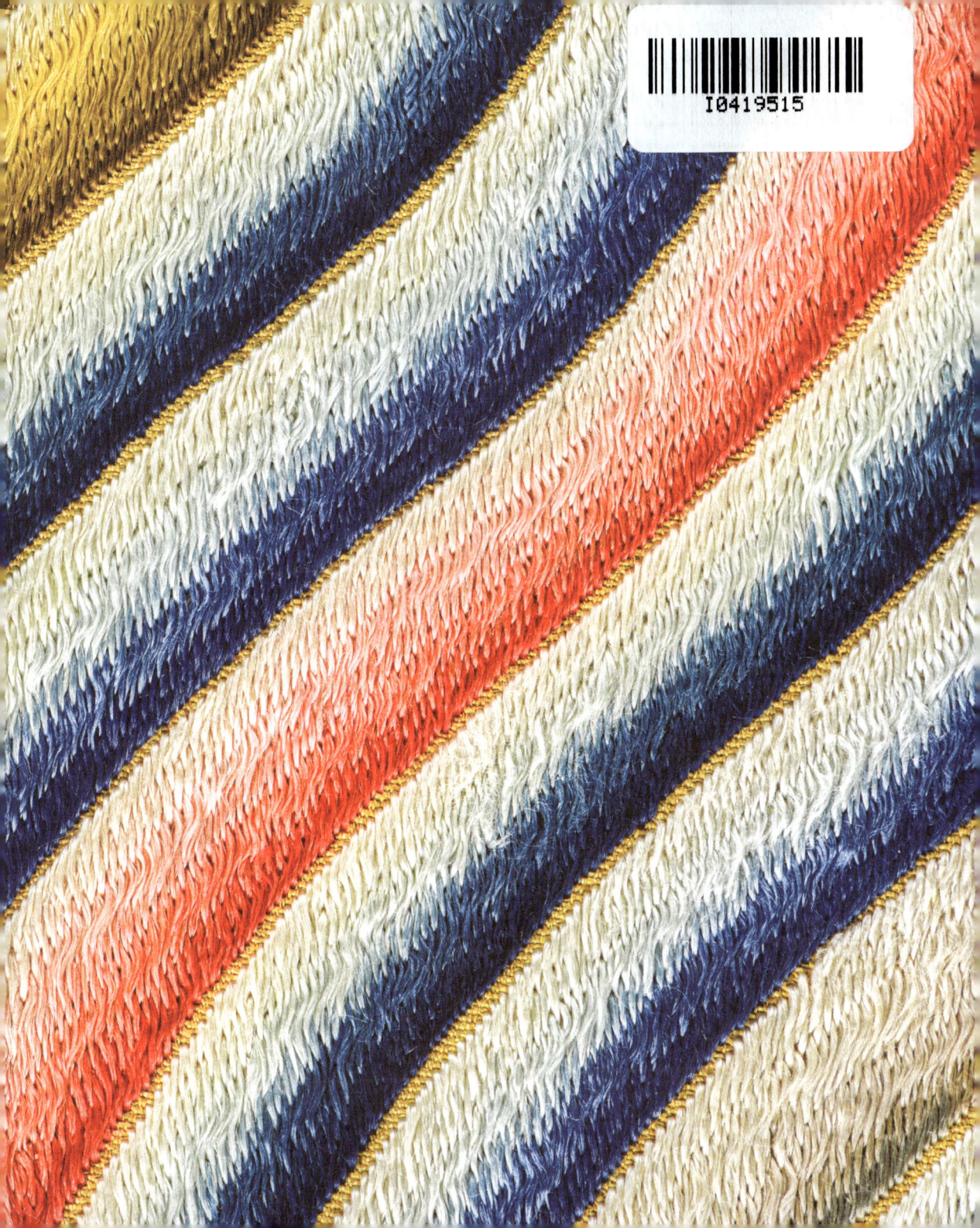

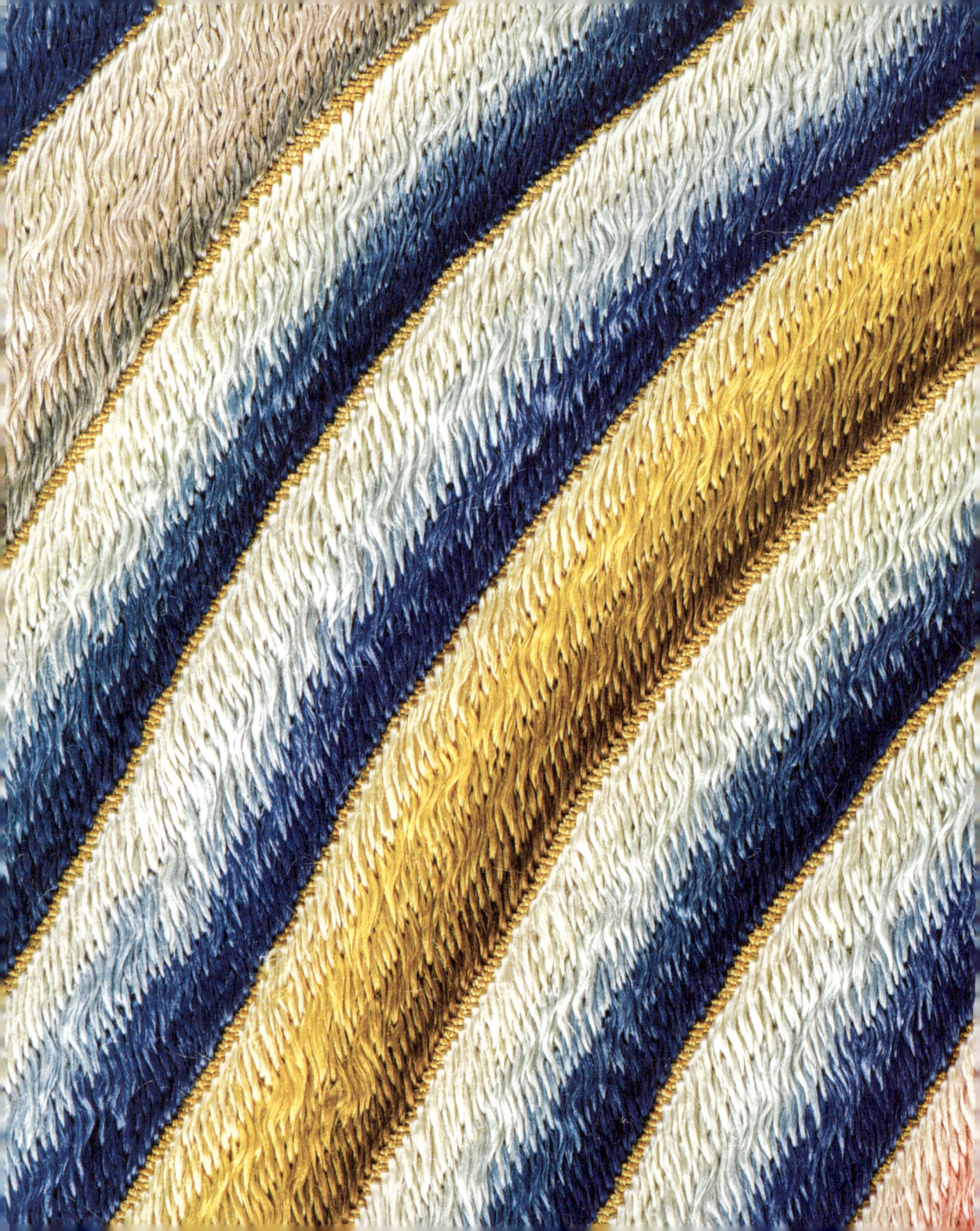

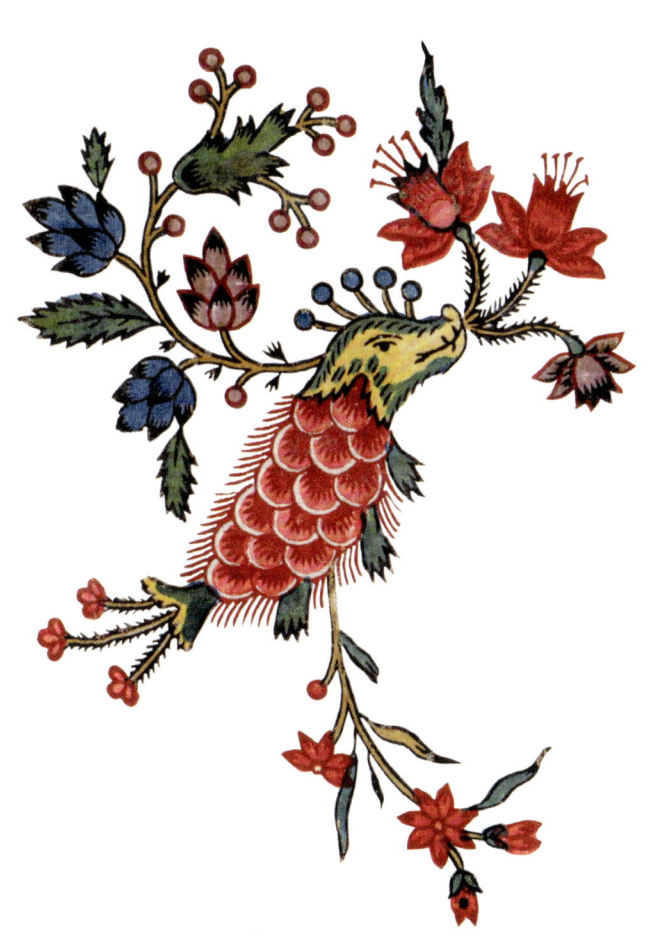

STEPHEN ELLCOCK

Stephen Ellcock is a London-based author, curator, researcher and online collector of images who has spent the last decade creating an ever-expanding virtual museum of art that is open to all via social media. His ongoing attempt at creating the ultimate social media 'Cabinet of Curiosities' has so far attracted more than 650,000 followers worldwide and increasing media attention, not all of which is unwelcome. He is the author of *The Cosmic Dance, Underworlds, Elements, All Good Things, England on Fire* (with text by Mat Osman), *The Book of Change, Jeux de Mains* (a collaboration with Cécile Poimboeuf-Koizumi), and the co-author of *Time for Magic* with Jamie Reid, John Marchant and Philip Carr-Gomm. Stephen has been variously described as 'the most inspiring dandy of the new, weightless world' and 'the soul of the internet'.

KARUN THAKAR

Karun Thakar has been collecting textiles and other objects for over four decades. He is drawn to forms of making and designs that speak of human creativity, skill and artistry across cultures and time. Of the tens of thousands of global textiles in his collection, many hint at hidden layers of meaning and unheard stories: of identity and belonging, trade, colonialism, migration, exchange and the wider human experience.

Karun is passionate about democratising art and bringing forward lesser-known narratives. These aims are reflected in the ways he works to share his collection with a wider audience. To date, he has organised five exhibitions at venues within educational institutions and six books present understudied objects in an accessible but academically robust manner. Textile research is notoriously under-resourced. In 2020, the Karun Thakar Fund was set up in collaboration with the Victoria and Albert Museum to address this imbalance, awarding substantial grants for the study of African and Asian textiles and dress.

Stephen Ellcock's

Book of Textiles

The Karun Thakar Collection

An inspiring journey through
the enigmatic world of pattern
and cloth

ACC ART BOOKS   **Hali**

Contents

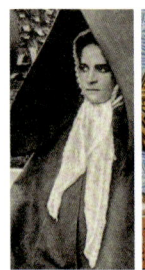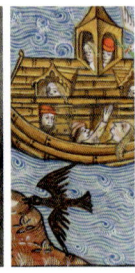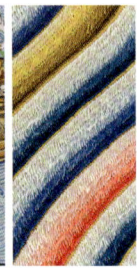

Introduction

**by Stephen Ellcock and
Karun Thakar**   **6**

A shared experience of collecting images
and objects, and the genesis of the *Book of
Textiles* and the Karun Thakar Collection

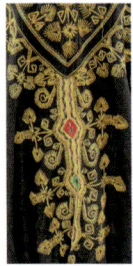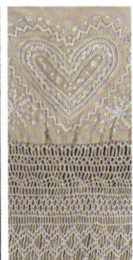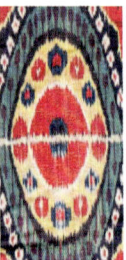

Costume

Chapter 3   **118**

Identity; Community; Status; Minority;
Society; Class; Court; Robes of honour;
Wealth; Hats

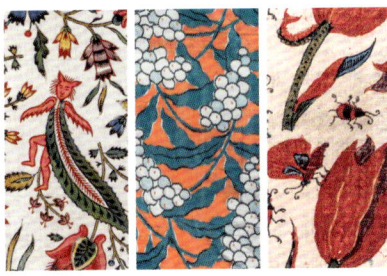

The Natural World

Chapter 1   **22**

Plants; Flowers; Gardens; Trees, Fruits;
Bushes; Superabundance; Animals;
Insects; Birds

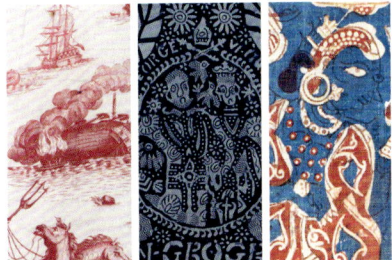

The Human Realm

Chapter 2   **70**

Human activity; Rites of passage; Birth;
Romance; Marriage; Death; Mortality;
Colonialism; War; Celebrations; Leisure;
Education; Storytelling; Expressions of life;
Deceit; Everyday objects; Covers; Bags;
Recycling

Belief, Myth & Magic

Chapter 4   **158**

Faith; Celebrations; Prayer; Enlightenment;
Protection; Pilgrimage; Ceremonial;
Devotion

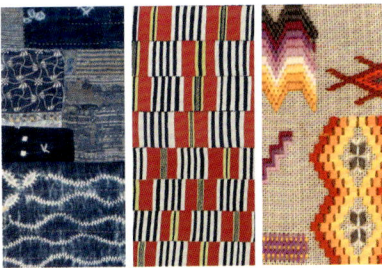

Patterns of Life

Chapter 5   **196**

Form; Function; Structure; Geometry; Colour;
Maximalism; Grid; Monochrome; Polychrome;
Composition; Meaning; Mark making;
Modernism; Colour field; Circles; Abstract

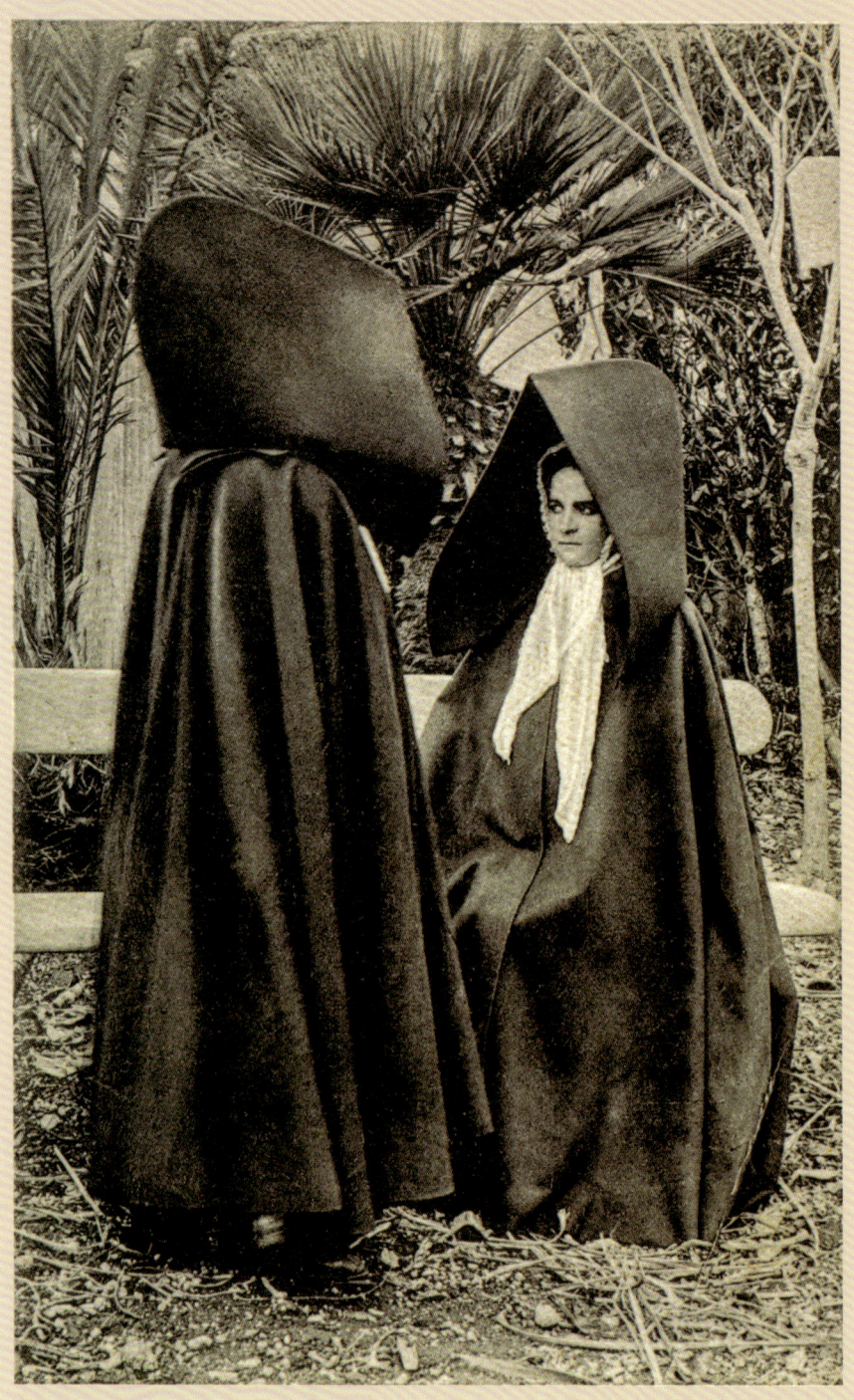

Gathering threads

Stephen Ellcock

I was born into a monochrome world, a black and white domain of achromatic palettes; of brown and anaemic, ash-grey staple foodstuffs; of off-white walls the colour of spoiled milk or tinned rice pudding; of washed-out flock and discoloured anaglypta; of furniture that came in various shades of sepia and burnt umber; of lustreless linoleum floors polished and worn to the point of obsolescence; of exhausted, once proud shag pile carpets that had long since lost the will to live; of olive-tinted heavy curtains that blocked out the light, stifled cheer and blighted the ambience of any room as effectively as the blast door of a nuclear bunker; in short, a world of apparent sensory deprivation.

The tectonic plates of social change were shifting unnoticed beneath our sensibly shod feet, and the first stirrings of the new-born counterculture, the technicolour sixties, and imminent sexual revolution may have been happening a mere thirty to forty miles away in newly 'swinging' London, the epicentre of this earth-shattering youthquake, but it may as well have been happening on the moons of Alpha Centauri for all the impact it had on our insular world of boiled sweets, tinned fruit and endless Sunday afternoons.

It would take another two or three years before the shockwaves of this revolution would hit the socially immobile backwaters of the rural home counties, but the environment we inhabited was not entirely monotonous, drab or starved of colour, flair, visual stimuli, and delight.

For example, both of my grandfathers created and maintained lovingly tended, immaculate flower, vegetable and fruit gardens and allotments, which were places of wonder, adventure, fantasy and great happiness. They were both, in certain ways, true horticultural artists, their achievements a combination of practical skills and carefully calibrated aesthetic judgement. To be a successful gardener requires a finely tuned awareness of colour, form, perspective, together with an aptitude for pattern making, combined with hard-won knowledge and practical nous.

Both of my grandmothers were similarly gifted and blessed with expertise and vision, but they found their creative outlet in textiles; in sewing, embroidery, knitting and crochet.

These arts demanded similar skills to those required of an accomplished gardener, but they also required additional skills – dexterity, playfulness, attentiveness to the smallest detail, an innate appreciation and understanding of the qualities and potential of different materials etc.

Between them my grandmothers created and crafted a remarkably diverse array of clothing, soft furnishings and household decorations – cushion covers, antimacassars, geometrically complex doilies, crocheted table- and placemats resembling an Arachne's web of latticework, and exquisite and delicately worked tablecloths, napkins and samplers ; whilst the hand-knitted Fair Isle jumpers, cardigans, cable-knit sweaters, baby clothes, bonnets,

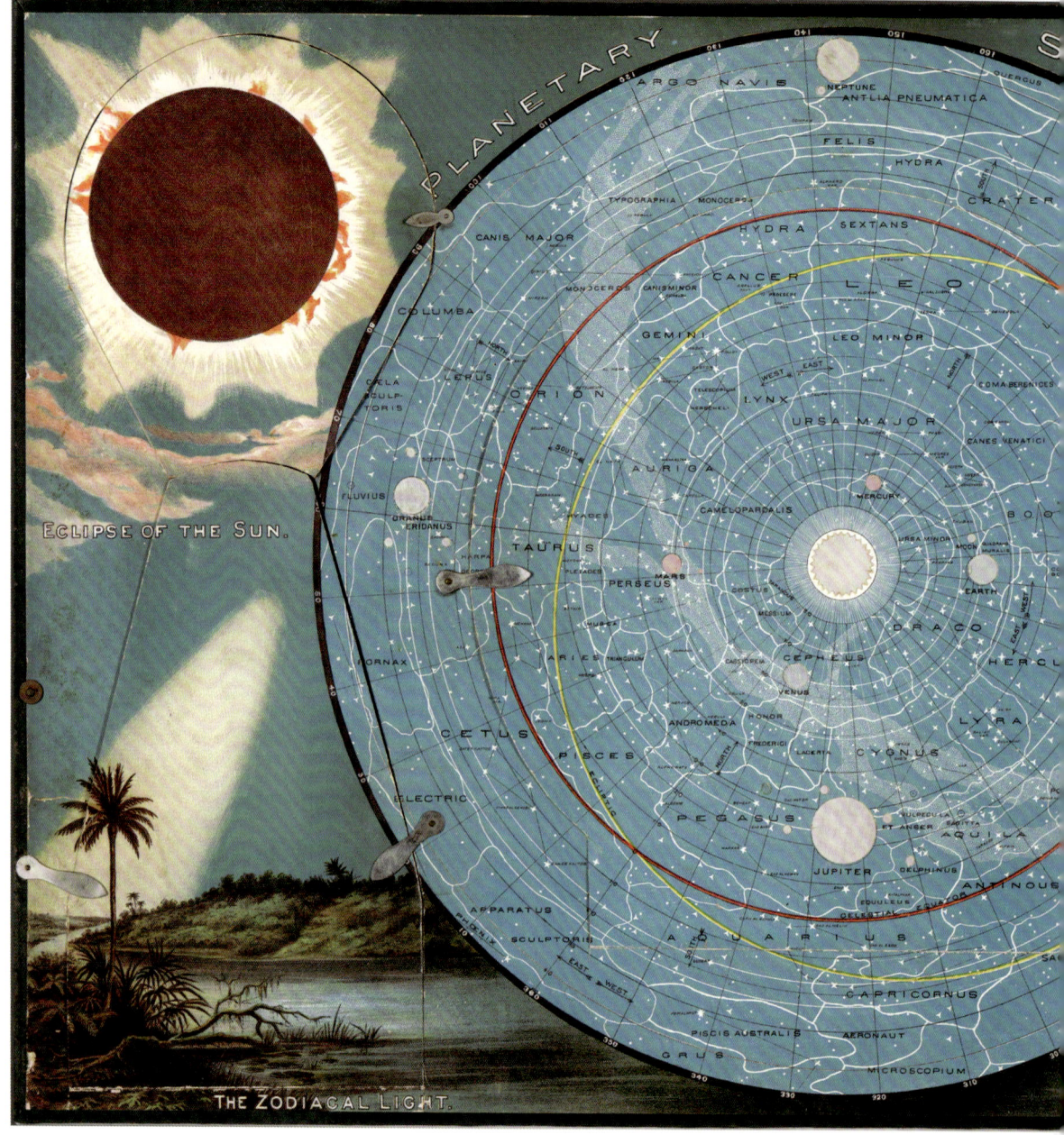

↑ **Map**

Planetary System. Eclipse of the Sun. The Moon. The Zodiacal Light. Meteoric Shower, Levi Walter Yaggy, Geographical Study Comprising Physical, Political, Geological, and Astronomical Geography, Western Publishing House, Chicago, circa 1887. David Rumsey Map Collection, David Rumsey Map Center, Stanford Libraries

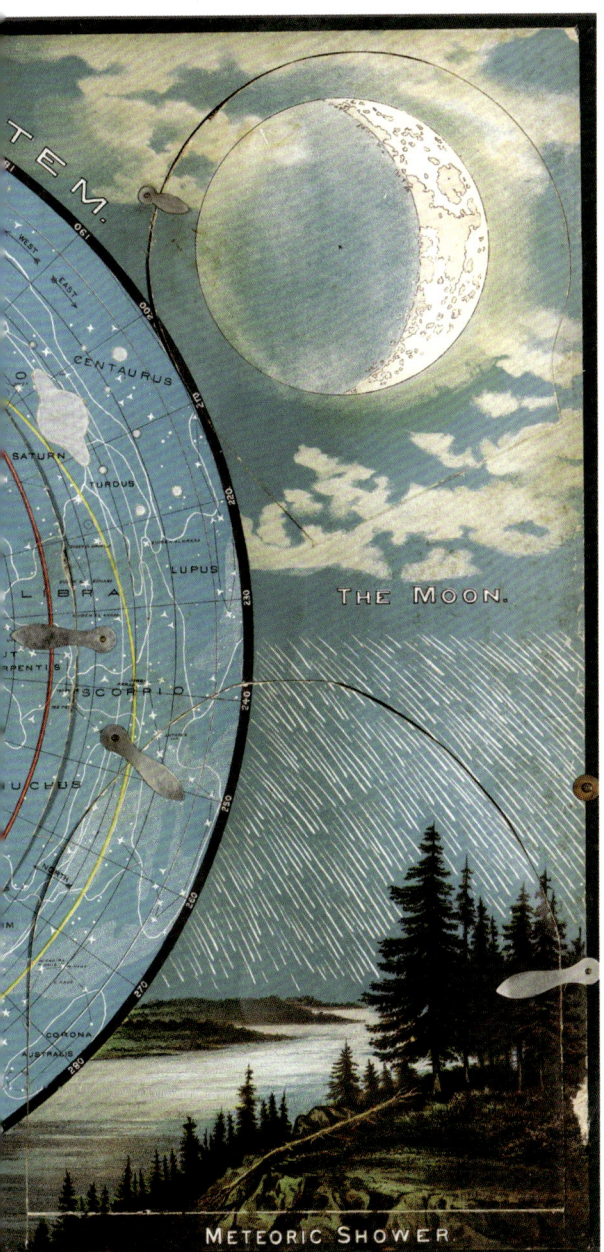

⋀⋀ **Postcard**
'Capote, Costume Popular, Fayal,
Azores'. Traditional clothing worn
until the 1930s

hats, gloves and mittens created by my paternal
grandmother were the equal of anything produced
by Westwood, Chloé or Ralph Lauren, and I have the
photographic evidence to prove it.

These creations were among the saving graces of
my early childhood, an introduction to abstraction and
creative thinking, to the possibility and importance of
beauty in the most unpromising circumstances, and
to ways of responding imaginatively to the socially
immobile world in which we found ourselves.

My grandparents' creativity sparked my infant
imagination in several different ways. I was obsessed
not only with the somewhat forbidding and
dangerous-looking contents of my grandfathers'
sheds but also with the enigmatic exoskeletal form
of my grandmothers' antique hand-cranked sewing
machines, which exuded far more mystery, allure
and fascination than any toy car, chemistry set
or rollerskate could possibly offer. These sewing
machines were, perhaps, the first sculptural objects
to trigger a genuine visceral, aesthetic response in me,
predating James Bond's Aston Martin (with its ejector
seat), the Daleks and the Batmobile by several years.

Gardening and textiles were my grandparents'
'visual culture', a source of fulfilment and enjoyment

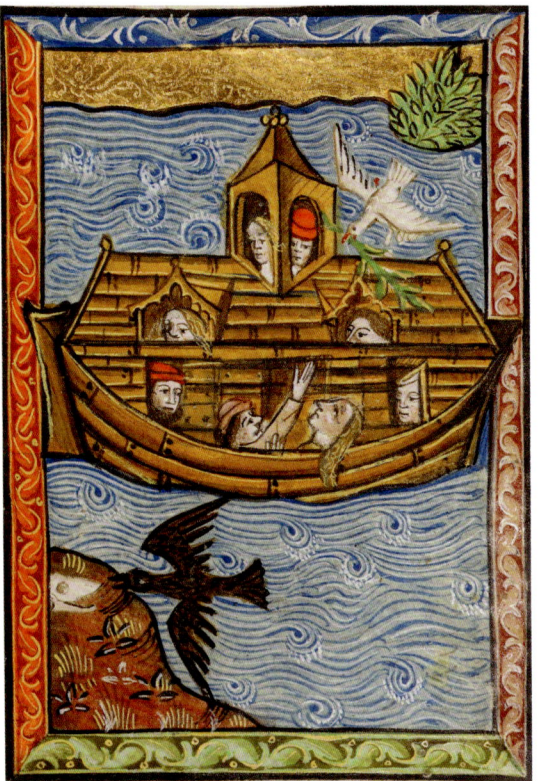

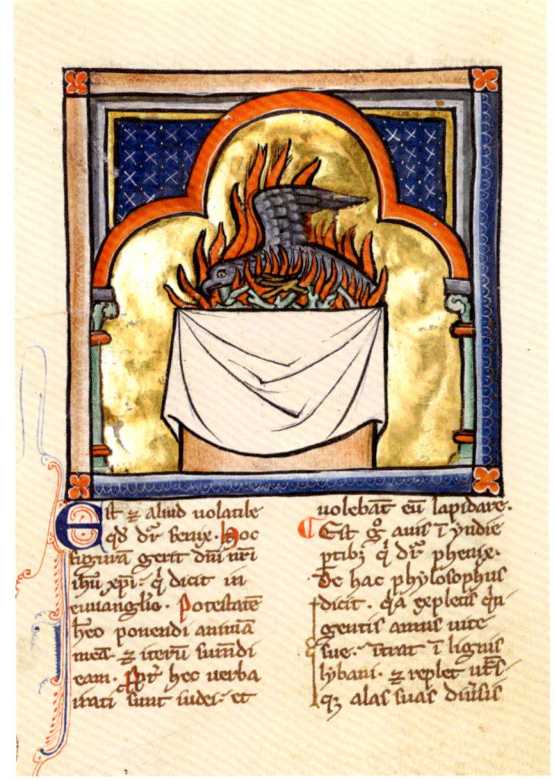

inextricably woven into the fabric of their daily lives. My grandparents would never have considered themselves craftspeople and would have scoffed at the very notion of themselves as any sort of artist, but they undoubtedly possessed uncommon skills and they brightened many more lives than they can have possibly imagined.

Tragically, the fruits of my grandmothers' labours are, as far as I am aware, long since lost – moth-eaten, fallen to pieces, tossed away, incinerated, consigned to landfill, bundled off in a house clearance van, or collateral damage in the internecine chaos of family strife, division and schism.

In retrospect, my grandparents' achievements were of great significance and immense value within the circles in which they moved, not least because they were responsible for bringing glimpses of loveliness and refinement into a dismal world, but their lives and achievements are very far from unique.

Textiles are the one art form with which it can be stated with some degree of certainty, that every human being on the planet is familiar.

The shared history of humankind, of civilisation and society is inextricably linked with the story and development of textiles. Cultural, social and economic history, the rise and fall of empires and of colonialism, the development of pan-global trade, the history of mass migration, relocation and urbanisation, the rise of capitalism and the foundations of the modern

←← Painting
Noah's Ark, unknown illuminator, circa 1480–90. The J. Paul Getty Museum, Los Angeles, Ms. 101, fol. 10, 2008.3.10

← Painting
A Phoenix, unknown illuminator, circa 1270. The J. Paul Getty Museum, Los Angeles, Ms. Ludwig XV 3, fol. 74v, 83.MR.173.74v

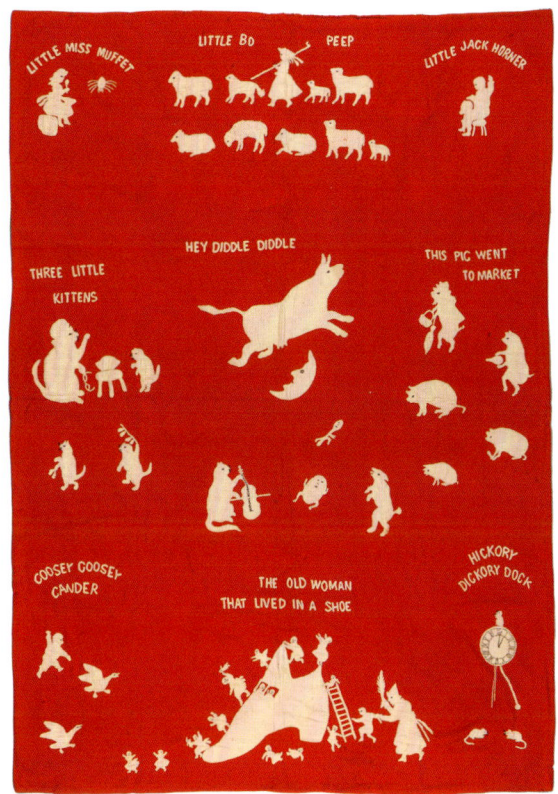

world are all inseparable from the history of textiles and textile production. Textiles have always been a catalyst for change, conflict, oppression, liberation, progress and interaction.

Textiles also provide vital benefits for humankind – most obviously in the form of clothing, shelter, protection, and as a means of spreading information but at the same time they are also a source of pleasure, joy, enchantment, allure and magic.

However, textiles tend to be regarded as the poor relation of the fine or applied arts. Textile artists and creators are usually dismissed as mere 'craftspeople', possessing neither the skill, the vision, the application, nor the mercurial 'genius' of the

↑ Hanging
Nursery rhymes depicted in cotton appliqué and embroidery on red felted wool, England, 1860s

11

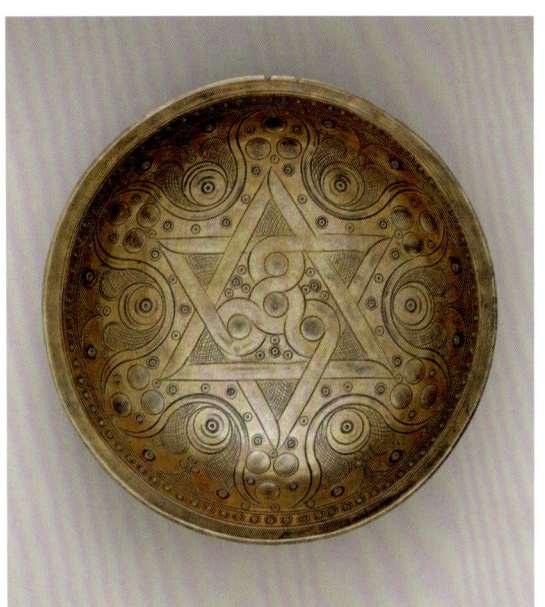

← **Metalwork**
Bowl, attributed to Afghanistan, 12th century. Metropolitan Museum of Art, New York, Louis E. and Theresa S. Seley Purchase Fund for Islamic Art and Rogers Fund, 2000, 2000.57

↙ **Photograph**
Lace glove cyanotype, Hippolyte Bayard, France, circa 1843–1846. The J. Paul Getty Museum, Los Angeles, 84.XO.968.9

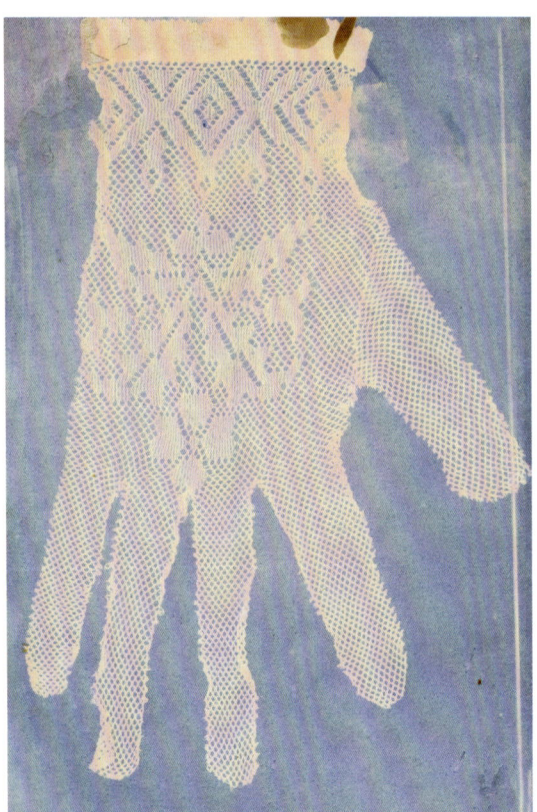

heroic artist of the popular imagination (almost all of whom, uncannily enough, turn out to be male). The identities of the incredibly talented artists responsible for the textiles that are currently held in the collections of major museums and collections worldwide are, alas, unknown, and unlikely to ever be discovered. They will be forever hidden, fated to be described as 'Unknown Creator' or 'Unidentified Artist'.

The majority of the anonymous textile artists whose work has survived would almost certainly have been women; some of whom would have been exploited or condemned to work in terrible conditions, forced or unpaid labour or domestic servitude. The majority of these women would also have been women of colour, with varying degrees of power, agency and cultural capital.

Textiles should be considered as vital and essential to humankind's cultural development and enrichment as any other comparable art form. They can stimulate the imagination, shed light on the 'Human Condition', and provide as much education, illumination and inspiration as any fresco, painting, mezzotint, drawing, iPhone self-portrait, or performance piece that you are likely to encounter.

→ **Robe**

Detail of a silk embroidered panel from a robe, China, 18th century

↘ **Illustration**

Table 5, dated Oct. 1, 1807, James Sowerby (1757–1822), A new elucidation of colours, original, prismatic and material; showing their concordance in three primitives: yellow, red and blue; and the means of producing, measuring and mixing them. With some observations on the accuracy of Sir Isaac Newton, London, 1809. Wellcome Collection, London

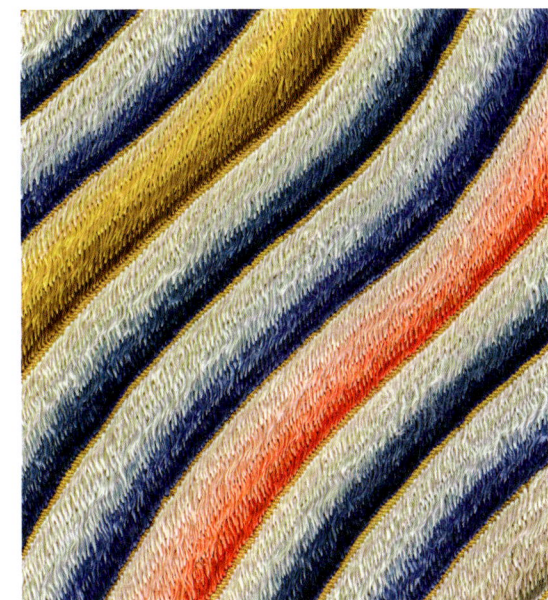

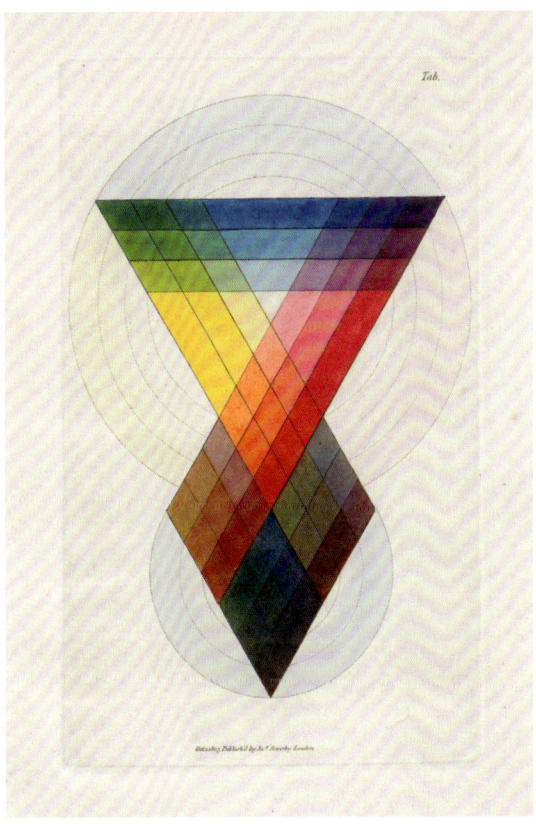

Sadly, when it comes to Culture, there is a well-established pecking order which places objects considered 'useful' and those created with practical purposes in mind below those works of art whose sole purpose is to be looked at, contemplated, gawped at, interpreted and adored.

According to the diktats of this self-appointed hierarchy of taste, textile art can be summarily dismissed as trivial and insignificant by the custodians and gatekeepers of 'High Culture'. This book therefore is intended as an opening salvo in a campaign to right this terrible misjustice.

Before I was introduced to Karun Thakar and his collection, my knowledge of textiles and textile art was patchy at best. I could barely tell my warp from my weft.

From our very first meeting, courtesy of a mutual friend, I recognised in Karun a kindred spirit, a fellow obsessive, blessed (or possibly cursed) with a taste for the beautiful, the bizarre, the extravagant and the extraordinary, combined with an overwhelming compulsion to share that obsession with as wide an audience as possible.

Karun and I are both impassioned and dedicated collectors, but our shared enthusiasms have manifested themselves in very different ways.

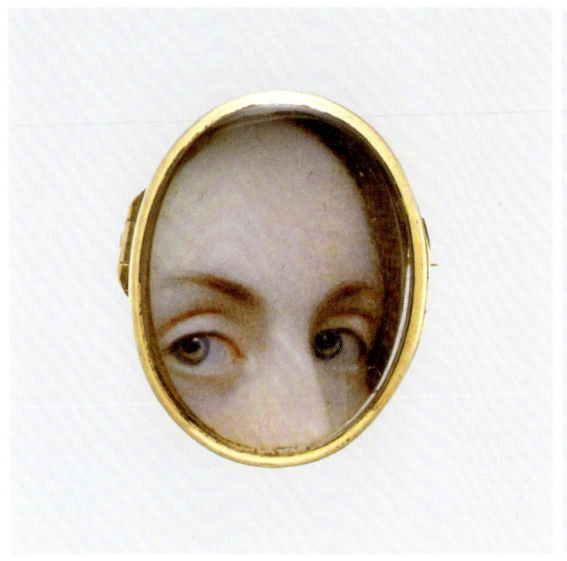
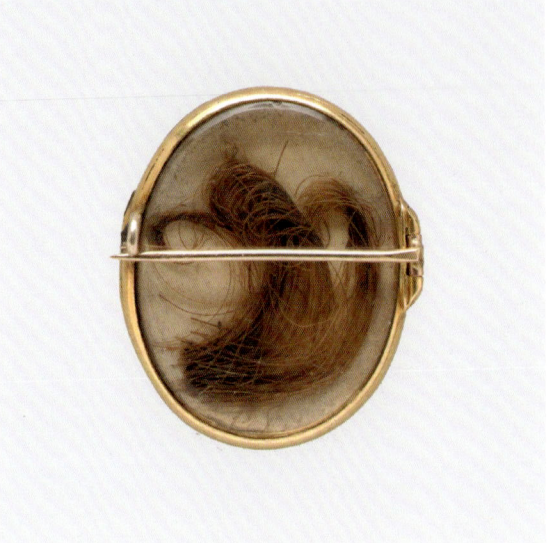

↑ **Painting**

Lover's Eyes, USA, circa 1840. The
Metropolitan Museum of Art, New York,
T. Johnson Fund, 1999, 1999.313

I understand the collecting impulse all too well
and it has got me into a lot of trouble and many
tricky situations in the past with landlords, creditors,
removal companies, ex-wives and girlfriends, among
others. Eventually, circumstances cured me of this
mania for hoarding, but my suppressed urges found
a new outlet in the form of social media, and I have
spent the past decade and a half creating an ever-
expanding virtual museum, in a vainglorious attempt
to create an infinite archive of visual treasures drawn
from as many different sources, eras, traditions,
genres and cultures as possible.

Karun, on the other hand, has, over the course of forty
years or so created one of the world's most important
private collections of textiles and other artefacts, a
remarkably diverse collection that is testimony to Karun's
energy, enthusiasm and extraordinary 'eye'.

In building our respective 'virtual' and physical
collections, both Karun and I are constructing our
own unique aesthetic universes, immune to trends
and influence, set apart from the mainstream, and
ignoring established hierarchies and canons of taste
and culture. Our collections encompass everything
from unimaginable opulence to recycled rags, from
the highest peaks of the highbrow to the vernacular
and lowly; from works of huge historical and cultural
significance to the most mundane artefacts.

Many of the humbler items in our collections
encapsulate the beauty and complexity of everyday
objects, objects that bear witness to the remarkable
skills and artistry of countless unknown artists from
every corner of the earth. In highlighting the work
of so many nameless, sometimes marginalised,
creators in his collections, Karun is engaged in a

hugely important, ongoing project of restitution, reclamation and recognition.

Karun is possessed with an almost evangelical passion to communicate his enthusiasm, his unique insight and wealth of knowledge. His mission is to educate and enlighten the wider world about the remarkably complex, endlessly fascinating, history of textiles. His target audience exists way beyond the rarefied, elitist world of hallowed palaces of culture, biennales, museum galas and art fairs inaccessible to all but the most privileged, venal or corrupt.

Despite significant advances in recent years, the history of textiles is still under-researched and largely unknown. There is so much more to learn, so many stories left untold, and so many gifted women waiting to be discovered.

This volume features just a small selection of textiles chosen from Karun's vast collection. In making our choices we have attempted to reflect the remarkable diversity and range of his interests and to do justice to his unique vision.

Working with Karun over the past few years has proven to be a constant source of surprise, delight and revelation. I have learned so much about social, economic and cultural history, and my appreciation for this often-overlooked art form, still regularly dismissed as inferior or as mere 'craft', continues to grow with each astonishing new discovery and fresh revelation.

↓ **Painting**

Design for The Magic Flute: The Hall of Stars in the Palace of the Queen of the Night, Act 1, Scene 6, after Karl Friedrich Schinkel, published by Ludwig Wilhelm Wittich

German 1847–49. The Metropolitan Museum of Art, New York, The Elisha Whittelsey Collection, The Elisha Whittelsey Fund, 1954, 54.602.1(14)

↓ **Photograph**

Waiting in the Forest – Cheyenne, 1910, cyanotype, Edward S. Curtis, USA, 1910. The J. Paul Getty Museum, Los Angeles, 84.XM.638.50

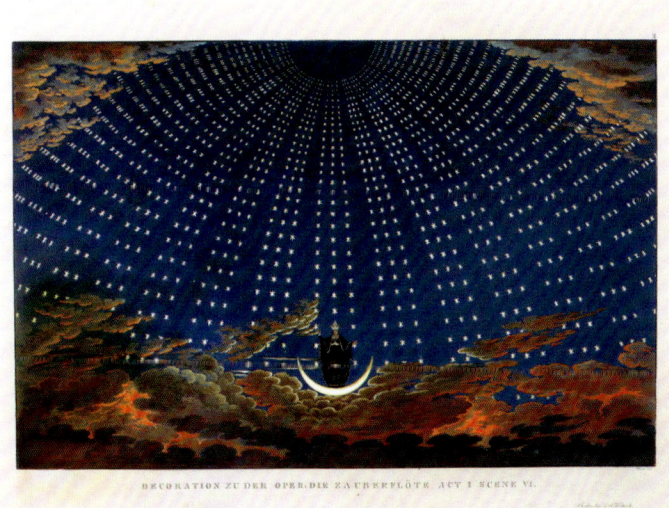

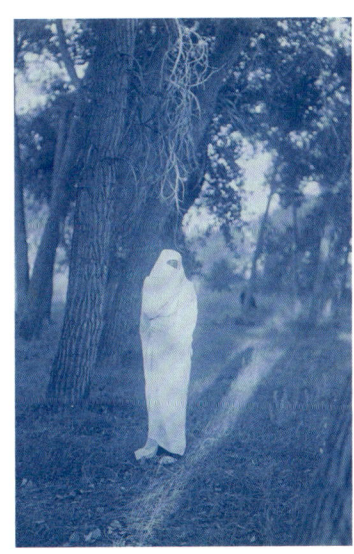

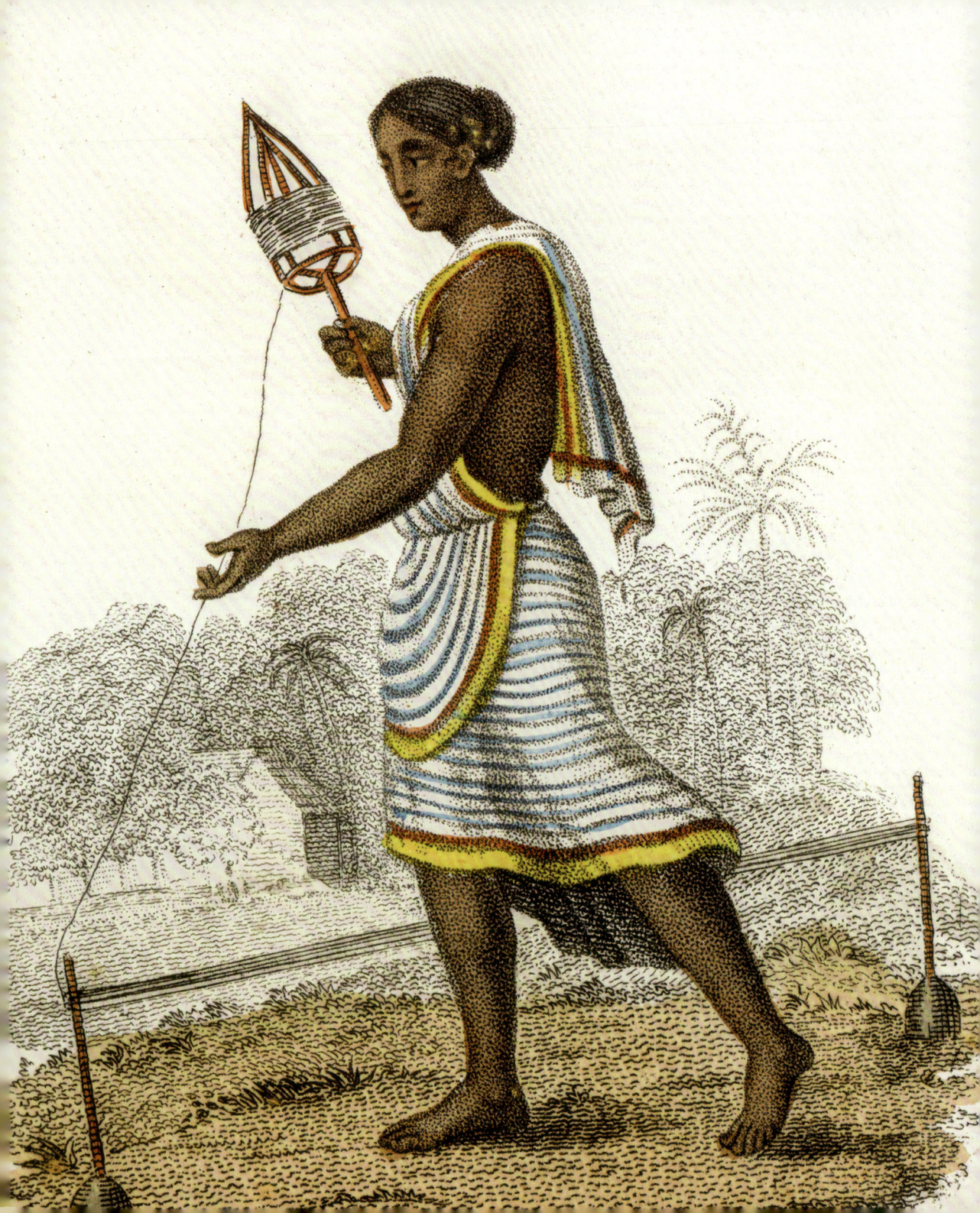

The Collection

Karun Thakar

Collecting and textiles have been with me since my early childhood. My mother ran a couture shop in Delhi, so stitching and hemming, cutting, patching and embroidery constituted a constant activity at home. I learnt quickly to judge the beauty, value and usefulness of textiles coming into the shop, and I recall spending my pocket money judiciously in the markets around the Red Fort on exceptional Banjara embroideries.

When I moved to the UK at thirteen years old, textiles and collecting gave me a sense of continuity and connection, familiarity and stability in a strange new, foreign and often hostile land. There was very little money, so I had to make my own clothes, using textiles to shape my new 'British' identity. I remember the Bay City Rollers, glam rock and 20-inch flares being my own rites of passage.

At the age of twenty-one I started to travel in search of textiles. With my late partner, Roy Short, I returned to India and eventually travelled through the whole subcontinent as well as Africa and Japan. Travelling extensively was a means of sourcing more material but also of learning: making connections between the people and places and the pieces I was buying.

I began visiting museums and other institutions; the most influential were the Victoria and Albert Museum and National Trust properties. Visiting these showed me how to live with a collection and introduced other forms of art – furniture, jewellery and ceramics – which I also started to collect. Reflecting on that time when I was busy travelling, visiting exhibitions and museums, forever reading and researching new purchases, it is surprising, and indeed satisfying, that my collecting journey seems to have come full circle; since I am now working on important projects with the V&A and the National Trust. While I used to read and revere the work of museum curators and academics from a distance, those same people are now part of a close network of experts that advise me on aspects of my collection. Their input is valuable since I have no team or staff that help me manage my collection on a day-to-day basis.

Yet working independently has its own rewards. Over four decades of collecting, I have learnt to trust my own instincts in selecting pieces which are both beautiful and important. I am drawn to aesthetic beauty, to forms of making and design that speak of human creativity, skill and artistry, but I am equally passionate about what a textile communicates about identity and belonging, production and trade, the lives of its makers and owners, and what it tells me about international themes of migration and exchange, and indeed the wider human experience.

Just as textiles have been integral to me and my own story, so they have been for people throughout history. Although textile-making has almost always been an anonymous form of art, textiles are also uniquely intimate – a material connection to those

17

who made them, wore them, touched them, saved them, infusing them with love, envy, hope and humour, and ultimately investing them with different types of value. For me, no other object captures and retains the essence of what it is to be human better than a textile, and the most beautiful pieces in my collection are the ones that hold meaningful stories within their folds.

Perhaps as a result of my own life experiences, I particularly connect with what are sometimes called outside or folk pieces, terms which I find problematic and pejorative. These textiles tend to be unfashionable, unknown in traditional collecting circles, and mostly not represented in institutional collections. I have never had an unlimited budget, and tended towards buying pieces which hint at hidden layers of meaning and unheard histories.

For example, an important part of my collection is dedicated to Indian cotton textiles, or chintz. Seen for many years as simply a decorative fabric, chintz has a lot to tell us and is far from superficial. Its histories are entwined with Indian mercantilism, colonialism and capitalism, trade wars, design innovation and migration, and lead all the way through to slavery in the Americas. Although these histories may be painful, for me these connections enrich my appreciation of chintz and take me beyond their joyous surface decoration.

Likewise my collection includes Asafo flags from Ghana which are both masterly works of design and making and poignant symbols of the West's well-rehearsed dismissal of Africa's contributions to art. The designs of these flags made by black artists were of a style seen as primitive by the same art historians who celebrated the appropriation of African artistic devices by Western artists.

As a collector of textiles, I am therefore a collector of stories, stories that I feel compelled to share. Over the past twenty years, I have worked hard to make my collection available: all five of my exhibitions

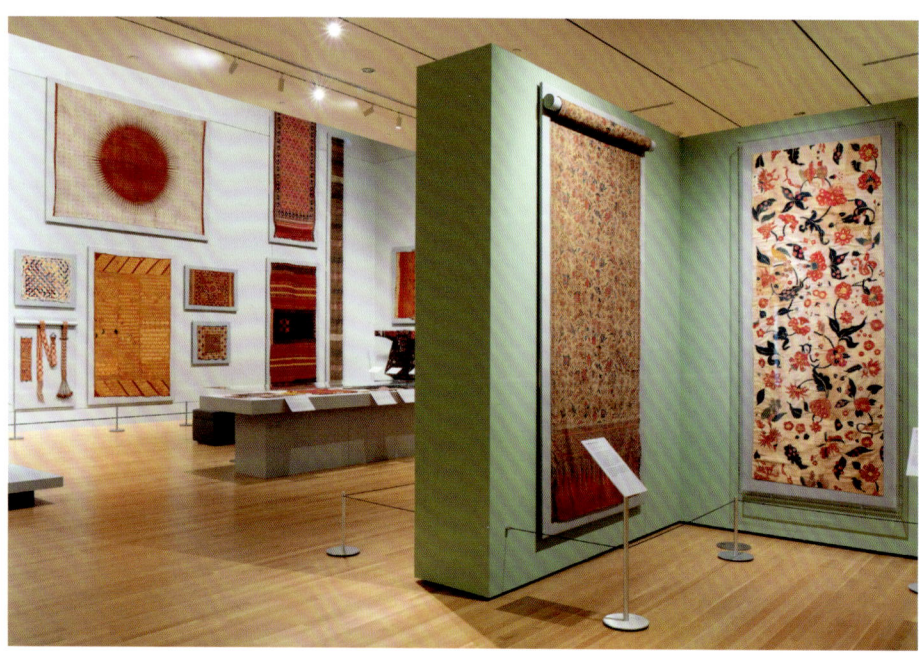

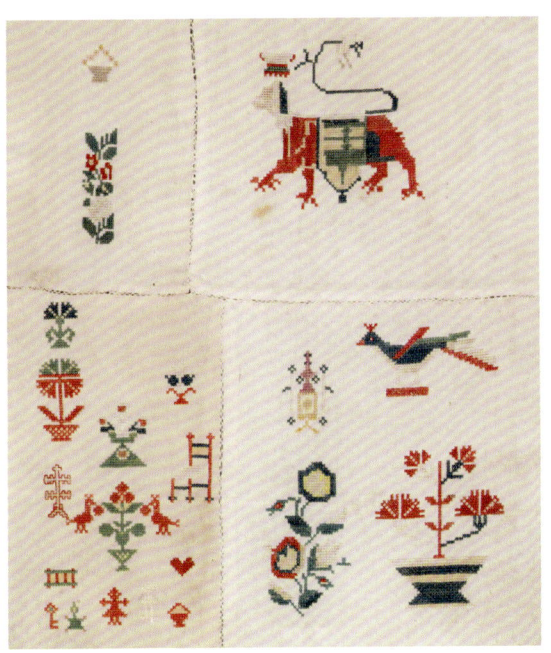

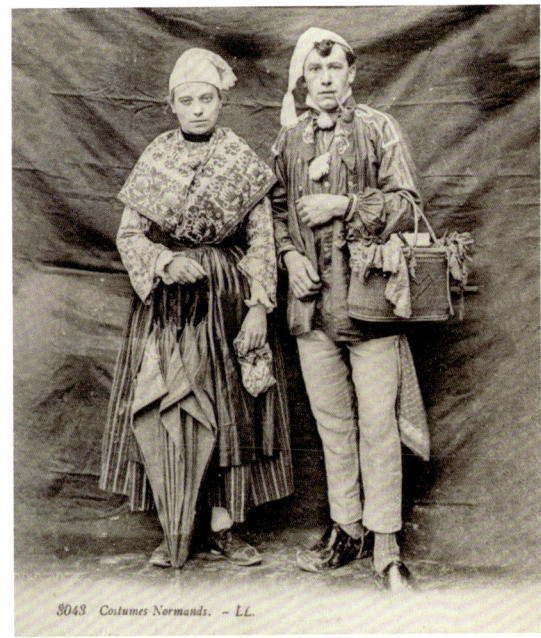

8043 Costumes Normands. — LL.

↑↑ **Engraving**
Preparing of the Warp for Weaving,
Frederic Shoberl, *The World in Miniature:
Hindoostan*, London, 1820s

↑ **Sampler**
Detail of an embroidered sampler,
German Pennsylvania, USA, late 18th
century

↗ **Postcard**
Costumes Normands, Calvados, France,
early 20th century

← **Exhibition**
Installation of 'Indian Textiles: 1,000
Years of Art and Design, The Karun
Thakar Collection' at The George
Washington University Museum and The
Textile Museum, Washington, DC, 2022

have involved international institutions connected
to education; and the six books I have published
to date are all aimed at broadening access and
awareness to a new audience. With past books
and three future publications focused on specific
areas of my collecting, the *Book of Textiles* offers new
and hopefully fresh perspectives on my collection,
and subaltern stories using textiles as the medium
between the past and the present.

It is hugely gratifying to see that interest in textiles
is so much greater than when I first started collecting,
when they were generally overlooked in favour of
more 'formal' art types. Twenty or thirty years ago
a collection like mine, made up of mostly everyday
textiles used by people far removed from the art
capitals of the world, would not have been considered
important. Today museums are increasingly working
to diversify and refocus their collections by acquiring
artefacts of the kind I have been collecting for over
four decades.

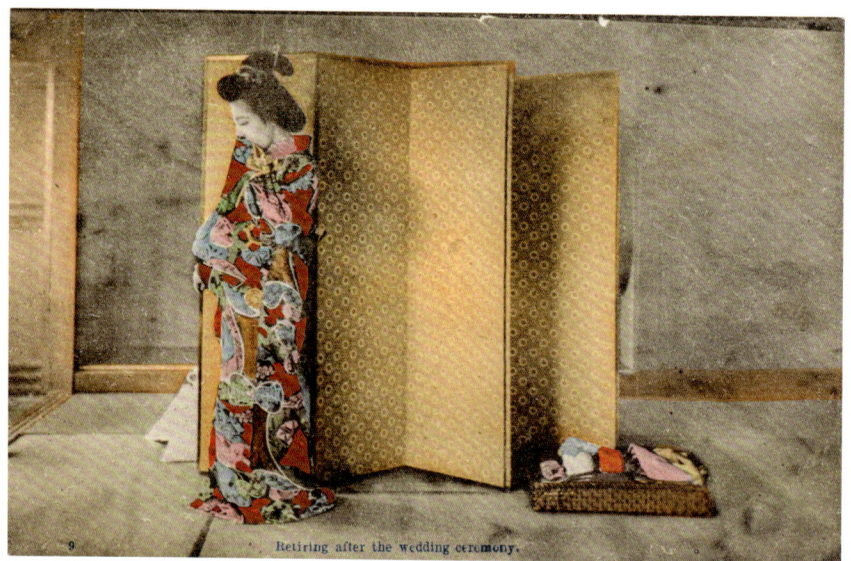

↑ **Postcard**
Retiring after the wedding ceremony,
Japanese Wedding Ceremony series,
circa 1910

→ **Cover**
Banjara cotton and silk embroidery,
Madhya Pradesh, India, early 20th
century. Bought by Karun Thakar in
Delhi in 1982

→ → **Home of a collector**
Karun Thakar's home with 19th-century
Central Asian ikat robes and an Uzbek
suzani on the bed alongside 16th- and
17th-century English oak furniture

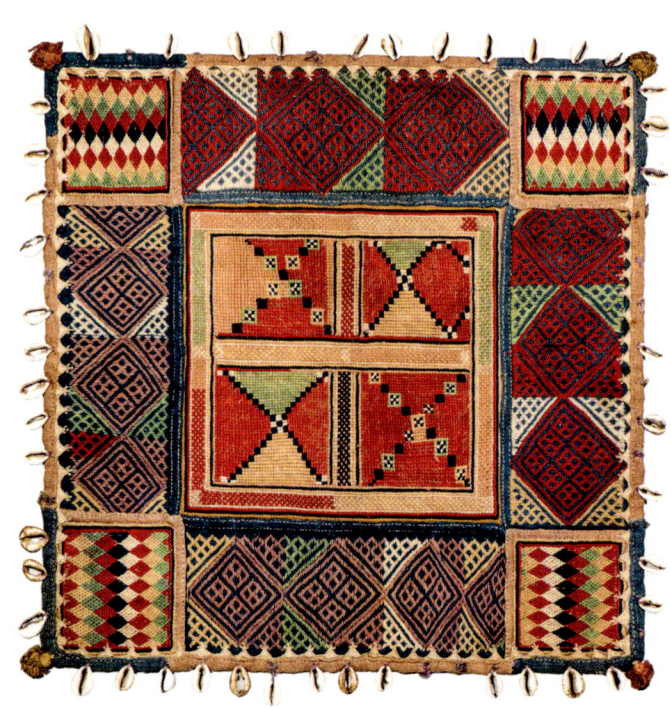

This is part of a wider move to start telling stories from a broader and more diverse section of society, to democratise museums and art, and build bridges with the past and tell lesser-known stories. As a result of this shift, I am now sharing my collection even further via collaborative shows with museums and heritage institutions in the US and UK, including the V&A and National Trust. I am particularly passionate about engaging younger and under-represented audiences with textiles. This motivated me to establish The Karun Thakar Fund for the Study of Asian and African Textiles and Dress at the V&A, which awards funding for scholars as well as community-based projects all over the world.

Collecting has forged new friendships and connections with people who have similar interests and the same collecting instinct. Stephen Ellcock is a fellow collector – he collects images, I collect objects. His curation of this new book has led me to see my collection in new ways. His enthusiasm for sharing the collection outside the confines of my specialisms perfectly aligns with my instinct to share these objects as widely as possible.

The textiles in this book represent a small part of my textile collection and collection per se. It is not comprehensive or global; these are simply the textiles bought by one individual. My own ambition and hope for this *Book of Textiles* is that it inspires new interest in textiles and shows them to be a profoundly important expression of the human spirit. For me it is also a celebration of all the makers and menders, dyers and weavers throughout history whose names are not known. And it is to them that I dedicate the book.

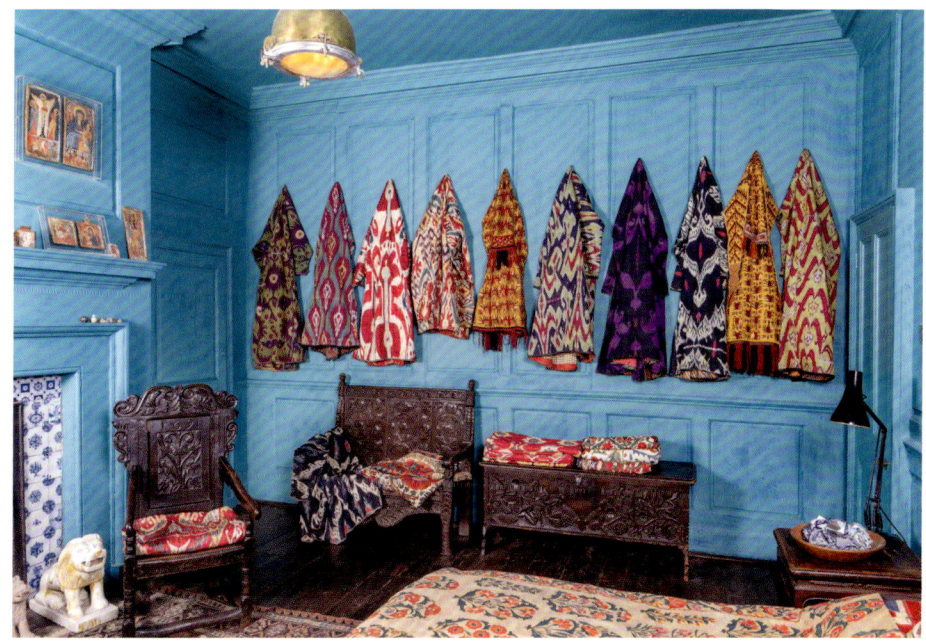

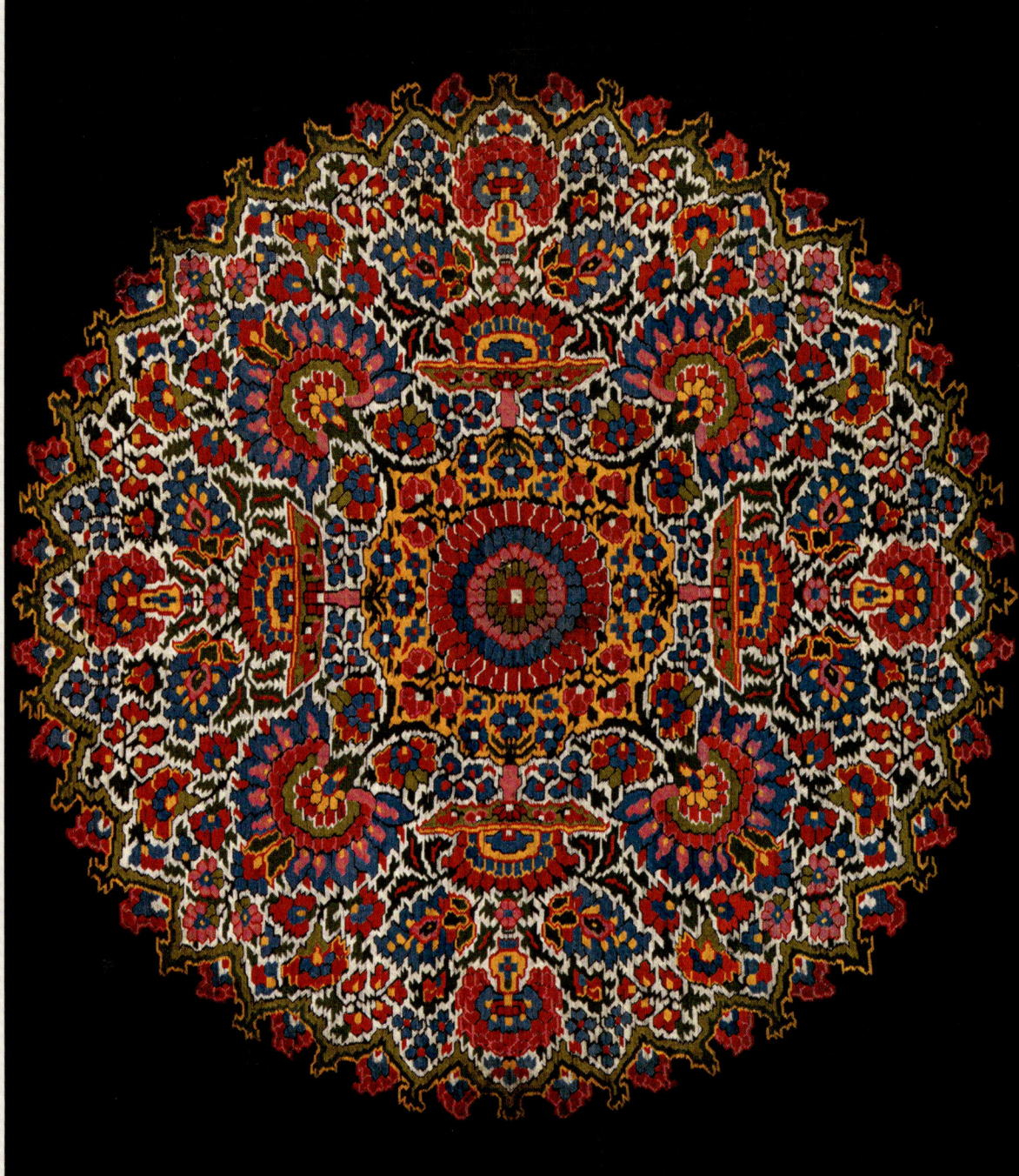

The Natural World

"Nature uses only the longest threads to weave her patterns, so each small piece of her fabric reveals the organization of the entire tapestry."

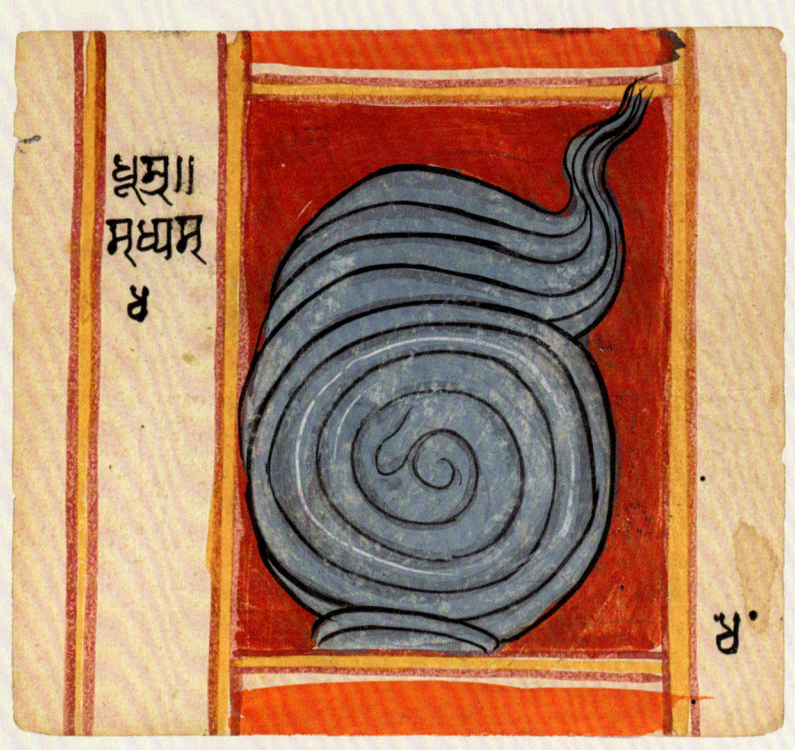

↑ Manuscript

Illustration from a manuscript on
astronomy, Rajasthan, India, circa 1800

The natural world is innately decorative, a quality that artists have taken advantage of since the birth of their craft. From the bulls painted in Lascaux to modern-day leopard-print jackets, plant and animal life has long been utilised as a tool for self-expression. Textiles owe their existence to the land in a more physical sense too; cotton, flax, silk and leather are essential components of clothing derived from the natural world.

It is not so surprising, therefore, that depictions of flowers, animals and birds often appear on the finished textiles as pleasing adornments. Designers would historically look to bestiaries and florilegia for inspiration, employing the ornamental shapes, colours and compositions of flowers, animals or landscapes in their work. Along with depictions of the moon, sun and other celestial phenomena, earthbound natural motifs that are instantly familiar to all are employed by textile designers. Animals were used as symbols of strength and power, with birds and fish connecting the earthly realms as well as suggesting a link to those beyond.

The further we as a society industrialise and urbanise our environment, the more we seem to crave the natural; be it in the clothing against our skin, the flowers we put in a vase, the small garden we cultivate in the backyard of a terraced house or the motifs with which we surround ourselves.

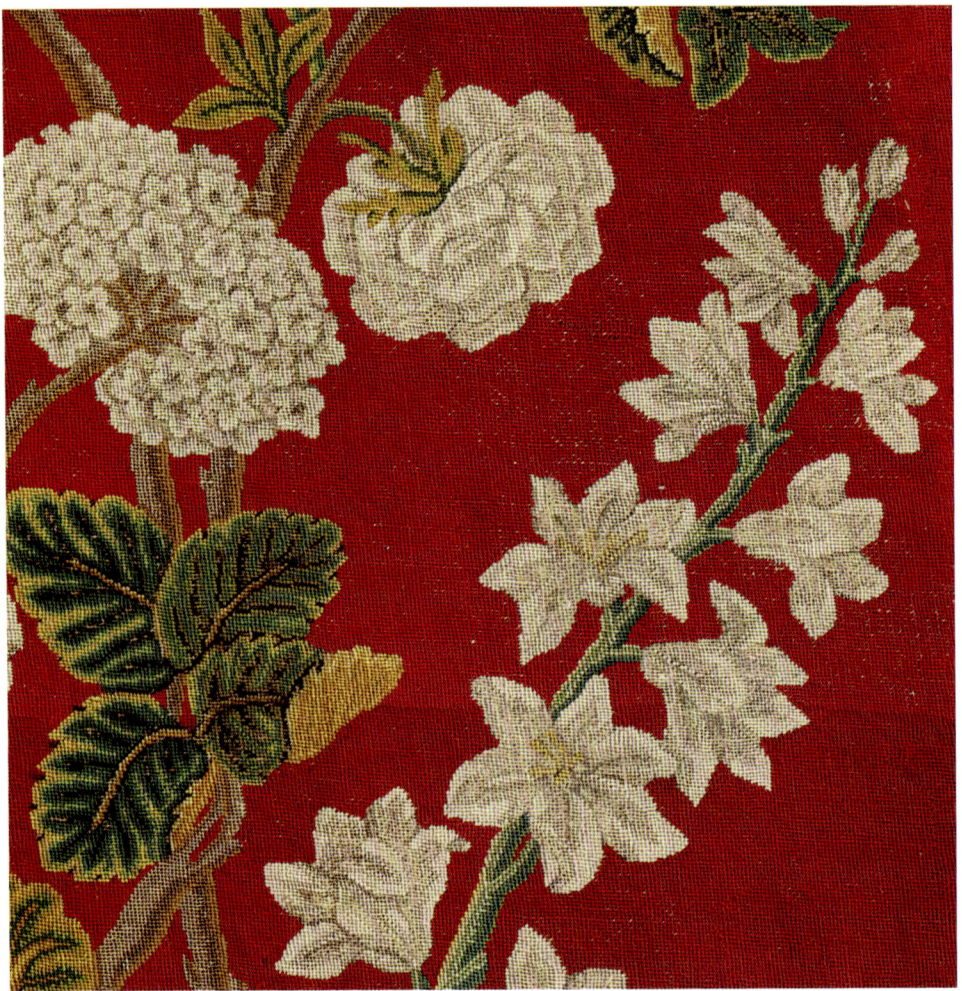

Flowers and textiles are a magic marriage since both are nature's perfect vessels to convey colour in every possible tone, depth and combination. Textiles can carry depictions of natural beauty – 'Rose is a rose is a rose is a rose', as Gertrude Stein wrote – or portray gardens with great symbolic and religious meaning.

↑ **Plants** *Flowers*
Silk embroidery, England, 18th century. The fineness of the embroidery creates a life-like quality in these blossoms set against a brilliant scarlet background

↓ **Plants** *Flowers*
Chintz bed cover for the European market, India, early 18th
century. Most of the flowers are designed to appeal to Western
taste but the central motif is a lotus blossom, a symbol ubiquitous
in Asia and an unusual feature on chintz from the 1700s

The Natural World

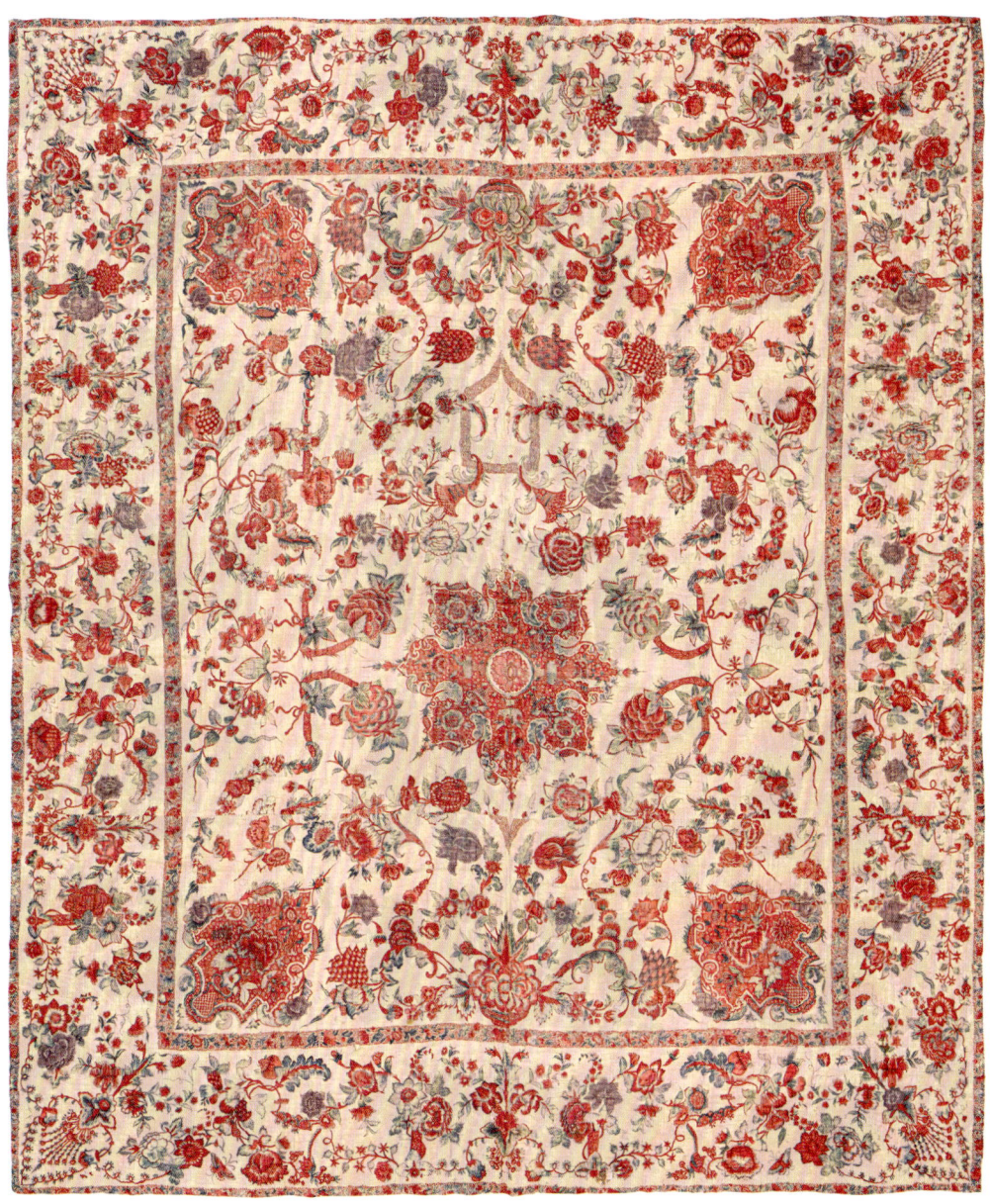

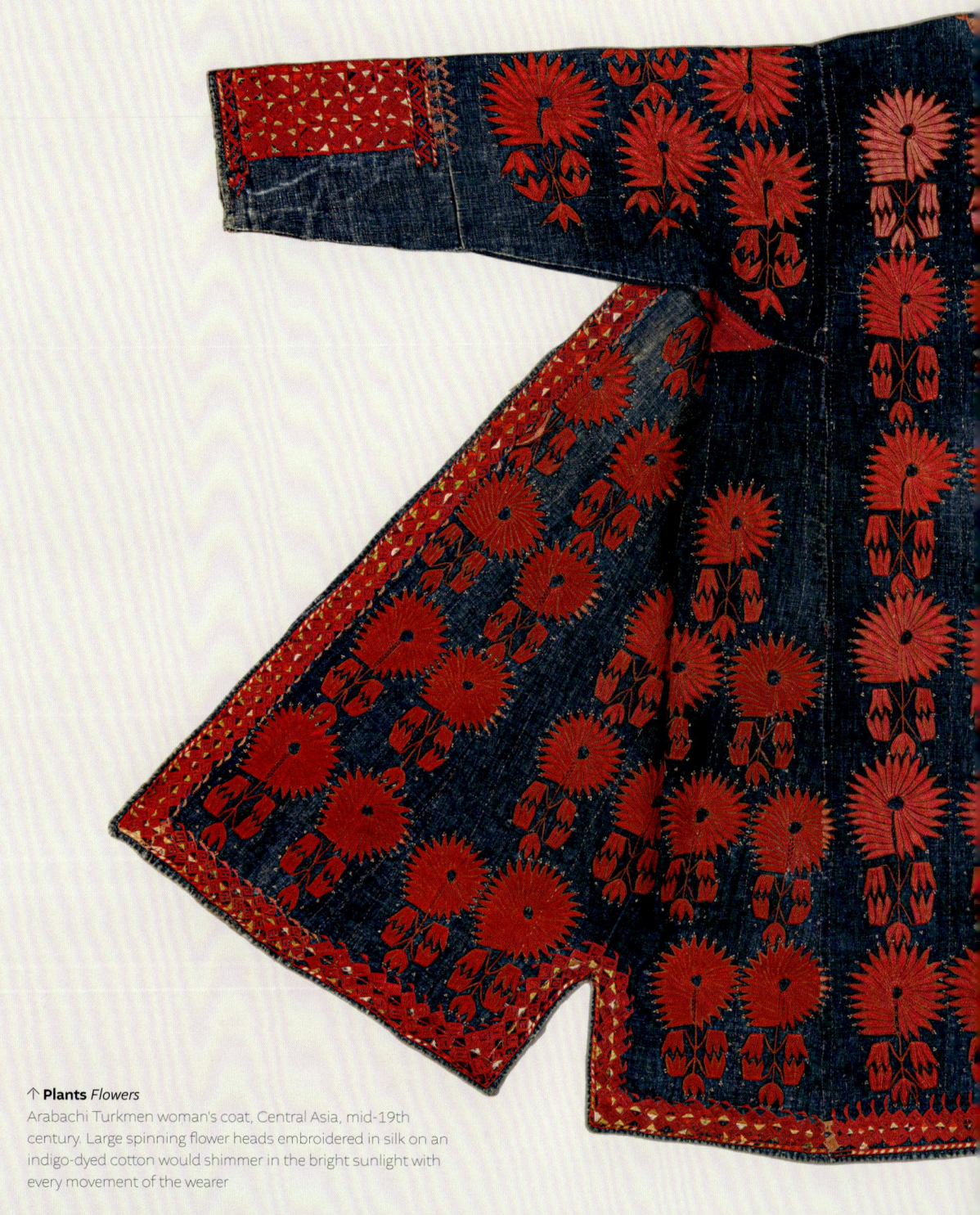

↑ **Plants** *Flowers*
Arabachi Turkmen woman's coat, Central Asia, mid-19th
century. Large spinning flower heads embroidered in silk on an
indigo-dyed cotton would shimmer in the bright sunlight with
every movement of the wearer

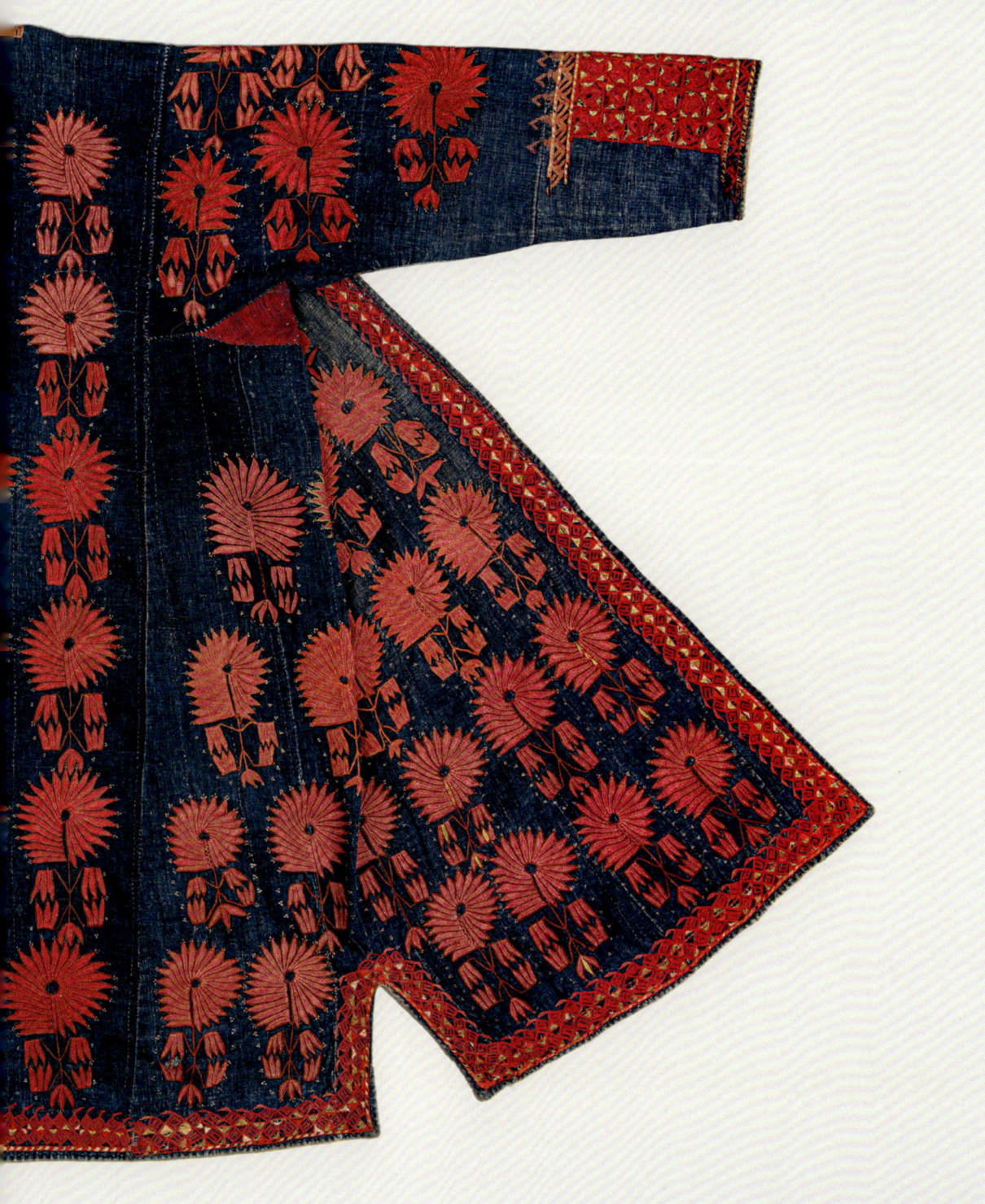

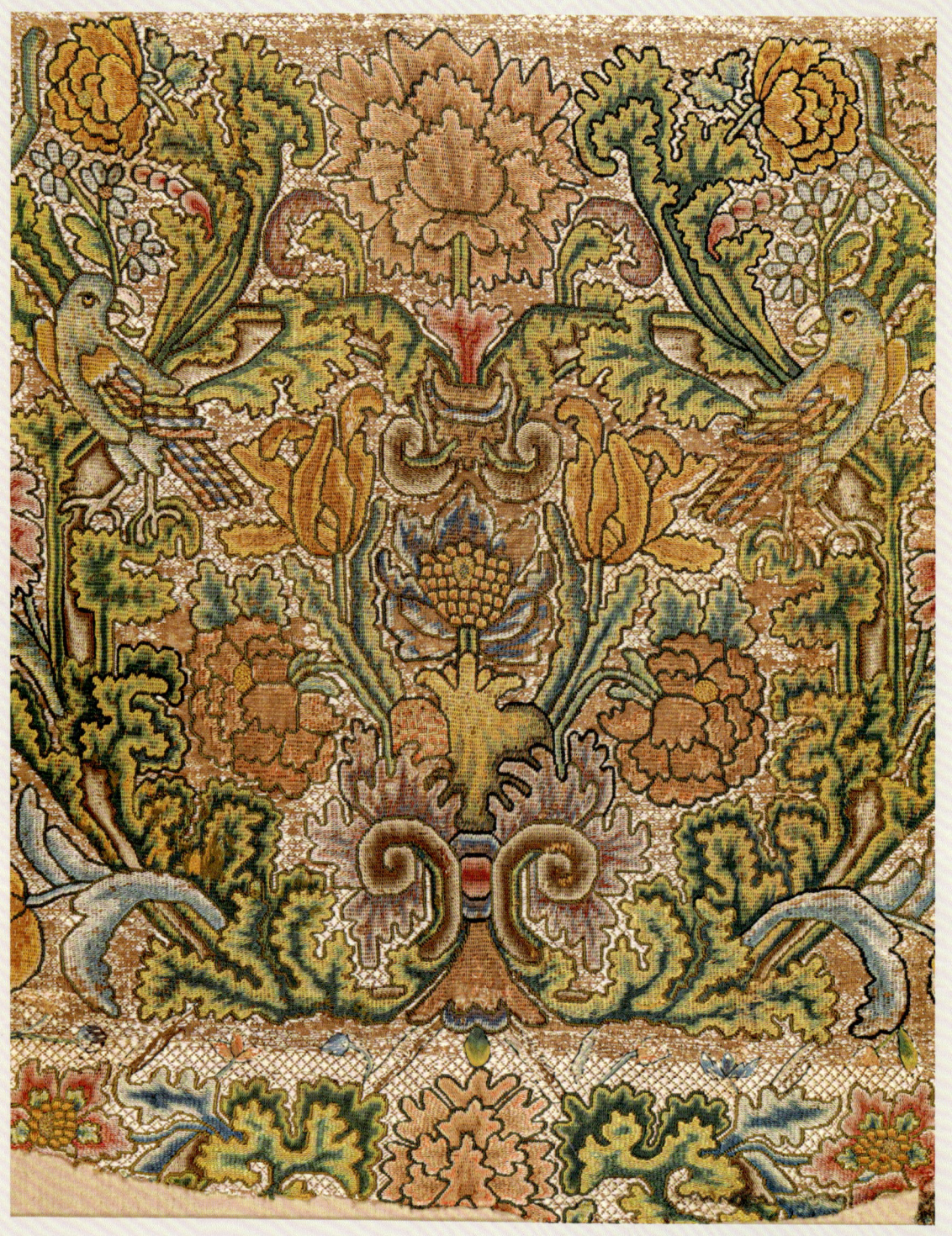

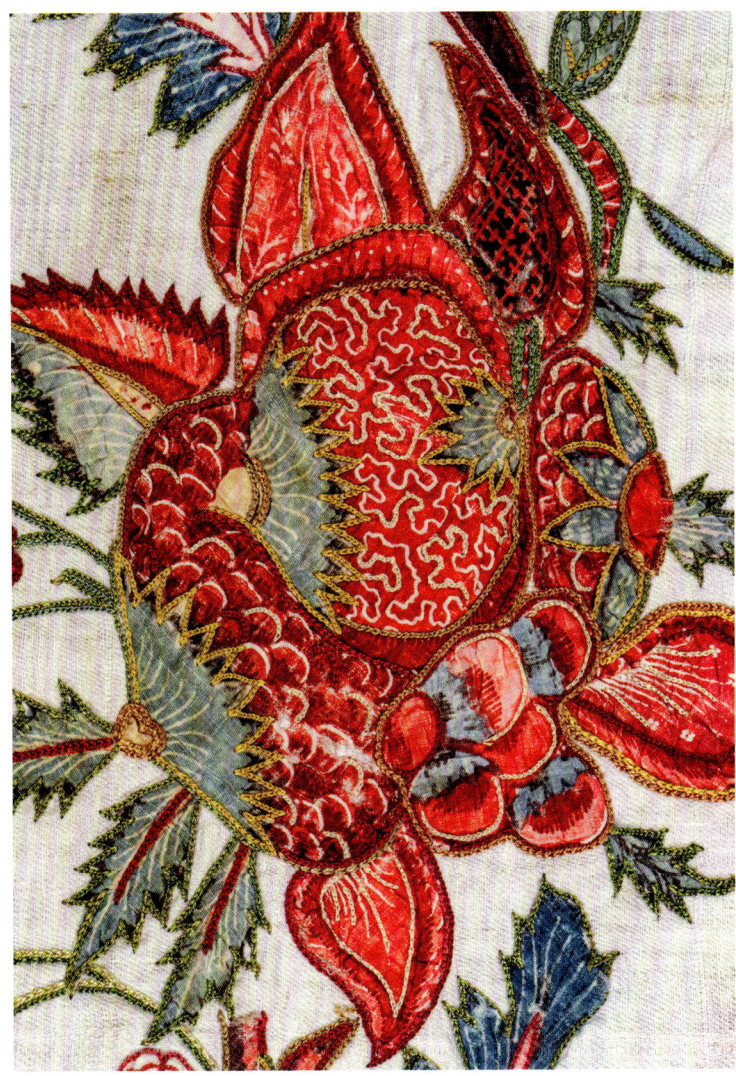

← **Plants** *Flowers*
Seat cover, England, 17th century. A cornucopia of flowers, foliage and a pair of parrots radiate abundance in a cover used on a chair or stool

↑ **Plants** *Flowers*
Bed hanging, France, mid-18th century. In France, Indian chintz was cut and appliquéd onto cotton with elaborate embroidery, which turbocharges the intense colour

↓ **Plants** *Flowers*

Batik sarong, Java, Indonesia, early 20th century. The technique of very fine wax resist slowly builds up layers of this complex pattern over many stages – note the small white dots throughout created by spots of wax applied with a special tool akin to a pen nib

→ **Plants** *Flowers*

Unfinished needlework, Italy, 17th century. This embroidery shows how a design was drawn onto canvas and gradually embroidered. The filigree-style ground pattern gives an embroiderer considerable freedom to interpret and embellish even within a professional workshop environment

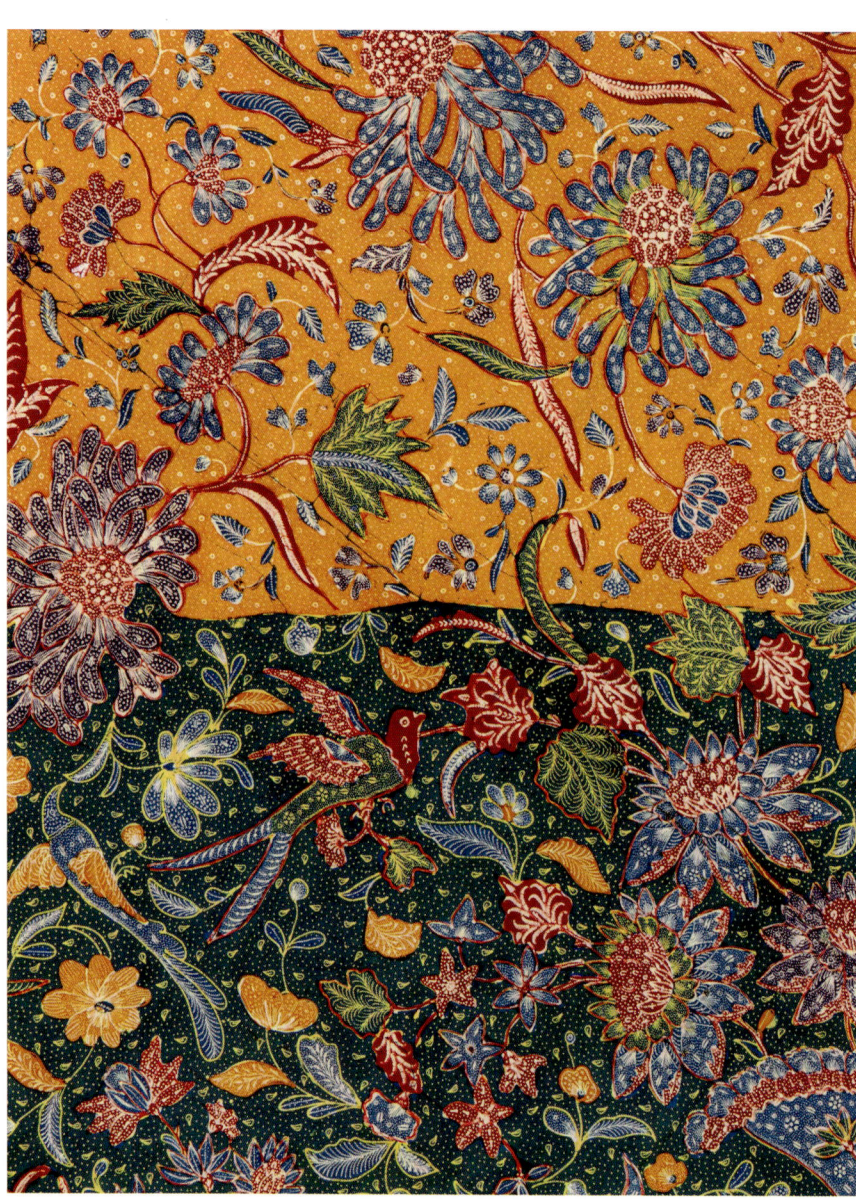

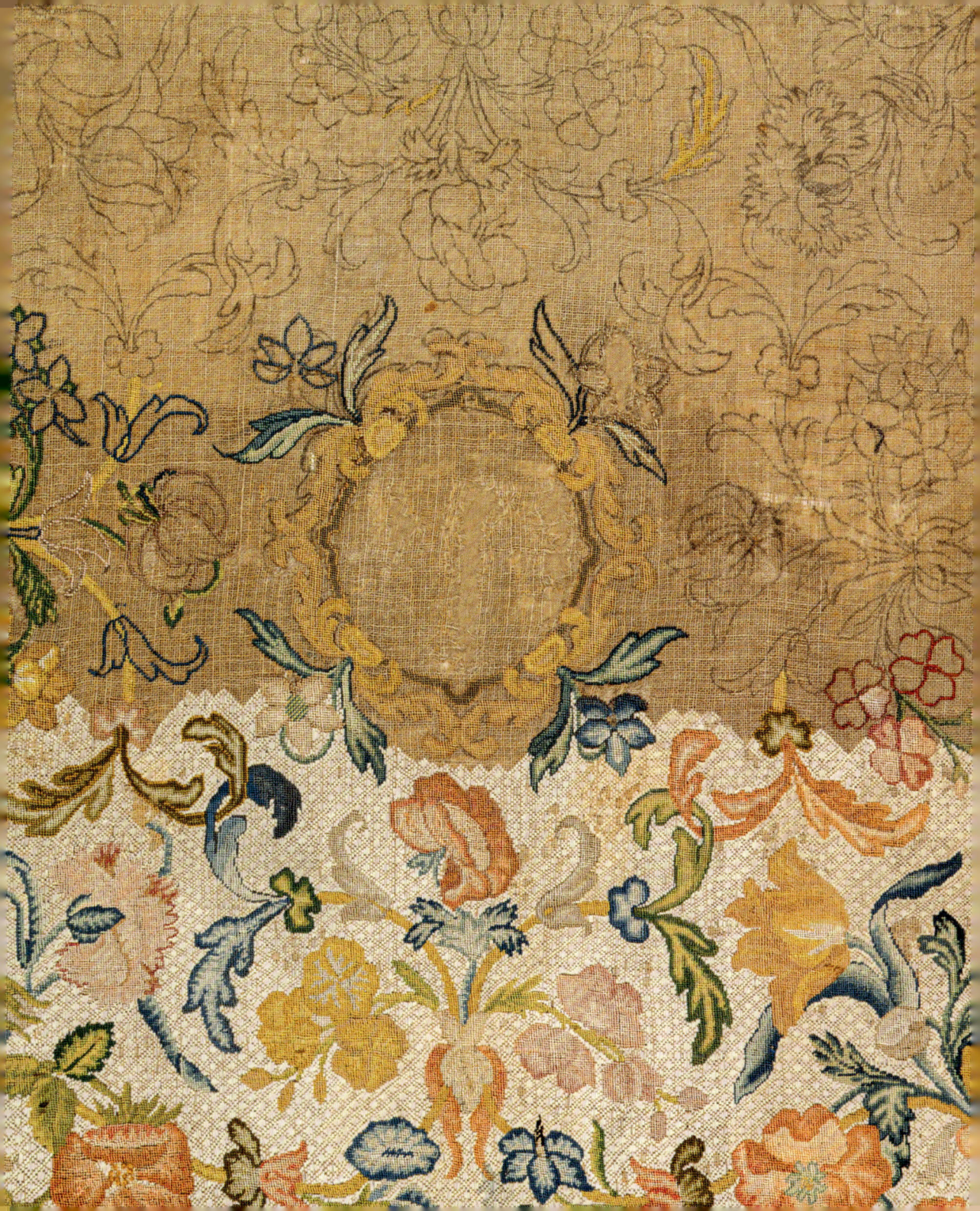

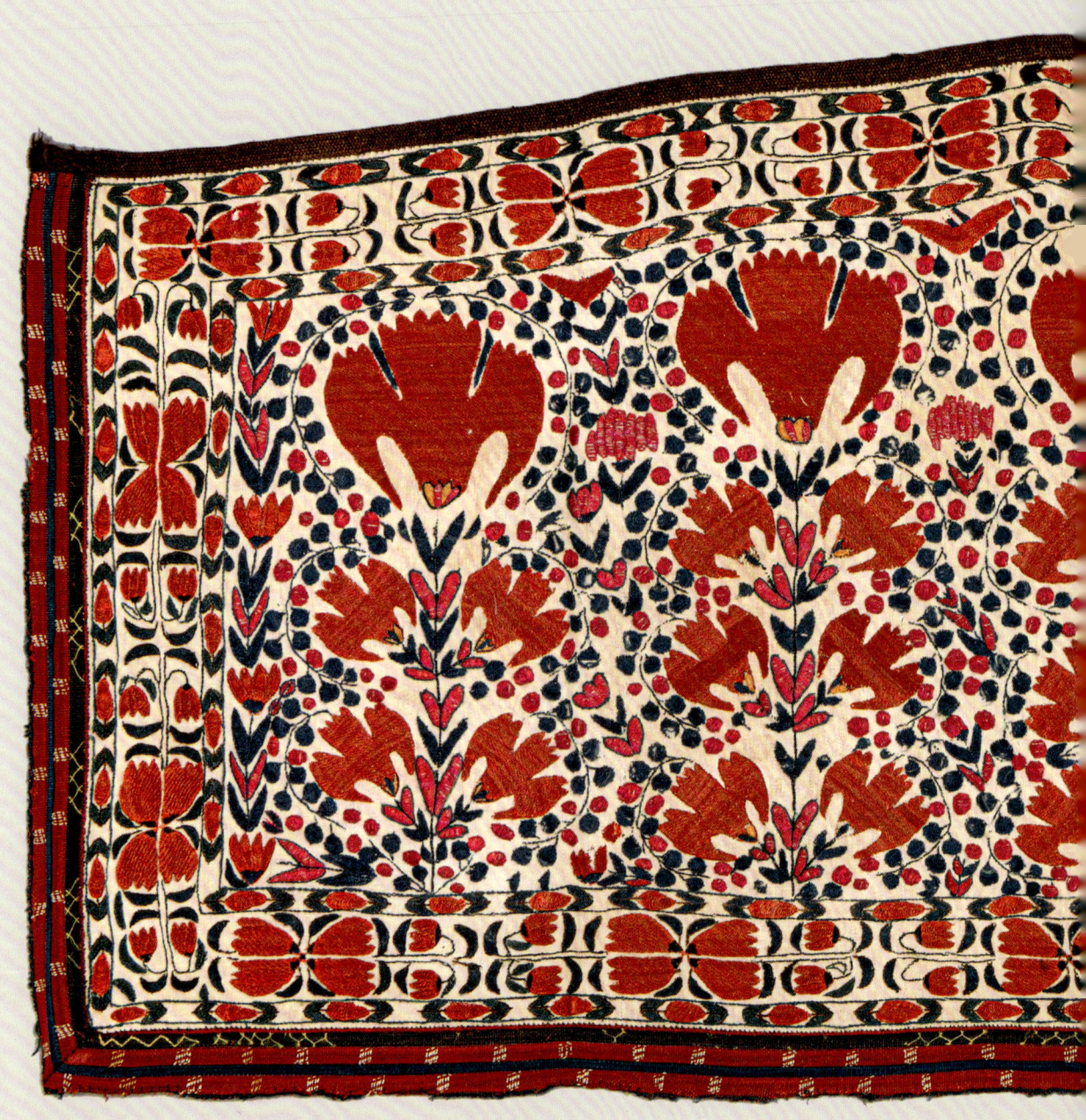

Tekke Turkmen asmalyk or wedding trapping, Central Asia, early
19th century. The flowers may represent new life and family and
are embroidered in silk on a cream woven wool ground. Made in
pairs by a bride to decorate the wedding litter on a camel, this
type of textile is a vision of beauty and fecundity

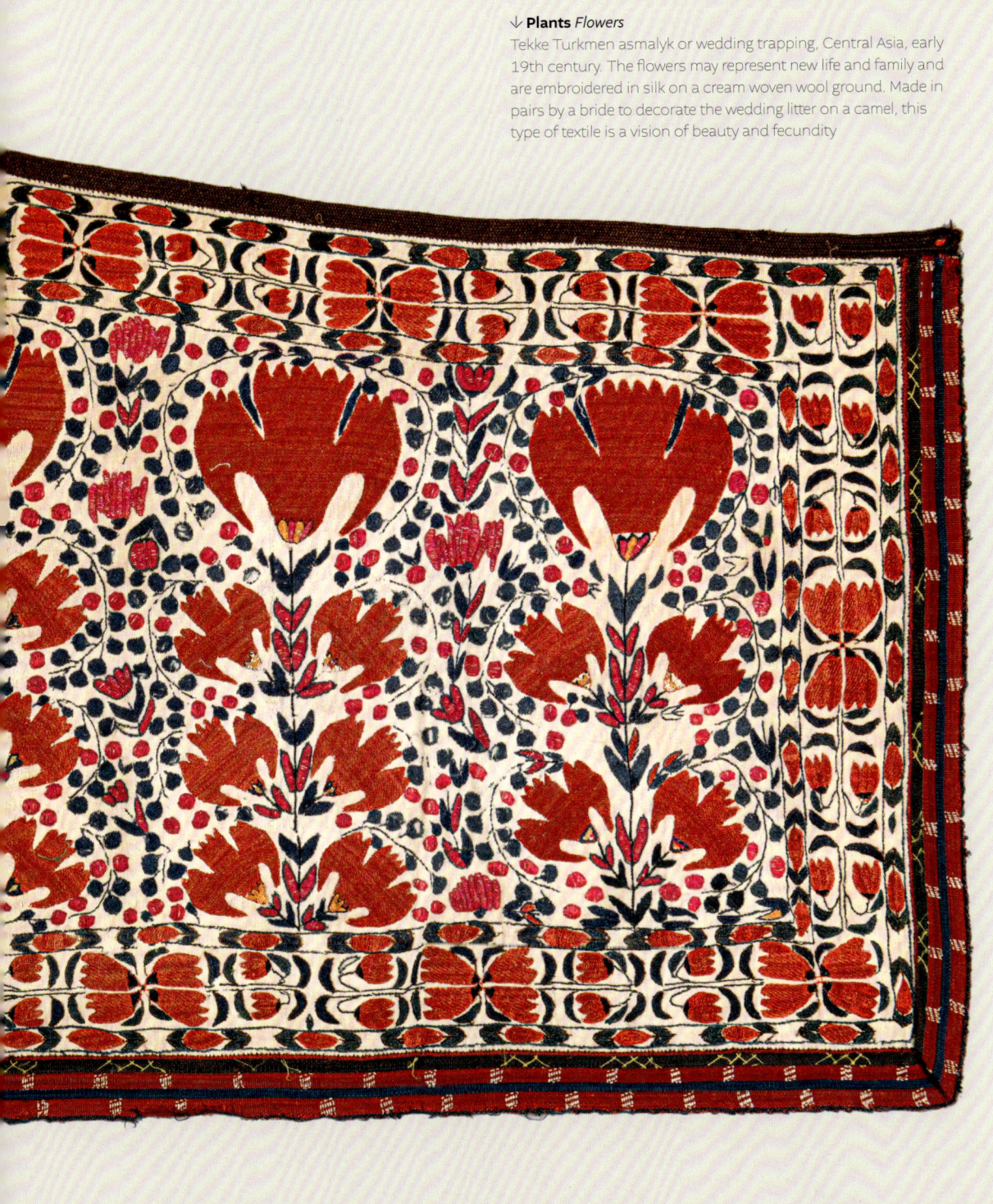

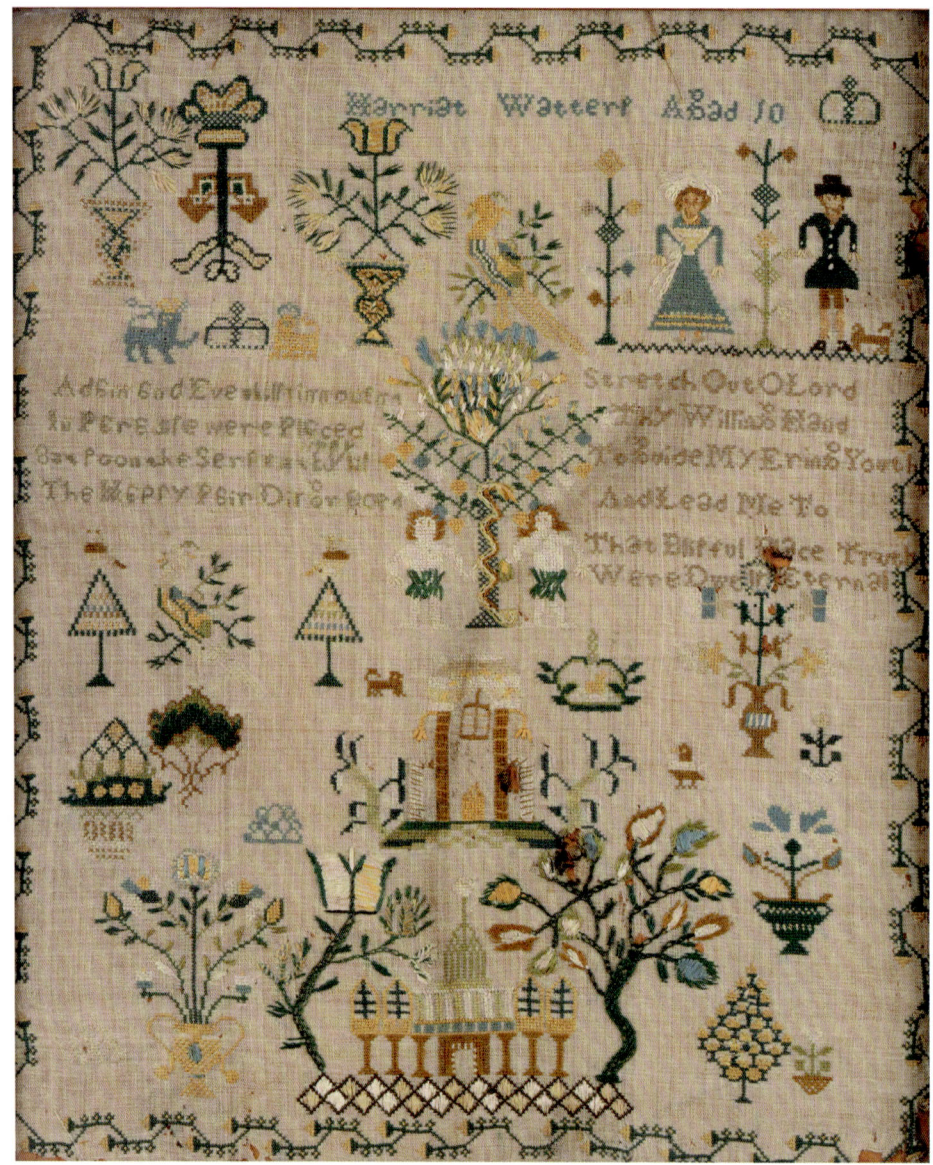

↑ **Plants** *Gardens*

Sampler, England, mid-18th century. The maker, ten-year-old Harriat Watterp, has depicted her parents and Adam and Eve under an apple tree among the plants, trees and flowering shrubs throughout this textile

→ **Plants** *Gardens*

Wedding shawl, Sindh, India, late 19th century. This bird's-eye view shows a garden with trees providing shade within a formal layout associated with traditional Islamic gardens. The small discs of mica imply water-filled canals

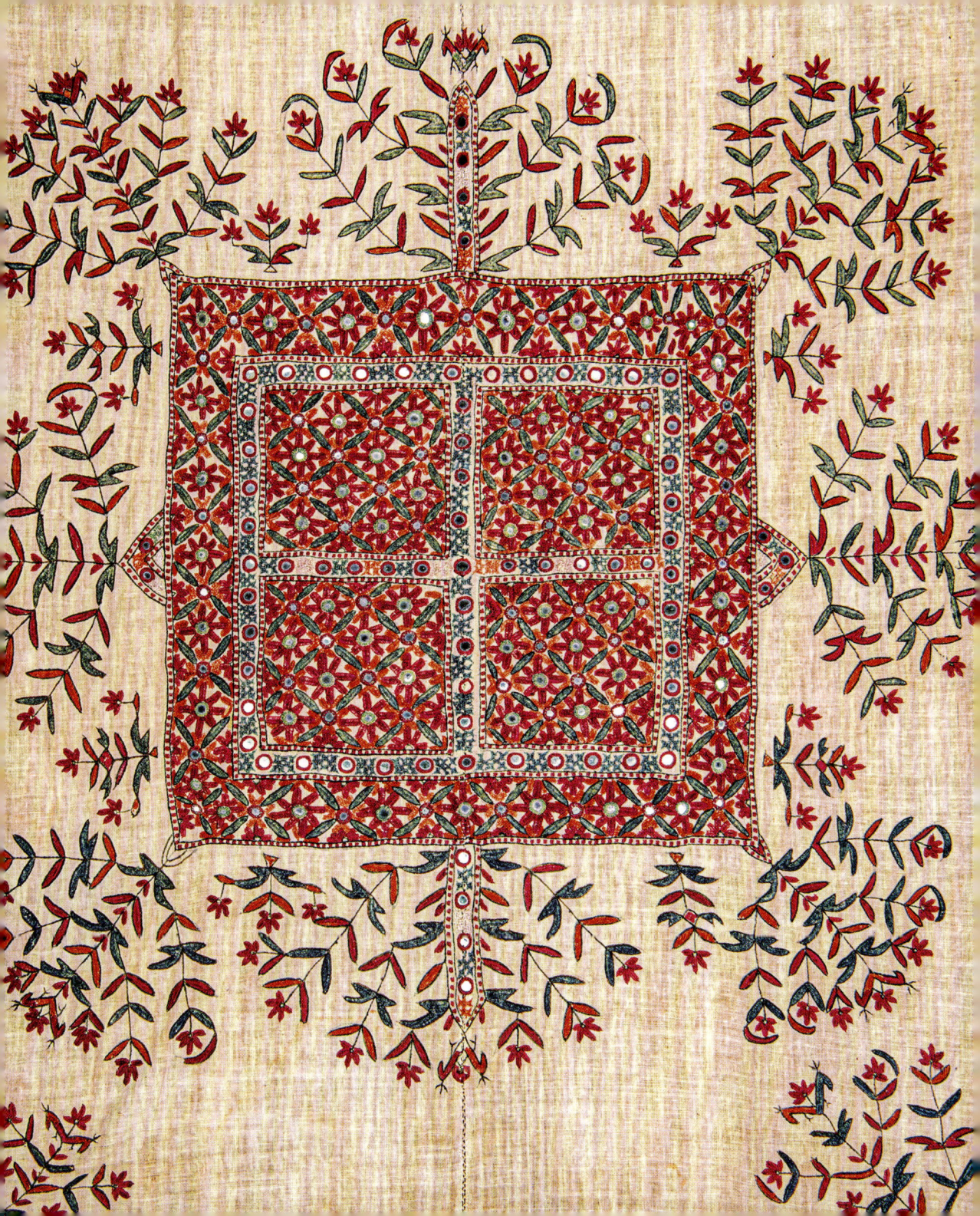

Trees are deeply rooted in many cultural, religious and philosophical traditions and laden with symbols, meanings and beliefs. The tree of life, the tree of knowledge, the tree as the connection between the heavenly and the earthly realms have always been transported into pictorial images, but the tree of life is of particular significance and frequence in textile arts. Whether providing shade, implying power or knowledge or giving shelter to animals and birds, trees are central to many traditional textile types, offering a point of both unity and difference.

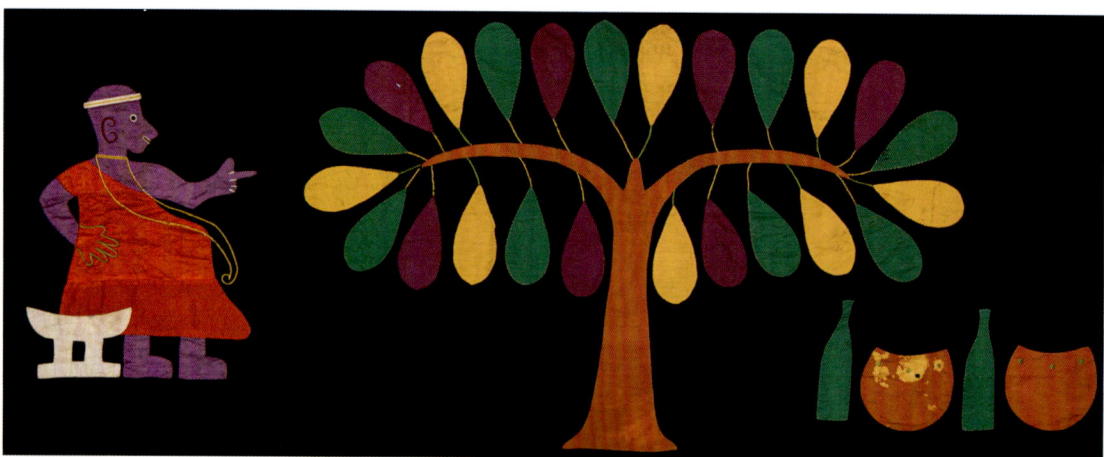

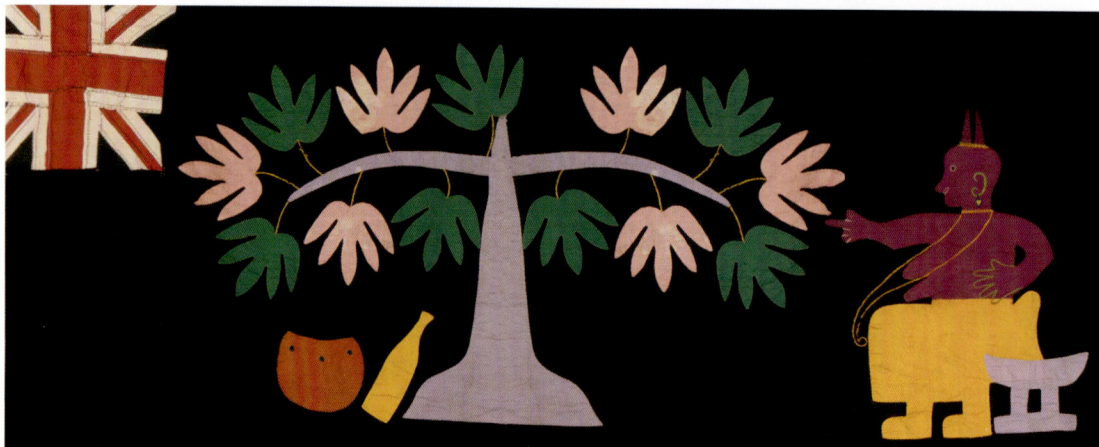

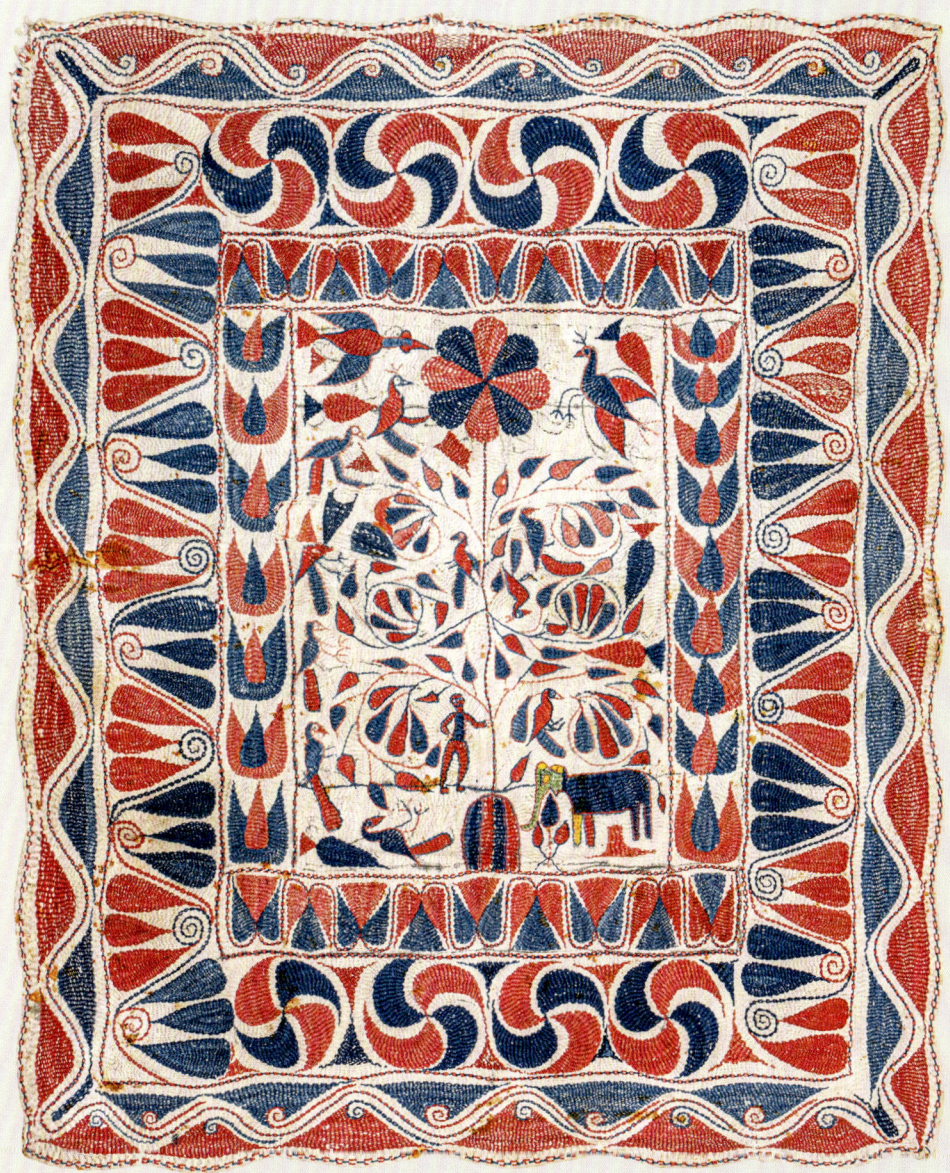

← Plants *Trees*

Details from two Asafo flags made by master flag maker Kobina Bodowah, Ghana, 1920s. 'Purist' robust simplified forms with minimal details created using complex appliqué and embroidery techniques are characteristic of Asafo flags. In both examples depicted here, priests point out offerings left under sacred trees

↑ Plants *Trees*

Kantha, undivided Bengal, late 19th century. Made by a woman using recycled threads created from old clothes, this embroidery has spinning wheels, a tree of life supporting a person, and various birds. This cover was not made for sale, but for use in the house in which it was created

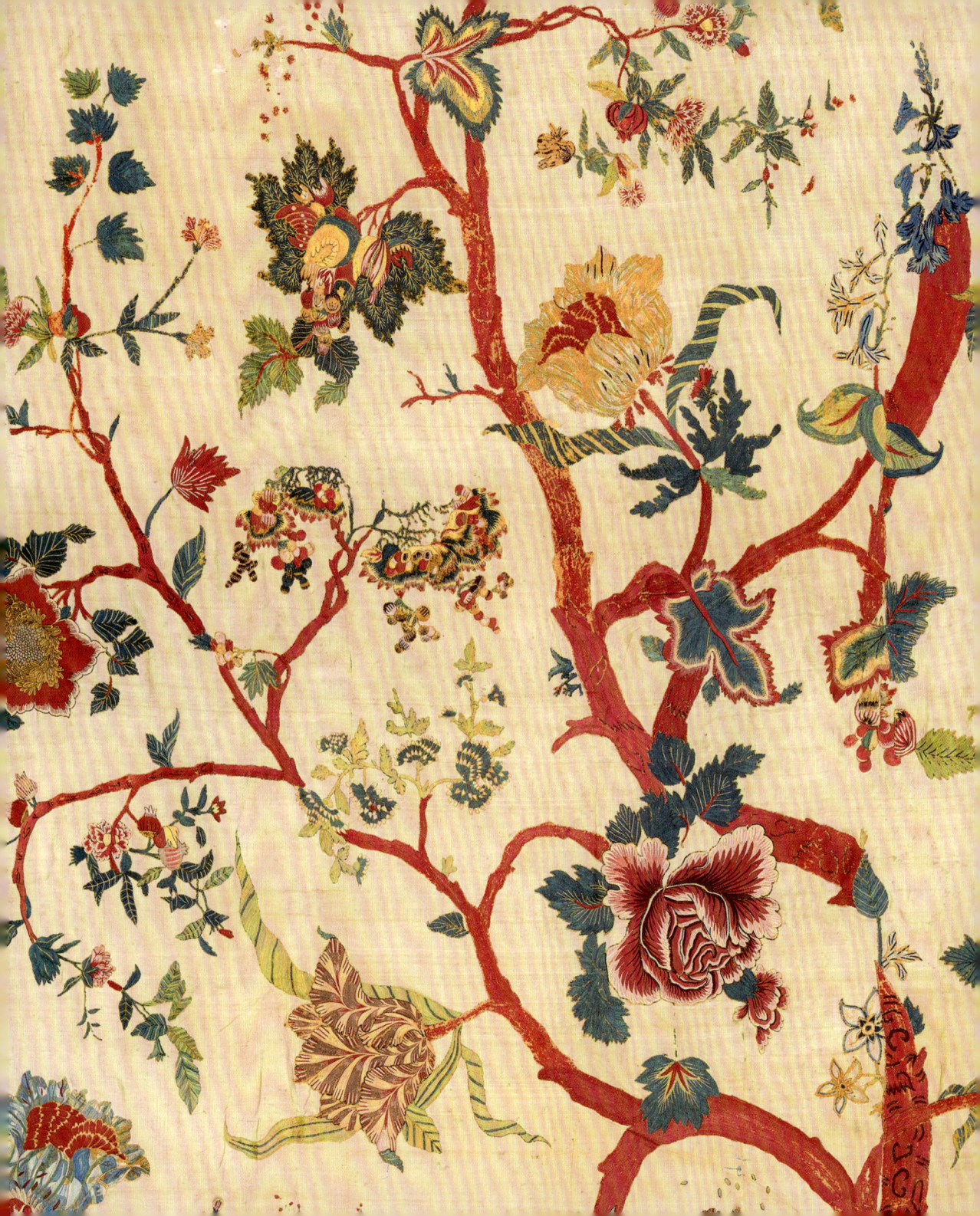

Plants *Trees*

← **Plants** *Trees*

Palampore or hanging for the European market, Gujarat, India, circa 1700. This was embroidered with a straight needle allowing for remarkable detailing. The design is inspired by imported botanical prints from the 1600s; colour and movement are encapsulated in the blossoming of the flowers

↓ **Plants** *Trees*

Palampore or hanging, India, circa 1715–25. The trees springing from rocky mounds focus the eye on a scene taken out of a contemporary Islamic miniature. It depicts a tiger attacking a deer. Their stances imply a direction of design that is balanced by the trees

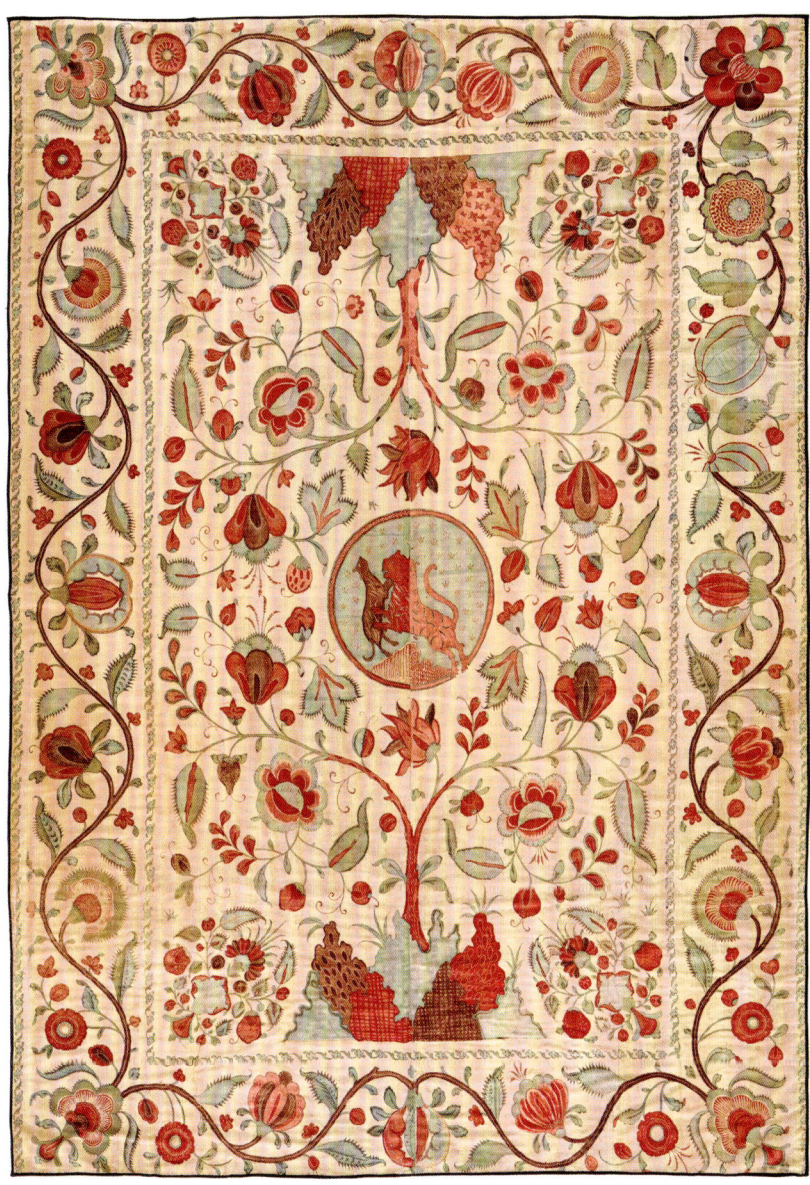

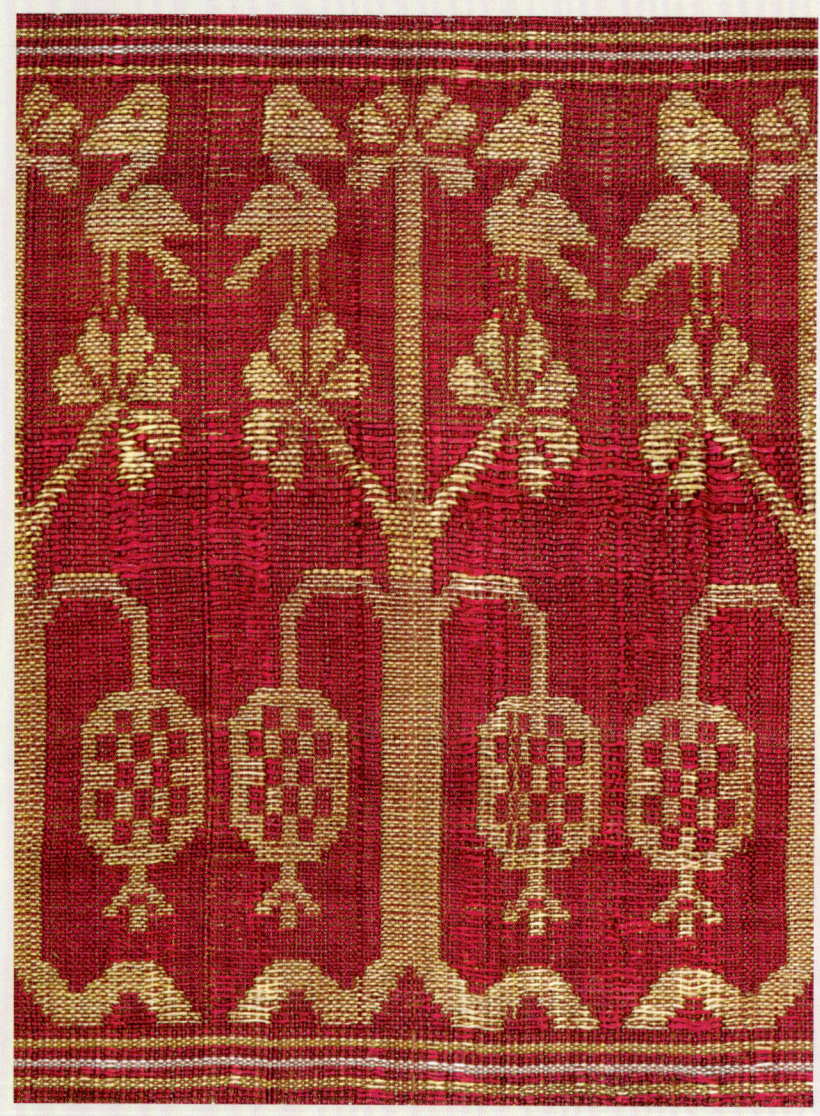

↑ **Plants** *Trees*

Silk sash, Morocco, 18th century. This complex woven sash includes a lot of precious metal thread and would have been wound around the body a number of times. Sashes such as this are associated with ceremonial costume. The trees bear heavy pomegranates, often seen as symbols of fertility

→ **Plants** *Trees*

Palampore or hanging, India, circa 1740–50. Made for the Western market, this hanging's twisting boughs and exaggerated scale are hallmarks of the best-quality chintz ordered to decorate beds and hang on the walls in grand houses in Europe

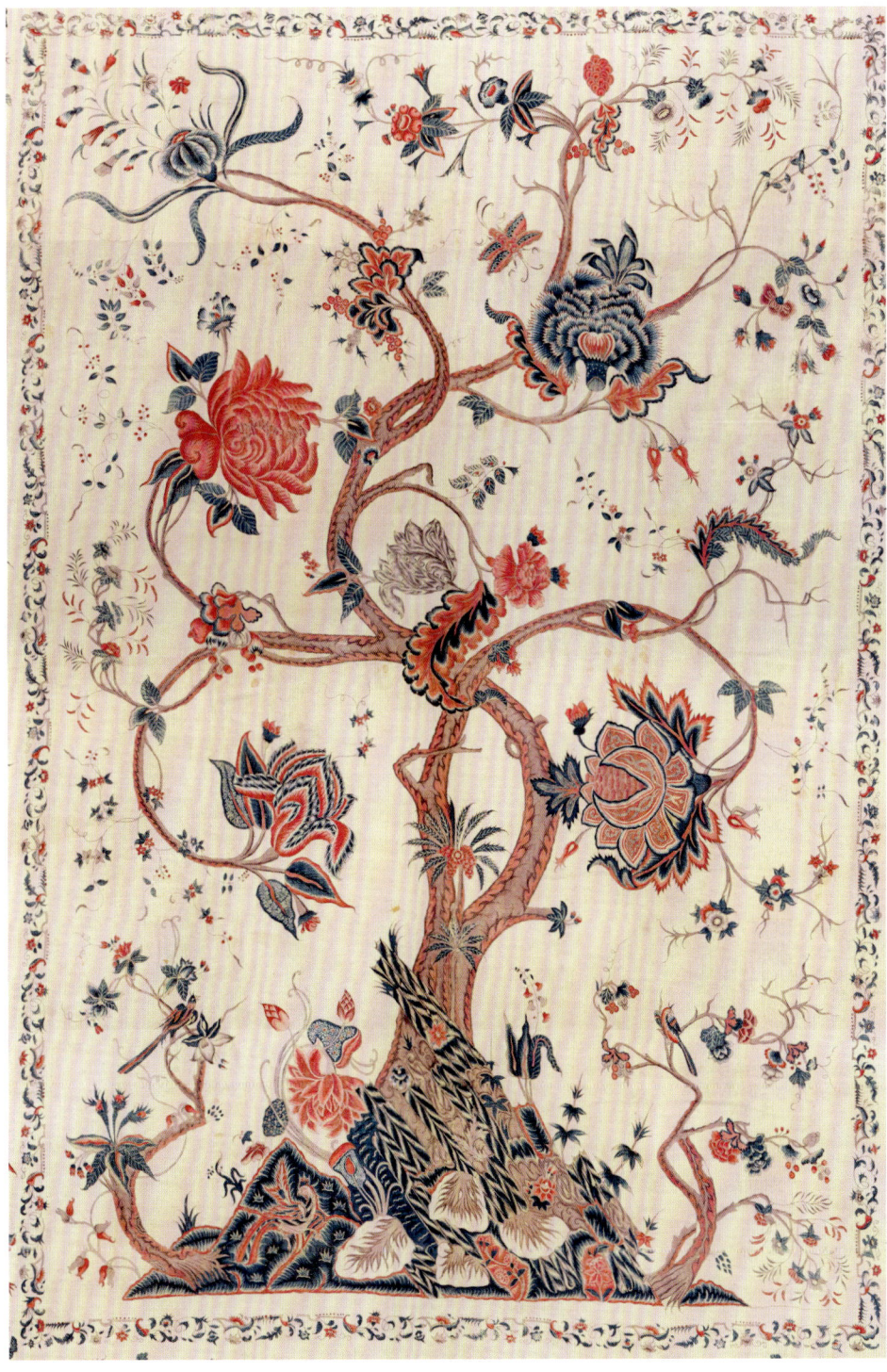

The Song of God: Bhagavad Gita, Chapter 15, verse 1, translated
by Swami Prabhavananda and Christopher Isherwood (1944)

"There is a fig tree
 In ancient story,
The giant Aswattha,
The everlasting,
Rooted in heaven,
Its branches earthward:
Each of its leaves
Is a song of the Vedas,
And he who knows it
Knows all the Vedas."

→ **Plants** *Trees*
Meisen kimono, Japan, early 20th century. A seam separates
two panels made with the ikat-style technique which gives the
blurred edges to the design. The loquat tree, depicted here, is a
popular tree in Japan, with the orange fruit widely eaten and its
leaves used to make tea

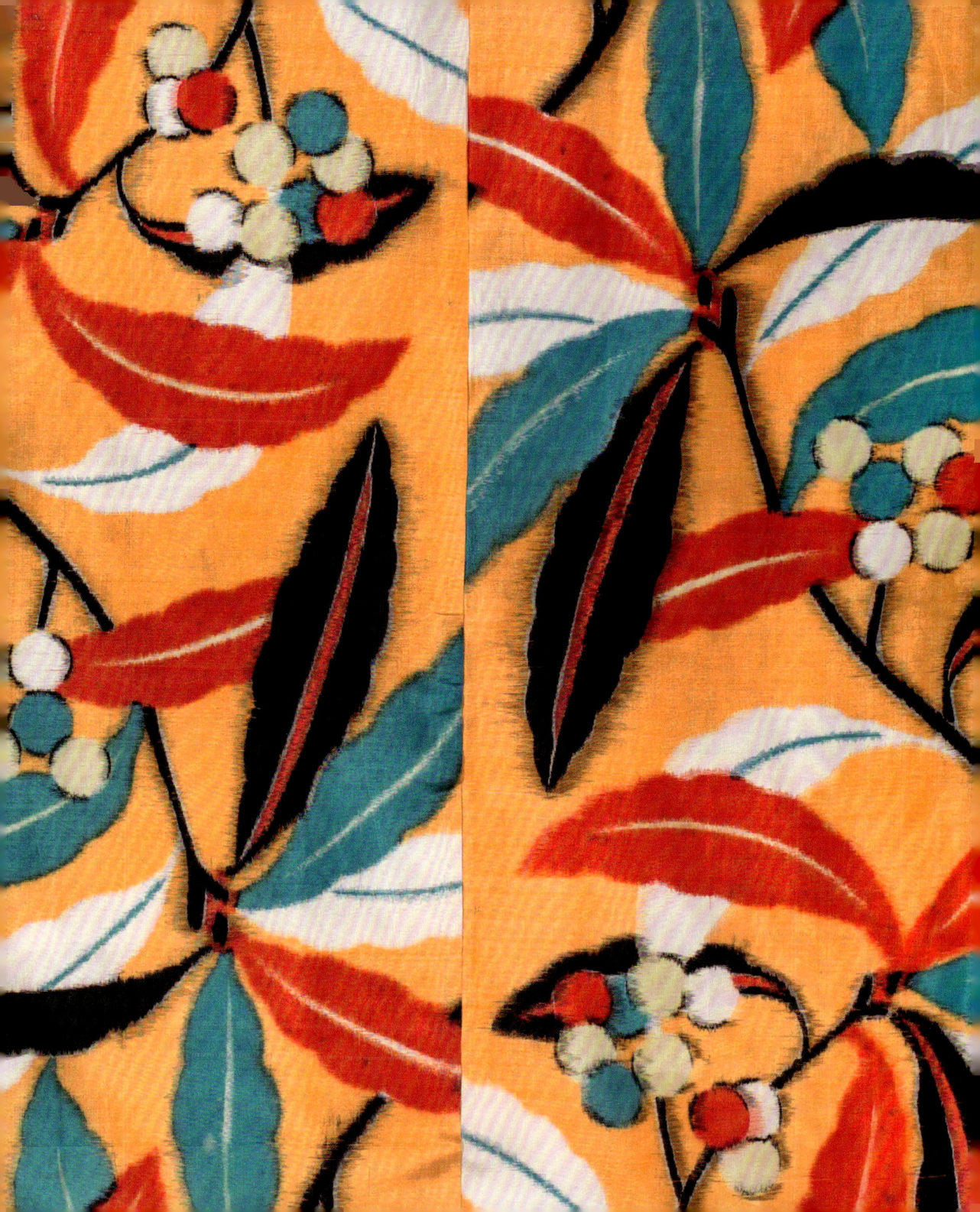

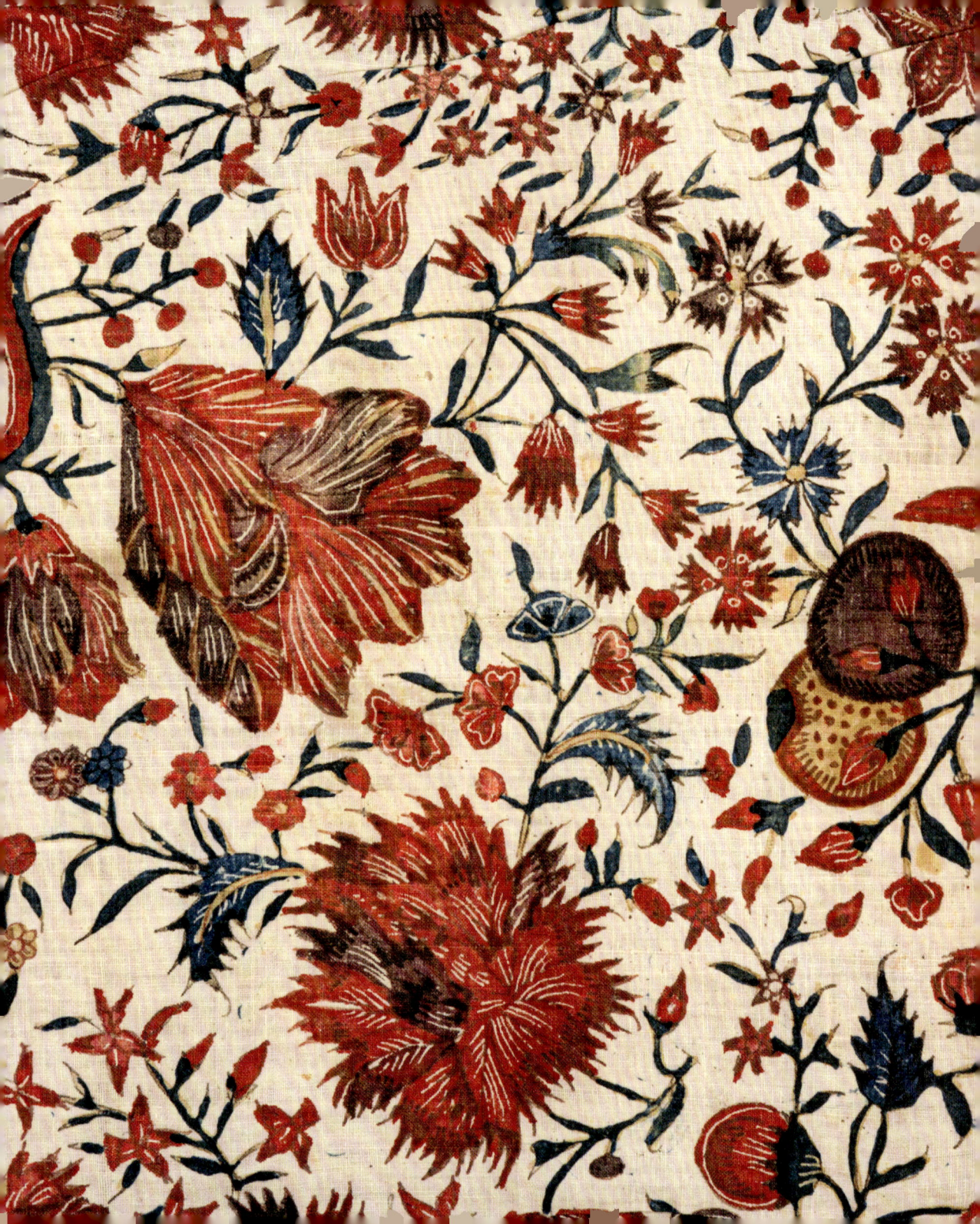

← **Plants** *Fruits*

Chintz panel, India for the Dutch market, mid-18th century. The cannonball tree has large fruits and fragrant flowers, and was introduced to Asia 300 years ago. It has become a sacred tree as it is associated with the canopy of the Shiva linga, an abstract representation of the Hindu deity

↓ **Plants** *Fruits*

Embroidered dress panel, Gujarat, India, early 18th century. Cashew were introduced to India by the Portuguese in the 1560s, and this is the earliest Indian depiction of the nut. This elegant yardage would have been cut up in Europe for dressmaking – several dresses of a similar style survive today

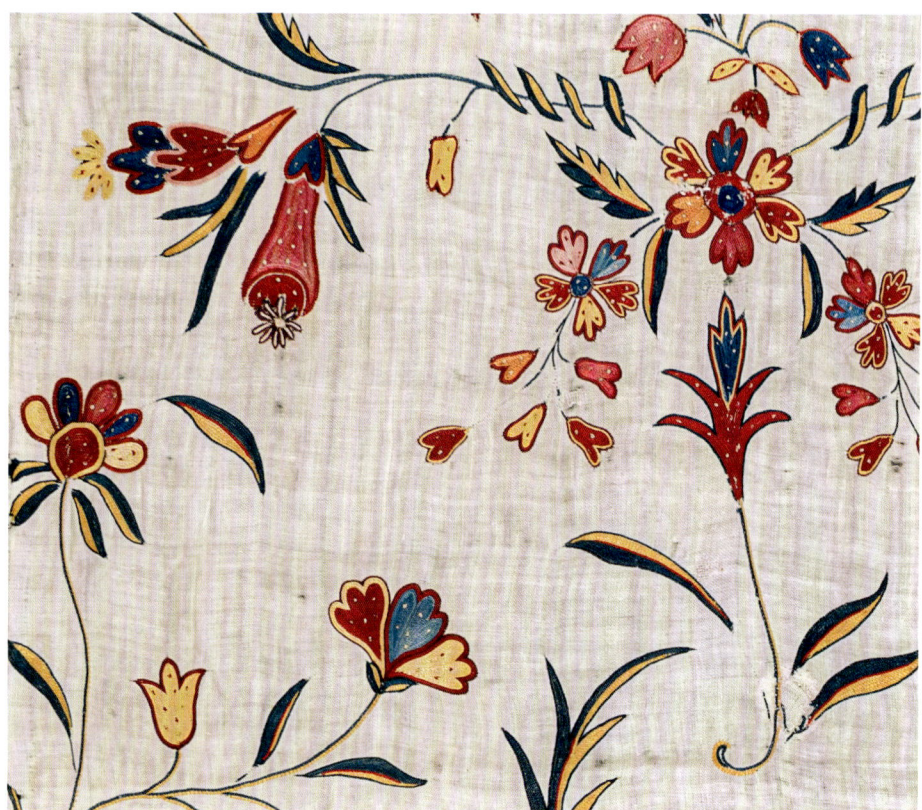

Fruit has a magical quality since it is sweet to eat and sustains us but also contains the seed of its own regeneration. The link between its flesh and seed is a source of inspiration in many textile traditions, where fruit is also used for dyeing and colouring. Sometimes, textiles and fruit also have shared tales of long-distance trade and exchange to tell.

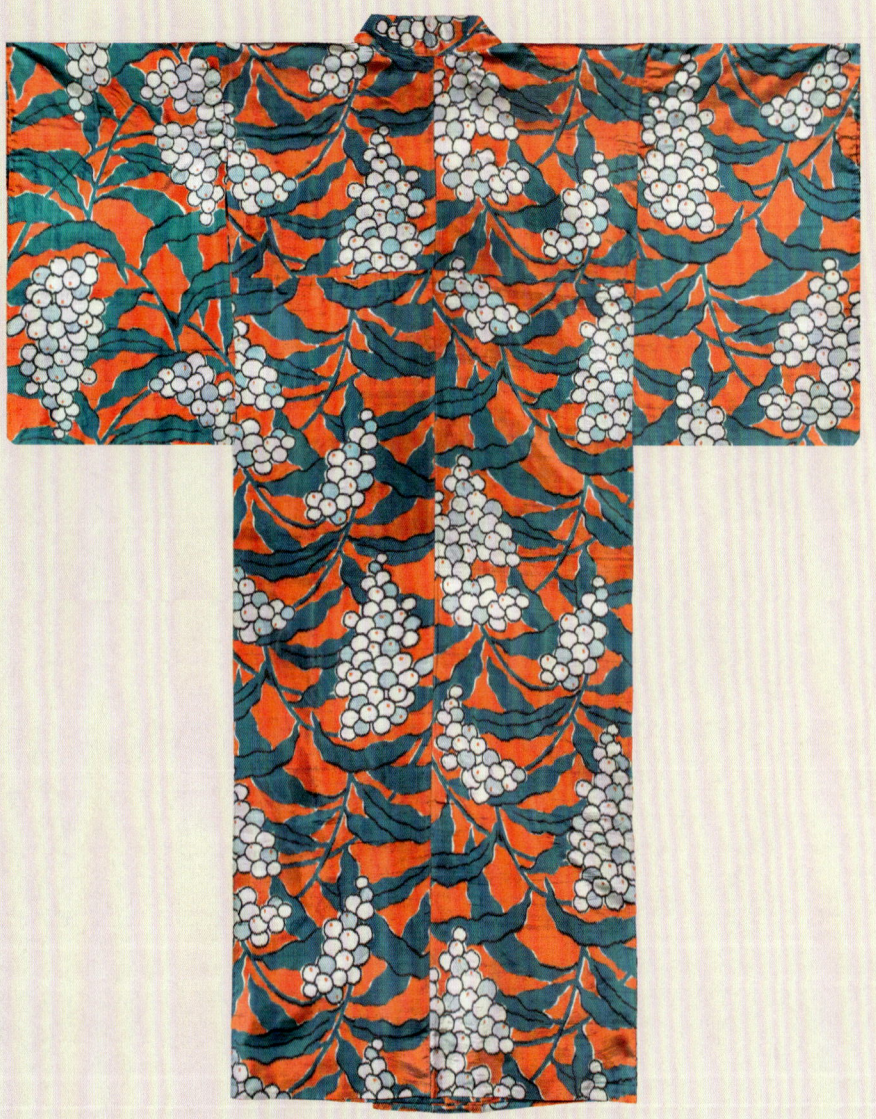

↑ **Plants** *Fruits*
Meisen kimono, Japan, early 20th century. As dress traditions
relaxed, women wanted to show individual taste via more modern
kimonos, which led to an explosion of innovation in small
weaving studios mixing Western fashion with Japanese style. Here
grapes and banana leaves make for a Hawaiian shirt-like design

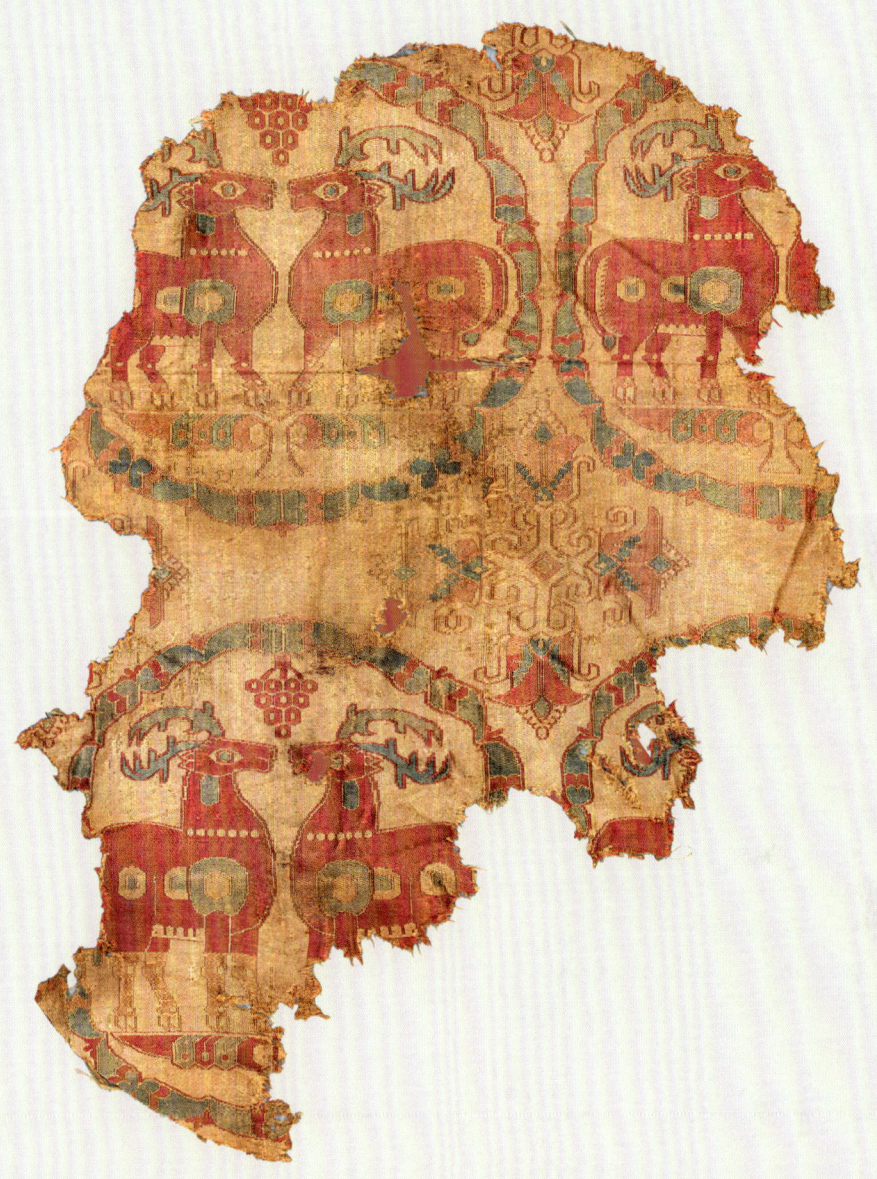

↑ **Plants** *Fruits*
Sogdian silk fragment, Central Asia, 6th–8th century. These horned confronted rams or deer seem to smell the bouquet of a bunch of grapes that hangs between them. The depiction of such animals suggested a divine connection for the member of the elite wearing or associated with the textile

↓↓ **Plants** *Fruits*
Silk embroidered table carpet, France (?), 17th century. A suggestion of abundance is made through an excess of fruit-laden branches and flowers. The sharp-eyed can make out tiny instances of words and letters in this rich yet highly unusual carpet. We can only speculate about its meaning

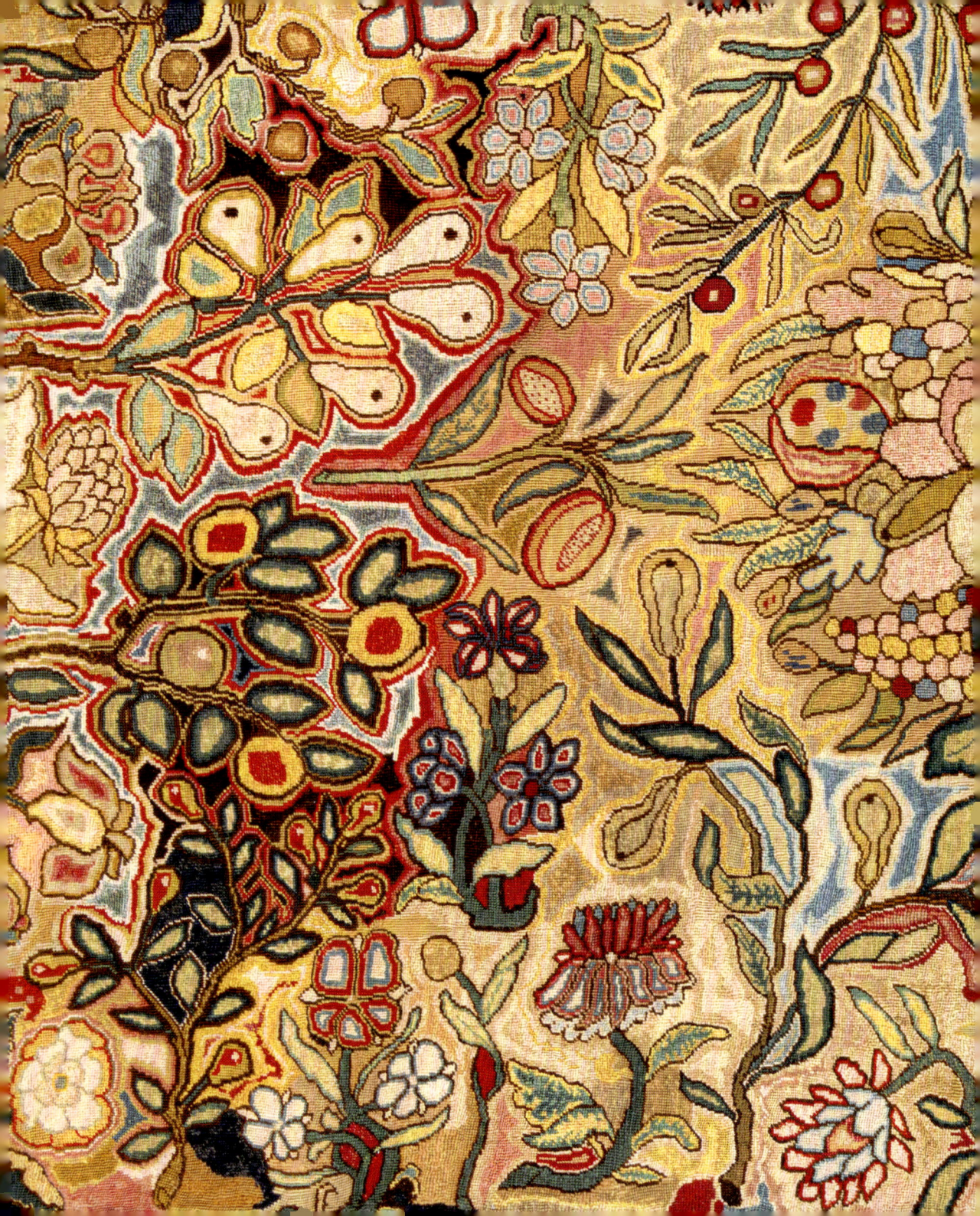

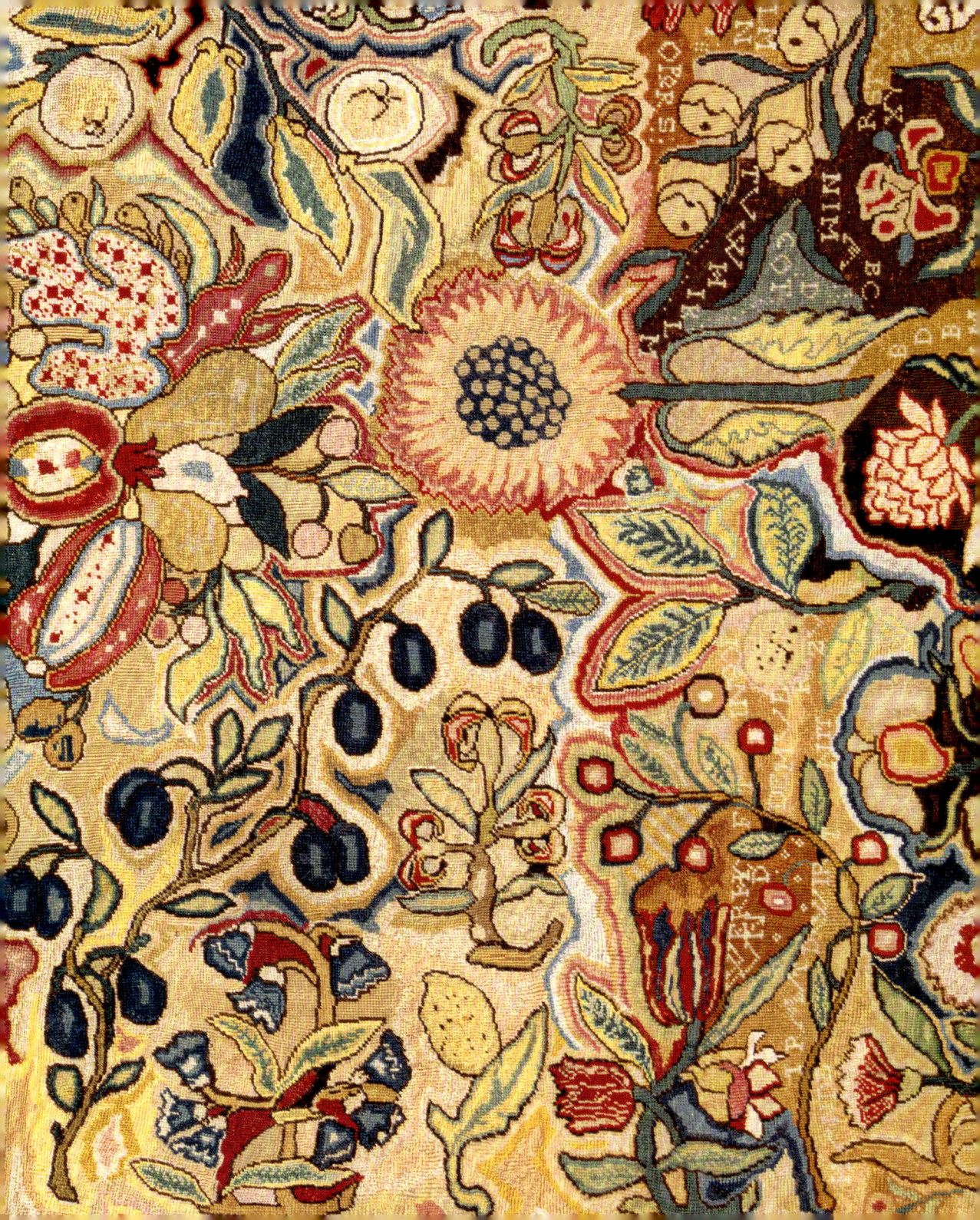

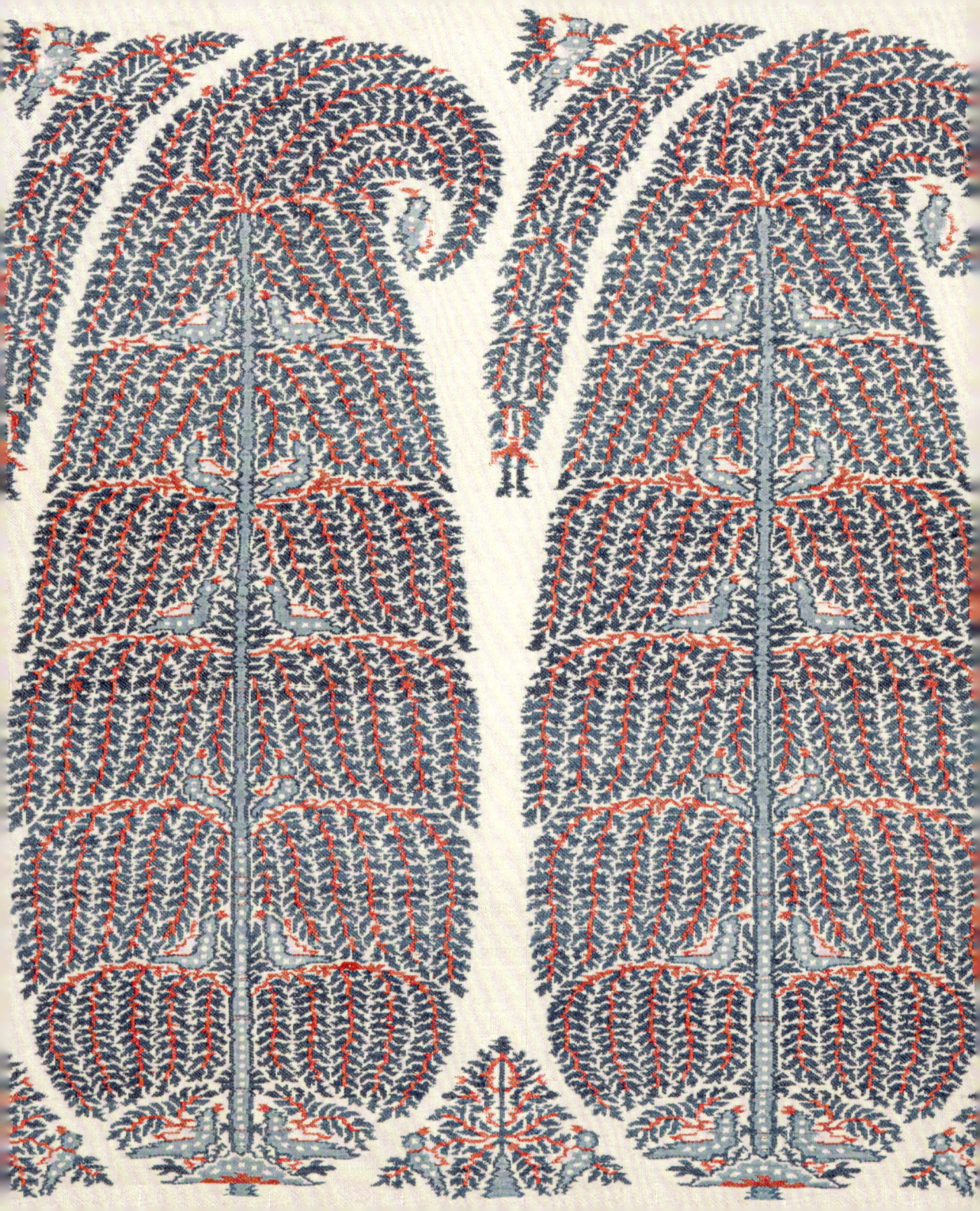

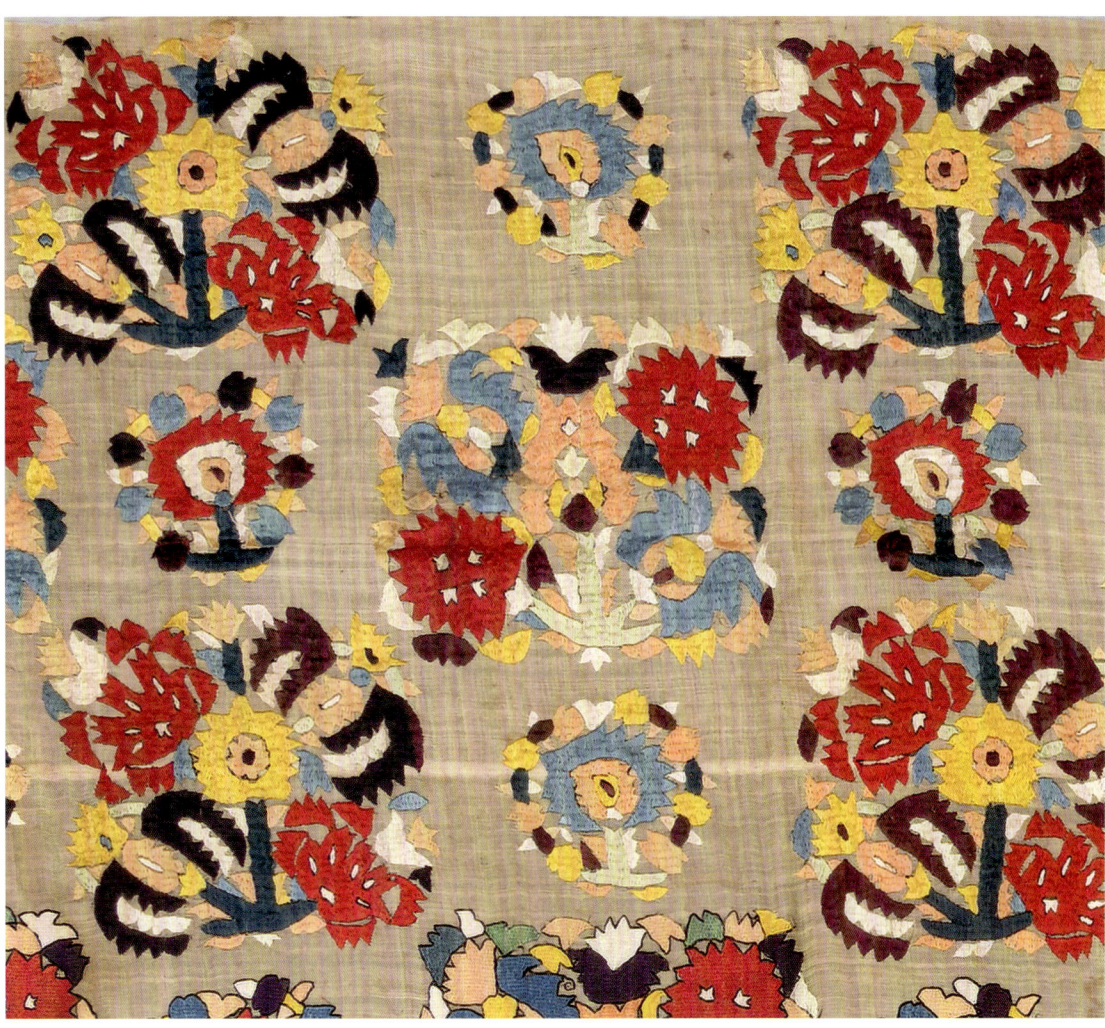

← **Plants** *Bushes*
Shawl, France, early 19th century. The flowering shrub or boteh is commonly known as the paisley pattern. In fact, it originated in Iran and India, and was widely copied into shawls in France and Britain to fulfil huge demand in the 19th century. Note here the small parrots hidden in the dense foliage

↑ **Plants** *Bushes*
Silk embroidered hanging, Tetouan, Morocco, 18th century. The use of masses of silk on a fine linen ground gives this hanging considerable weight, allowing it to drape elegantly as a bed- or window cover. The bushes are made up of easily identifiable individual flowers with contrasting colours

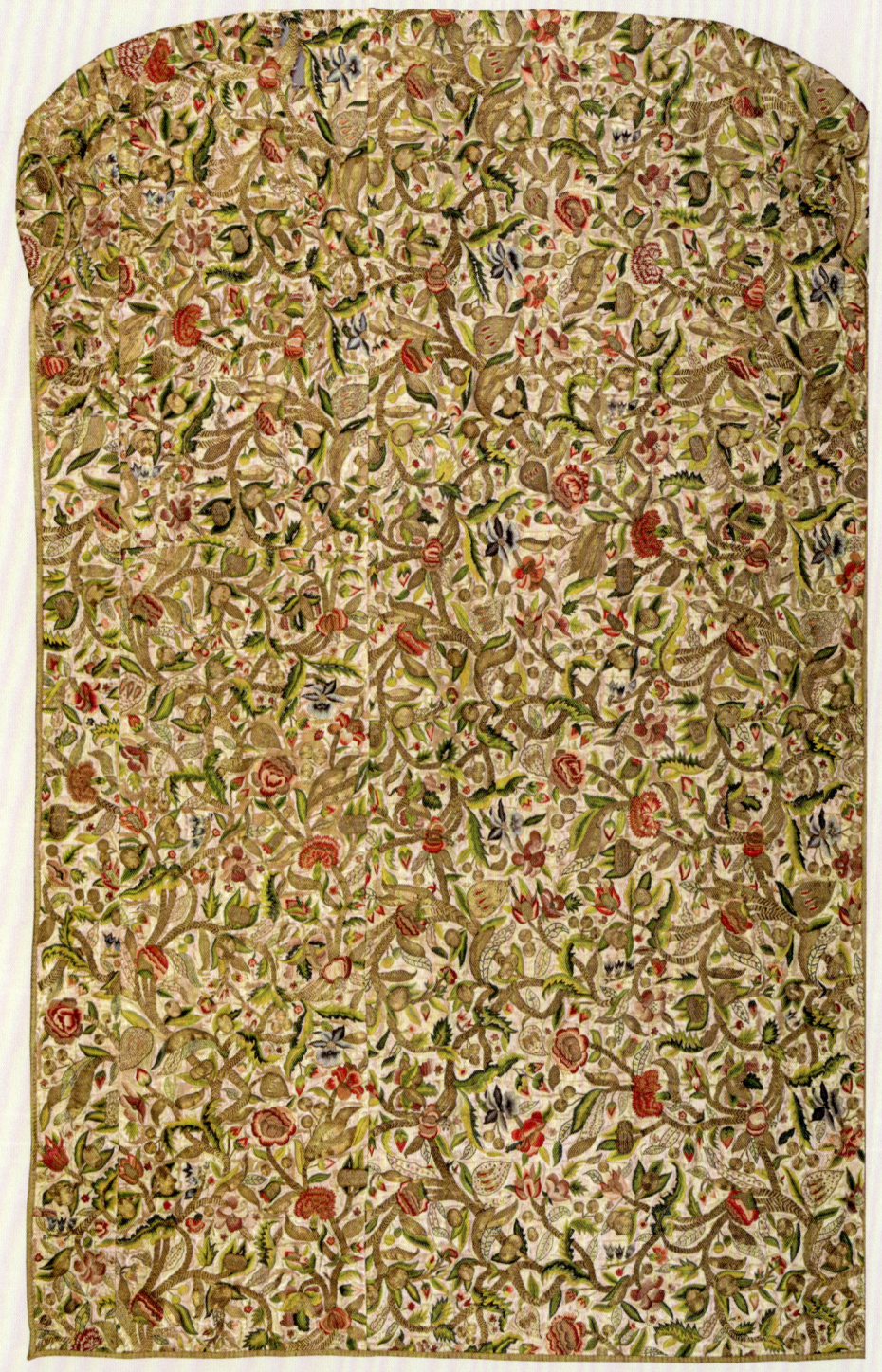

← **Plants** *Superabundance*

Embroidered bed cover, England, mid-18th century. The full glory of spring is suggested in this design, everything bursting with life and in full bloom. Silk is used alongside silver and silver-gilt metal thread to help convey this sense of excess and luxury

↓ **Plants** *Superabundance*

Kantha, undivided Bengal, late 19th century. The central lotus and surrounding trees and plants show the cycle of life, full of energy and a rich, fertile garden. This is far from the scarcity of resources that may be implied by the use of recycled threads

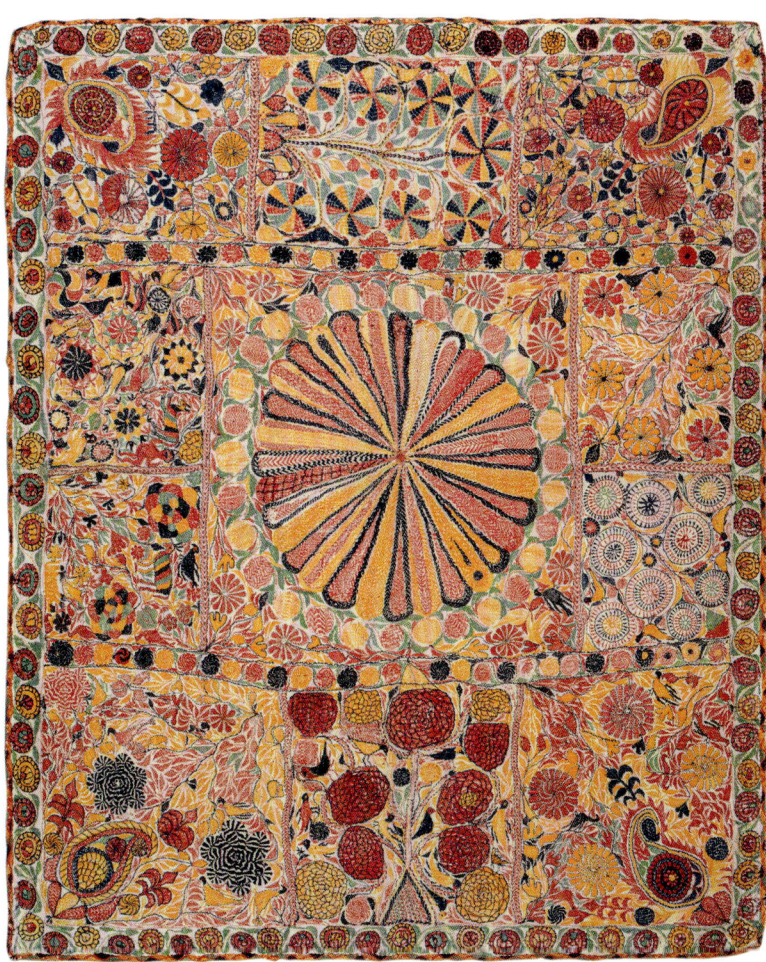

Superabundance is a maximalist form of decoration. It is well suited to depictions of nature, as it suggests wealth, luxury and extravagance through a sense of abundance and lushness. This translates to the surface of an object being packed full of ornamentation and for plants to be overburdened with lush fruit and huge rich flowers creating an almost fantastical environment.

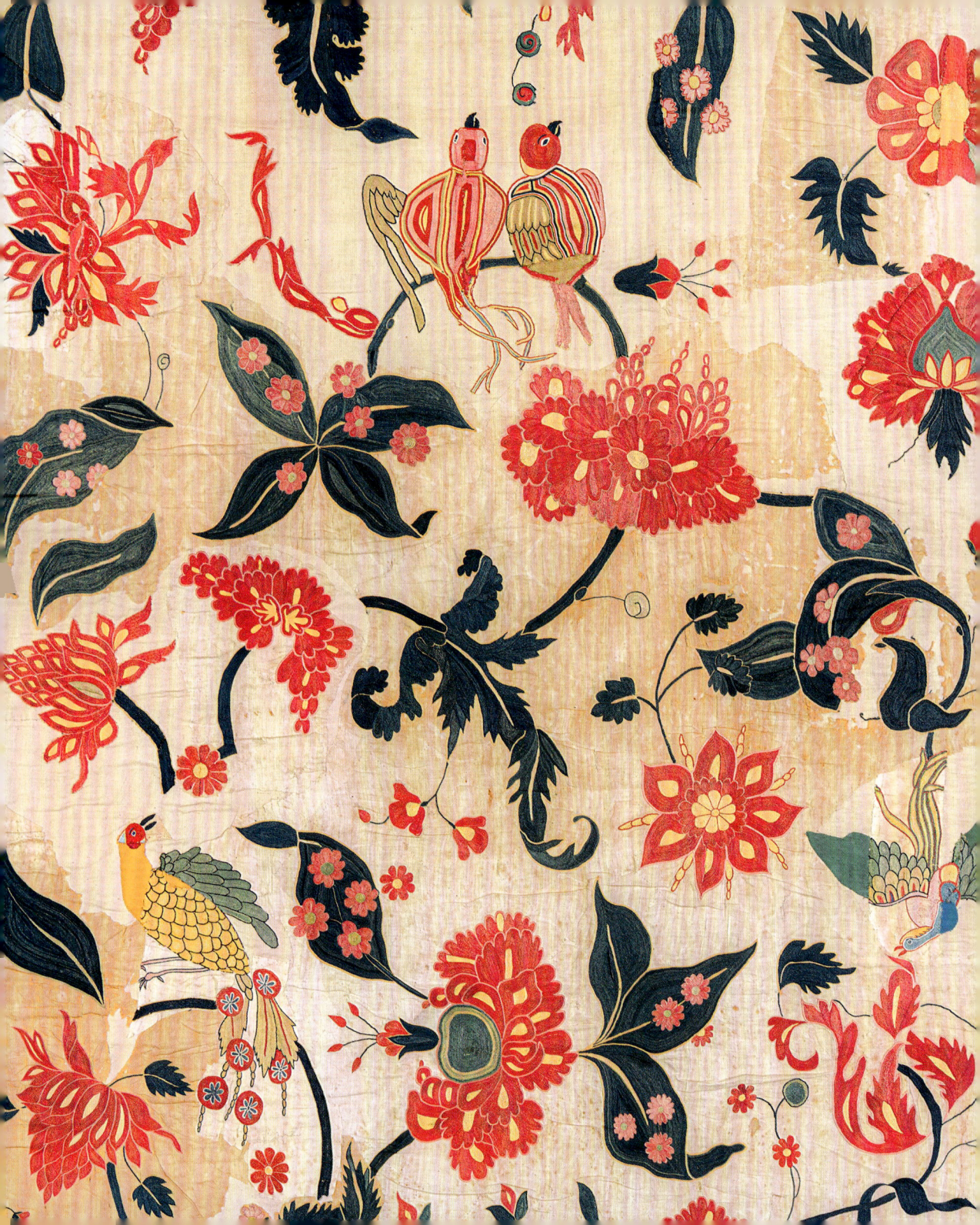

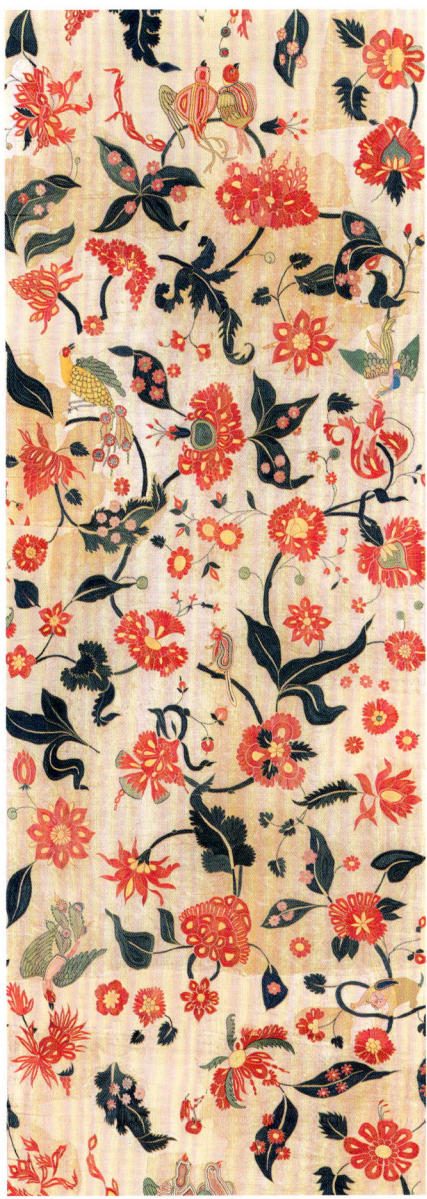

← **Plants** *Superabundance*

Embroidered bed hangings, Gujarat, India, 17th century. Made up from lots of small fragments, these panels belong to a set of hangings made for Ashburnham Place in southern England. Other parts are in the Victoria and Albert Museum in London and the Met in New York. Made in professional workshops for export, this textile sees birds, enormous flowers and twisting leaves form a lush canopy of a forest that is hyper real. The silk becomes like paint and creates shadow and depth throughout

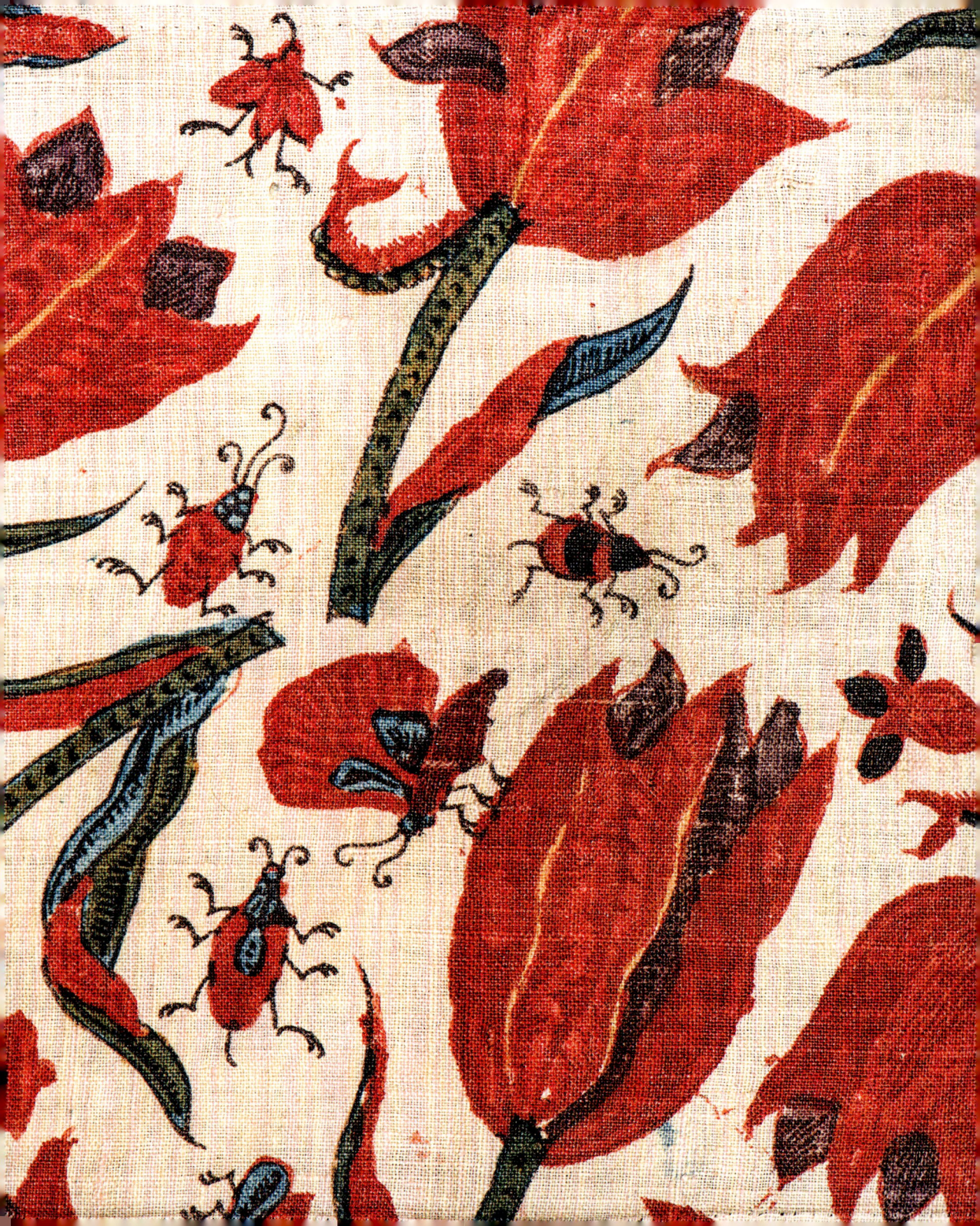

Animals are depicted in many guises in textiles, reflecting differences in cultural and religious traditions. While birds are sometimes seen to represent a connection with the heavens, interestingly insects also have a role as metaphors and prey. Animals in depictions are more than heraldic emblems, admired for their strength, agility, loyalty or wisdom. They evoke emotion and empathy and can be a vehicle for expressing human relations, earnestly or through satire.

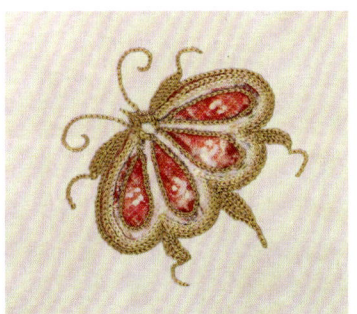
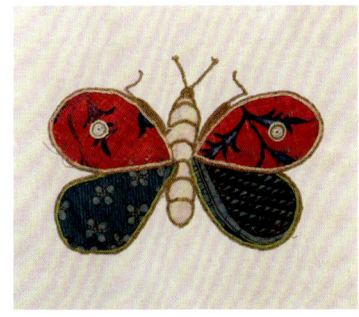
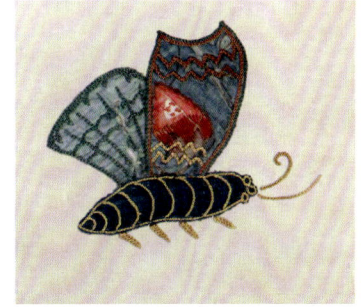
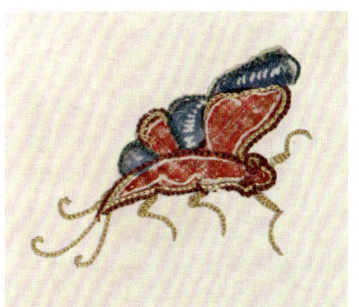
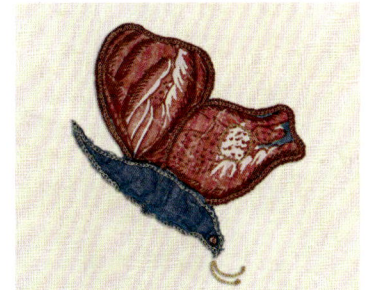
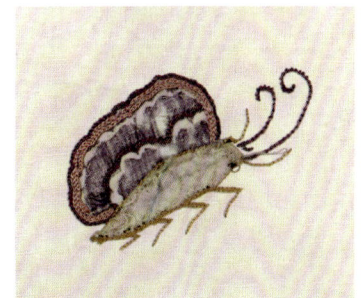

← **Animals** *Insects*
Chintz panel, India for the Dutch market, early 1700s. The craze for tulips, or tulip mania, is captured in this fragment preserved and found in Japan. The ladybirds and beetles are less typically part of tulip mania iconography but a lively addition

↑ **Animals** *Insects*
Embroidery, France, mid-18th century. The butterflies are made from small scraps of Indian chintz, showing the residual value of the cloth and the inventiveness of the embroiderer. Insects consume scraps; here they are made from the same

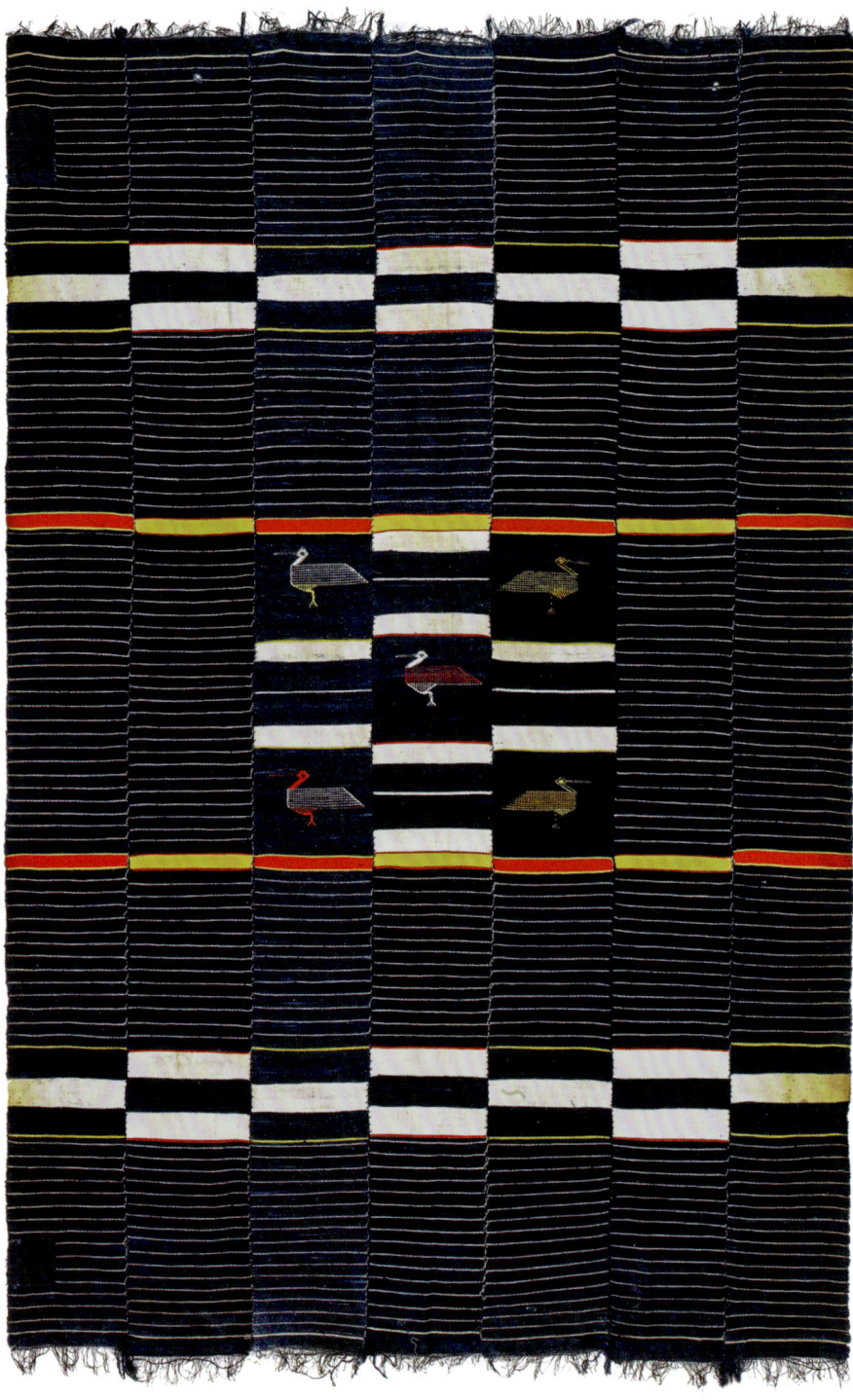

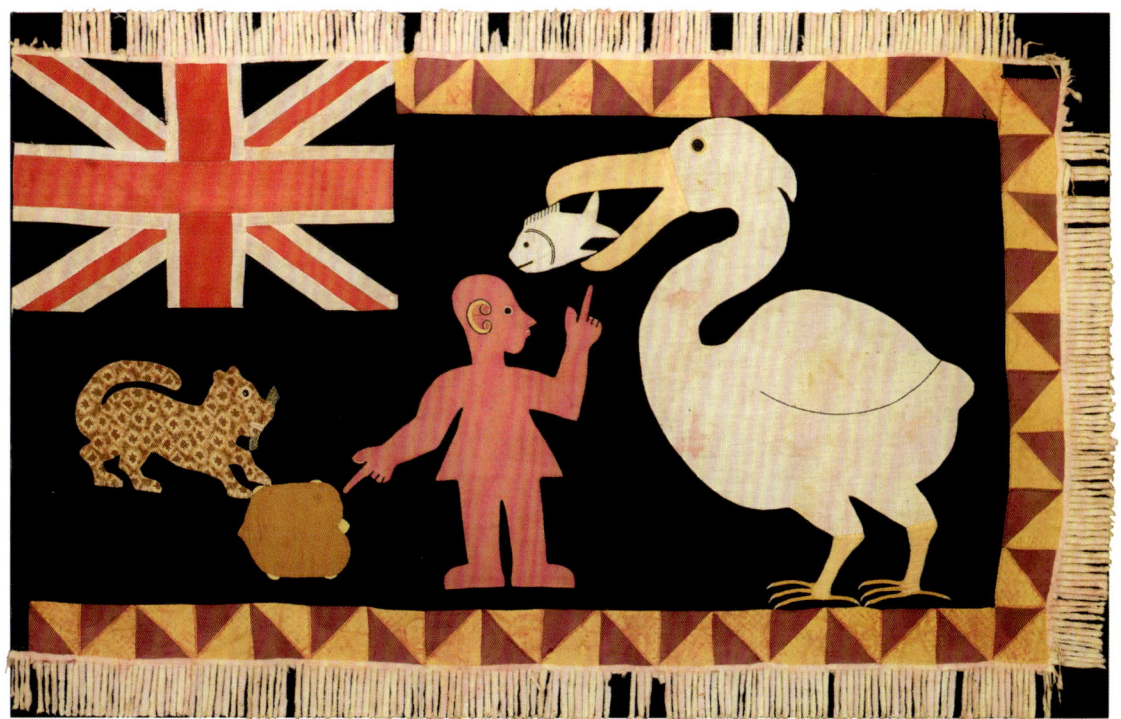

← **Animals** *Birds*
Blanket or wearing cloth, Ivory Coast, first half 20th century. The austere formality of the narrow lines cages five long-billed water birds in the centre of this rare depiction of the natural world in a West African textile. The birds would have been visible when the cloth was wrapped around the wearer

↑ **Animals** *Birds*
Asafo flag, Ghana, 20th century. This double-sided flag would have been used in a procession and depicts two local proverbs, one on the front and one on the back. On this side we see the pelican eating a fish backwards, meaning that problems must be approached in the right way

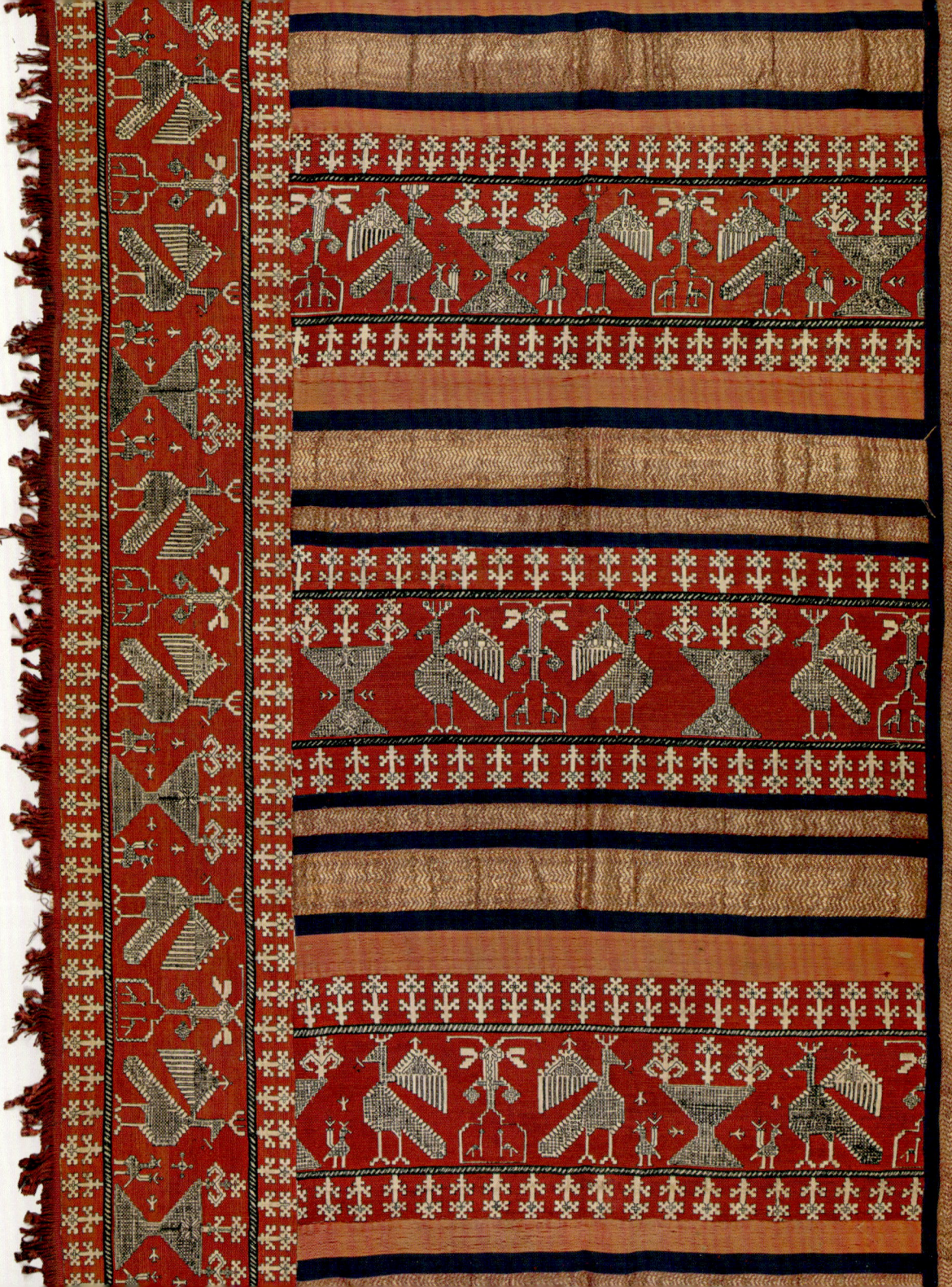

← **Animals** *Birds*

Hanging, Azemmour, Morocco, 18th century. This curtain is made using sections of a long embroidered band with metal-thread brocade. Winged and crested birds flanking vases is a common motif across the Mediterranean from the 16th century

↓ **Animals** *Birds*

Chief's beaded tunic, Ndop, Cameroon, 19th century. Hidden in the beaded surface are pelicans with curved necks and crocodiles. The lining helps identify the place and date of this prestige object

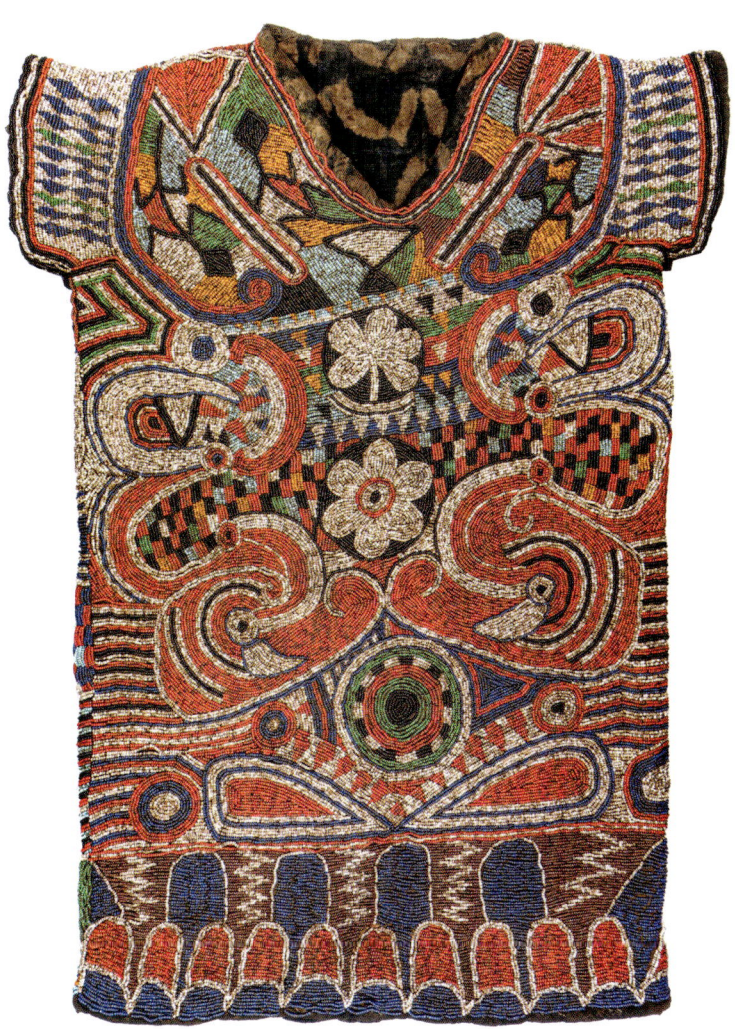

↓↓ **Animals** *Animals*

Quilt, USA, dated 1916. Embroidery gives the maker great control over the curves in the drawing of figures and flowers done on a fine cotton ground. Probably taken from a pattern published in a magazine or pattern book, the design favours naive small-scale sketches of animals close to home. Only a few vignettes are not repeated and a home is at the centre

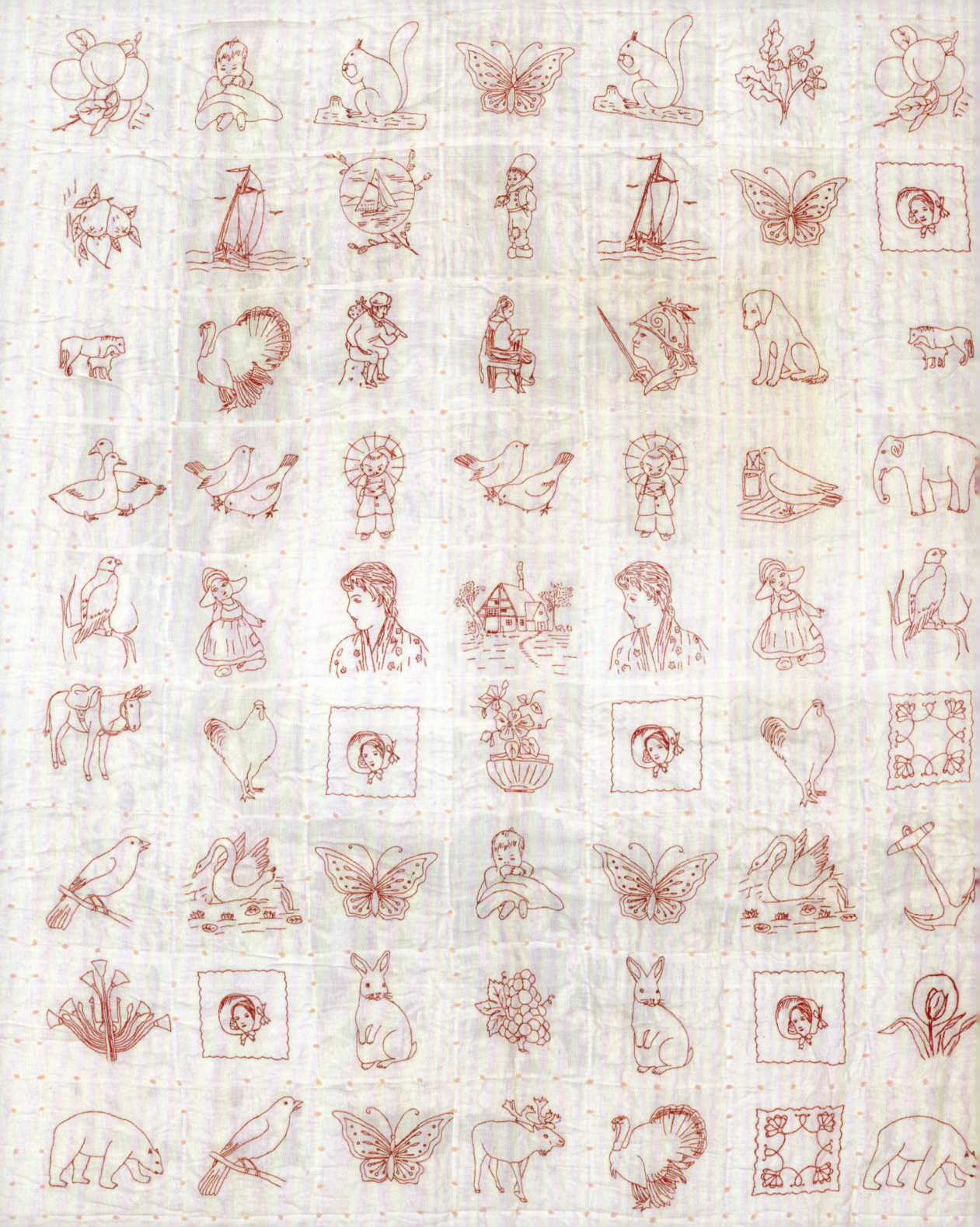

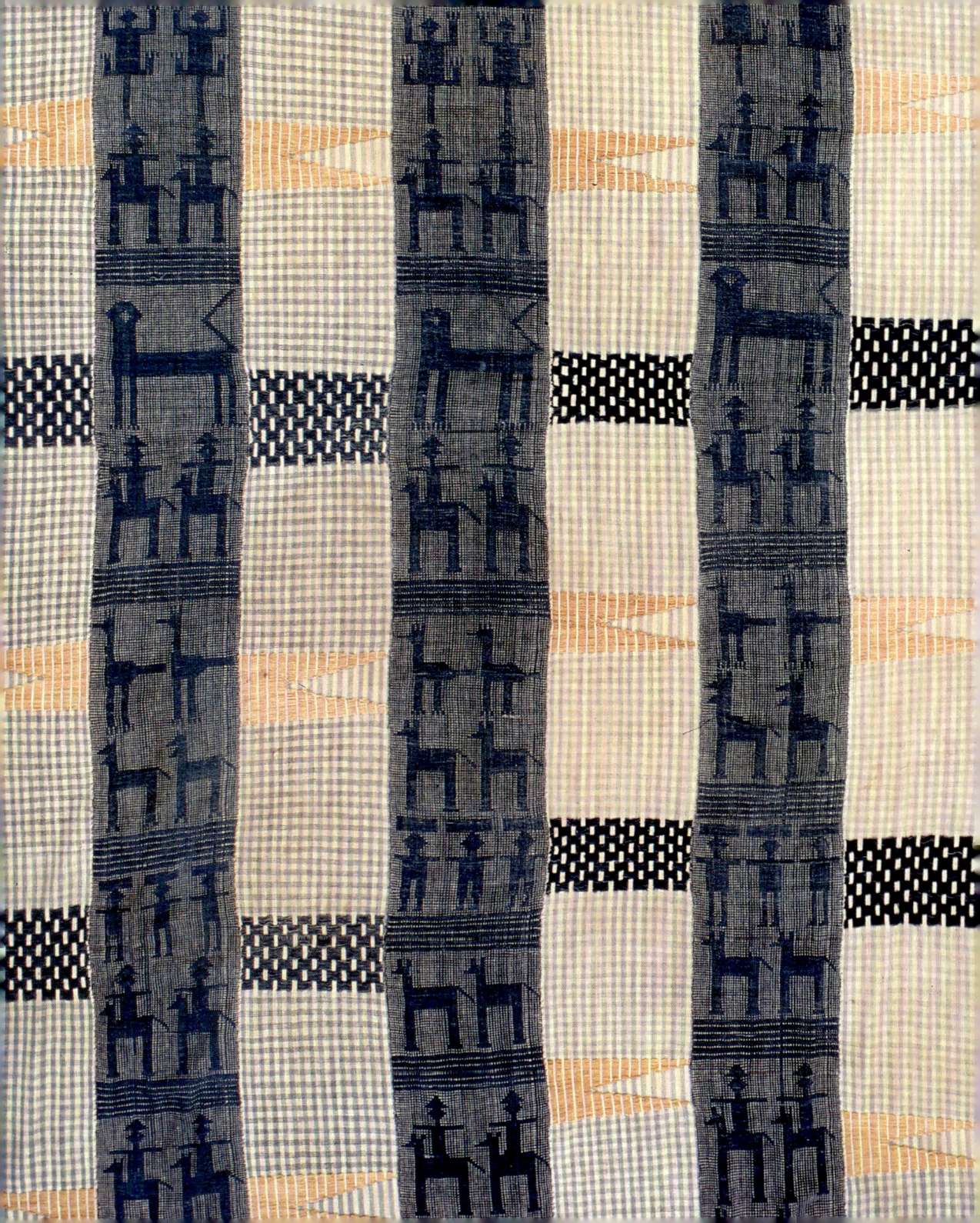

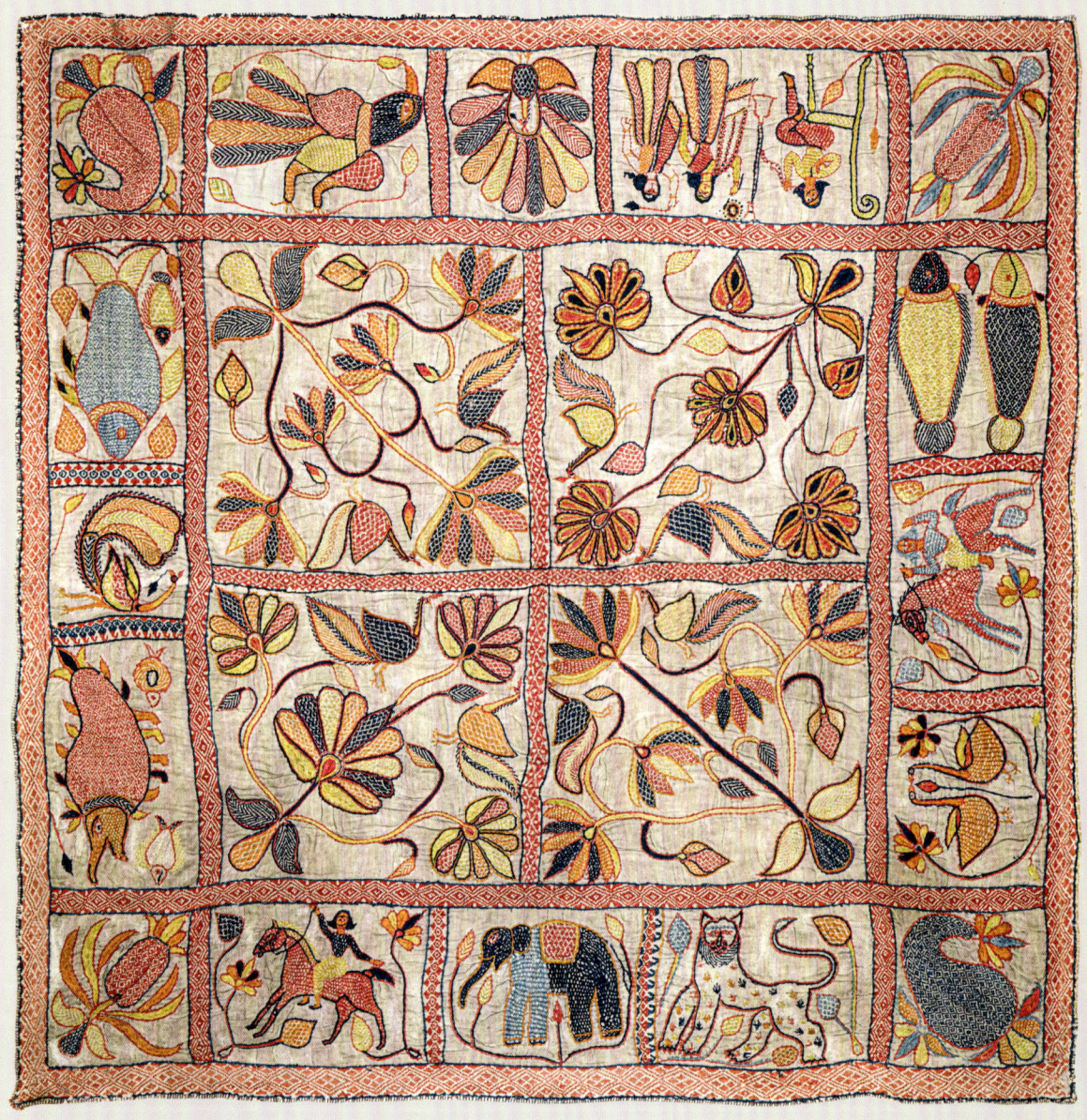

↑ **Animals** *Animals*
Kantha, undivided Bengal, late 19th century. In the border there
are sea dragons, elephants and riders, fish, which are seen
as symbolic of good fortune, and a sea monster or Makara.
Depictions of Makara are used to protect temples and liminal
spaces, guarding against malign spirits and influences

↑↑ **Animals** *Animals*

Shawl, Nigeria, 19th century. One of only two known examples, this shawl has numerous animal motifs in the narrow stripes. Note the way that many of the animals have different features and characteristics, from humps or saddles to heads facing backwards

↓ **Animals** *Animals*

Display cloth, Nigeria, 20th century. Made using resist dyeing in the Wukari region for trade to neighbouring Cameroon, this textile shows a leopard, a symbol of royal power, alongside crocodiles with birds or turtles

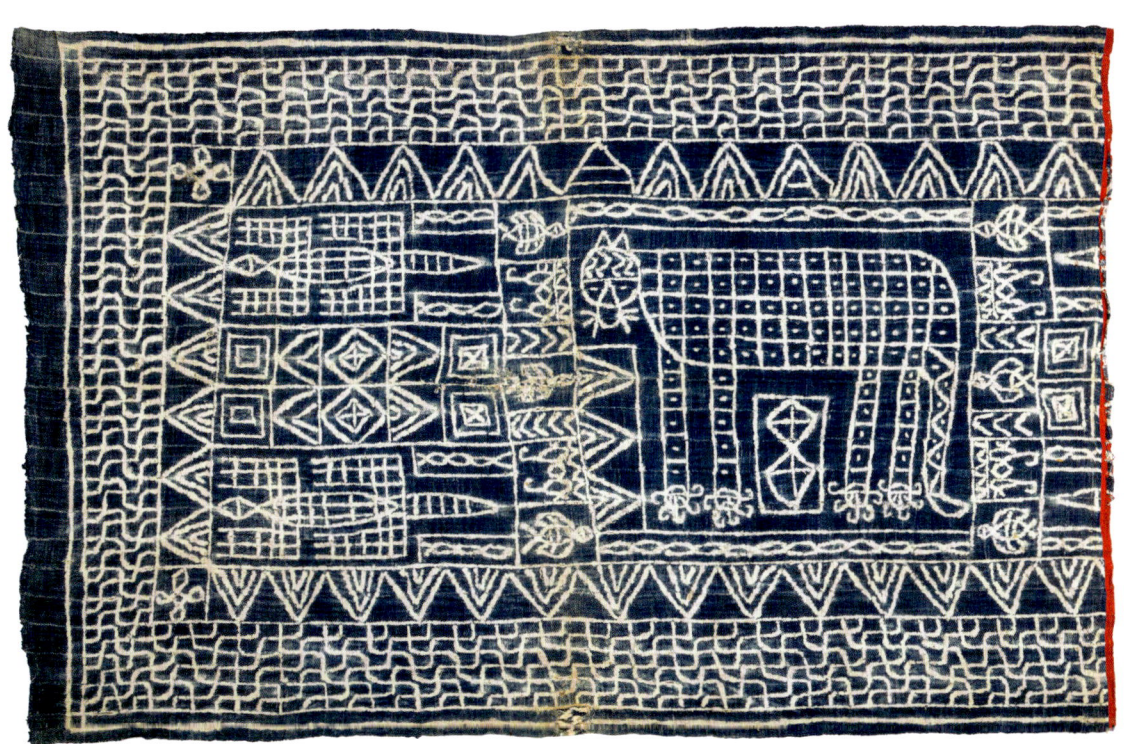

Mythological beasts are part of the origin stories and legends of most societies. Textiles are common sites of depictions of such fantastic creatures, some of which occur nowhere else, testament to the creativity of textile designers throughout history.

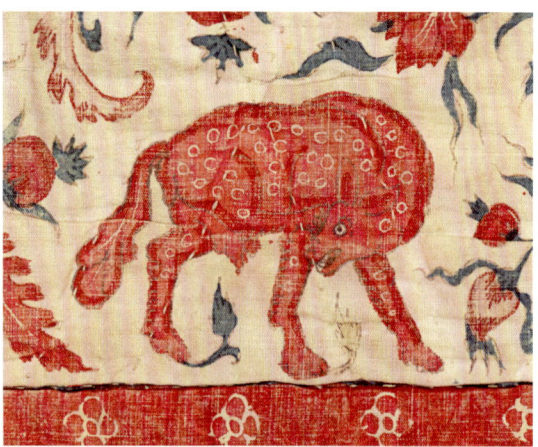

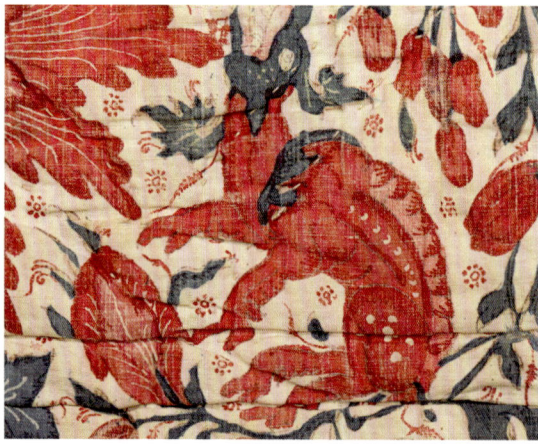

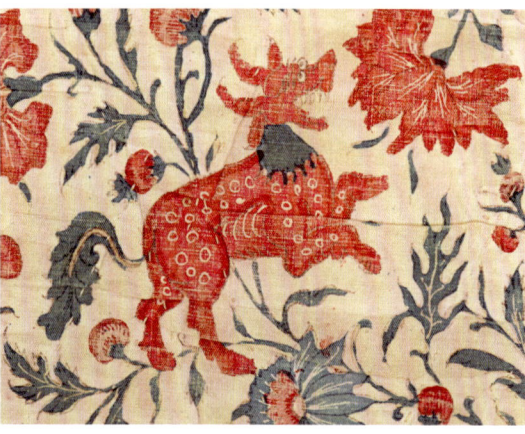

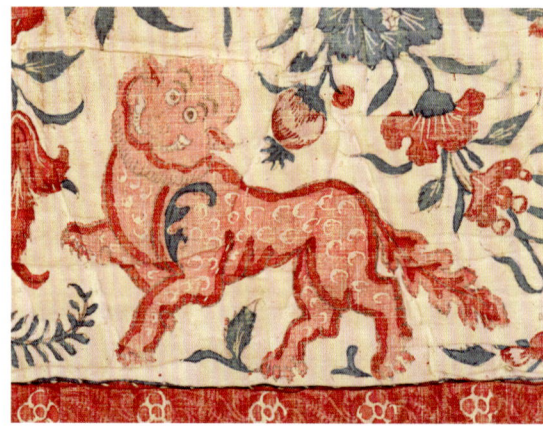

↑ **Animals** *Animals*
Chintz quilt, India but quilted in France, 18th century. Hiding in the undergrowth are hybrids of various animals. The elements are inspired by Chinese and Persian traditions and are hand drawn by their maker

→ **Animals** *Animals*
Printed fabric fragment, France, 1780s. This is a known pattern called *Les Coquecigrues*, manufactured by the famous Oberkampf Manufactory in eastern France. The elf-like figure blends seamlessly into the plant fronds and flowers

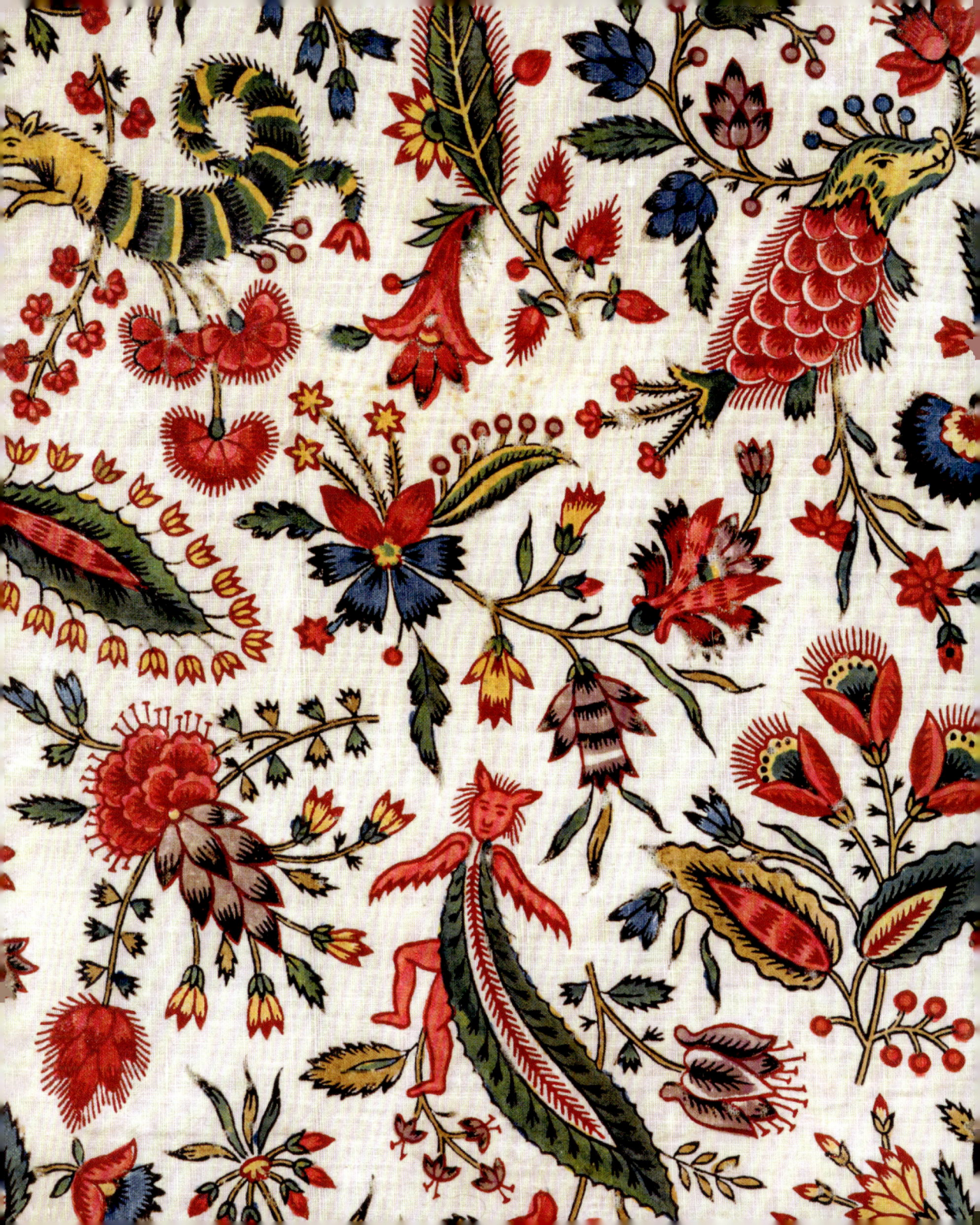

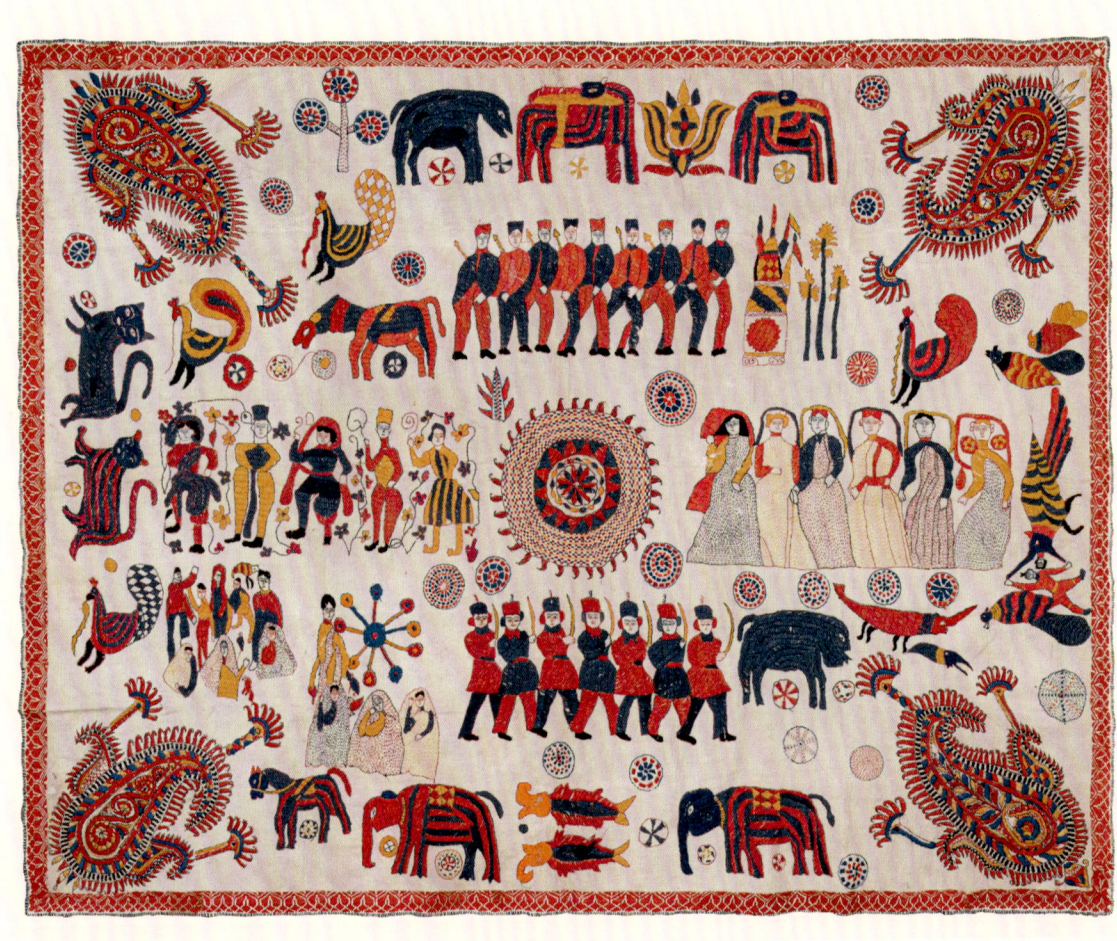

The Human Realm

"Fine art is that in which the hand, the head, and the heart of man go together."

← **Human activity** *Celebrations*
Kantha, undivided Bengal, 20th century. In this embroidered cover, a family is celebrating a wedding. We also see companies of soldiers and stylised flora and fauna, as well as images taken from religious texts, such as the Makara, a mythological sea creature, devouring a man

↑ *The Two Paths*, John Ruskin (1859)

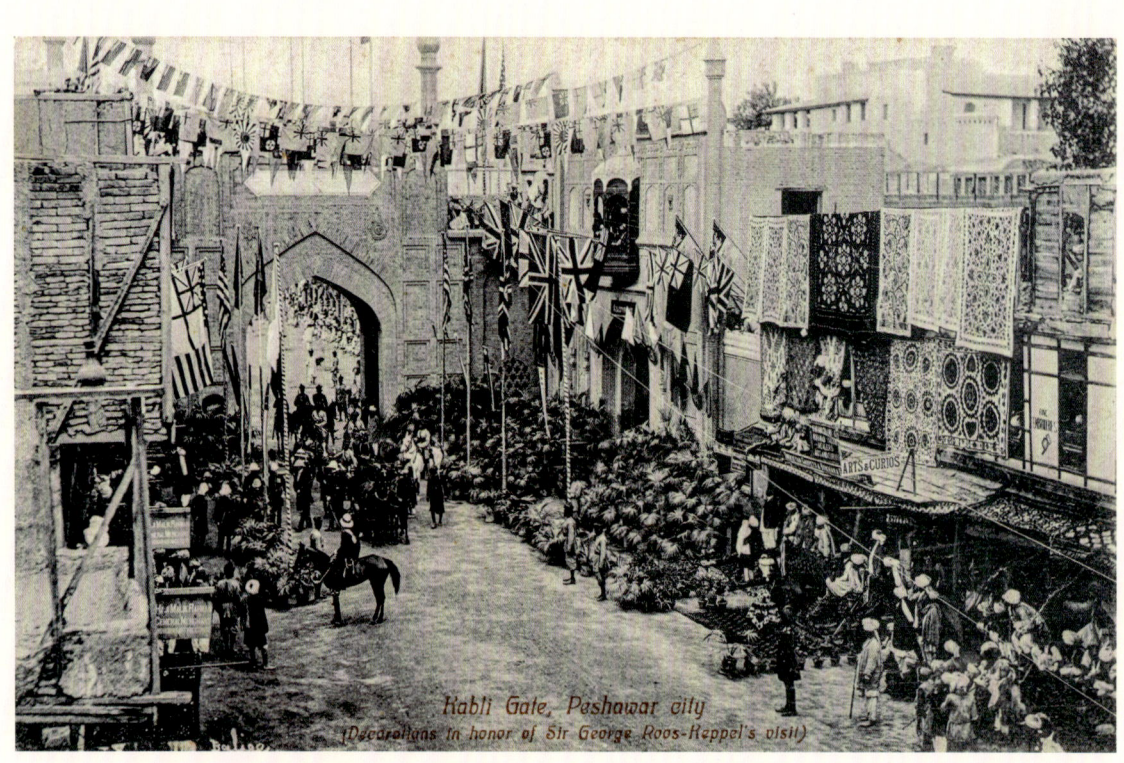

↑ **Postcard**
Photograph showing the Kabuli Gate, Peshawar, during the
visit of Sir George Roos-Keppel, circa 1910

The textile industry has always been grounded in human interaction. Its trade has long spread across the globe, with cultural exchange facilitating the furnishing of homes, the clothing of labourers, the signifying of social rank and much else. Through such global reach was cultivated a trade of exploitation, in which empires of cotton enslaved labourers while generating such wealth that entire cities came into being.

Kris Manajpra's concept of colonialism as a mat, or 'interlocking weave' of connection, is useful in understanding the complex nature of the textile trade in the imperial world. As a tool of control, the industry aided colonial dynamics – for example, in England's exclusion of Ireland from the wool trade in 1699. Textiles could equally be employed as symbols of resistance, as in the Asafo flags, part of the regalia of the Fante people of Ghana. Today, cloth is still employed in protest, as banners or slogan T-shirts, as well as in celebrations and to decorate rites of passage.

The social dynamics inherent in textile history are evident in gendered associations; needlecraft has always been considered a female pastime, for example. This has bled into the language we use: 'distaff' means both the staff used in spinning wool or flax, and work associated with women. Similarly, we speak of the 'spindle side' versus the 'spear side' of the family, and the term 'spinster' is still used to refer to an unmarried woman. Textiles both reflect and shape human society; as a historical resource, therefore, they provide valuable insight into our past.

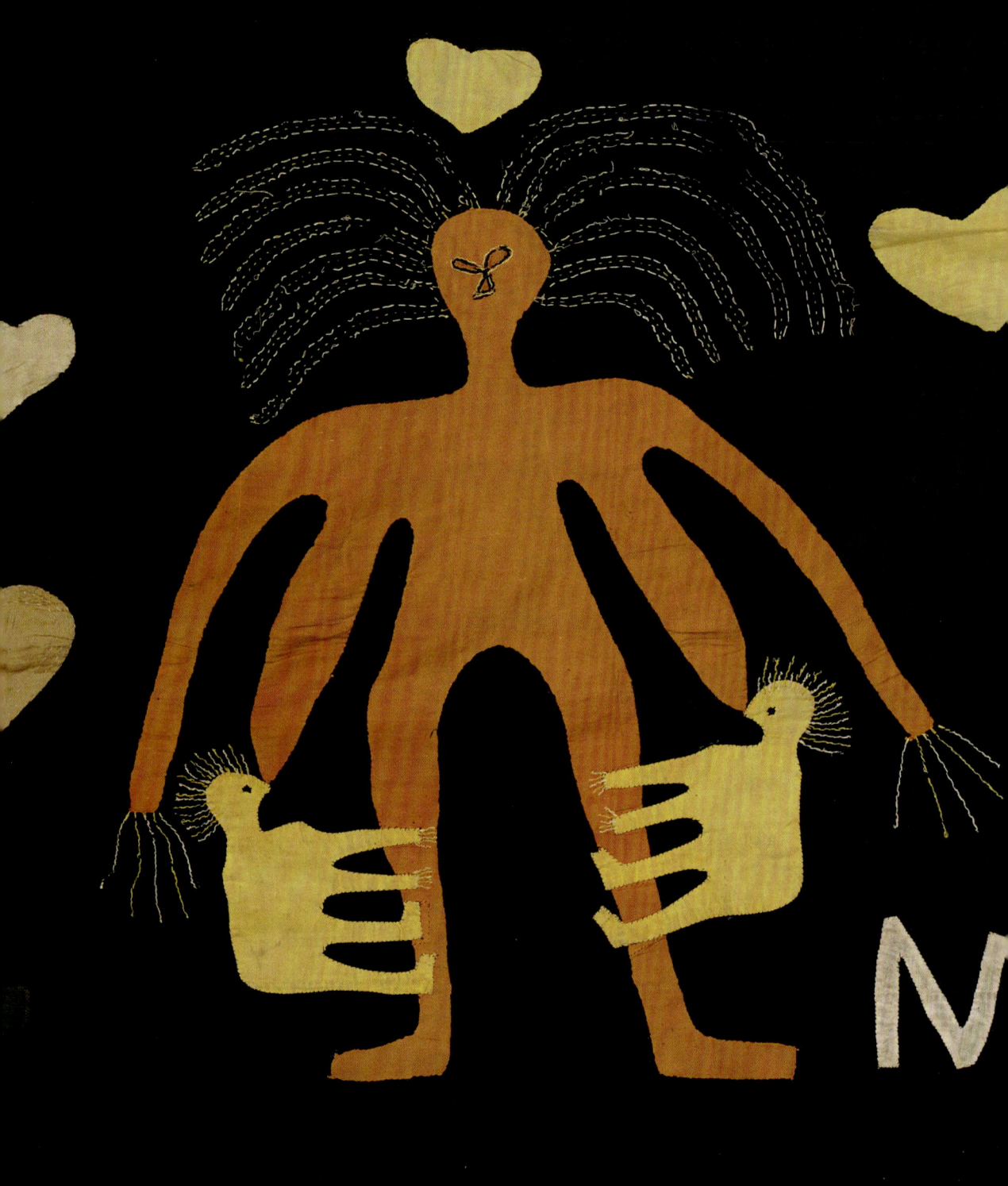

← **Rites of passage** *Birth*

Asafo flag, Ghana, 19th century. The exact meaning of this flag's aphorism is unclear. It features a human mother suckling children that could be mistaken for quadrupeds

↓ **Rites of passage** *Birth*

Toile de Jouy, France, 18th century. The rare blue ground print shows a washer woman feeding her child. These fabrics often had an element of satire and social commentary as seen here with the mischievous dog licking the dishes

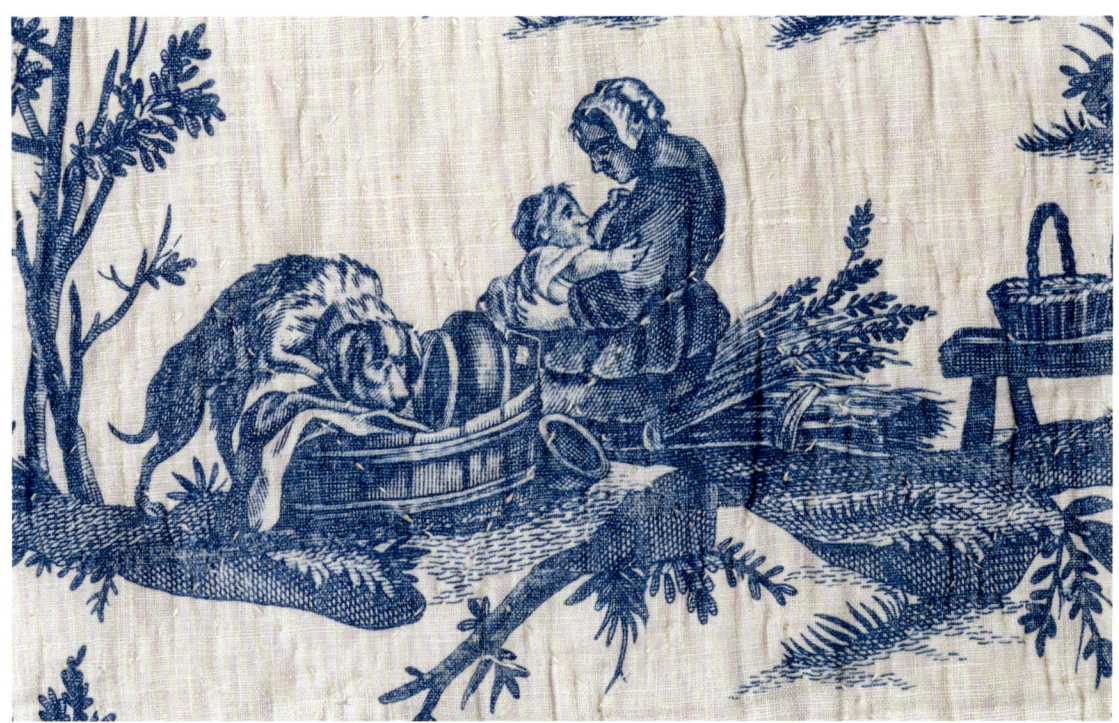

Rites of passage are marked in different ways depending on culture and historical traditions. Largely focused on birth, coming of age, marriage and death, these celebrations often feature textiles. Sometimes they simply hang in the background, forming a backdrop to proceedings. At other times, they serve as a canvas for commemoration or formal vehicles of transformation and initiation. In this way, textiles can become emblems of these critical passages in our lives.

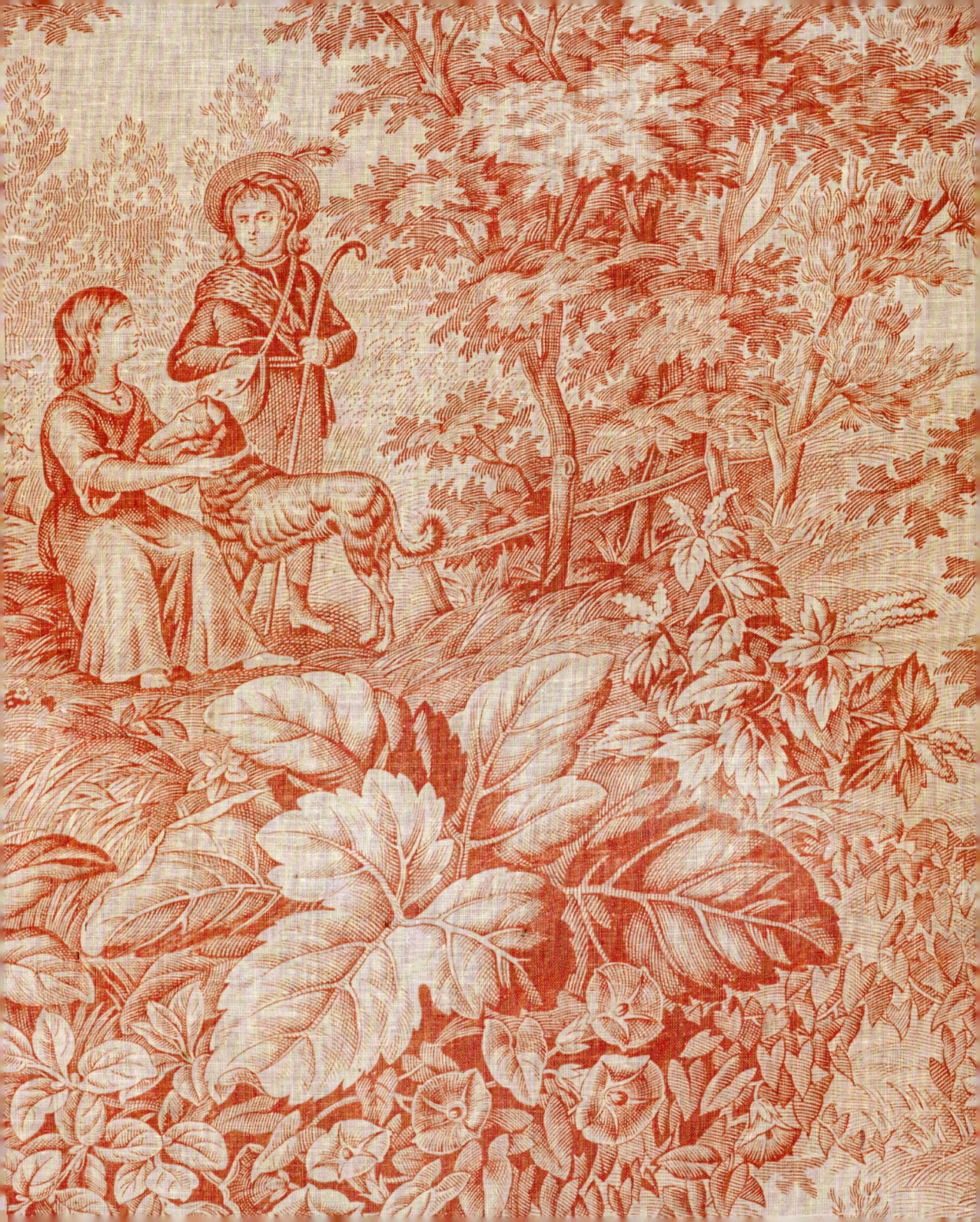

← **Rites of passage** *Romance*
Toile de Jouy, France, 19th century. This copperplate print conveys the ideals of a simple life lived well. Christian emblems are also present, such as the cross and the dog, the latter symbolising fidelity

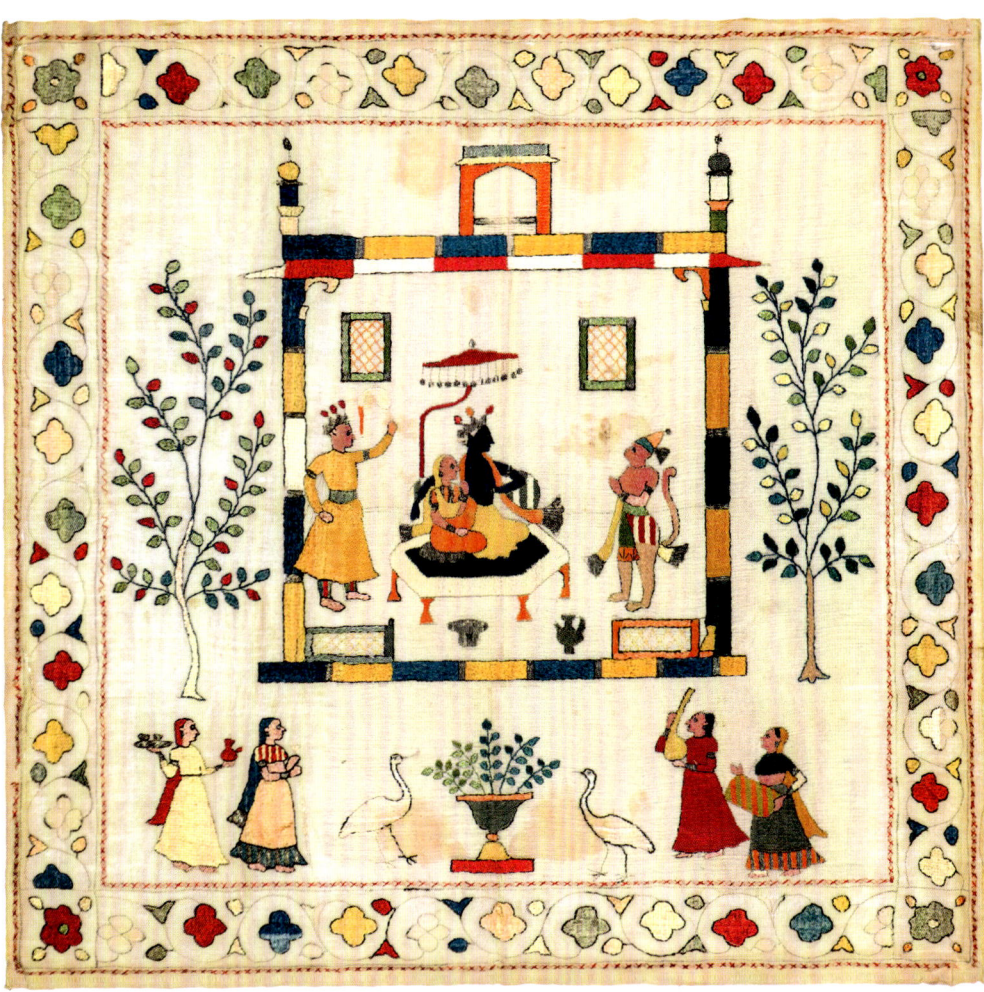

↑ **Rites of passage** *Romance*
Chamba rumal embroidery, Himachal Pradesh, India, 19th century. This scene from the Indian epic, the *Ramayana*, shows the deity Rama, whose blue colour identifies him as an avatar of Vishnu, one of the principal deities of Hinduism, embracing and protecting his wife Sita

↓↓ **Rites of passage** *Romance*
Embroidered valance, England, 16th century. Jealousy is captured in the central scene of this panel. While this ménage à trois is front and centre, someone's dogs are in the pond chasing the swans, which in England at the time were all the property of the king

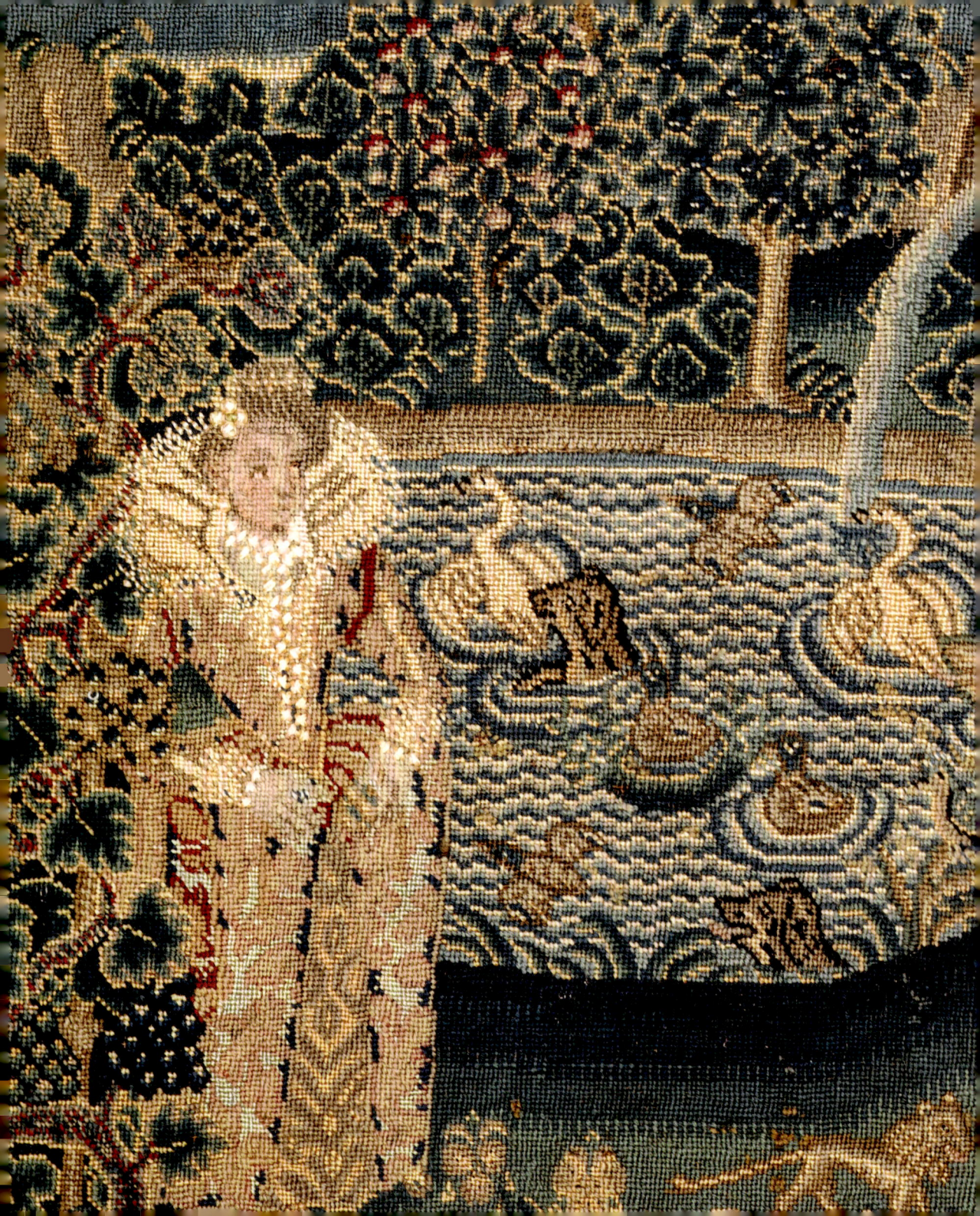

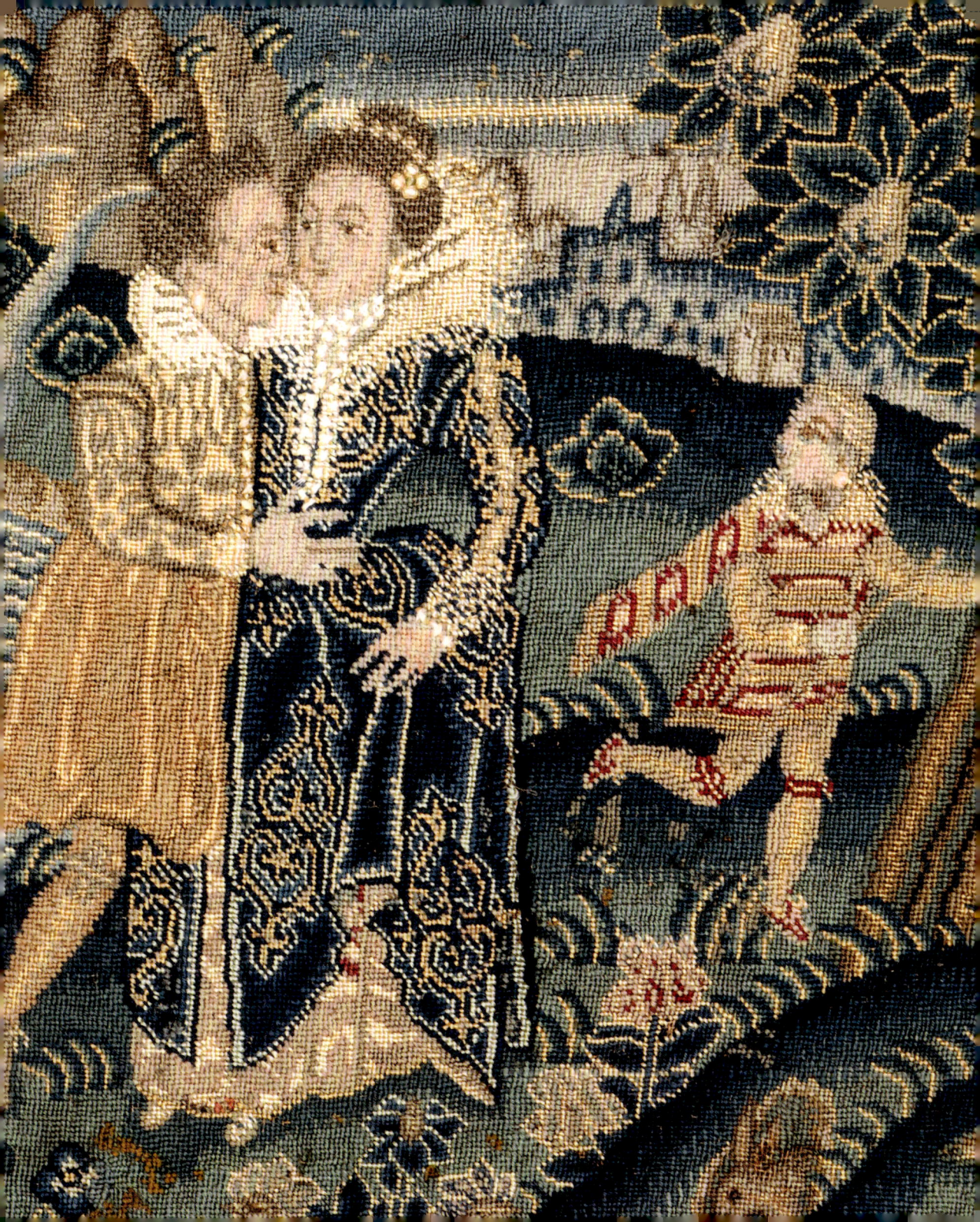

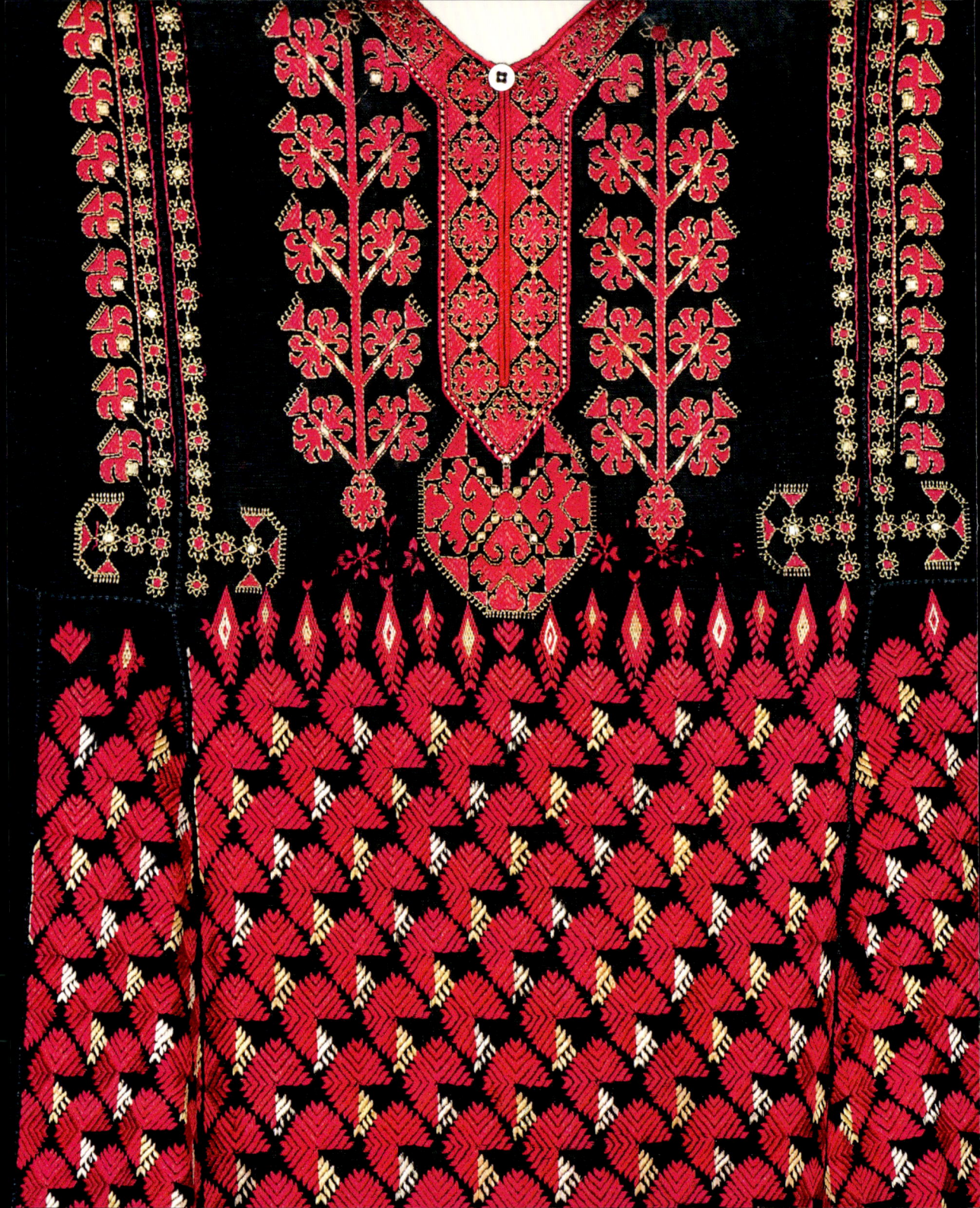

← **Rites of passage** *Marriage*
Wedding dress, Swat Valley, Pakistan, circa 1900. The imported silk and cotton would have been bought at the local market by a family preparing for a wedding. The contrast between the deep blue and bright scarlet makes for an eye-catching garment

↓ **Rites of passage** *Marriage*
Wedding hanging, Mali, 20th century. Made by Oumar Bocoum, this prestigious hanging was used in an important wedding ceremony. It was meticulously planned, as it is woven in thirteen narrow strips which were then assembled, matching seamlessly

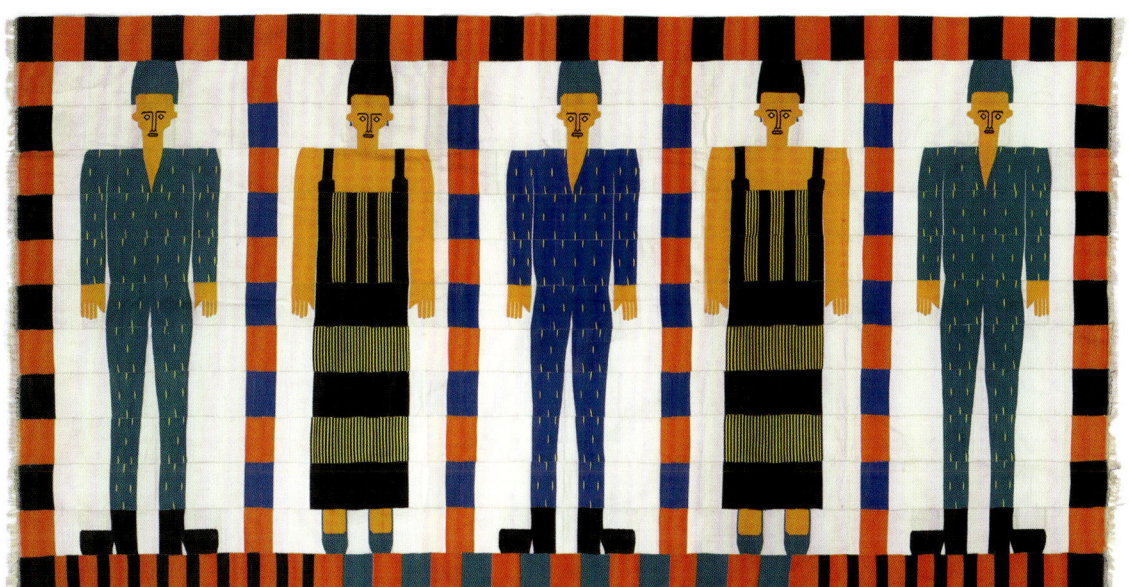

↓ ↓ **Rites of passage** *Marriage*
Phulkari, undivided Punjab, 19th century. Specifically made for a wedding, this shawl captures the rich colours, elaborate processions and architecture associated with the region's nuptials in its riotous and rich decoration

The wedding is universally understood as one of the most important rites of passage in a person's life. In many societies marriage implied the creation of a dowry for the bride, which would often consist of a number of textiles. Whether aspects of the wedding outfits or a prescribed suite of textiles, these would most likely be made by the bride and her relations. They brought not only wealth and value into her new home, but demonstrated her skill at weaving or embroidery and may well have been used to decorate rooms associated with the marriage celebrations.

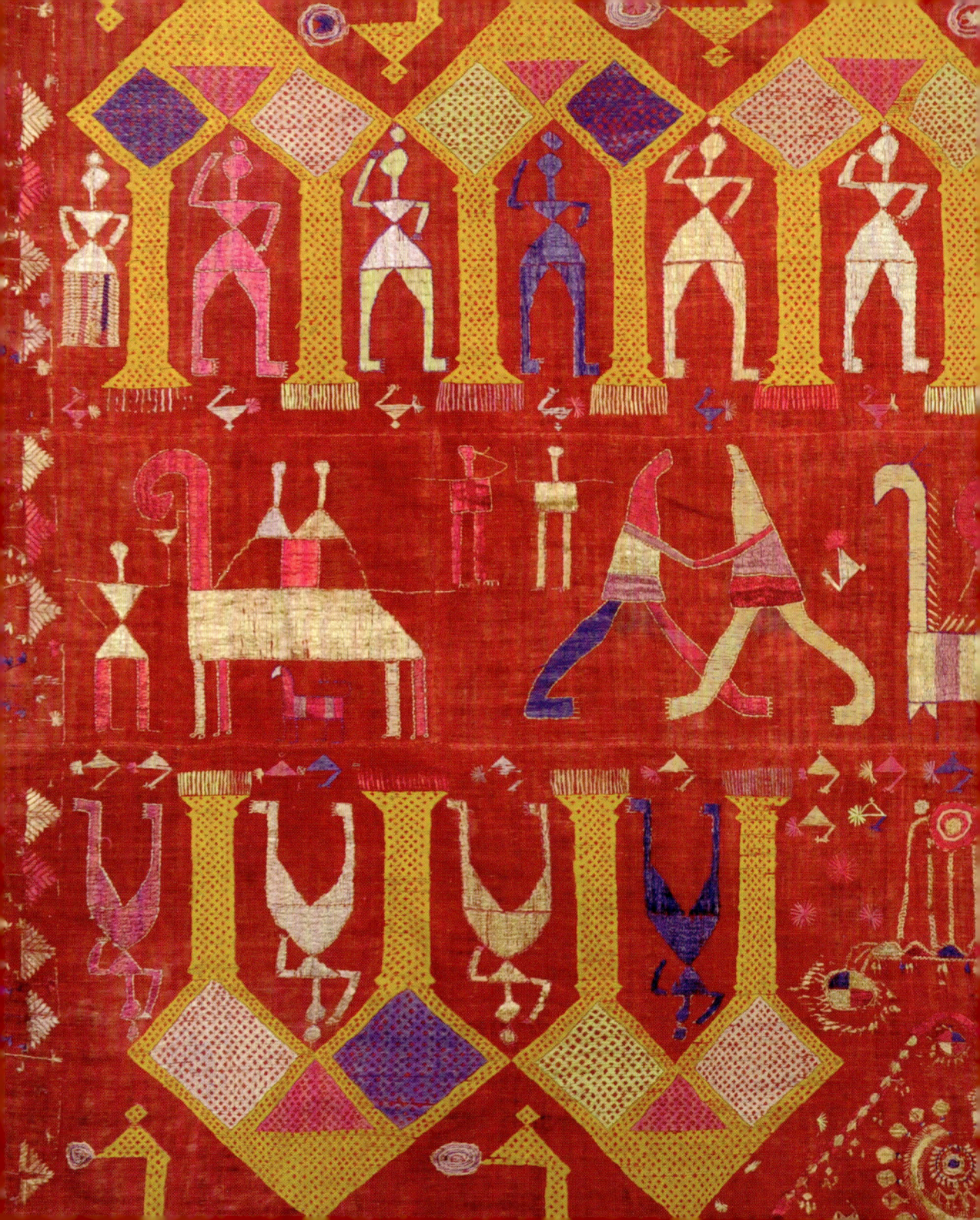

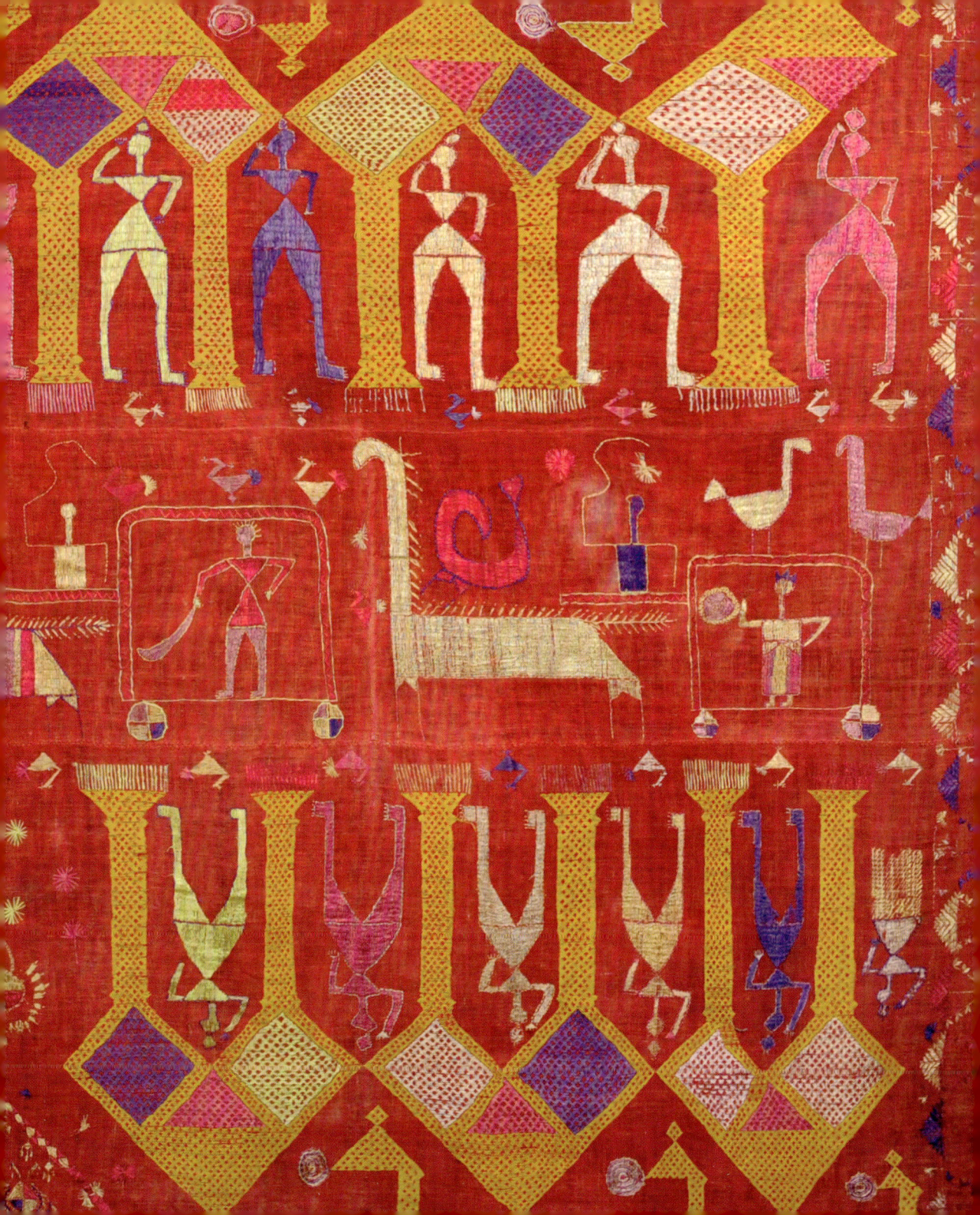

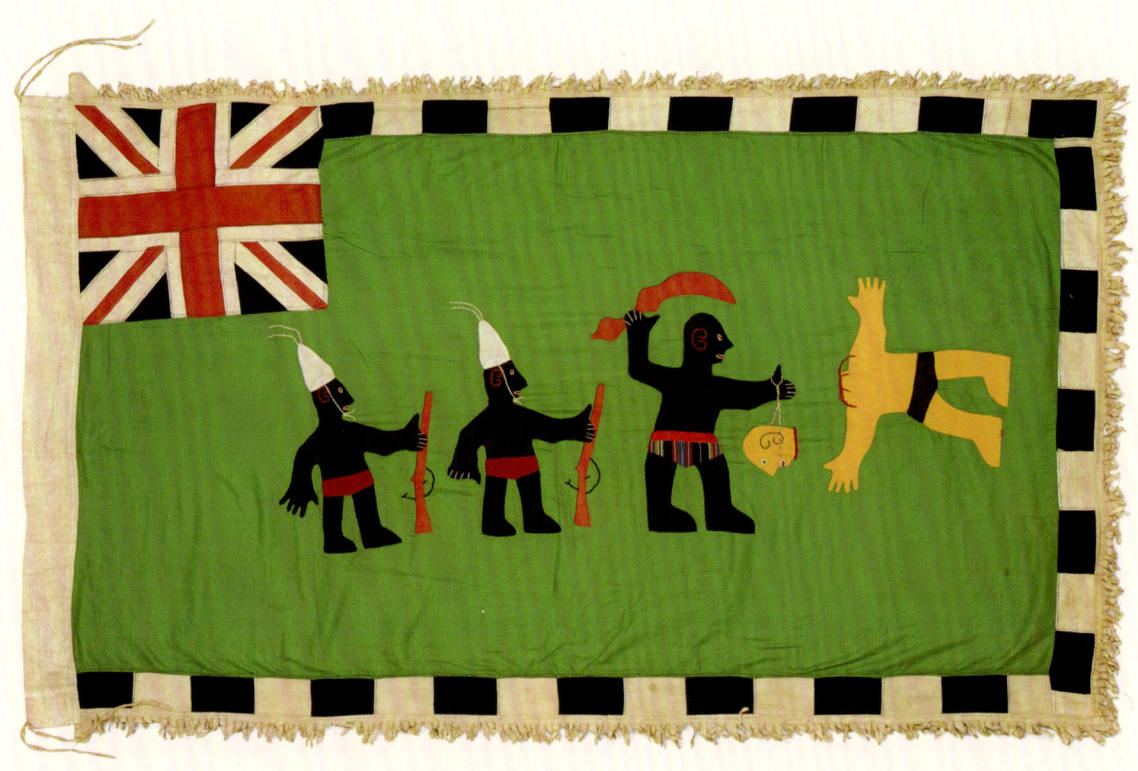

↑ Rites of passage *Death*
Asafo flag, Ghana, 19th century. The Union Jack demonstrates
that this flag is from pre-independence Ghana, so before 1957.
The decapitation is a statement of power aimed at rival Asafo
military companies

↓↓ Rites of passage *Marriage and mortality*
Kantha, undivided Bengal, 19th century. This cloth records
a Bengali murder case of 1873, where a woman, Elokeshi,
depicted here in various places with long black hair, was
accused of infidelity and murdered by her husband

↓ **Rites of passage** *Marriage and mortality*
Kantha, undivided Bengal, 19th century. While this kantha
depicts the stages of life centred on marriage and death, the
cloth itself also reflects this cycle since it is made using threads
recycled from the clothes of deceased family members

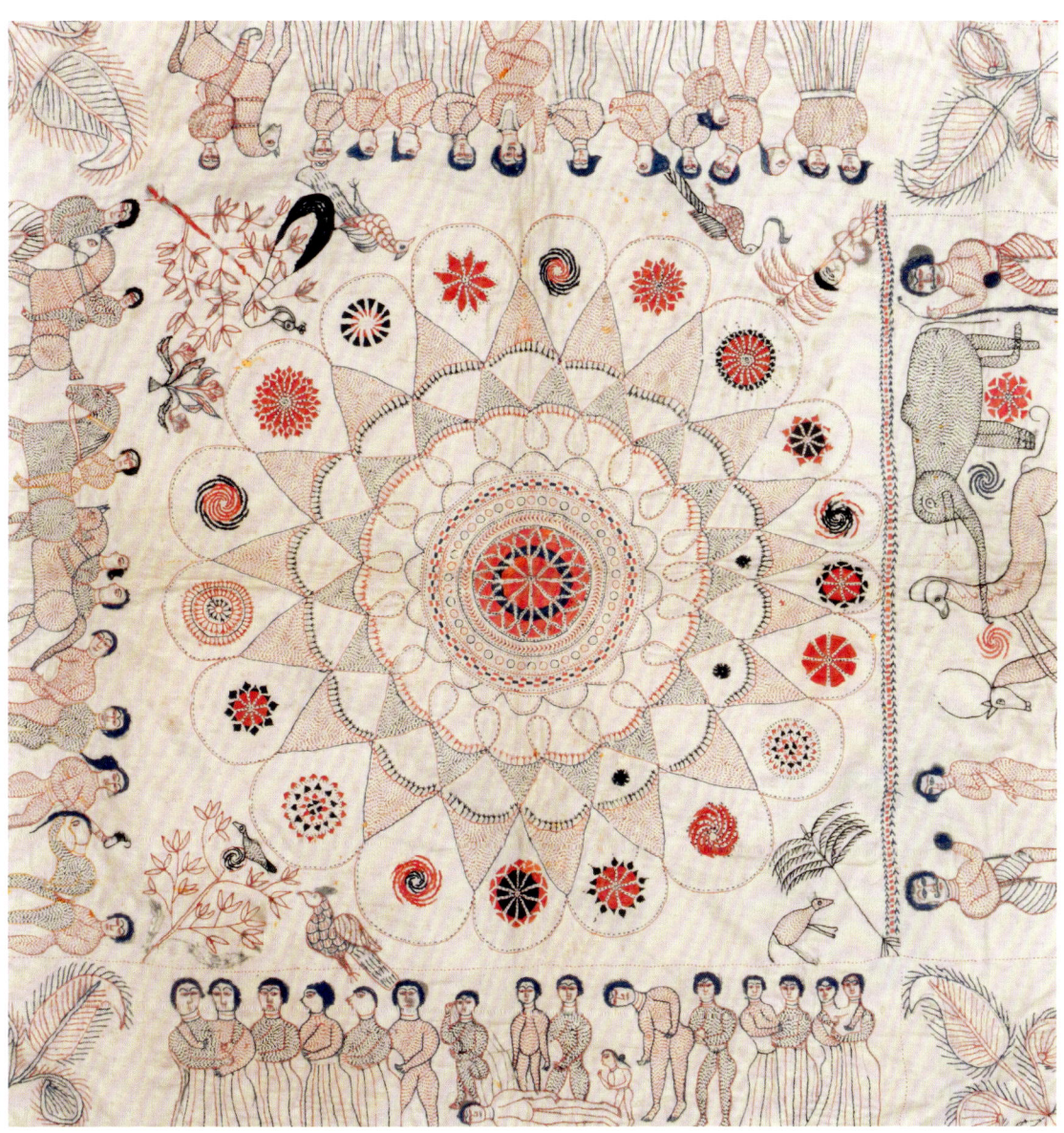

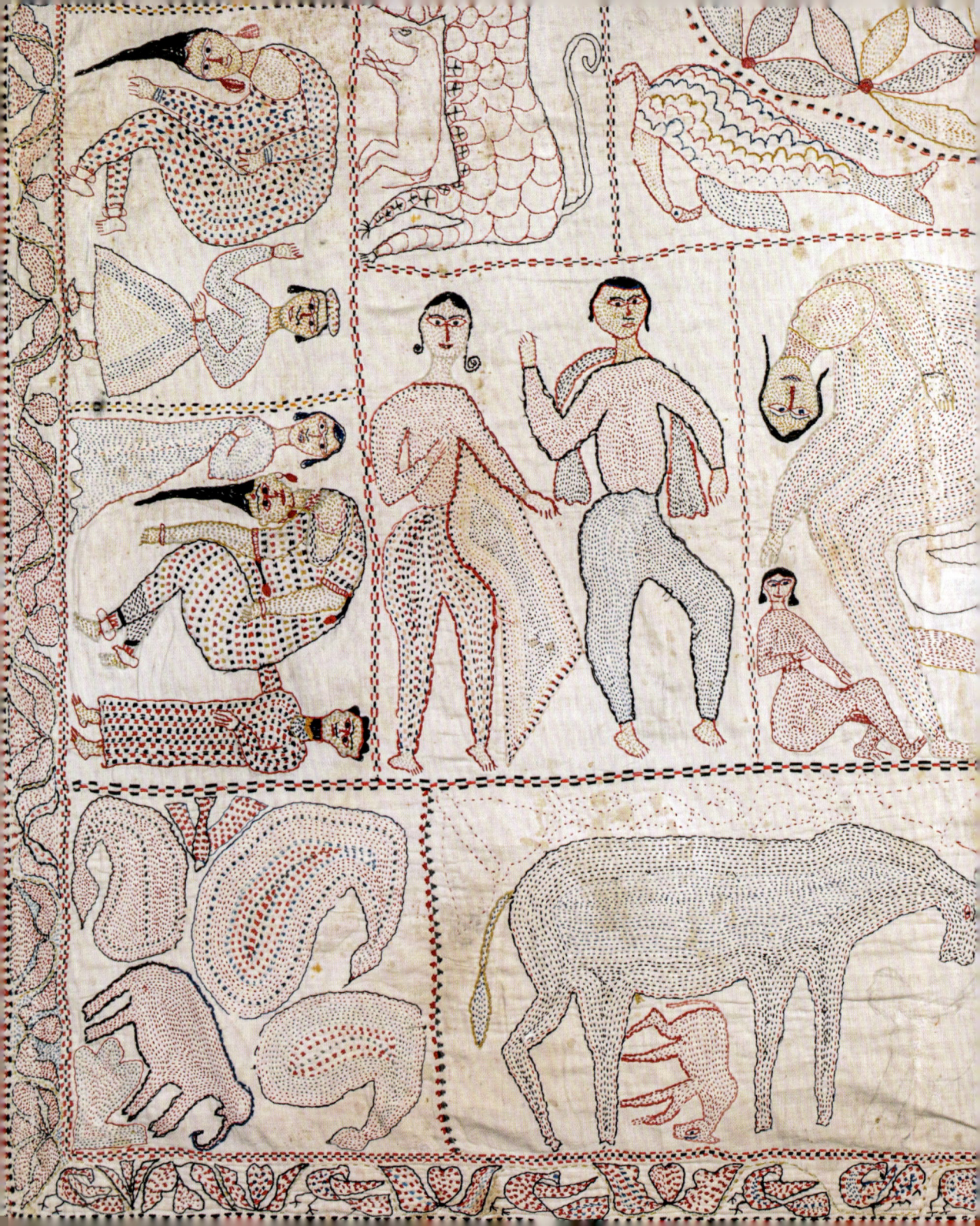

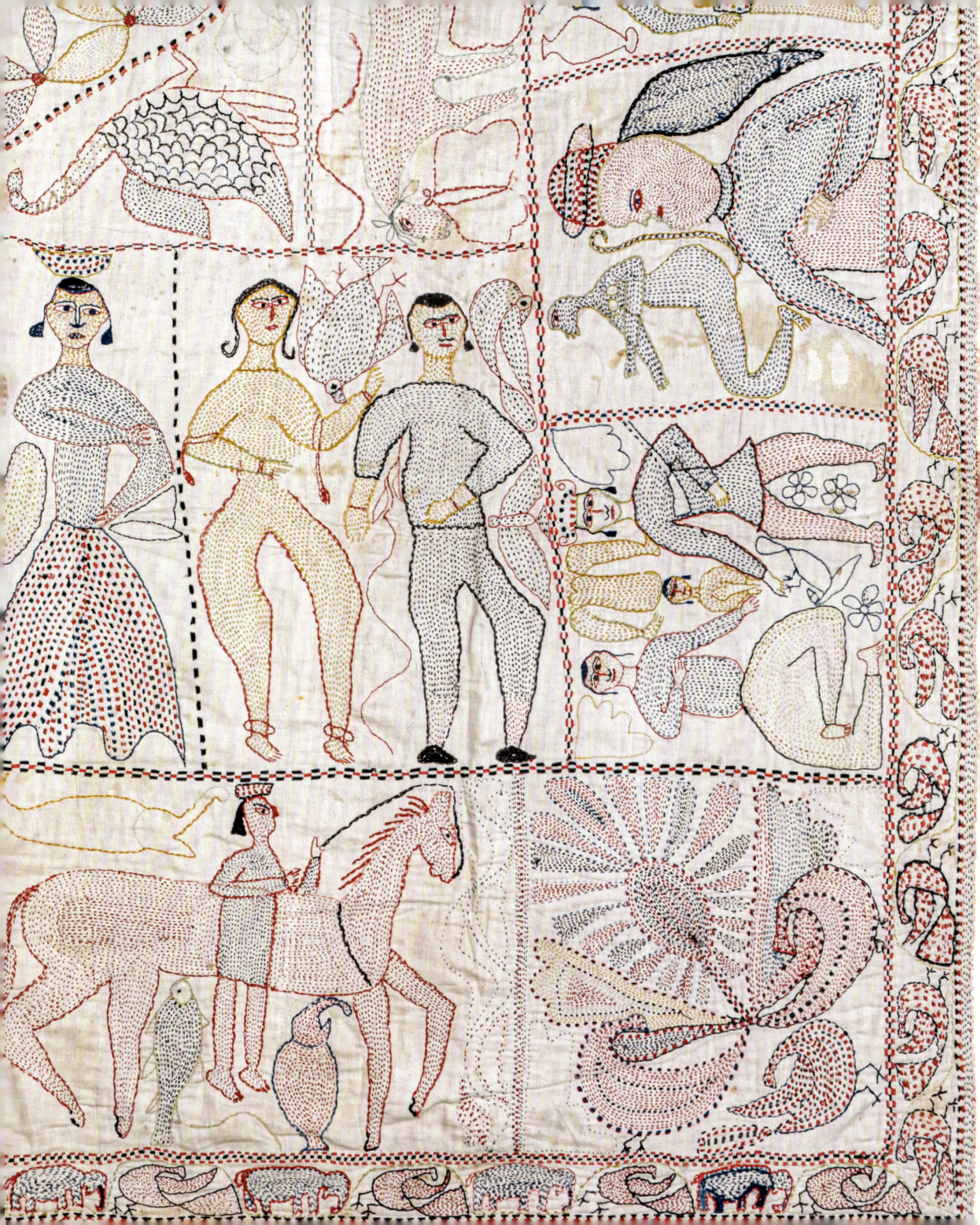

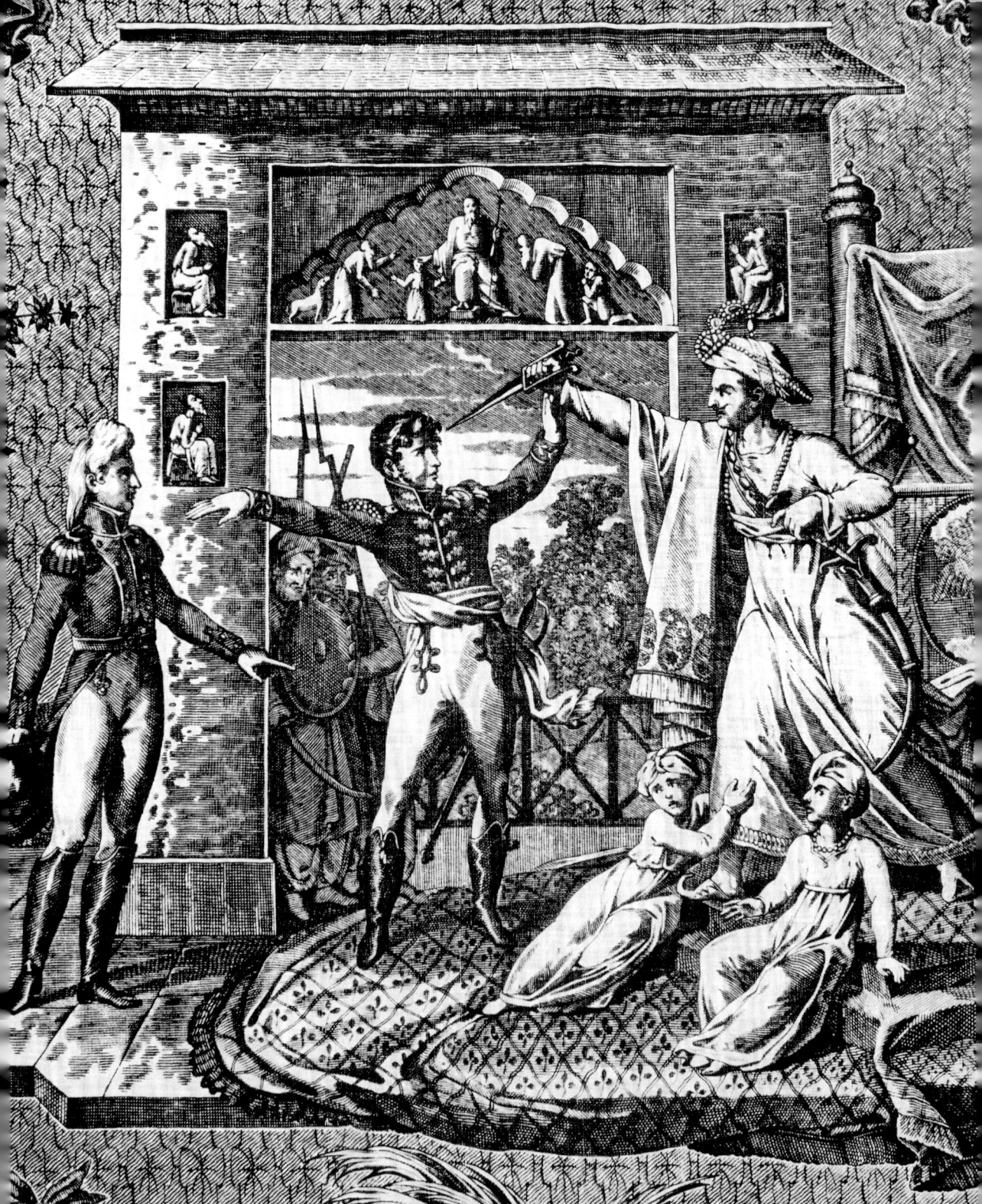

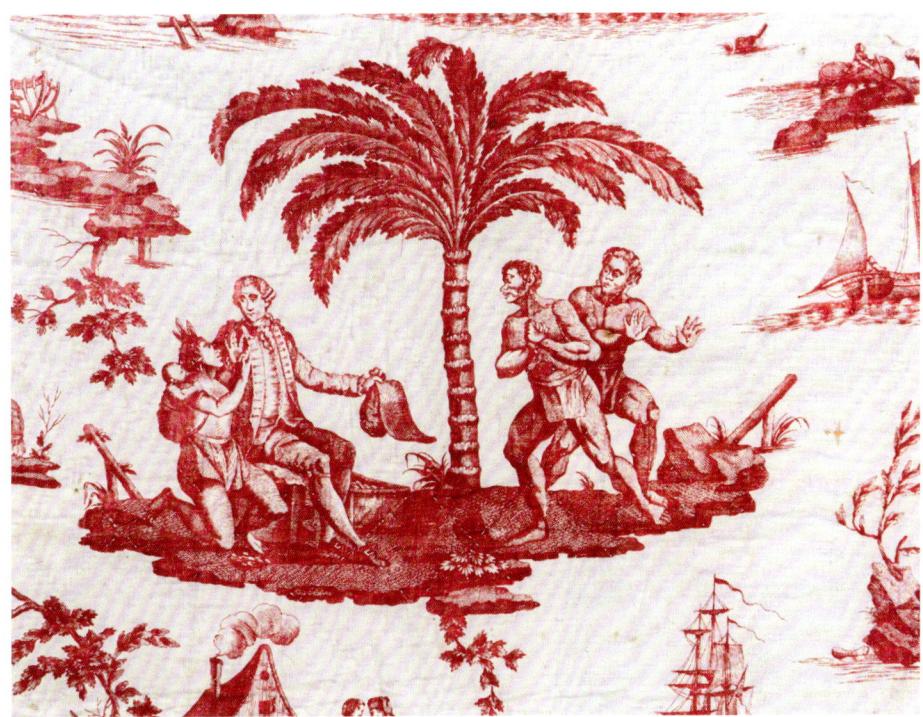

← **Human activity** *Colonialism*

Toile de Jouy, France, 19th century. This fabric shows the assassination of French General Jean Baptiste Kléber in Cairo. Appointed by Napolean to command in his absence, he was killed by a Syrian student in 1800. Napolean's invasion of Egypt is sometimes seen as the first act of European imperialism

↓ **Human activity** *Colonialism*

Toile de Jouy, France, circa 1785. This scene is taken from a little-known textile print called *Neptune or the Empire of the Sea*, produced in Nantes by the Petitpierre et Cie workshop. This tells the story of Western sea power (see next page) but also the resulting colonial expansion

Colonialism The textile trade, especially in cotton and wool, is closely linked to colonialism. Cotton grown in colonies such as the American South, India and Egypt was a cornerstone of European economies during the Industrial Revolution. These powers exploited these regions for cotton to supply their burgeoning textile mills, and aggressively promoted their products in these distant markets. Wool was a significant commodity from settler colonies like Australia and New Zealand, which supplied vast amounts to British mills and was sold into the Middle East. The integration of cotton and wool into the colonial trade networks underscores how colonialism reshaped global trade patterns.

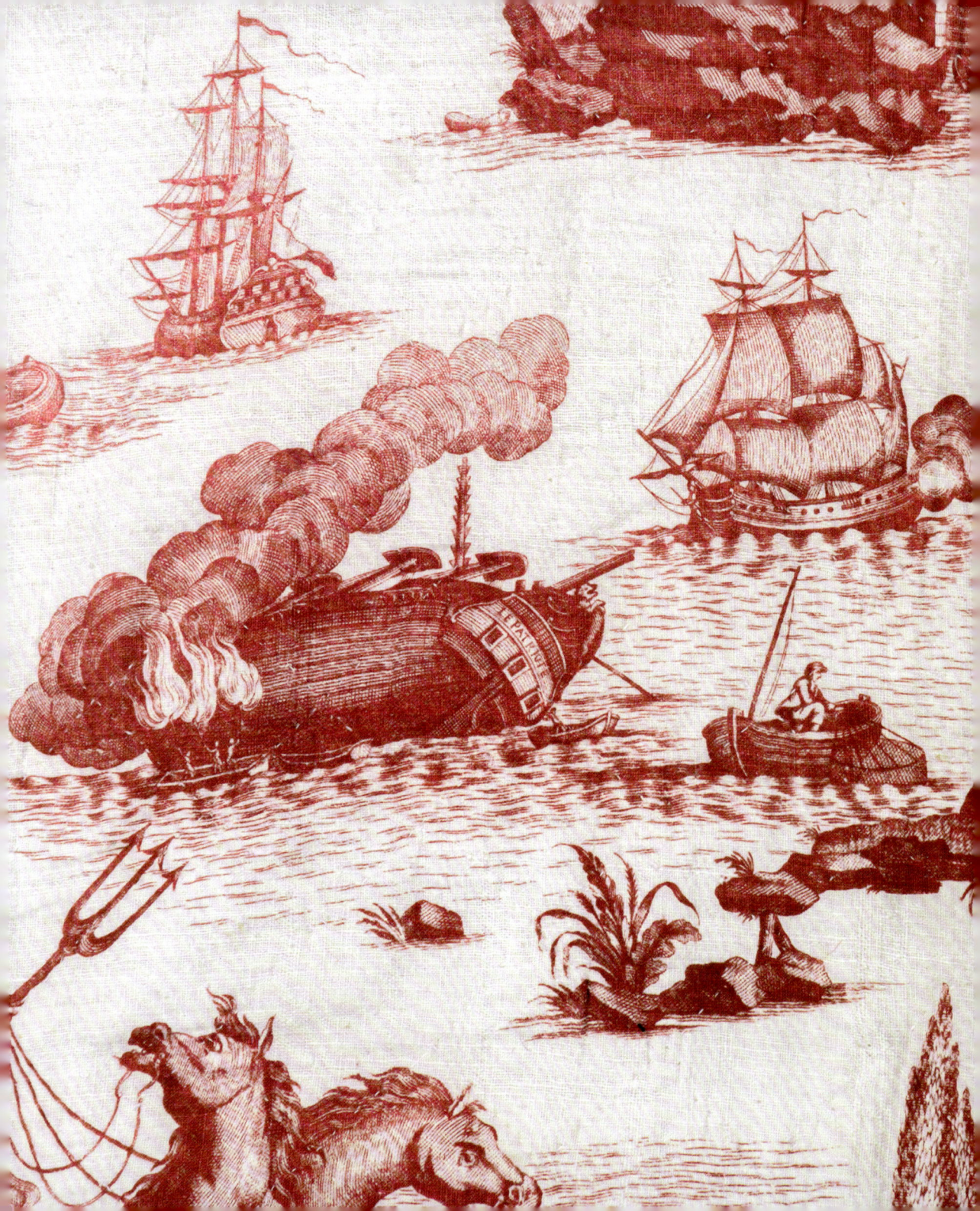

← Human activity *War*
Toile de Jouy, France, circa 1785. This is another scene from *Neptune or the Empire of the Sea*, here showing the destructive power of naval warfare and the allegorical challenge to the god Neptune's ascendency of the ocean

↓ Human activity *War*
Asafo flag, Ghana, circa 1910–20. This flag tells of how contributions from Ghana to the British war effort meant that there was a ready supply of reconnaissance planes for the fledgling Royal Air Force during the First World War

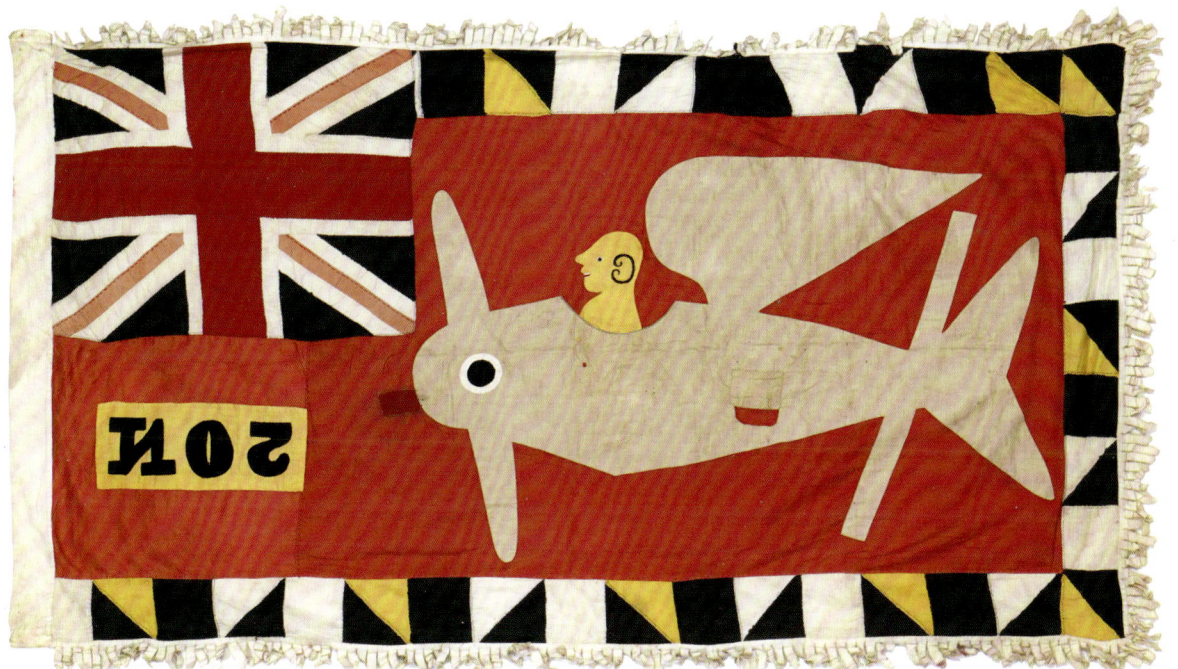

↓↓ Expressions of life *Celebrations*
Woman's wrapper, Yoruba, Nigeria, mid-20 century. This resist-dyed cloth celebrates the Jubilee of King George and Queen Mary in 1935, who can be seen in the central roundel. Probably used at a ceremony, the words just out of view read 'everything is seen by God'

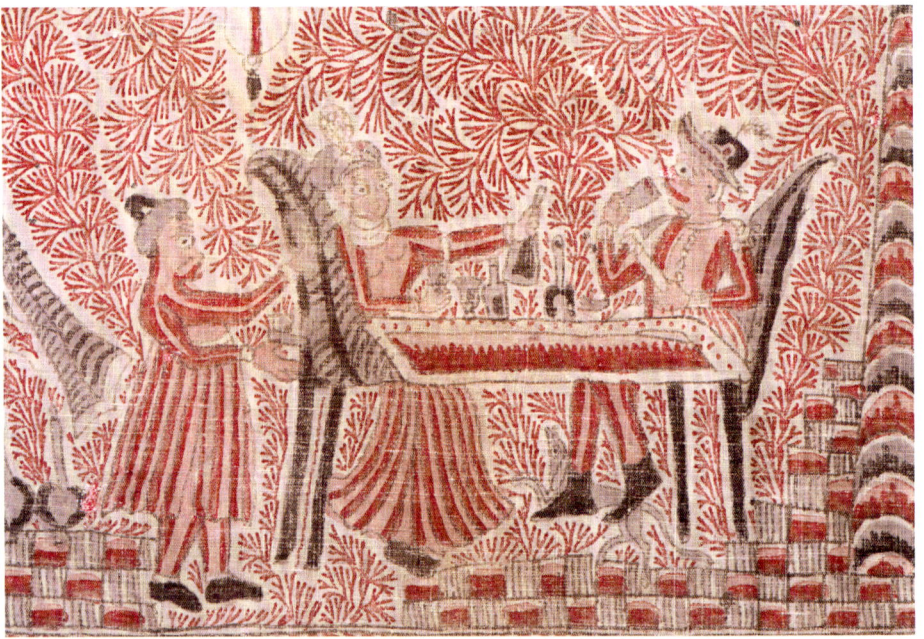

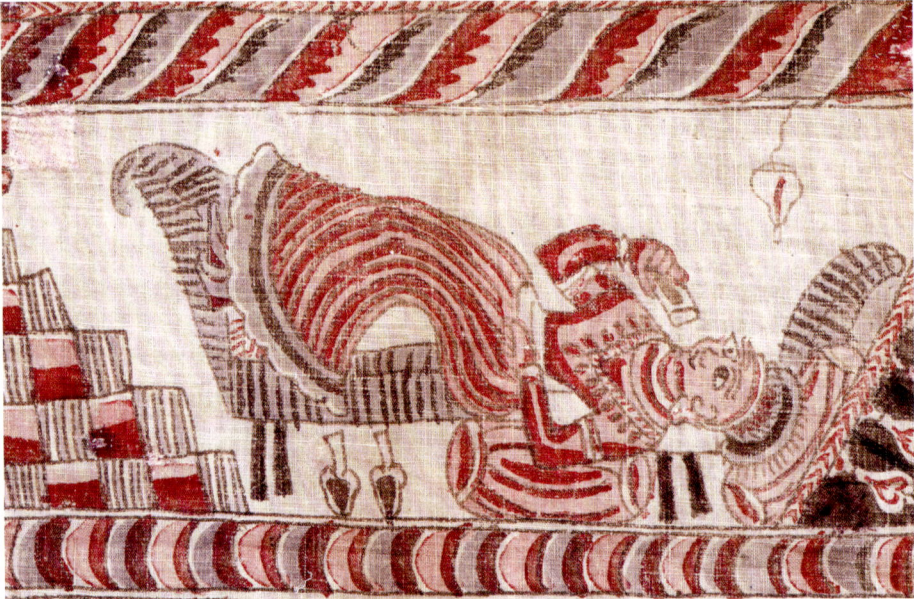

↑ **Expressions of life** *Celebrations*
Chintz hanging, India, 18th century. These vignettes can be read
on two levels: simply as scenes of European soldiers partying
with their wives, and secondly as a comment on the debauchery
of the ruling power, so drunk they cannot stay on their feet

↓ **Expressions of life** *Celebrations*

Toile de Jouy, France, 18th century. These scenes are taken from a toile length showing scenes of rural life. There is a noted, perhaps patronising, focus on the workers' desire to drink and make merry

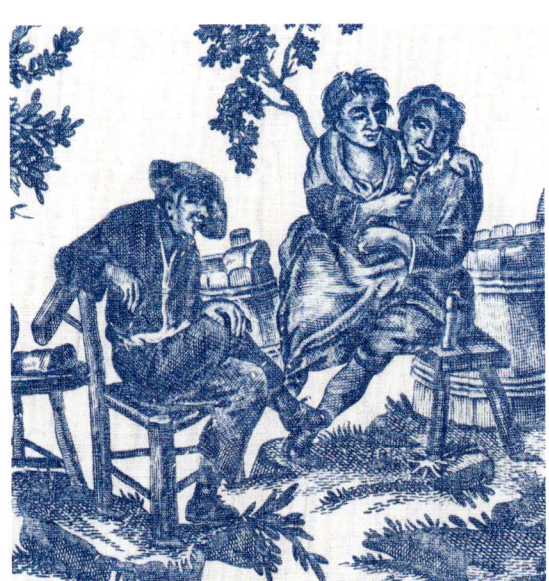

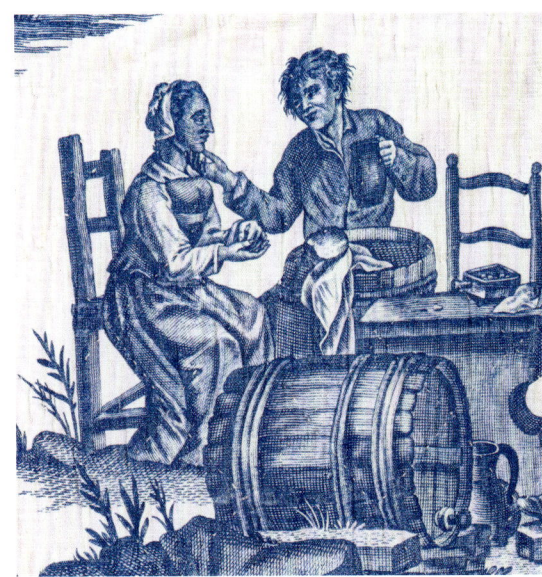

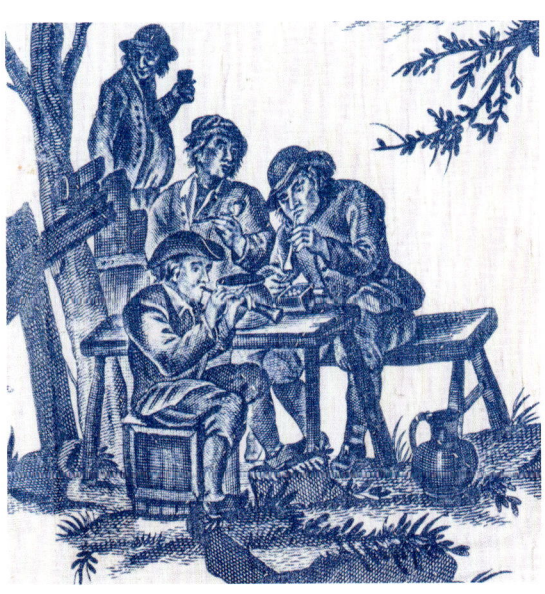

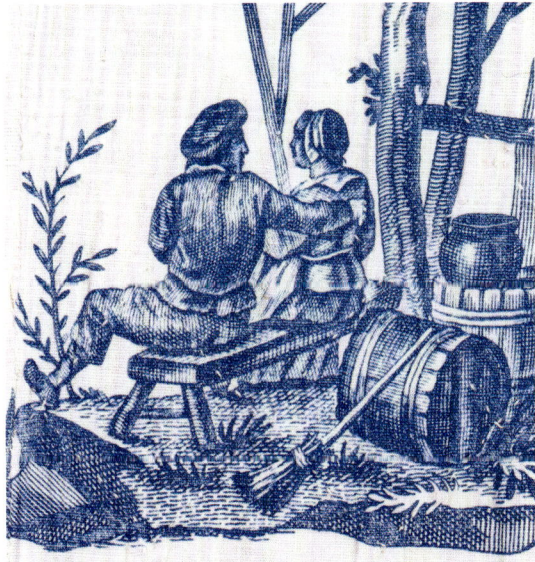

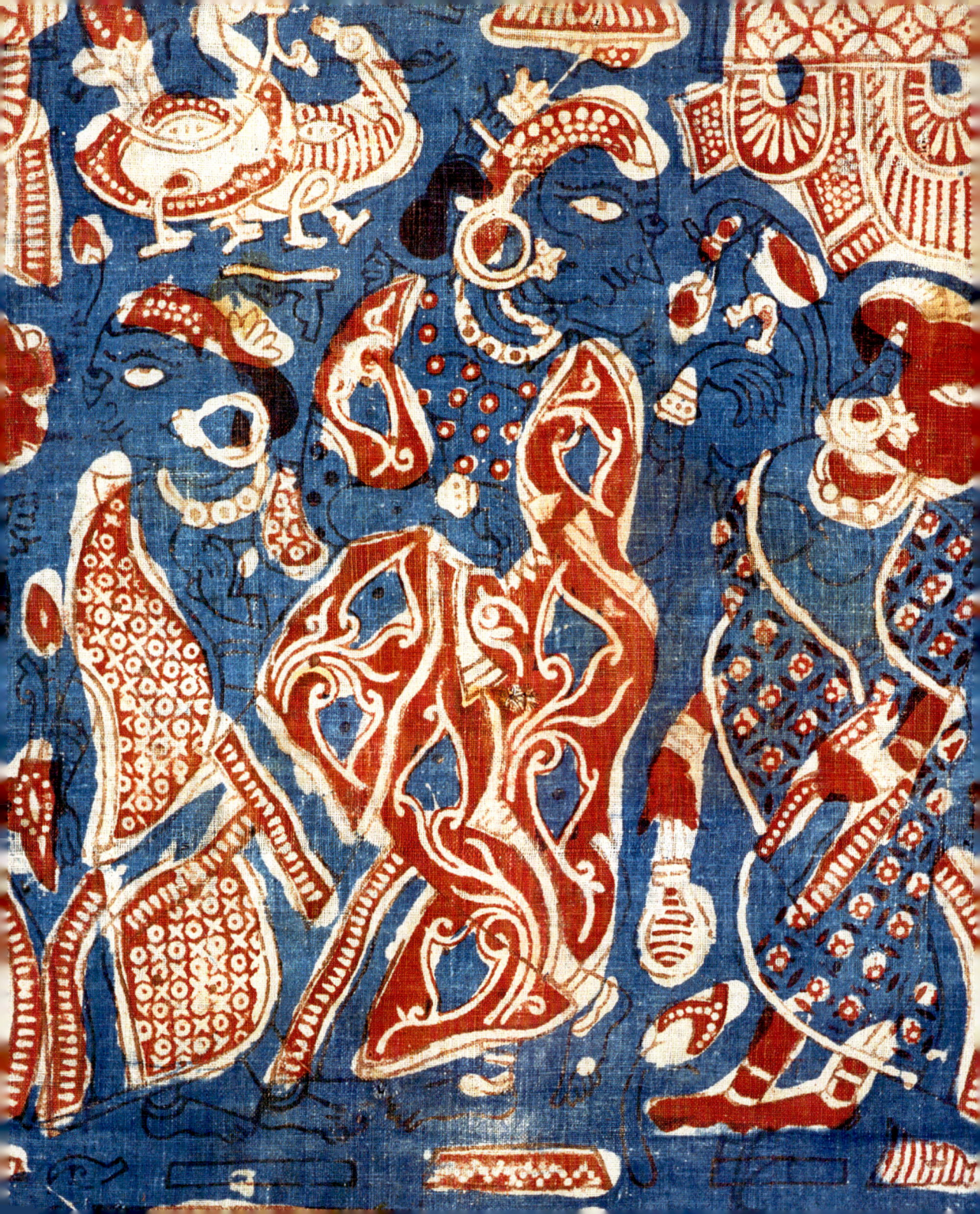

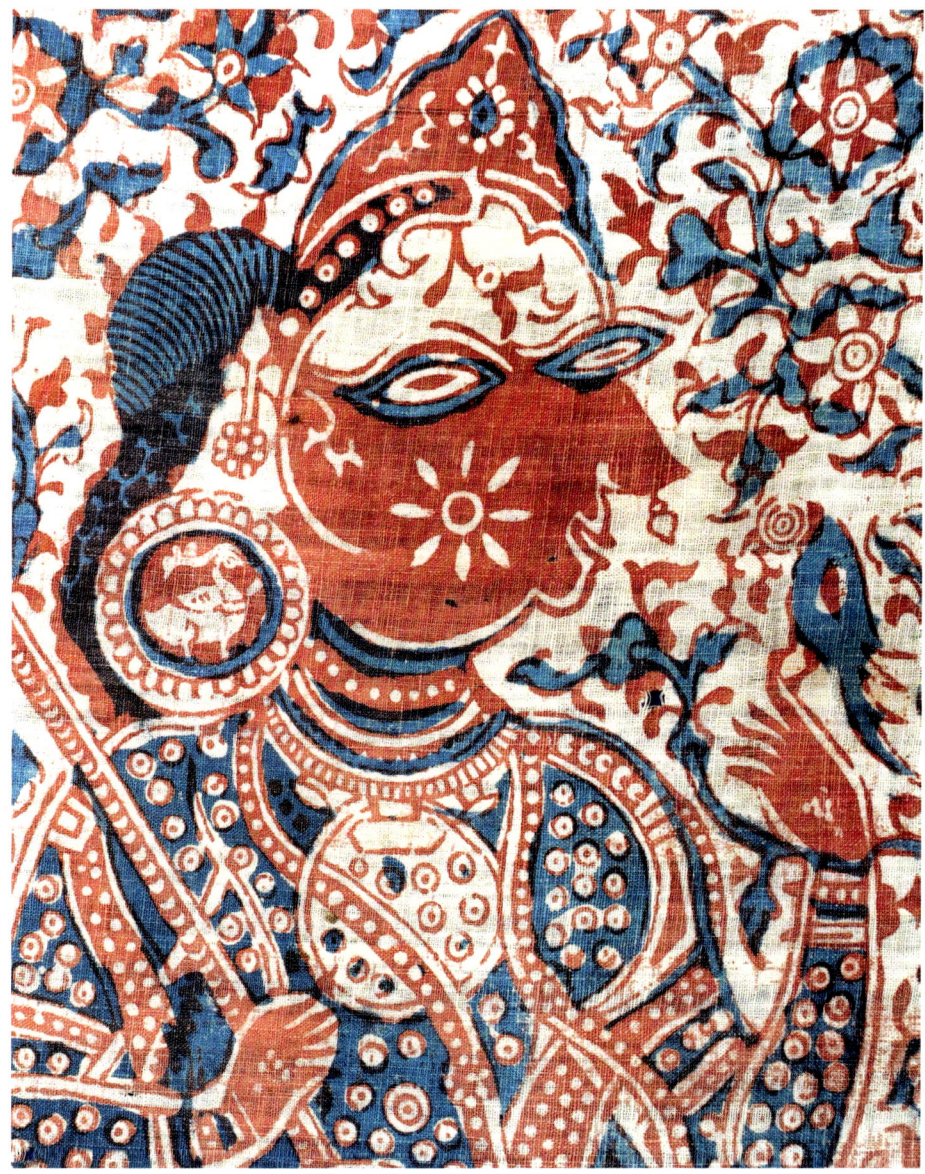

↙↗ **Expressions of life** *Celebrations*
Chintz hangings, India, 13th–15th century (left) and 1450–1650 (right).
Found in Indonesia, these block printed textiles feature women dancing,
wearing elaborate cotton clothing and jewellery. These textiles are locally
known as 'maa' and are used in certain ceremonies

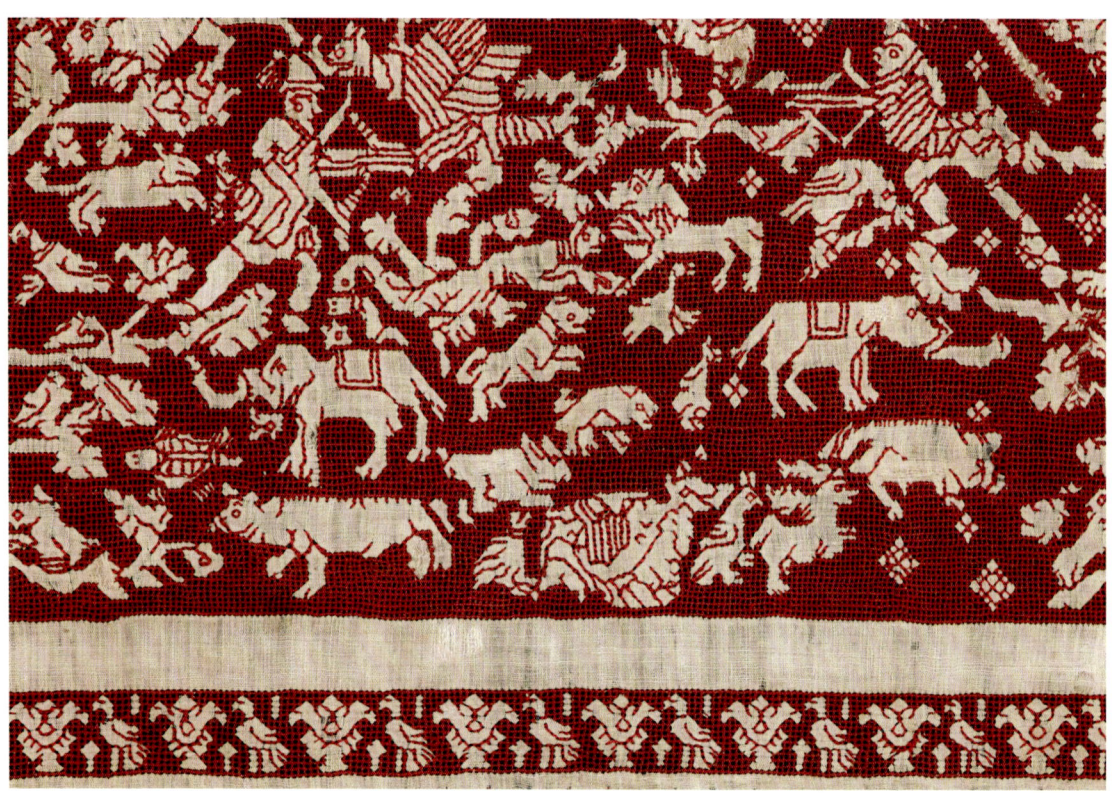

↑ **Expressions of life** *Leisure*
Frieze, Italy, 17th century. Hunting is often seen as a royal or aristocratic sport. Here men holding crossbows hunt boar, lions, tigers and perhaps elephants. The pattern is created by the areas left free of any silk stitches

→ **Expressions of life** *Leisure*
Chintz hanging, India, 18th century. The Indian hunt for tigers involves elephants decorated with textiles, as well as a retinue of servants emphasising the royal or princely status of such activities

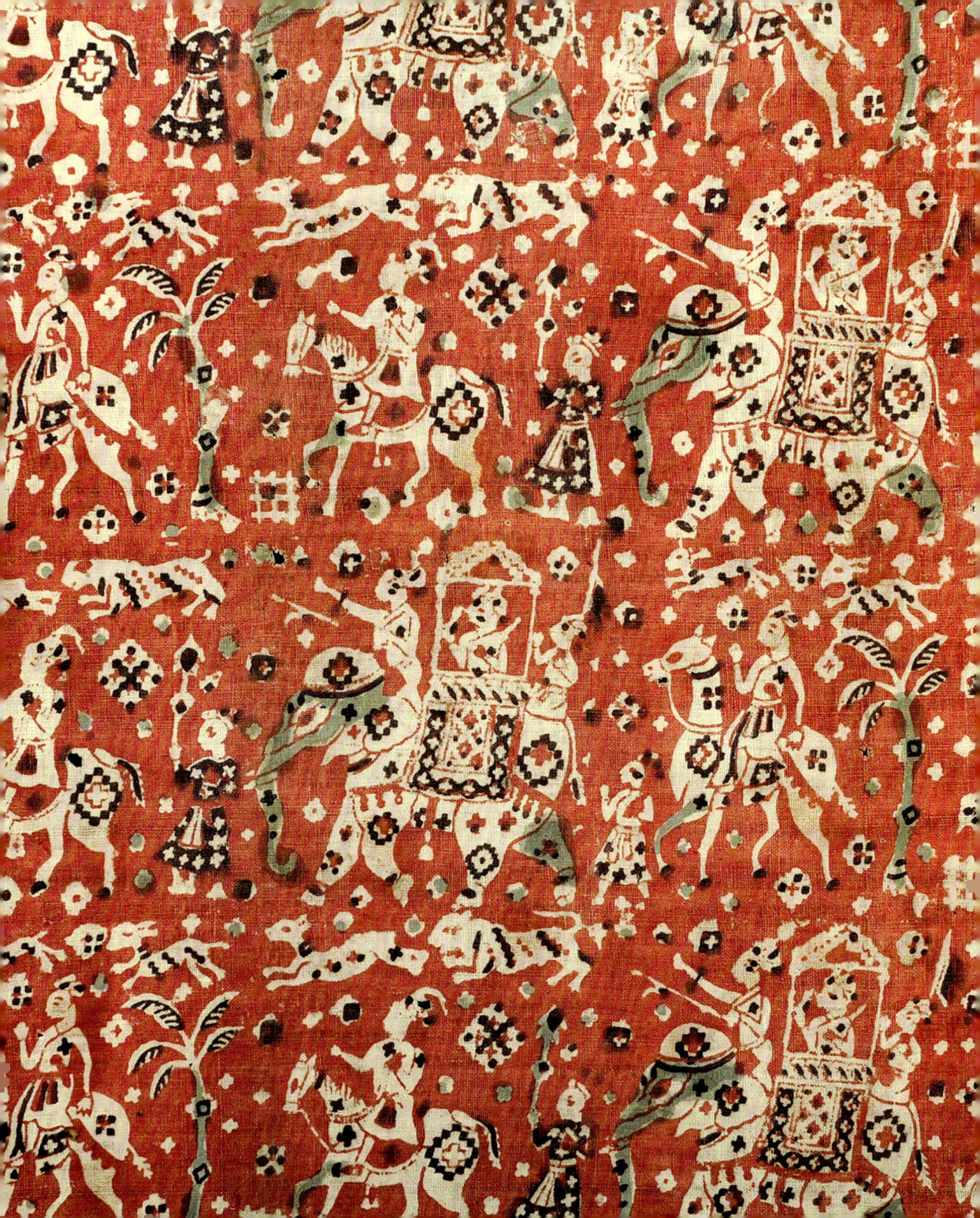

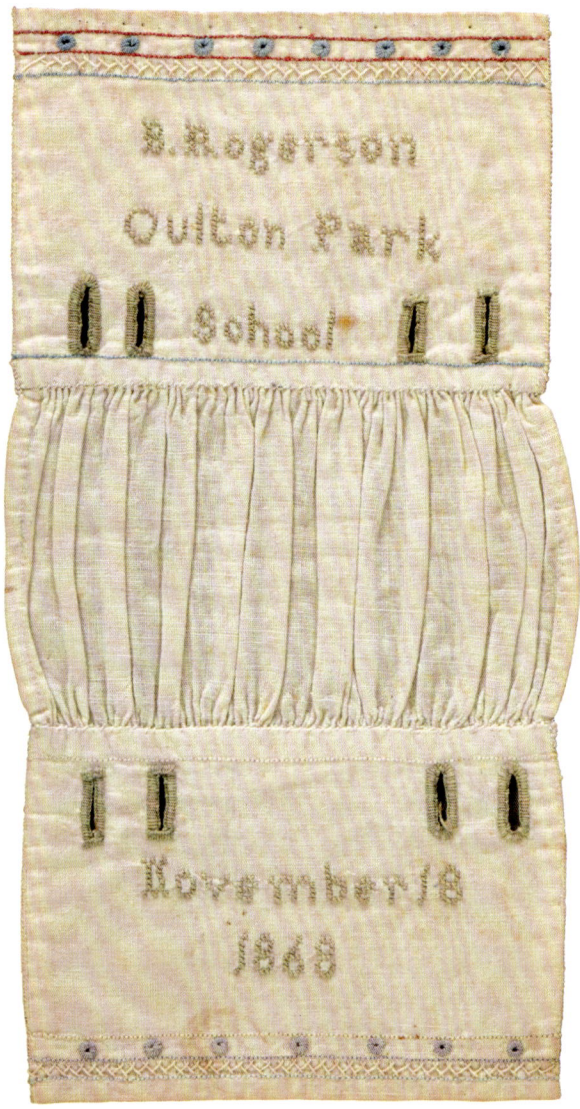

↑ **Expressions of life** *Education*
Sampler, England, dated 1868. This is a buttonhole and sleeve
sampler made by B. Rogerson at Oulton Park School. Girls
like her would have entered domestic service after primary
education, where such sewing skills were valued

→ **Expressions of life** *Education*
Smocking sampler, England, circa 1920s. Gathering and pleating
was a means of coping with excess material, while allowing
for growth and movement at work. Note the names of the
decorative stitches suggesting that this was a teaching aid

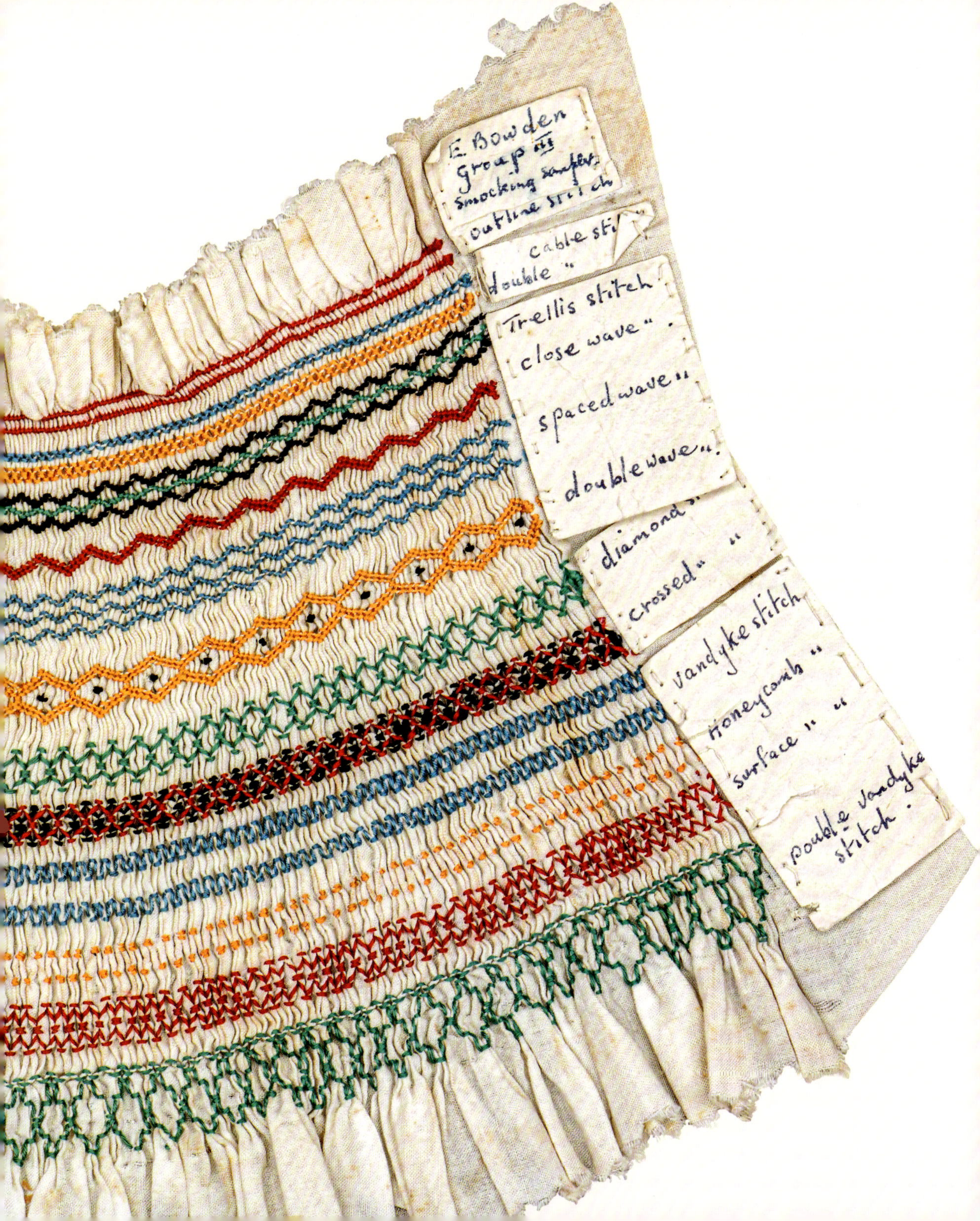

E. Bowden
Group
smocking sampler
outline stitch

cable stitch
double "

Trellis stitch
close wave "

spaced wave "

double wave "

diamond "

crossed "

vandyke stitch
honeycomb "

surface " "

Double vandyke
stitch.

↓ **Expressions of life** *Storytelling*
Chintz hanging, India, 18th century. This is a scene from a story cloth showing a fortune teller or magician performing with baskets that hide balls, a scorpion, snakes and a bird, among other things. A standing assistant is playing a drum to attract spectators and customers

→ **Expressions of life** *Storytelling*
Embroidered coat, India, circa 1830–50. This coat depicts a story from Persian poet Nizami's *Khamsa*: the story of Fitnah carrying the ox upstairs. She starts when it is a calf. As the calf grows, so does her strength, and ultimately she can carry an ox on her shoulders

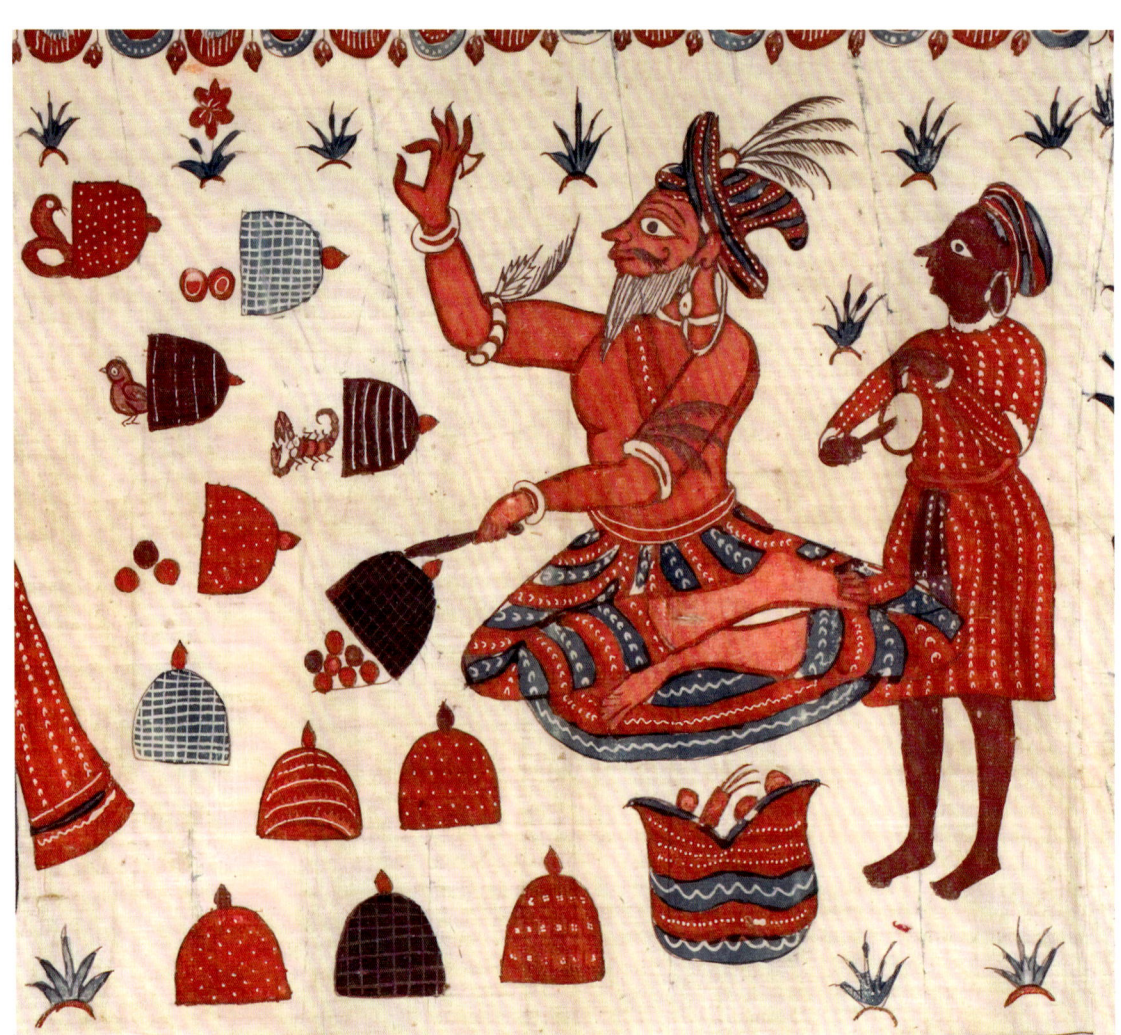

↓ ↓ **Expressions of life** *Storytelling*
Chintz hanging, India, 18th century. At over seven metres long, this story cloth depicts over 40 separate scenes from the life of Manikkivacakar, a famous south Indian poet of the 9th century

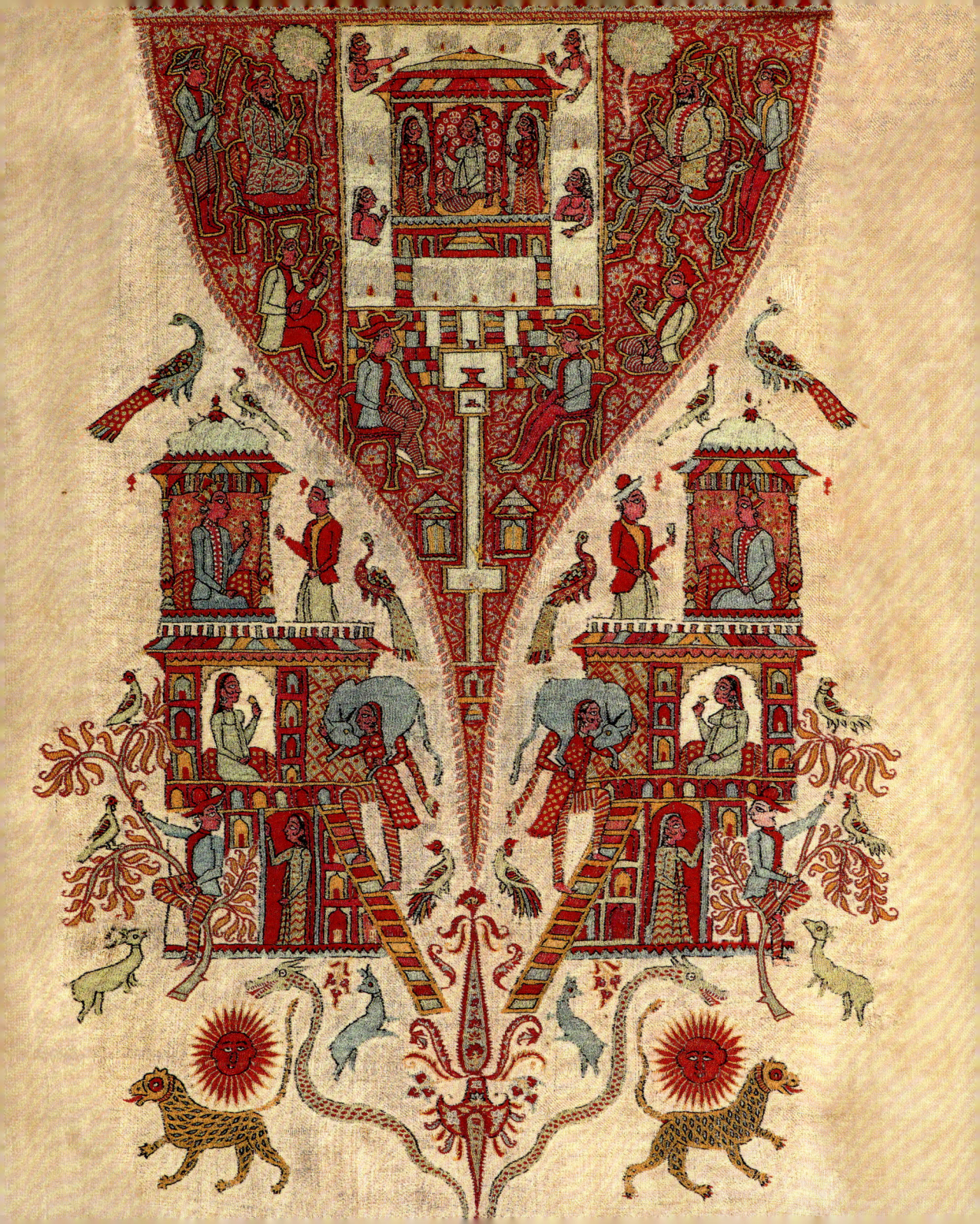

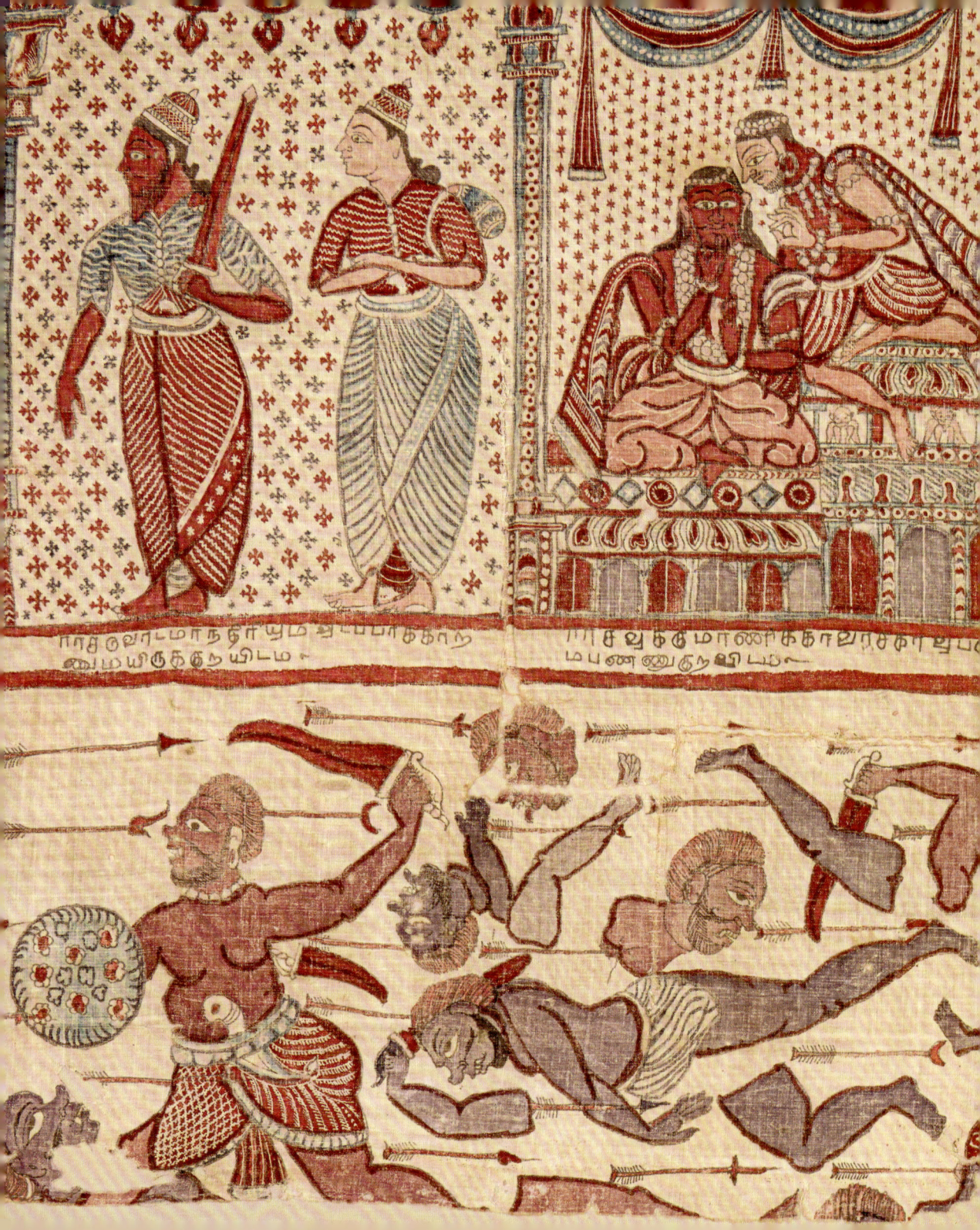

மாதுரவாடமாநதிரியும அபாபாகுகாந
யமயிருக்குக விடம

சிவுக்குமாணிக்காலர்சகாஉப
மபணையுகுர விடம

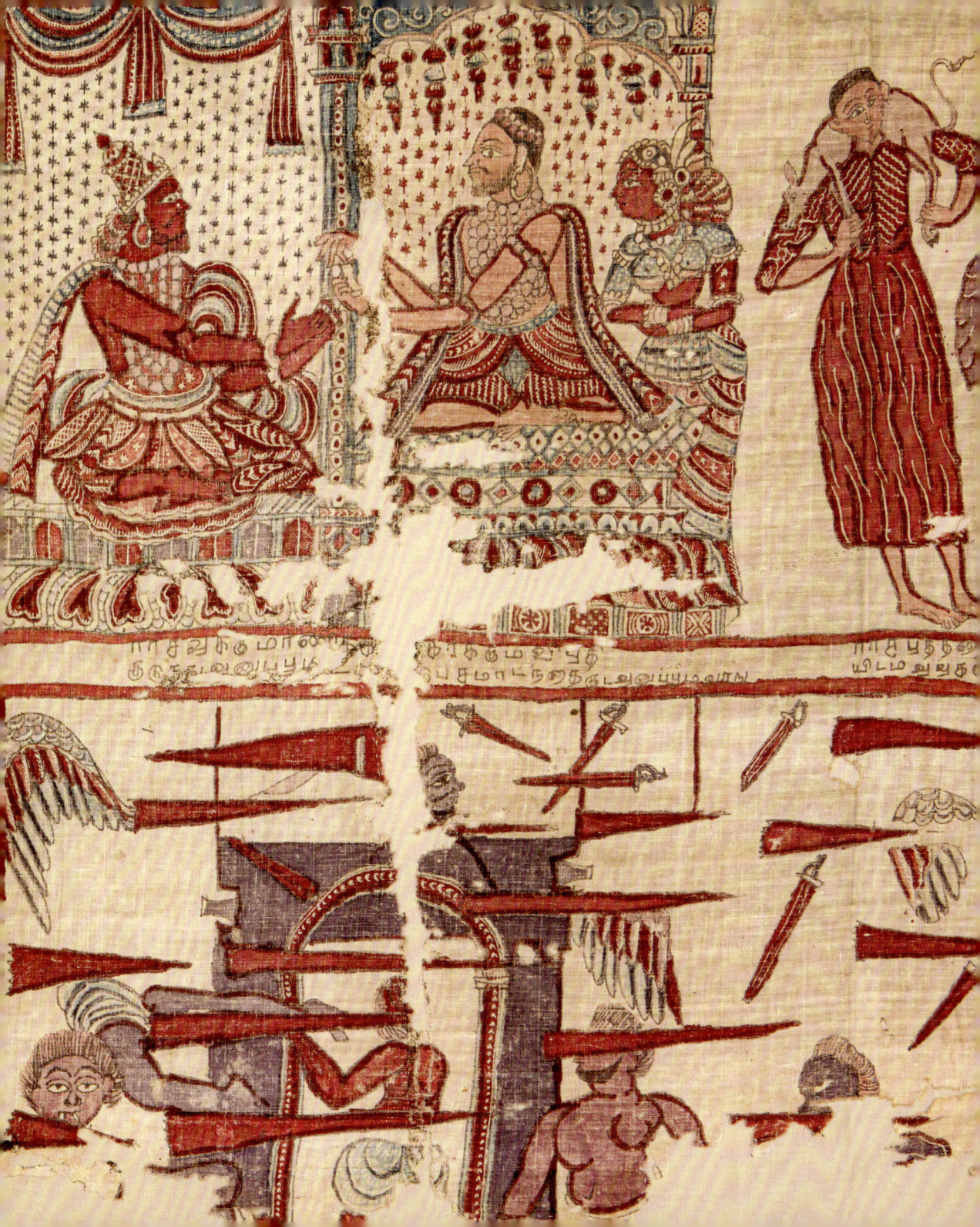

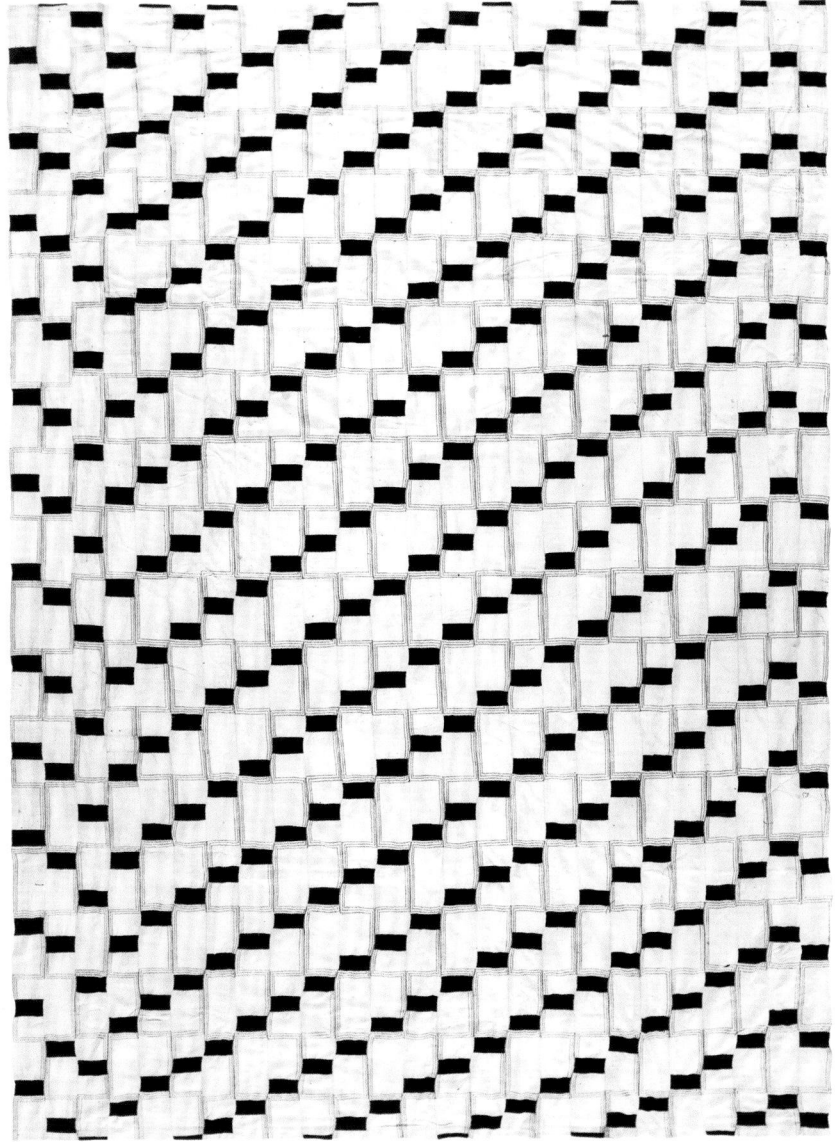

← **Expressions of life** *Deceit*
Mashru, India, 19th century. This fabric has a sumptuous sheen that implies the finest of materials. Looks are deceiving, however, as it is a mix of cotton and silk – a way to create the impression of a luxury textile for a more accessible price

↑ **Expressions of life** *Deceit*
Liar's cloth, Nigeria, 19th century. The depicted lines on this cloth shift and confuse the eye. Made of narrow woven strips, such a textile would often be commissioned by a chief

↓ **Everyday objects** *Covers*
Wrapping cloth, Japan, 20th century. Simple indigo-dyed cotton is decorated with a white cotton running stitch in a technique called sashiko

→ **Everyday objects** *Covers*
Door cover, Japan, 20th century. Sashiko is used to quilt and reinforce indigo-dyed cotton, and this type of threshold cover is ubiquitous throughout Japan

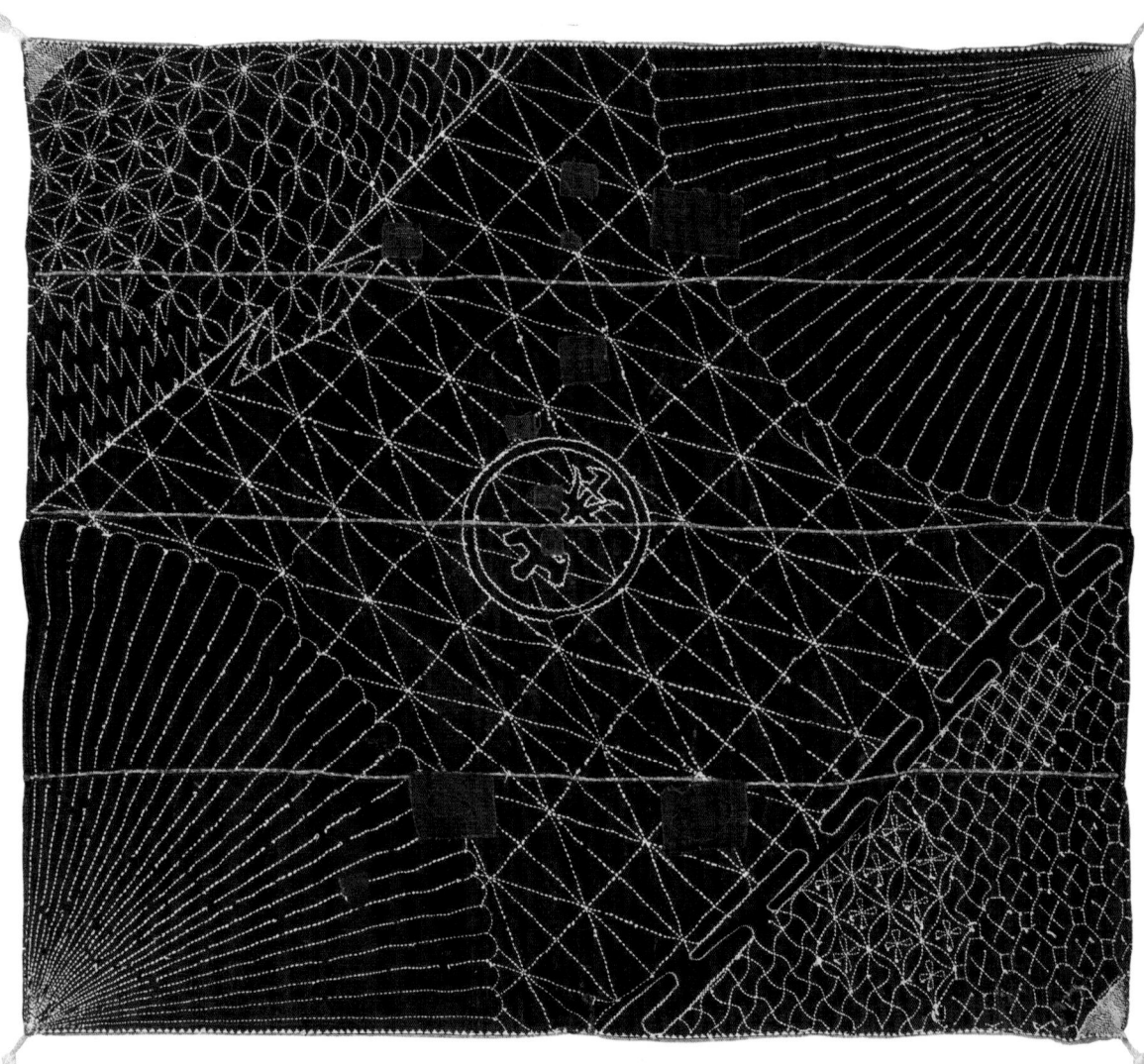

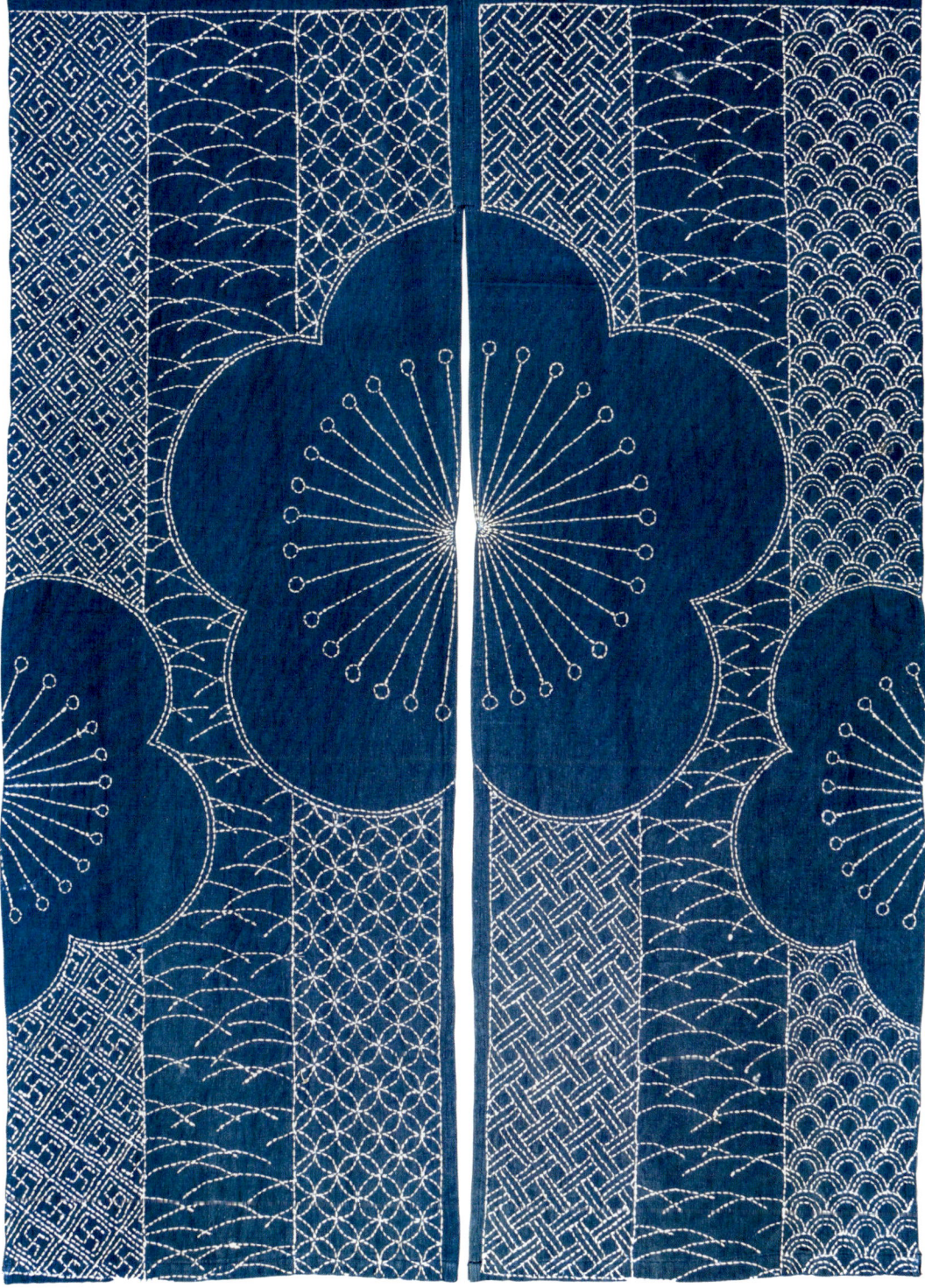

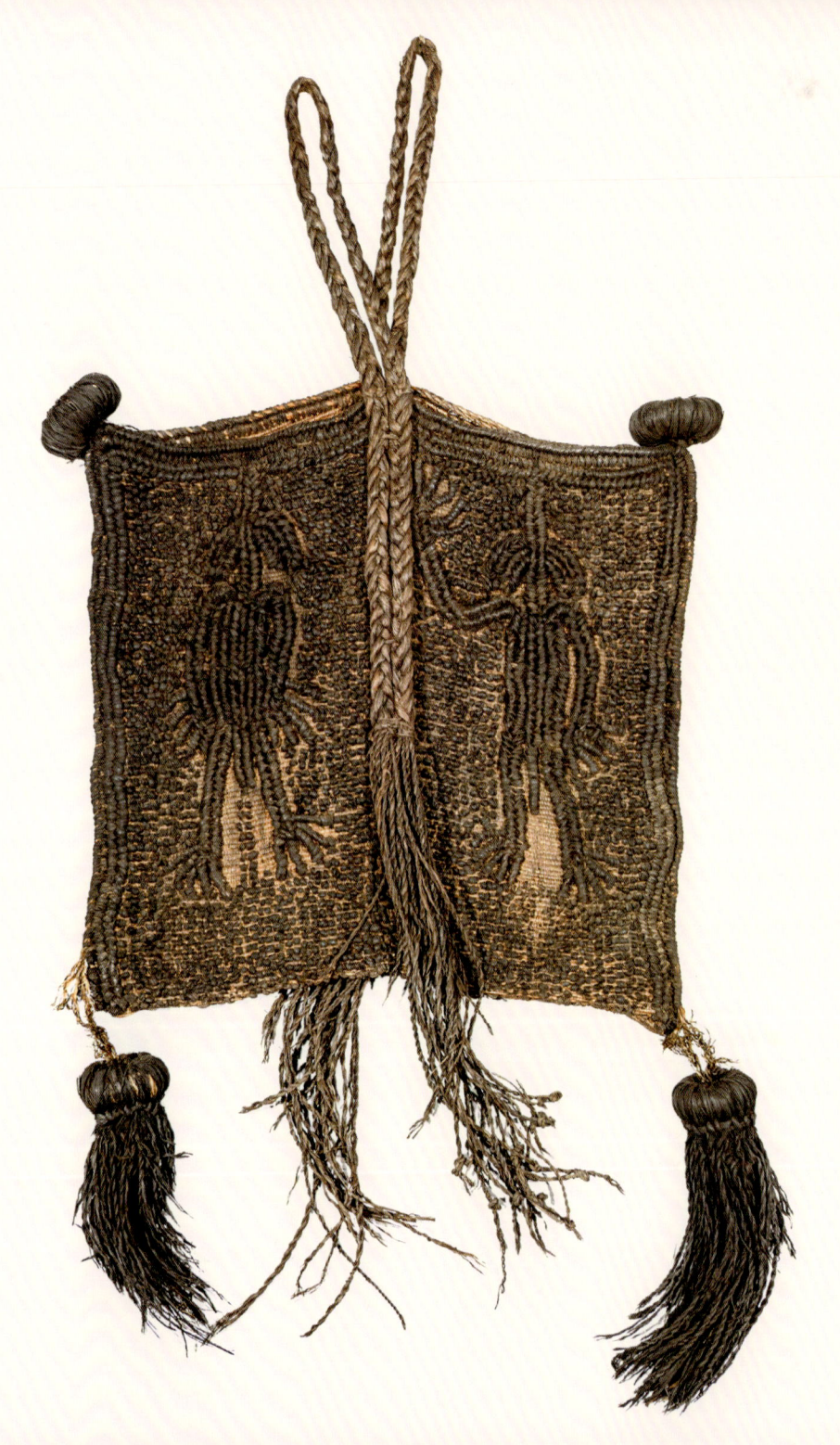

← **Everyday objects** *Bags*
Raffia woven bag, Cameroon, early 1900s. This unusual bag features two embroidered male figures with crested hair styles and elongated extremities

↓ **Everyday objects** *Bags*
Bag, Hazara, Afghanistan, 20th century. The harlequin-like silk embroidery is made of four triangular flaps joined together and is endlessly adaptable

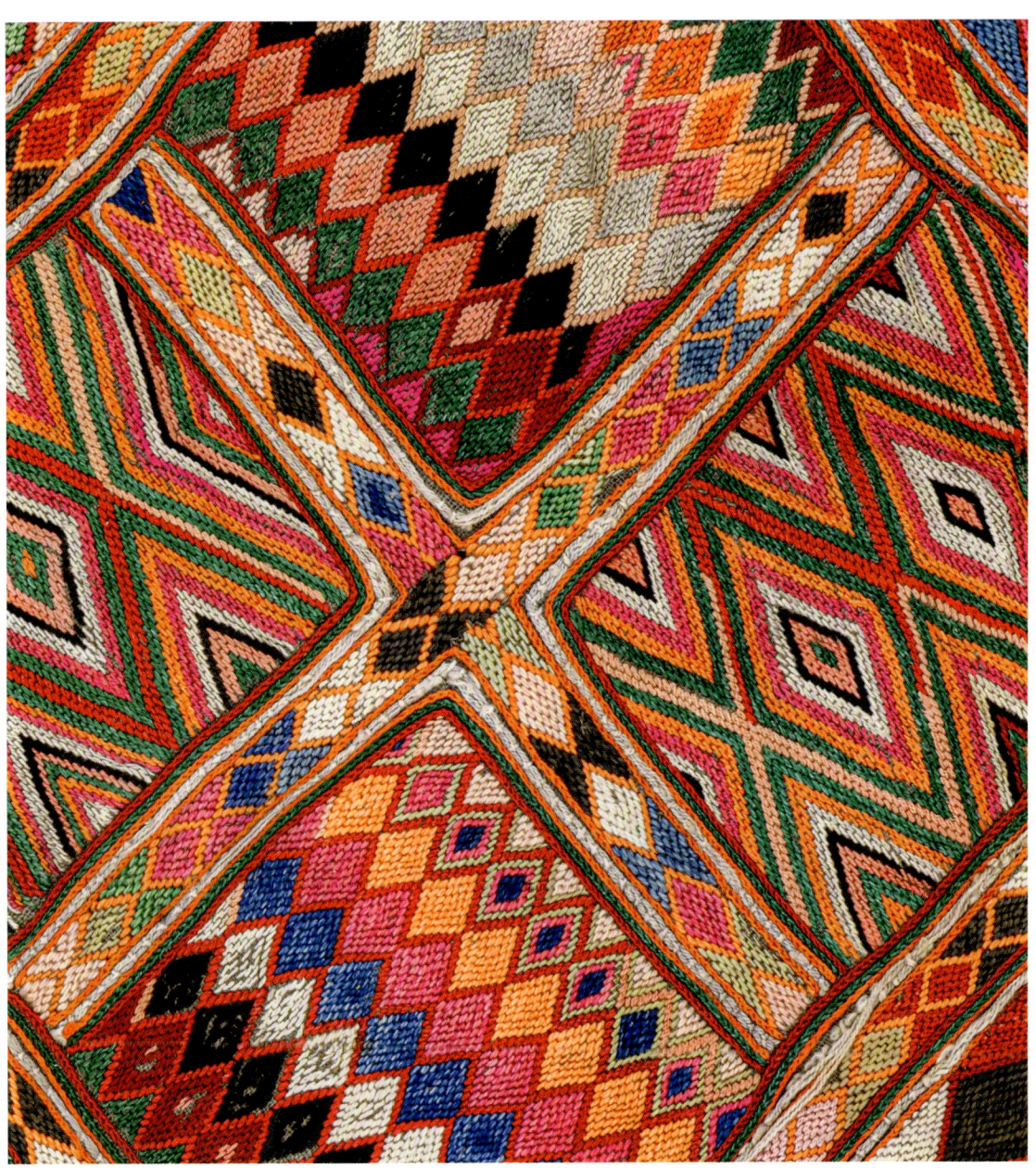

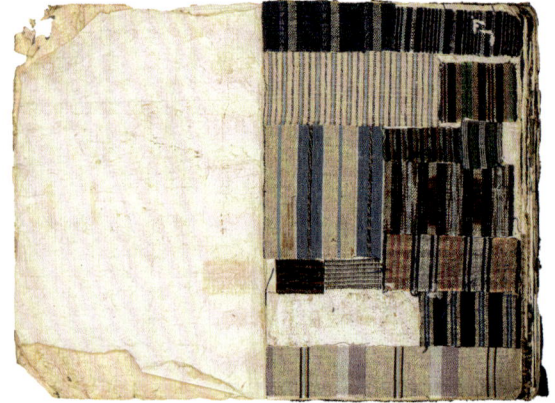
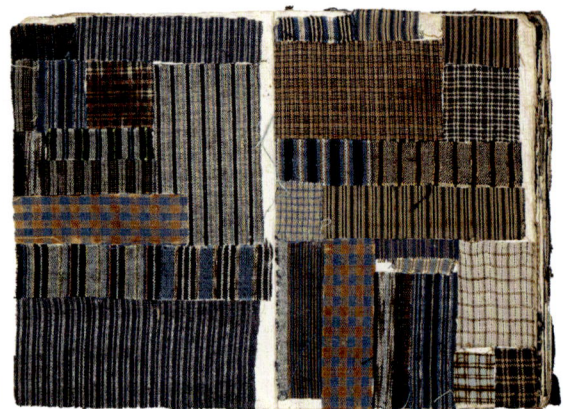
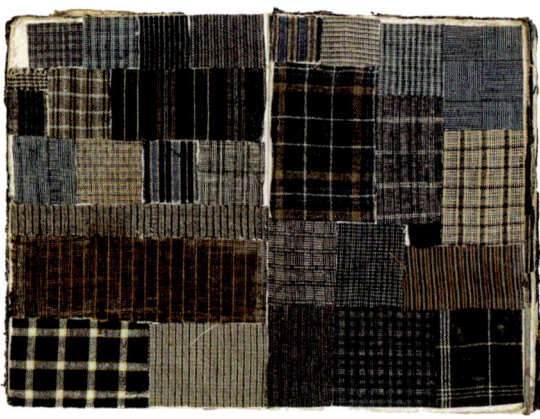
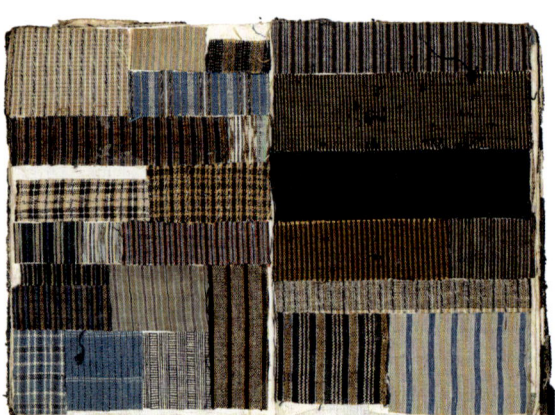
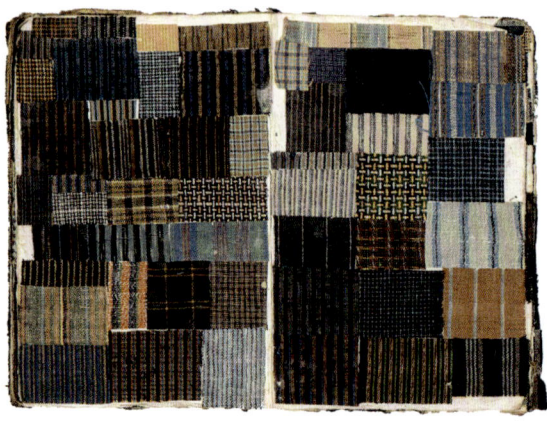
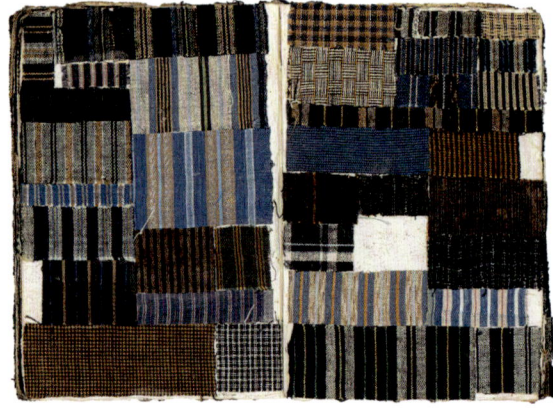

← **Everyday objects** *Recycling*
Books, Japan, late 19th century. These albums are called shimacho and are handmade books containing remnants of cloth. They are made by weaving families as a way of recording previous designs and preserving old textile fragments

↓ **Everyday objects** *Recycling*
Balls of thread, Japan, early 20th century. These are strips of cloth ripped from silk and cotton kimonos, saki, to be used to weave a certain type of cloth, ori, which is called sakiori and made entirely from recycled rags transformed into thread

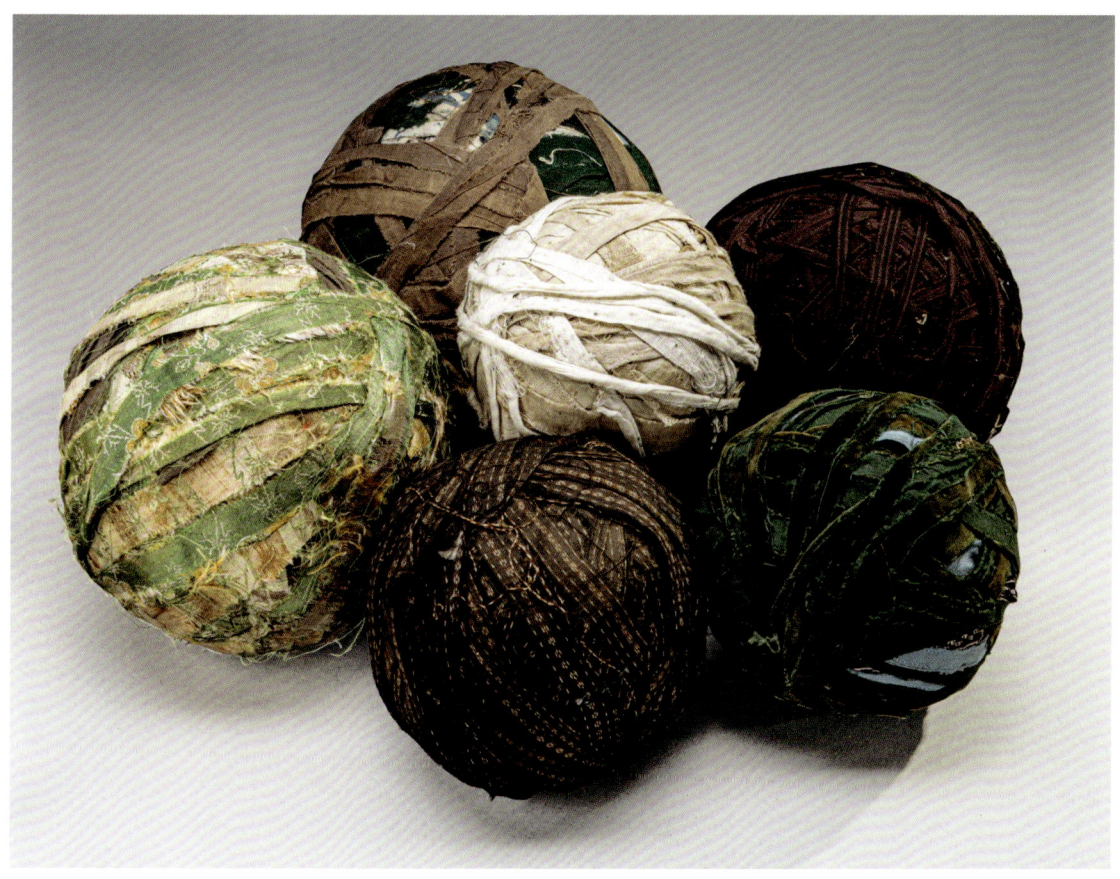

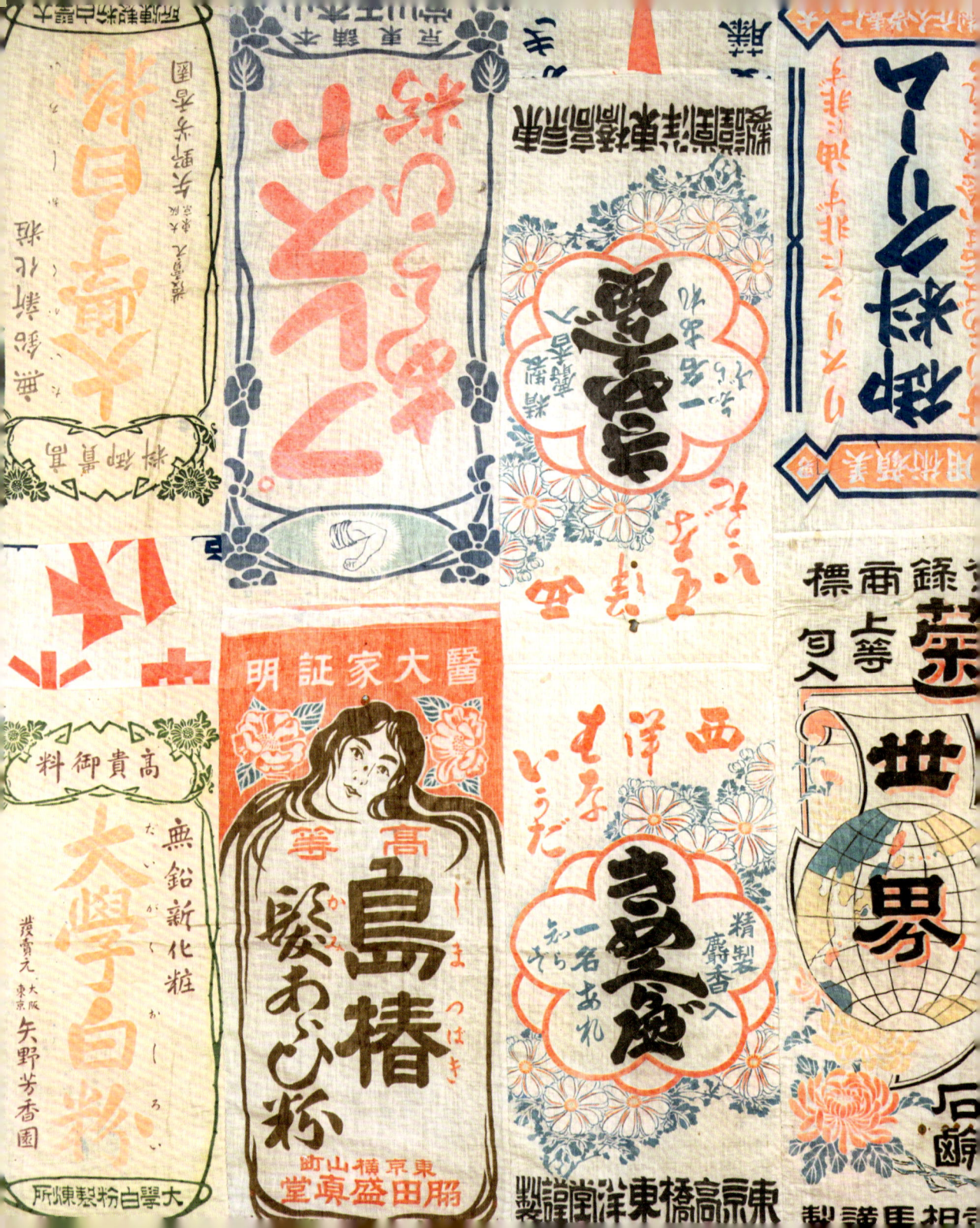

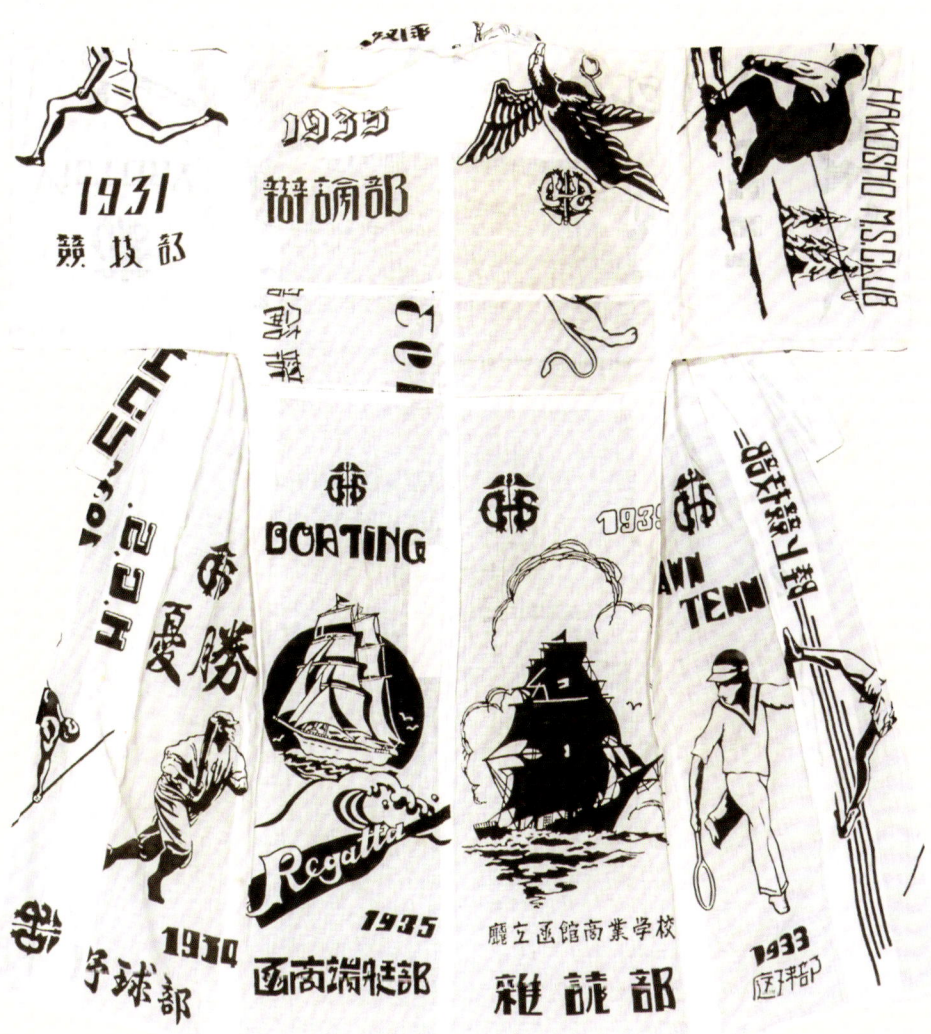

← Everyday objects *Recycling*
Curtain, Japan, 1920s. Printed cotton advertising signs for make-up have been stitched together to form a curtain that would hang outside a shop

↑ Everyday objects *Recycling*
Kimono, Japan, 1930s. Made from college sports towels, this garment captures the Japanese principle of mottainai, which promotes respect for resources and a hatred for waste

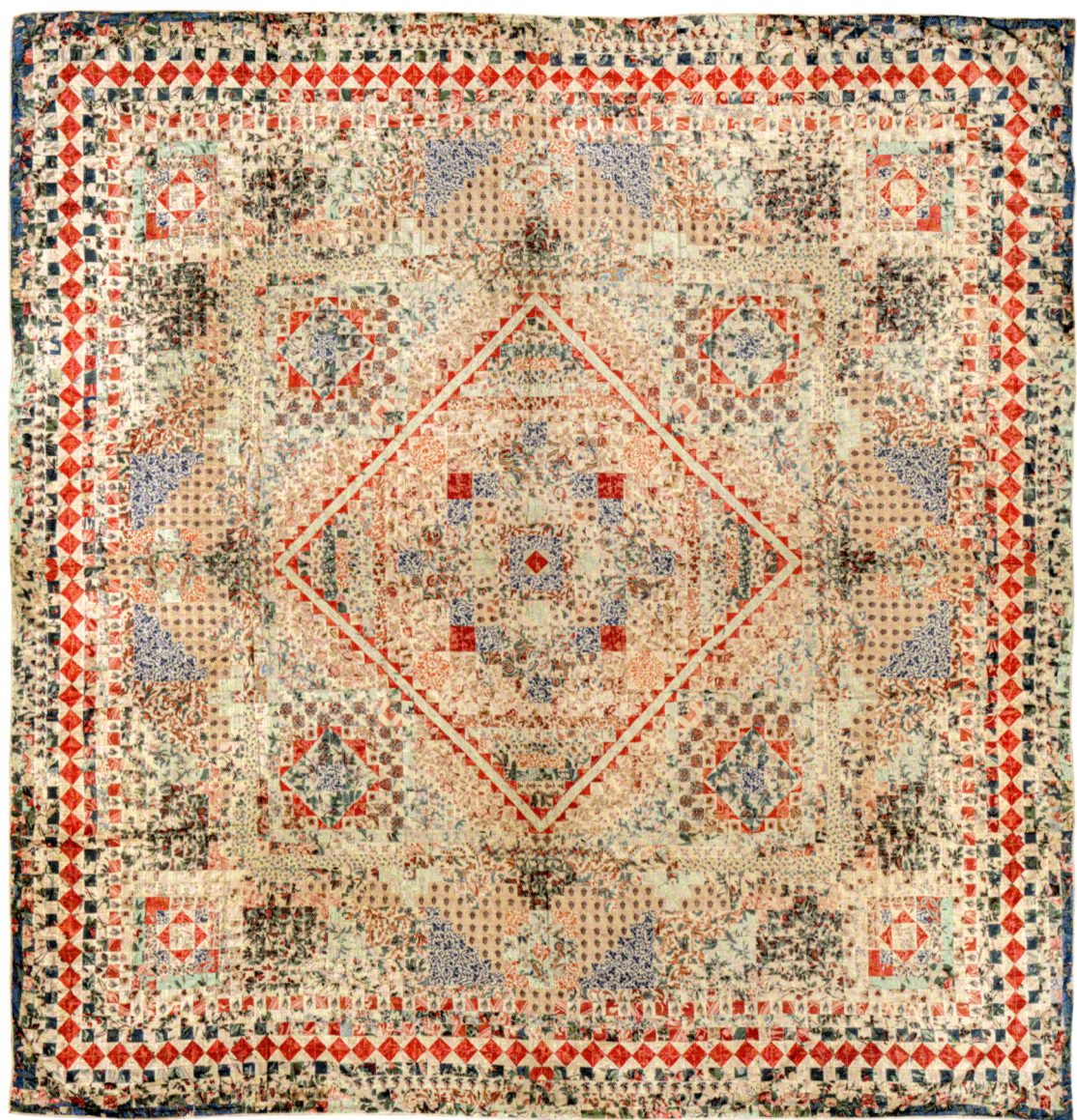

↑ →**Everyday objects** *Recycling*
Patchwork quilt, England, circa 1850. Made from European
fabrics dating between the late 1700s and the early 1800s,
this quilt would have taken many years to create. Over 7,000
patched pieces were originally cut out and applied to a paper
backing

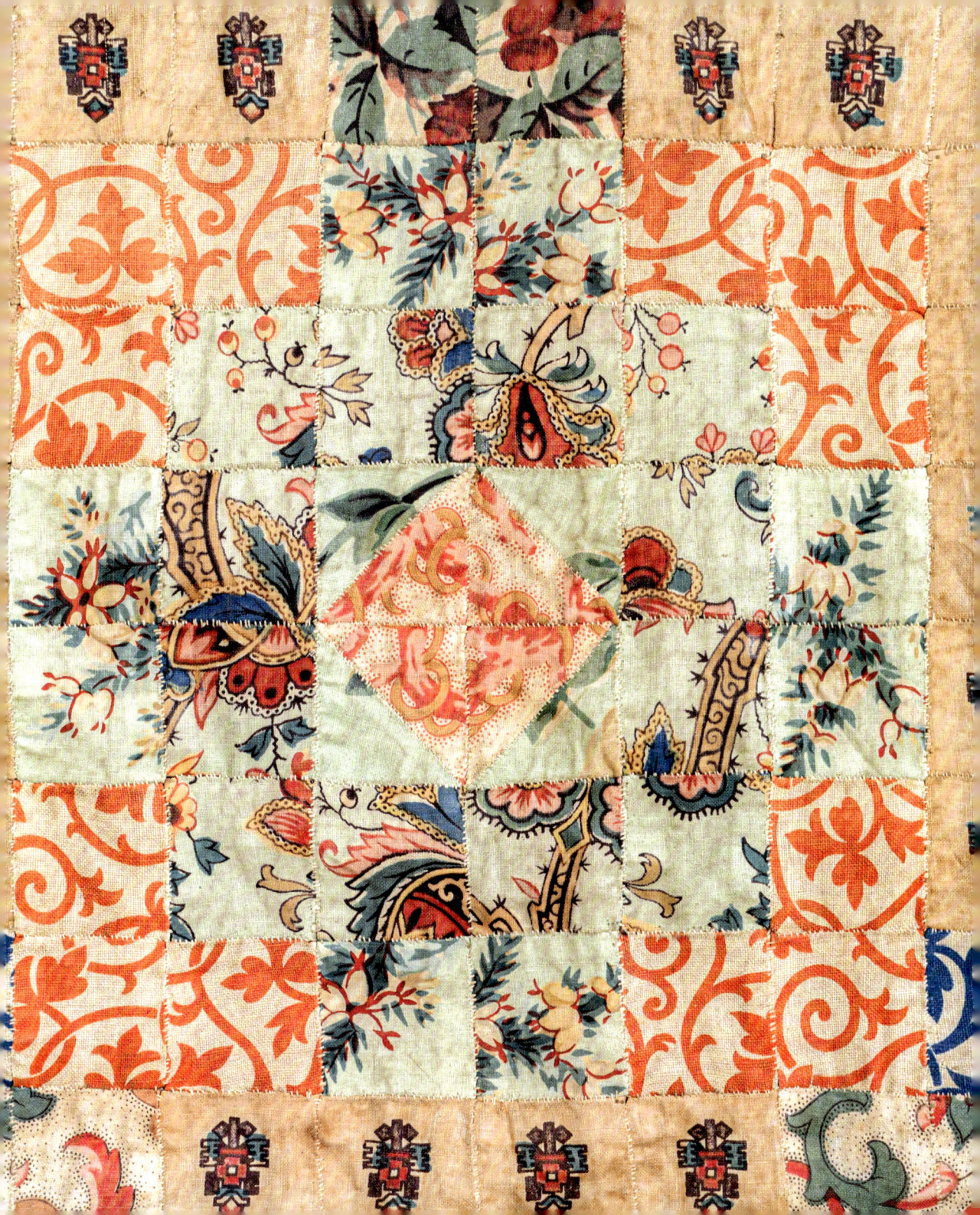

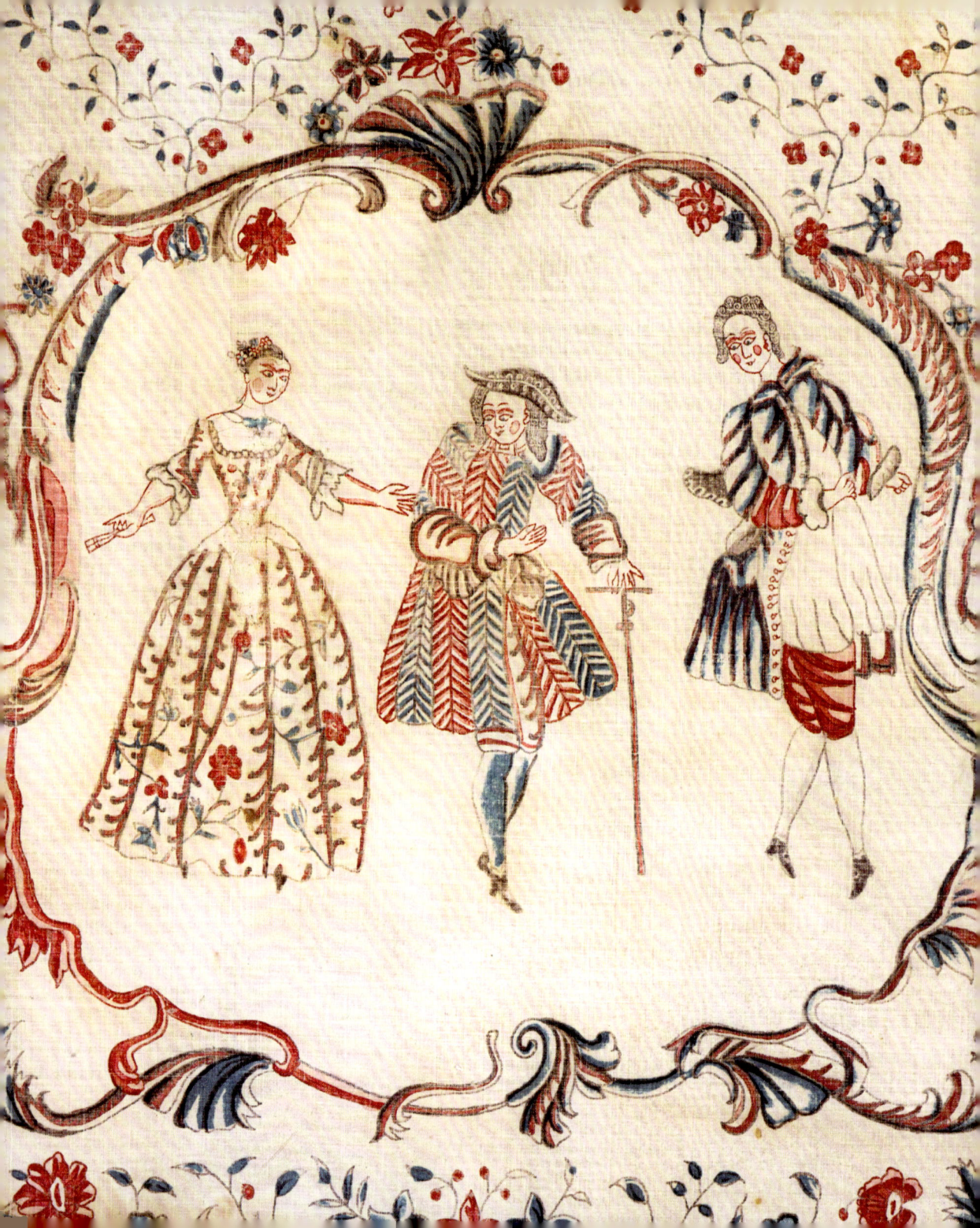

Costume

"Vain trifles as they seem, clothes have, they say, more important offices than merely to keep us warm. They change our view of the world and the world's view of us."

← **Human activity** *Celebrations*
Chintz, Coromandel Coast, India for the Dutch market, 1750s.
Intended for use as a woman's skirt, this cloth has a design of
three figures wearing elaborate costumes. It is taken from a
satirical French/Dutch print from the 1720s, and the scale of
the figures implies their importance to the designer

↑ *Orlando*, Virginia Woolf (1928)

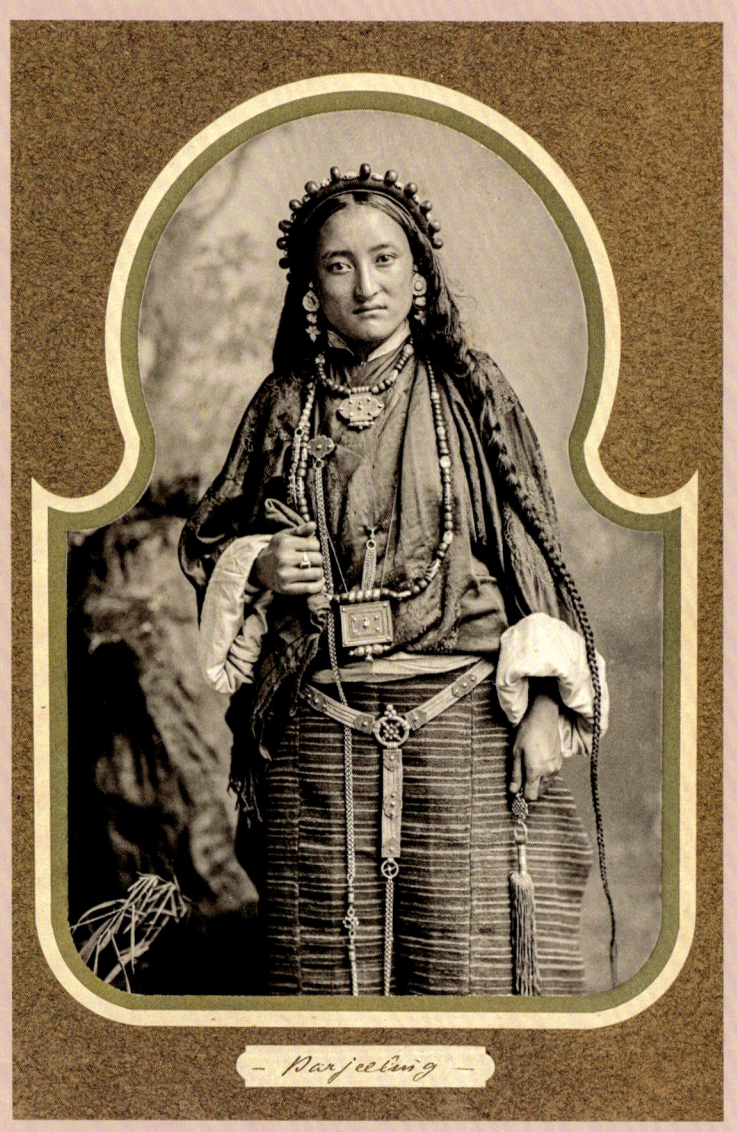

Darjeeling

↑ **Postcard**
Photograph of a woman named Lhamo, a name she
shares with a female deity, taken in the Johnston and
Hoffman photographic studio, Darjeeling, India, 1880s

The earliest known sewing needles date back fifty to sixty thousand years, and scholars have estimated that the first forms of clothing were worn up to 500,000 years ago. Apparel has since become a global industry, and 'fashion' can be seen as the consumerist by-product of this increasingly industrialised trade. Through clothing choices, wearers of textiles communicate something of themselves.

It should be emphasised that, in many periods of our history, the style, cut, material and even colour of clothing was designated by strict sumptuary laws, so you were what you wore. With such prominence granted to dress and textiles it is unsurprising that cloth and dye trading constituted a large part of international commerce over millennia.

Growth and industrialisation, through developments in transportation and the introduction of mechanised sewing machines, have given rise to necessary criticism of the ethical and environmental consequences of the textile manufacturing process. The use-and-discard mentality is being challenged in a number of ways. A useful comparison might be the Japanese boro textile, with its origins in the Edo period – reinforcing old, worn-out textiles with scraps of discarded cotton, linen or hemp. More economical than purchasing new clothing, this process, through the layering method, provided wearers with warm textiles where cotton was not available. Typically dyed with indigo, boros are beautiful heirlooms that pass down through generations.

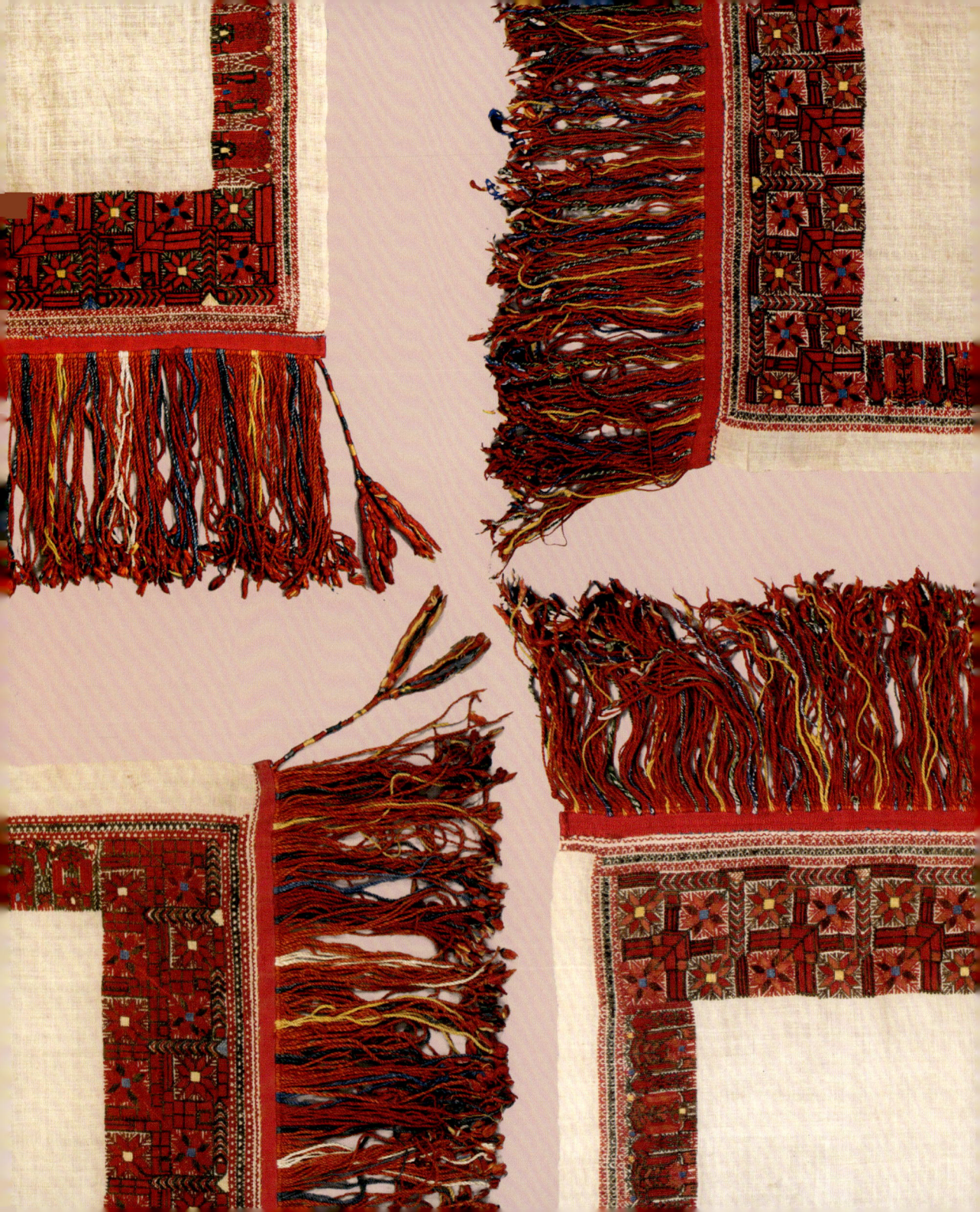

← **Identity** *Community*
Details from four Palestinian shawls, Ramallah, 19th century.
The linen shawls are embroidered with silk and have elaborate
tassels

↓ **Identity** *Community*
Ainu attush robe, Hokkaido, Japan, 19th century. This coat
is made from elm-bark fibre embellished with appliqué designs
in cotton

Costume

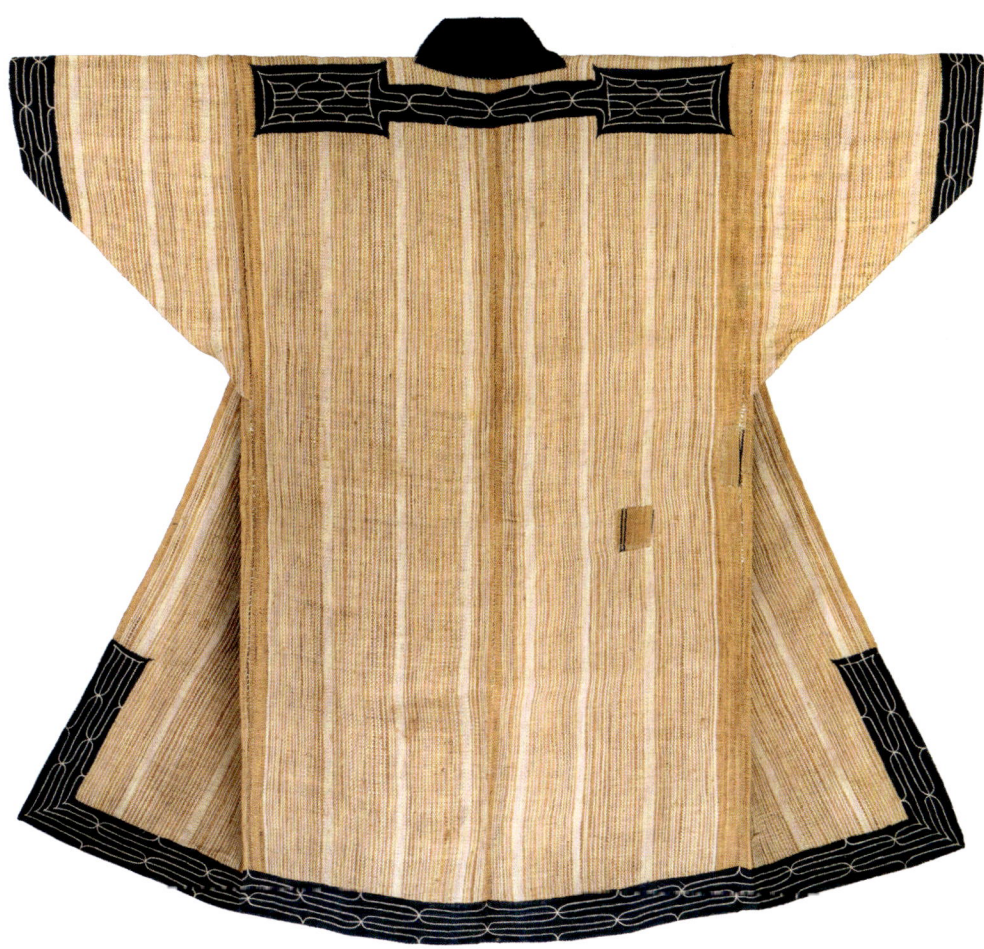

Identity Clothing has long been used as a means to create group identity. Whether this is used to form a sense of cohesion
and unity within a group or to provide a sense of belonging to a larger nation of people, clothing and costume are an important
way for people to express both individuality and integration. Subtle variations are a means of establishing hierarchy and
subdivisions within these larger communities of people.

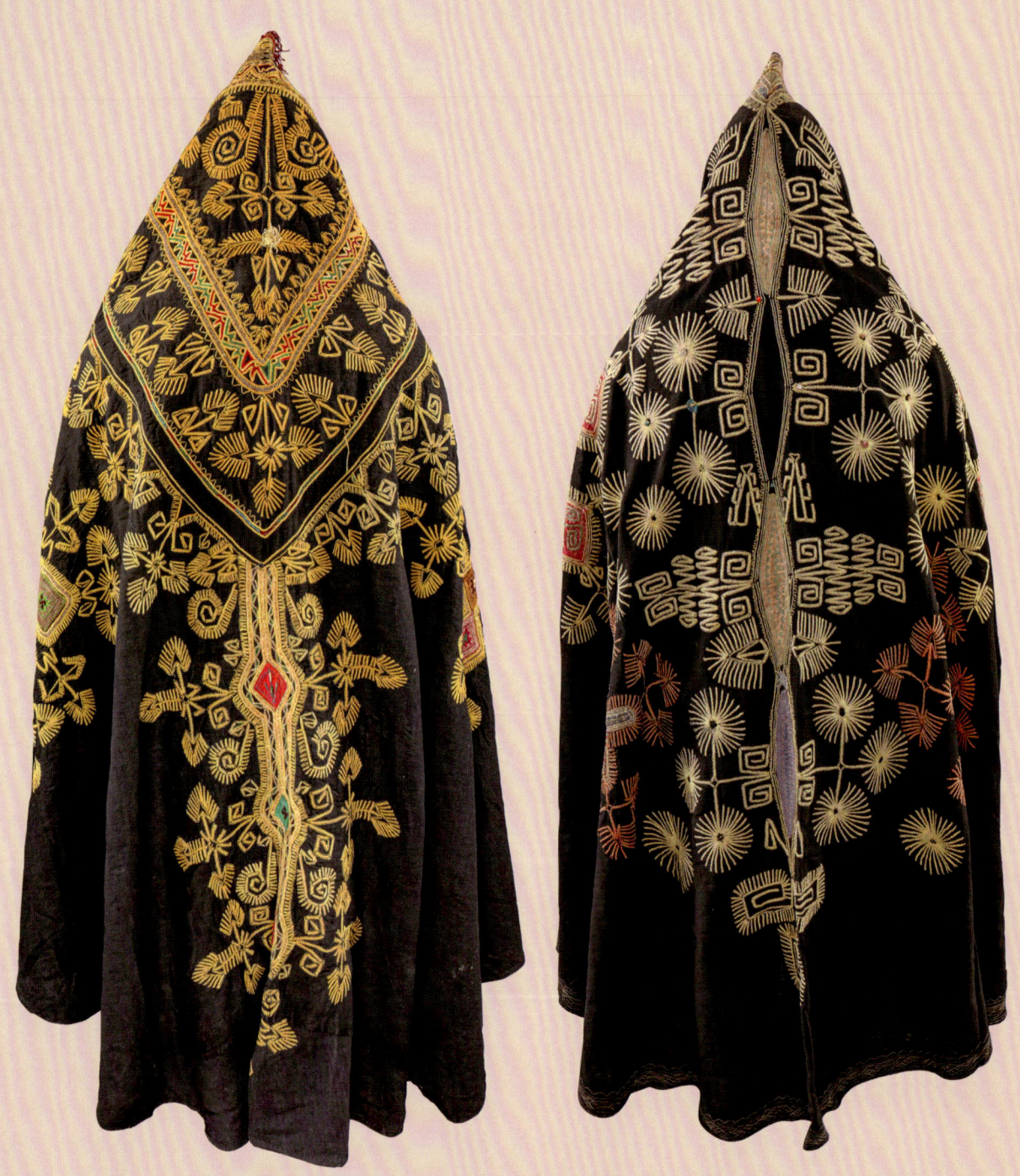

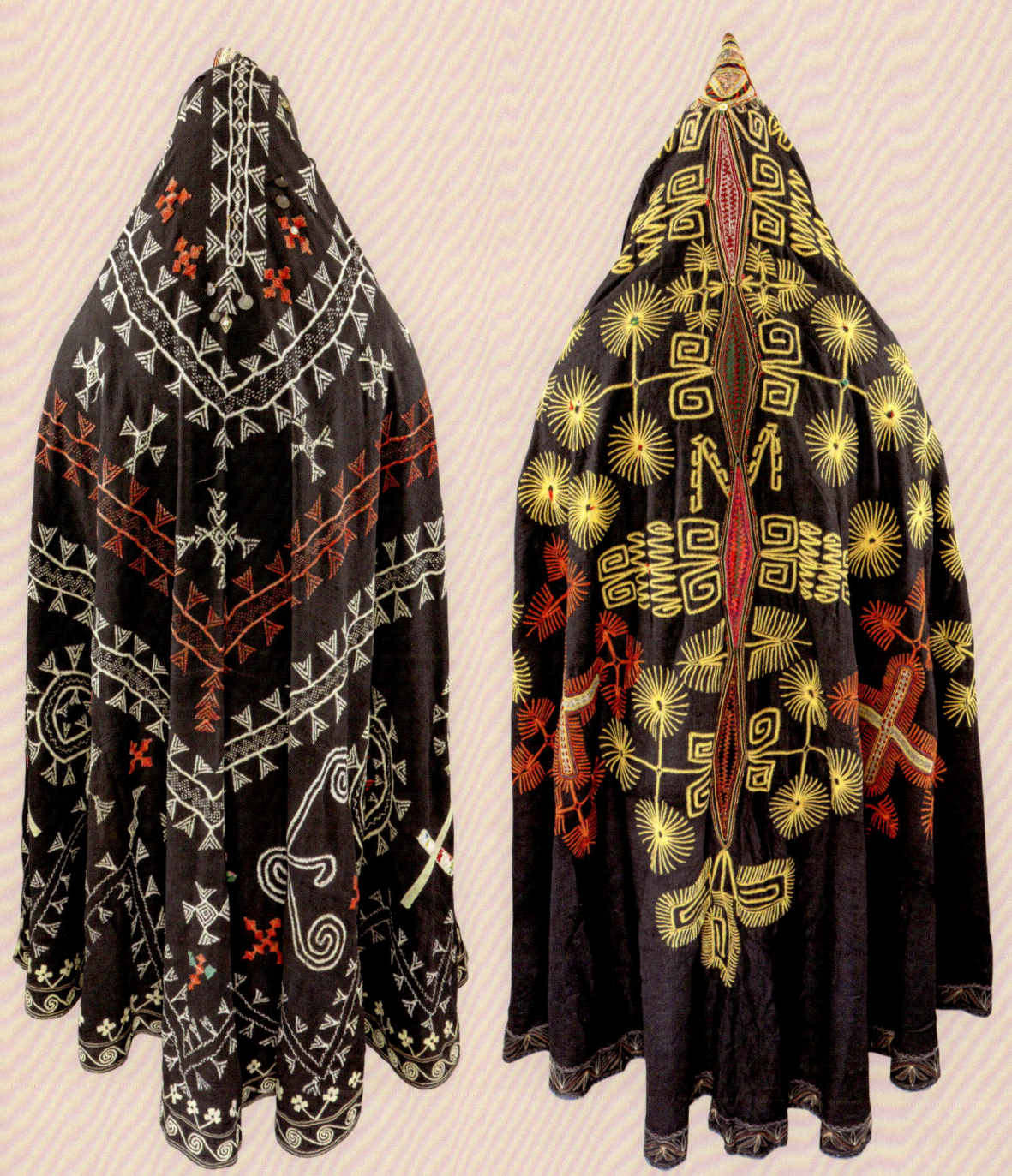

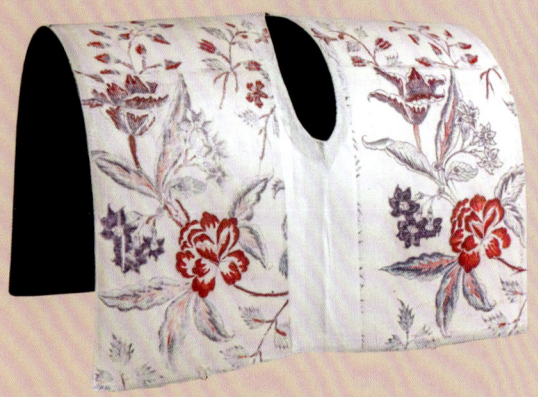

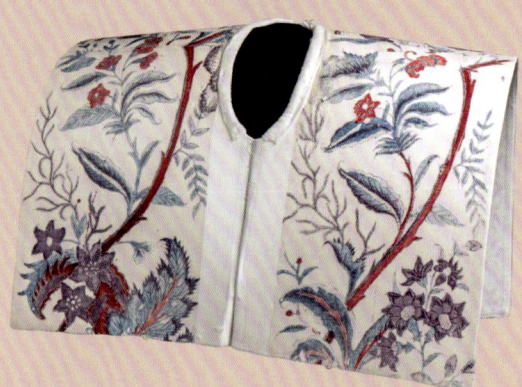

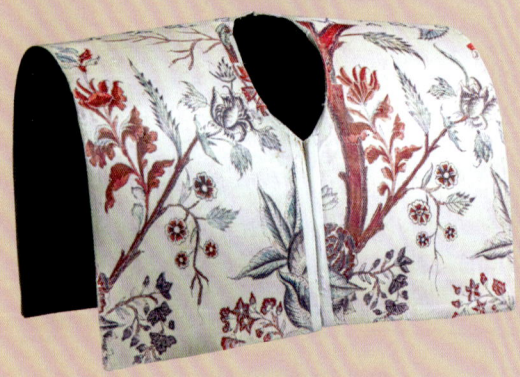

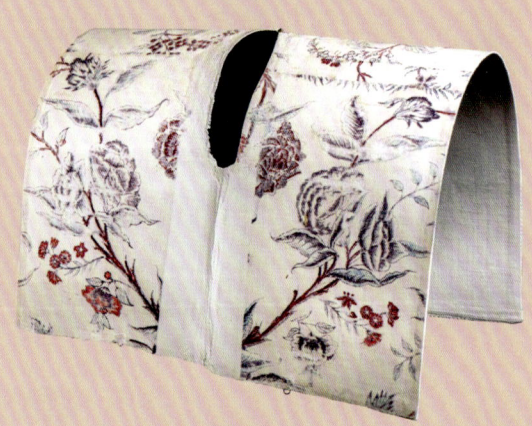

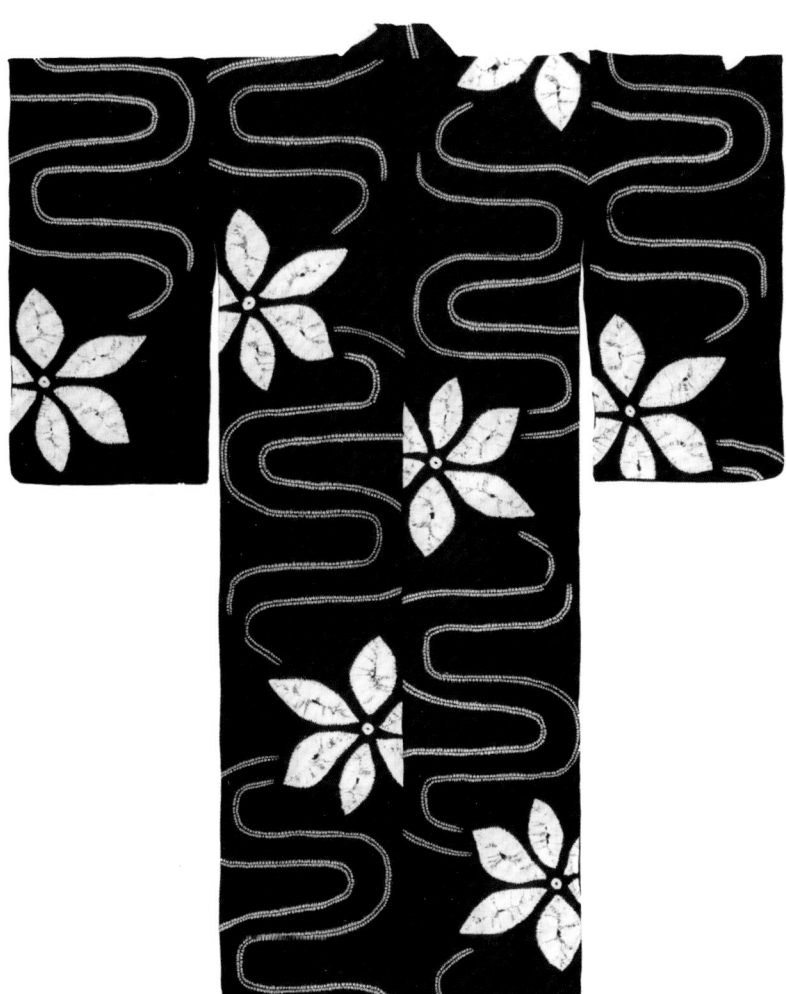

← **Identity** *Community*
Kroplaps, the Netherlands, 18th century. With some slight regional differences, these very distinctive stiff, starched breastcloths were once worn by women throughout the Netherlands. They were made out of imported Indian chintz

↑ **Identity** *Community*
Kimono, Honshu, Japan, late 19th century. Decorated using the shibori shape-resist dyeing technique, unlined short cotton kimonos or yukata were originally used in bathhouses, but became widely popular as casual summer garments

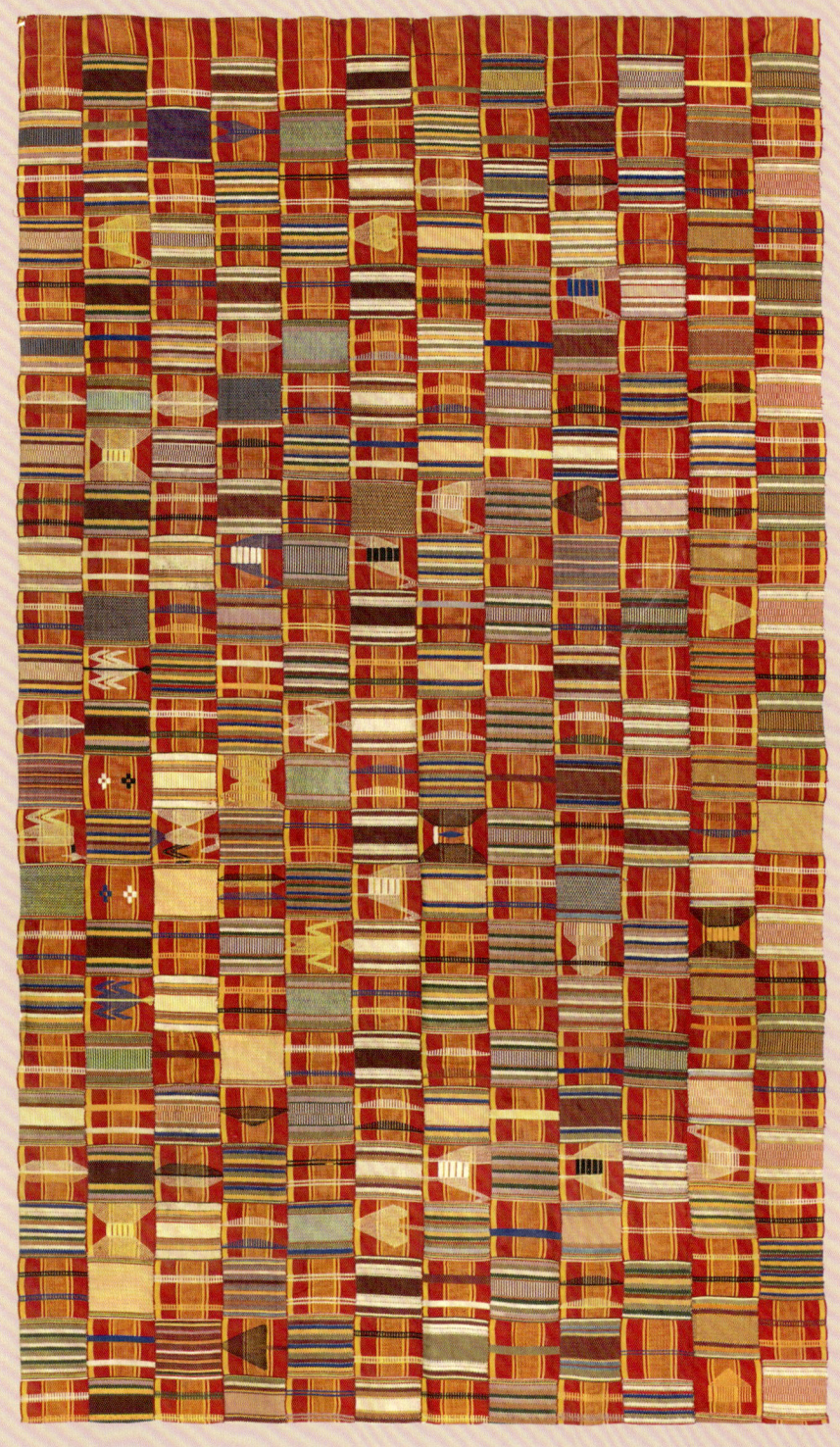

← **Identity** *Status*
Ewe woman's cloth, Ghana, early 20th century. Such narrow-strip-woven cotton cloths were used as wraps by women in Ghana. The complex weave with supplementary weft-float designs indicates that this is a special cloth, denoting status, and as such made for a dignitary or royalty

↑ **Identity** *Status*
Sul-ma, woman's woollen dress, Ladakh, India, late 19th/early 20th century. This style of garment, made from strips of snambu woollen cloth patterned with tie-dyed circles and cruciform motifs, was originally exclusive to the Ladakhi royal family, becoming more commonly worn late in the 19th century

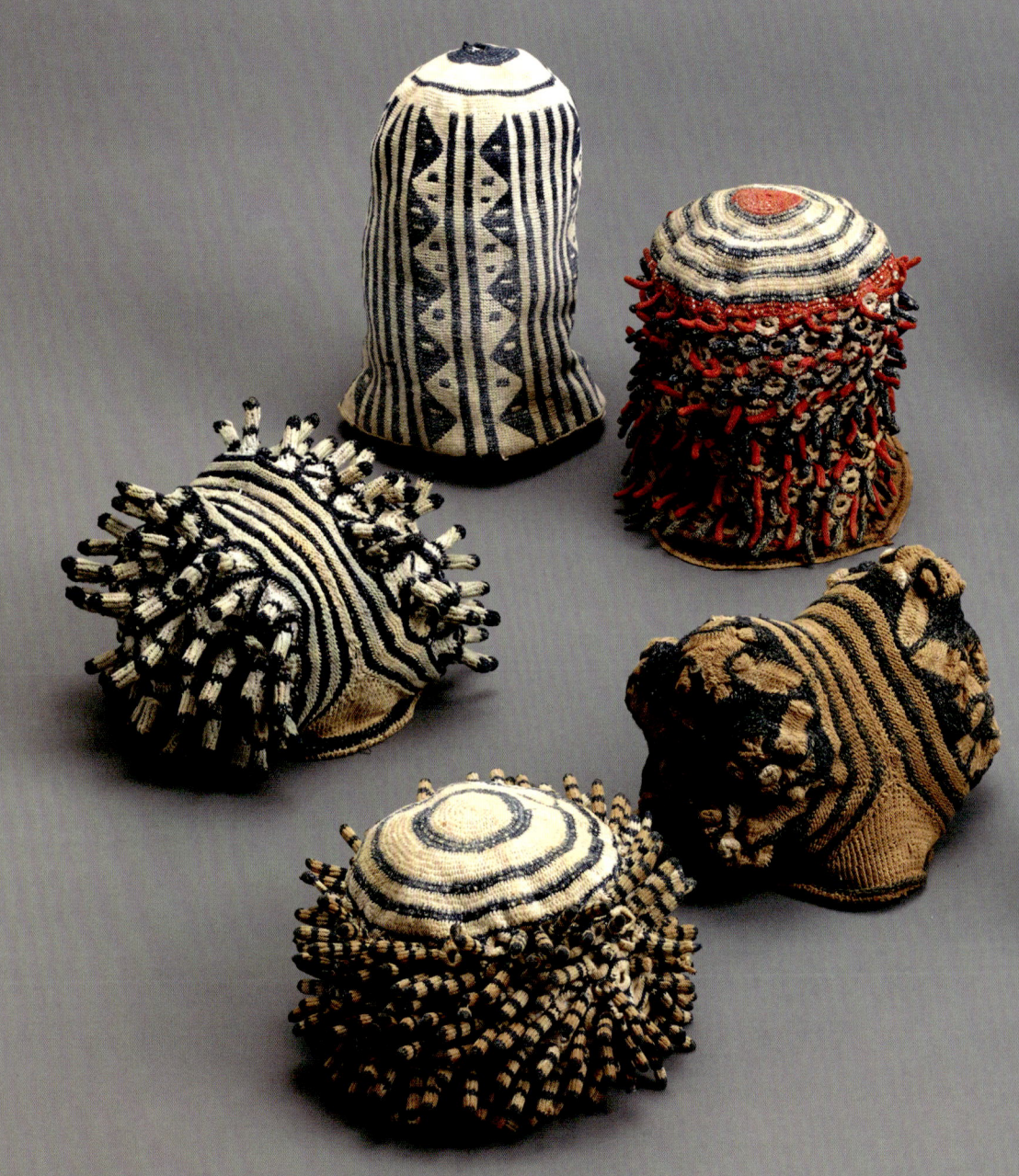

↓ **Identity** *Status*
Chief or senior officials' hats, Ashetu grasslands region,
Cameroon, 19th century. Some of the forms are derived from
the hair styles in the region, but the hats are reserved for sole
use by high-ranking males.

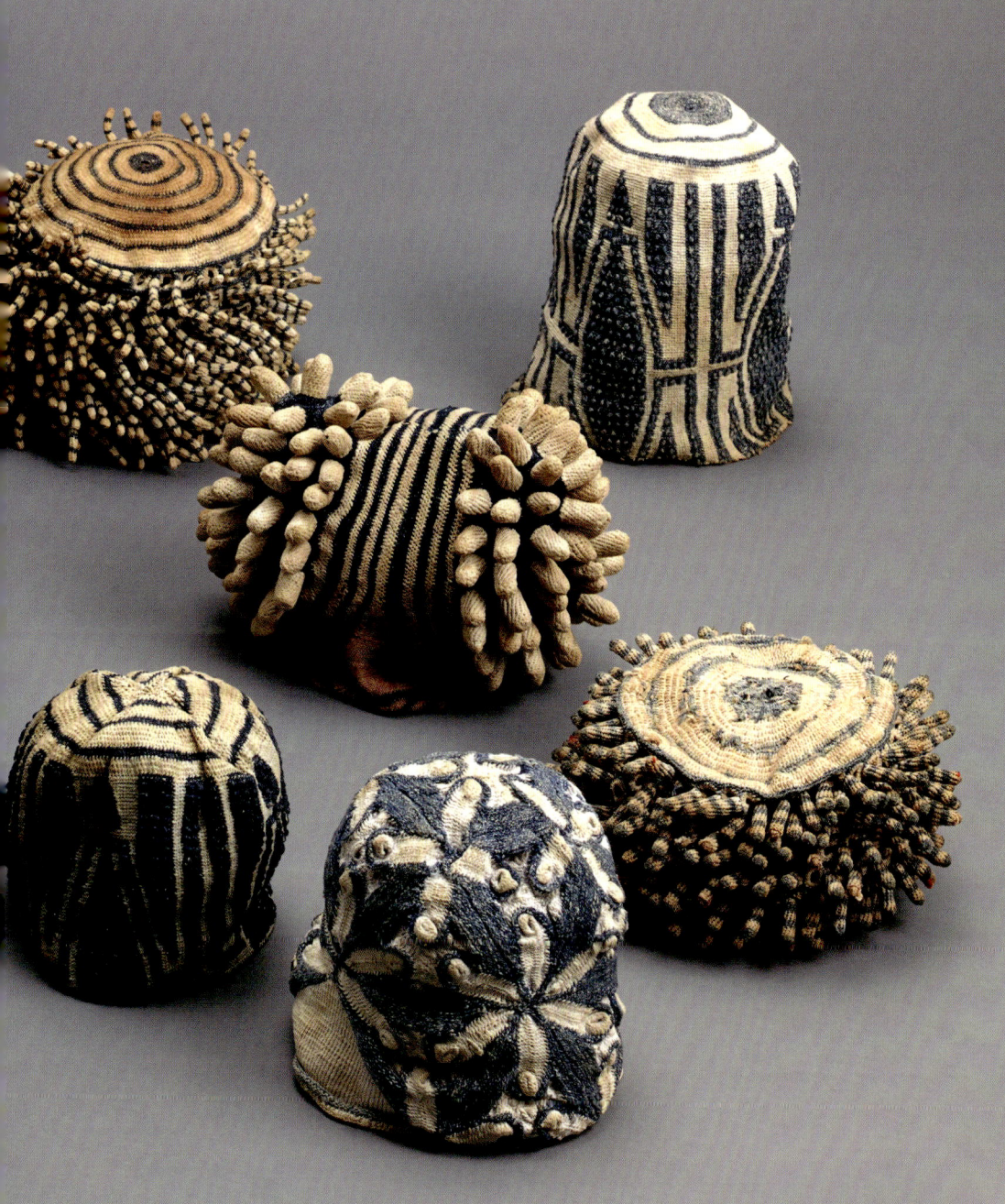

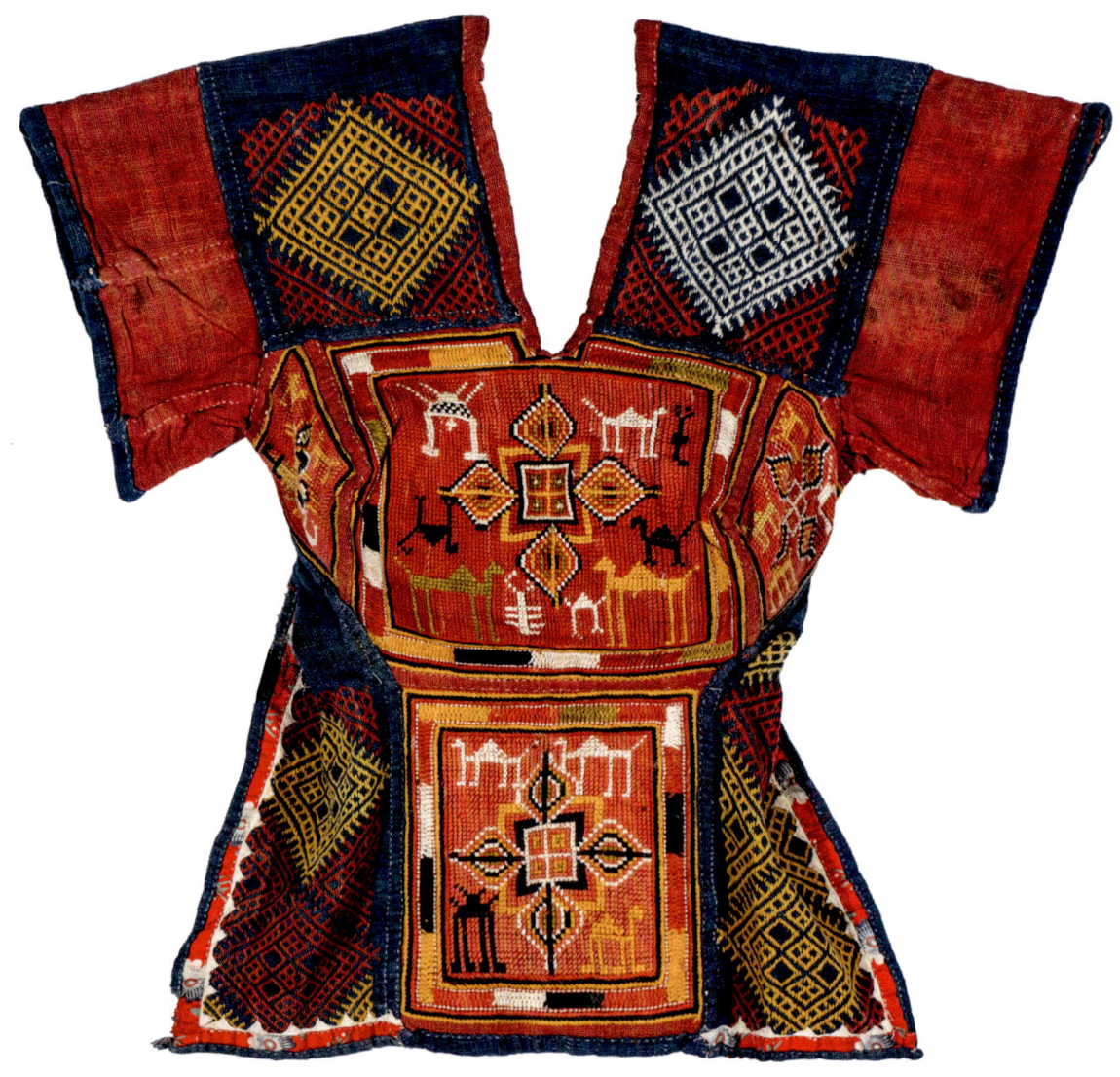

↑**Identity** *Minority*
Banjara woman's choli, Kutch, India, 20th century. Women
from the nomadic Banjara community are identified by
brightly coloured embroidered dresses tied at the back. In this
example the embroidered panels feature animals

→**Identity** *Minority*
Silk belt, Morocco, 19th century. Jewish brides in Morocco
wore elaborate silk belts wound around the waist at wedding
ceremonies

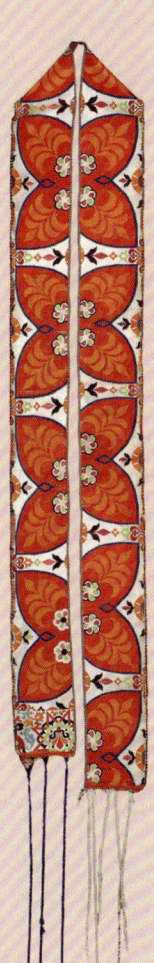

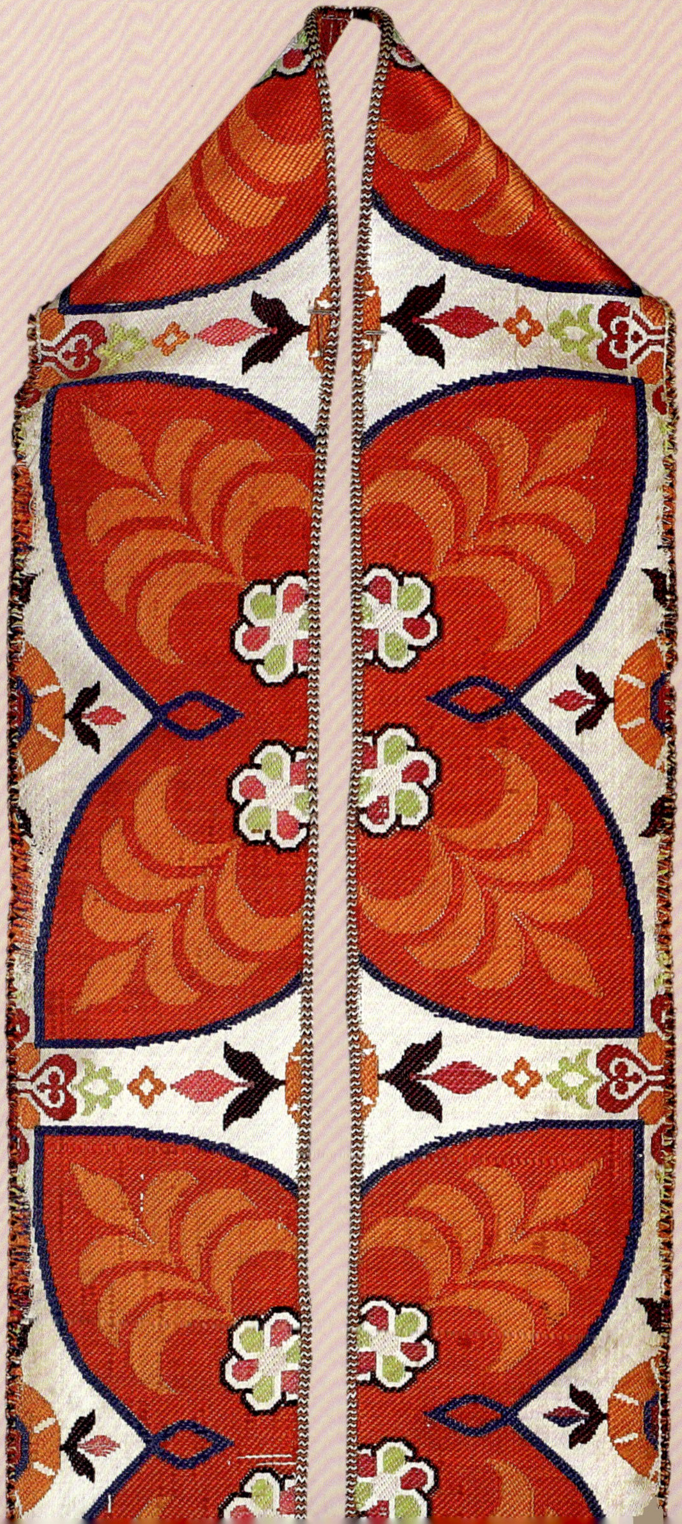

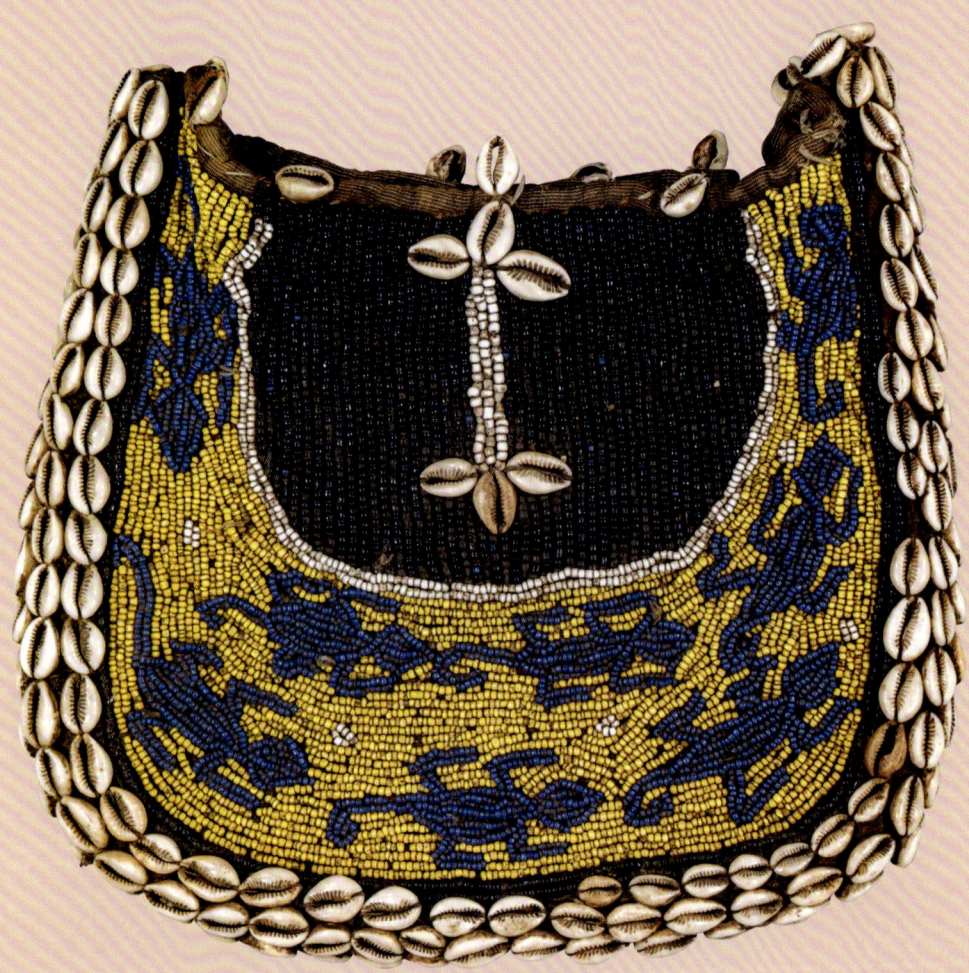

↖**Identity** *Status*
Hat, Cameroon, 19th century. The use of trade beads and cowrie shells, which would have been imported and therefore expensive, elevates this hat to a high-status item. Cowrie shells are thought to have been the first pan-African currency and thus convey wealth

→ **Identity** *Status*
Wari or Tiwanaku four-cornered hat, Peru, circa 500–900 CE. Finely knotted hats with square crowns, four sides and pointed tips are associated with two ancient cultures of the Andes: the Wari and the Tiwanaku. The hats signalled high standing

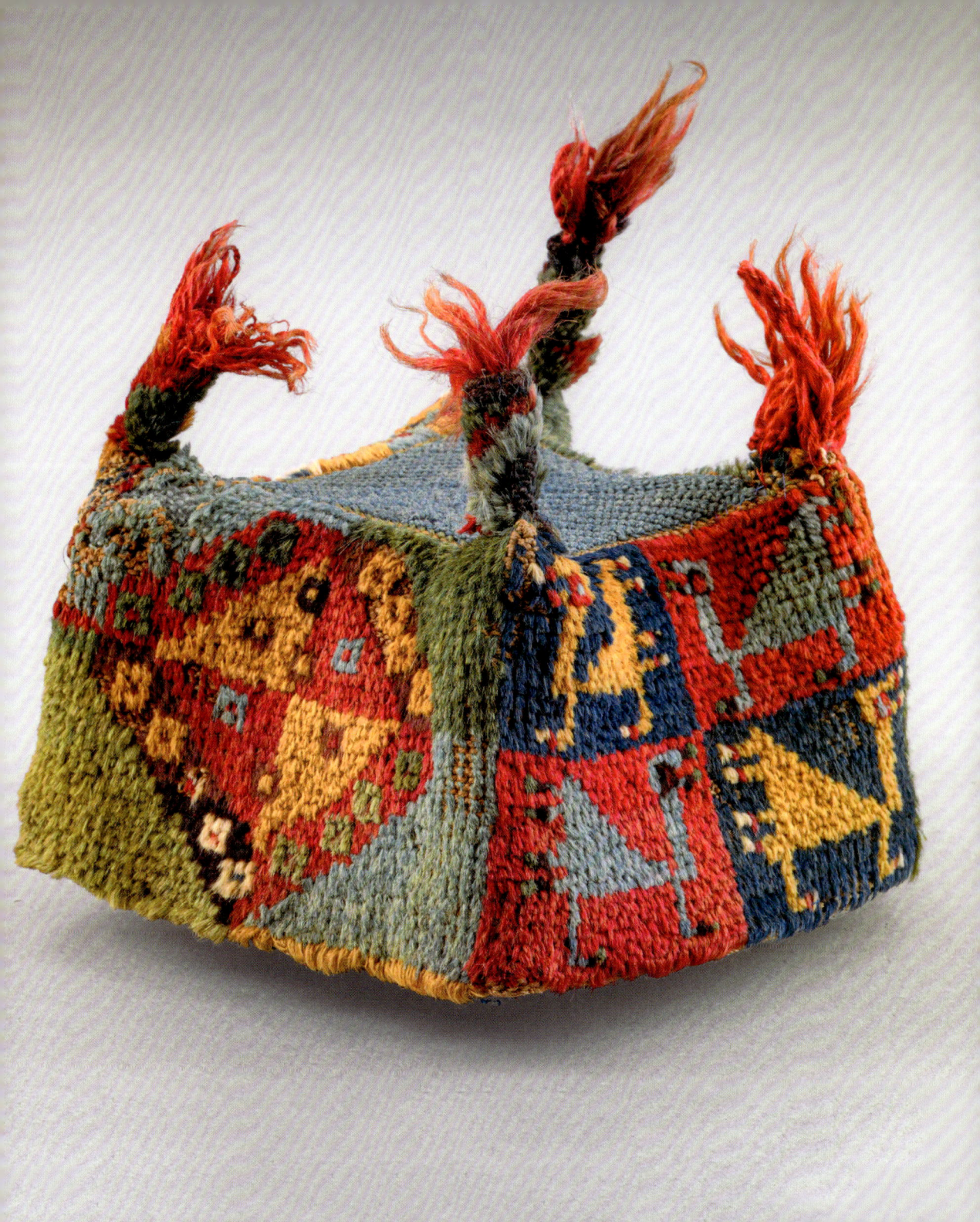

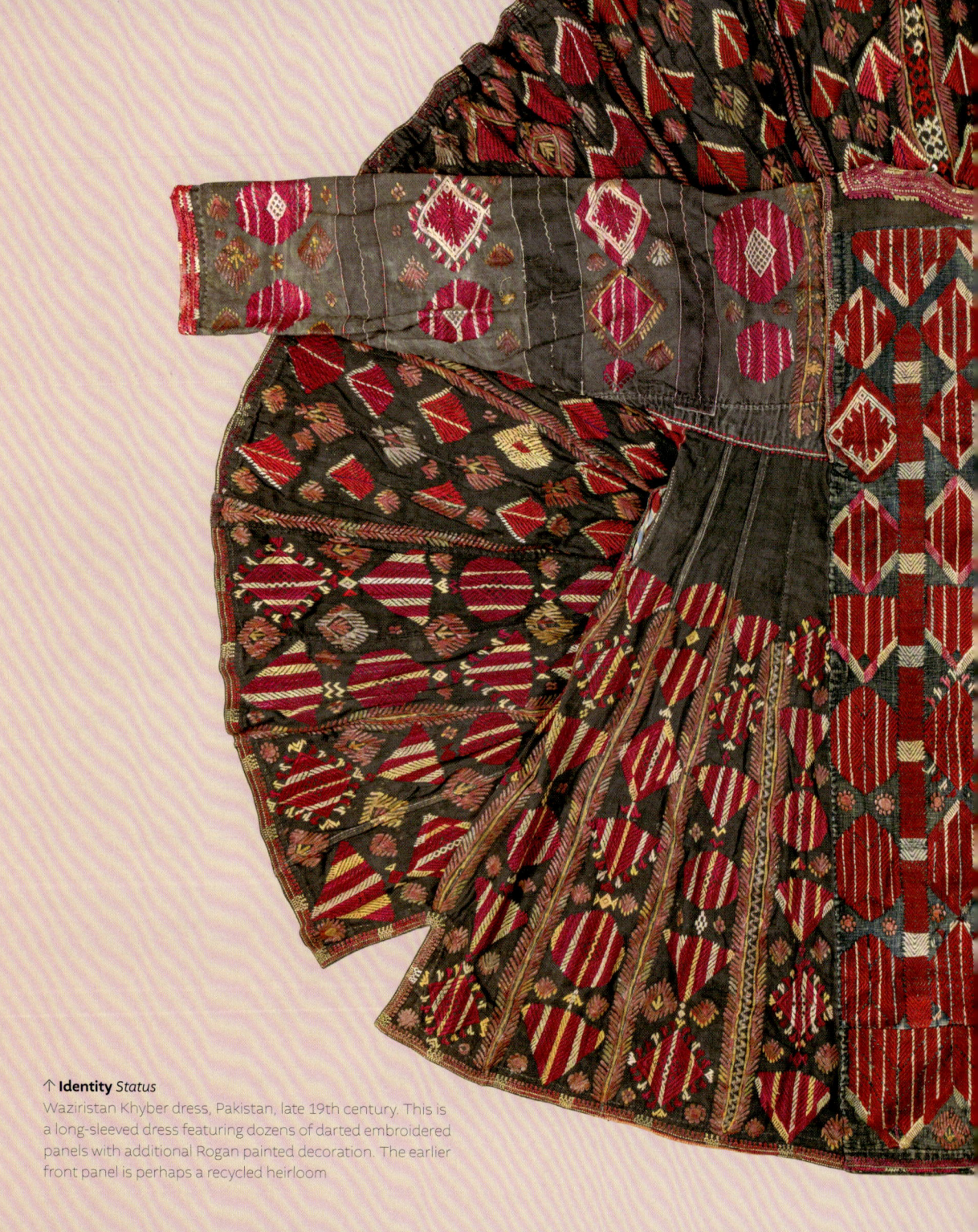

↑ **Identity** *Status*
Waziristan Khyber dress, Pakistan, late 19th century. This is
a long-sleeved dress featuring dozens of darted embroidered
panels with additional Rogan painted decoration. The earlier
front panel is perhaps a recycled heirloom

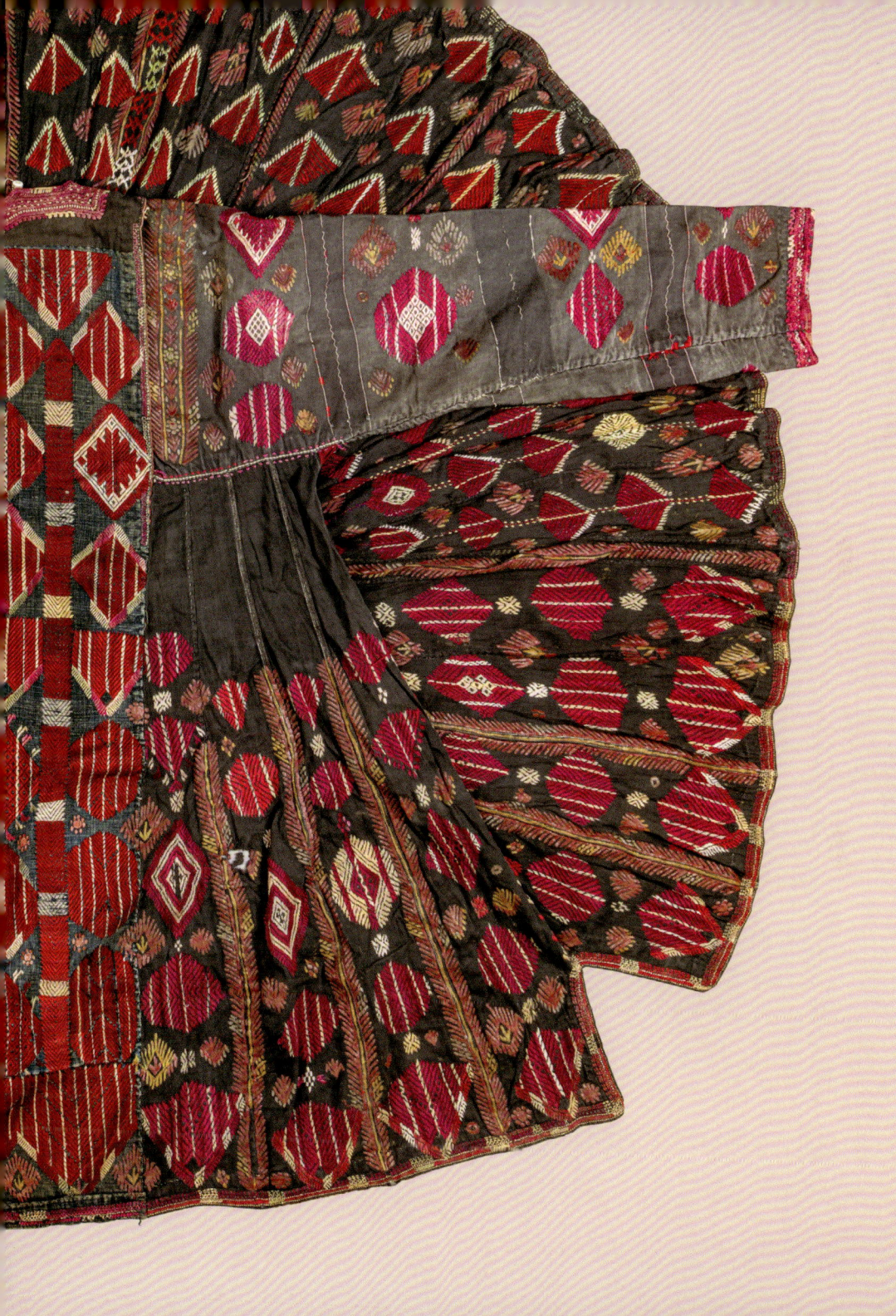

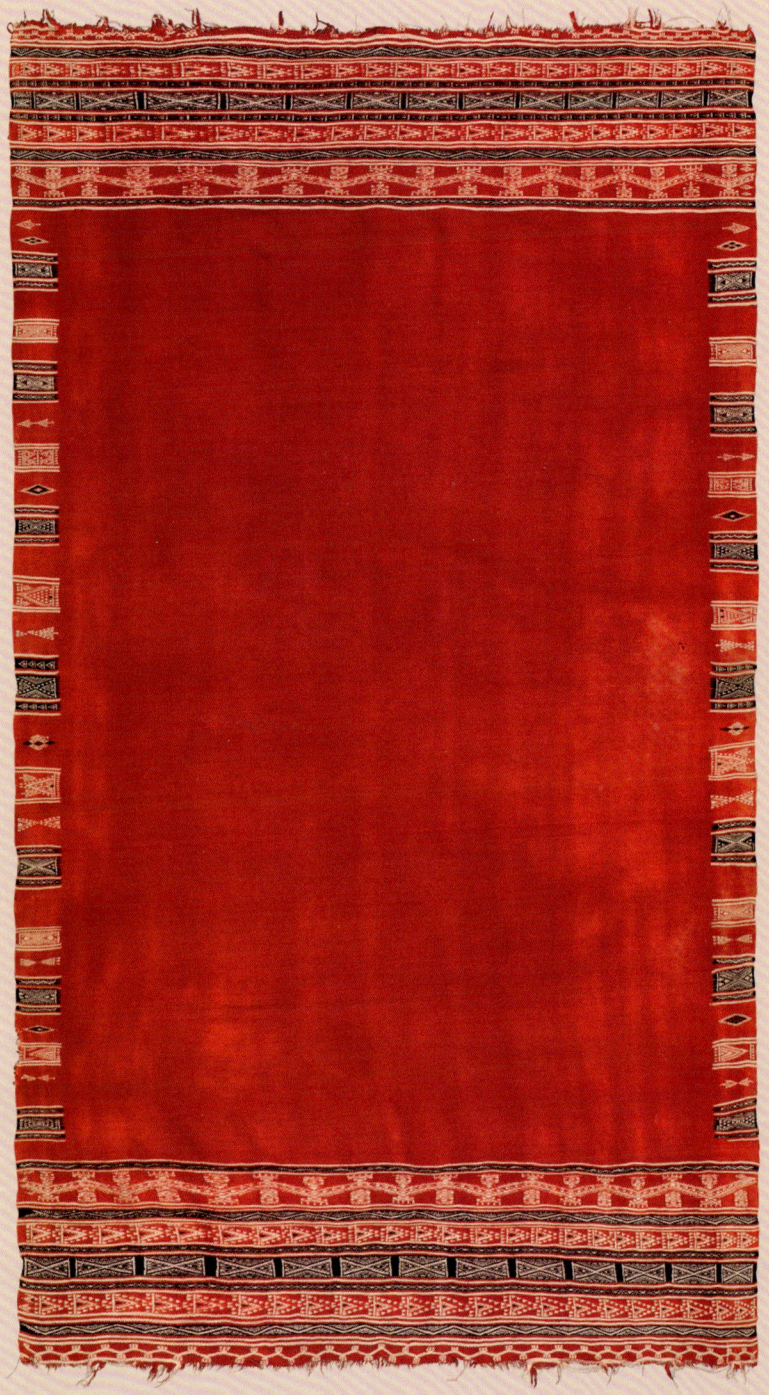

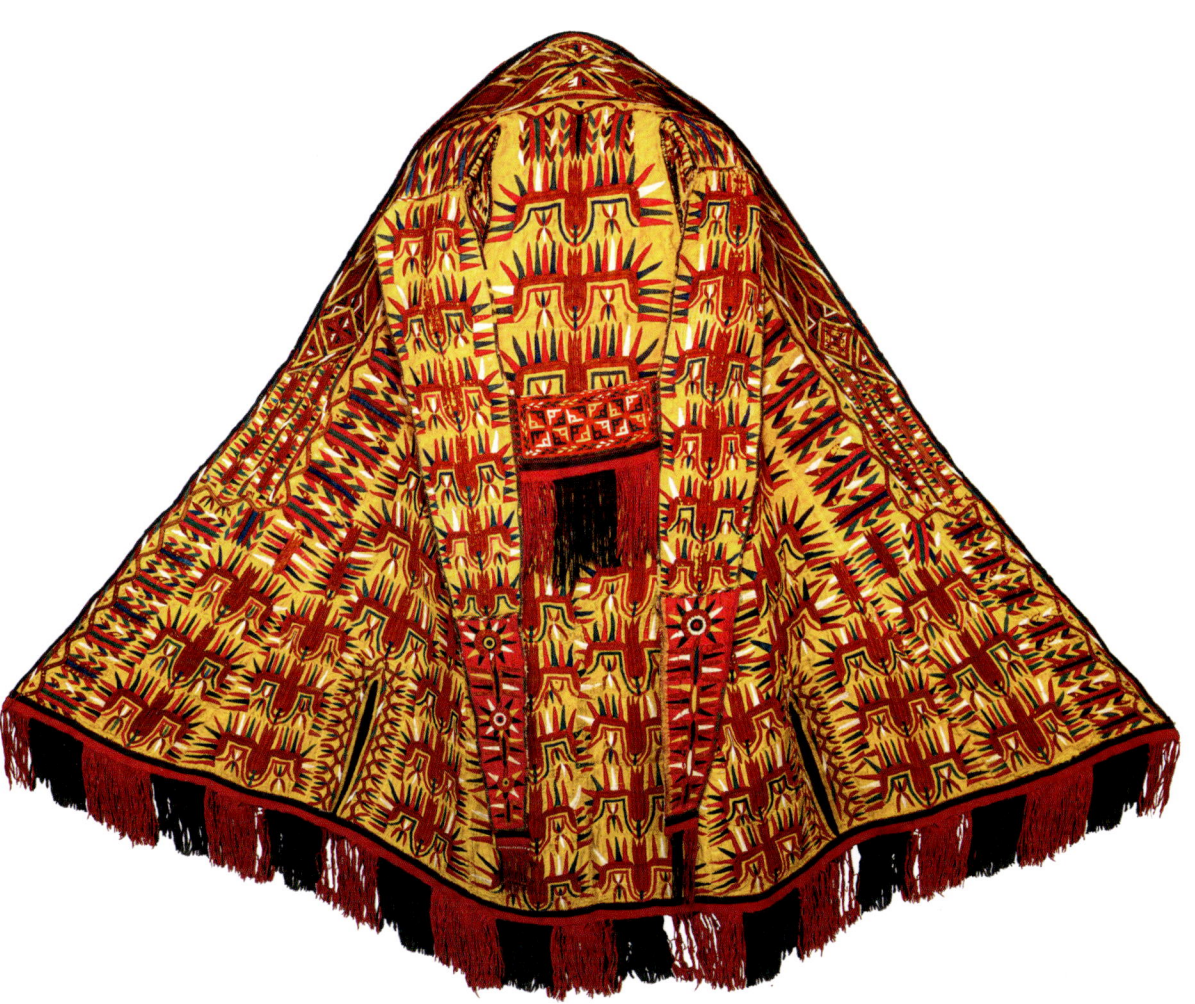

← **Identity** *Status*
Bakhnug, south Tunisia, 19th century. This red shawl marks
the transition of a young girl into a married woman. The
fish symbols on its sides made in extra weft-float brocade
symbolise good fortune

↑ **Identity** *Status*
Tekke chyrpy or mantle, Turkmenistan, 19th century. The
yellow silk indicates that this garment was worn by a married
woman. The scale and profusion of tulips across the whole
ground is noteworthy

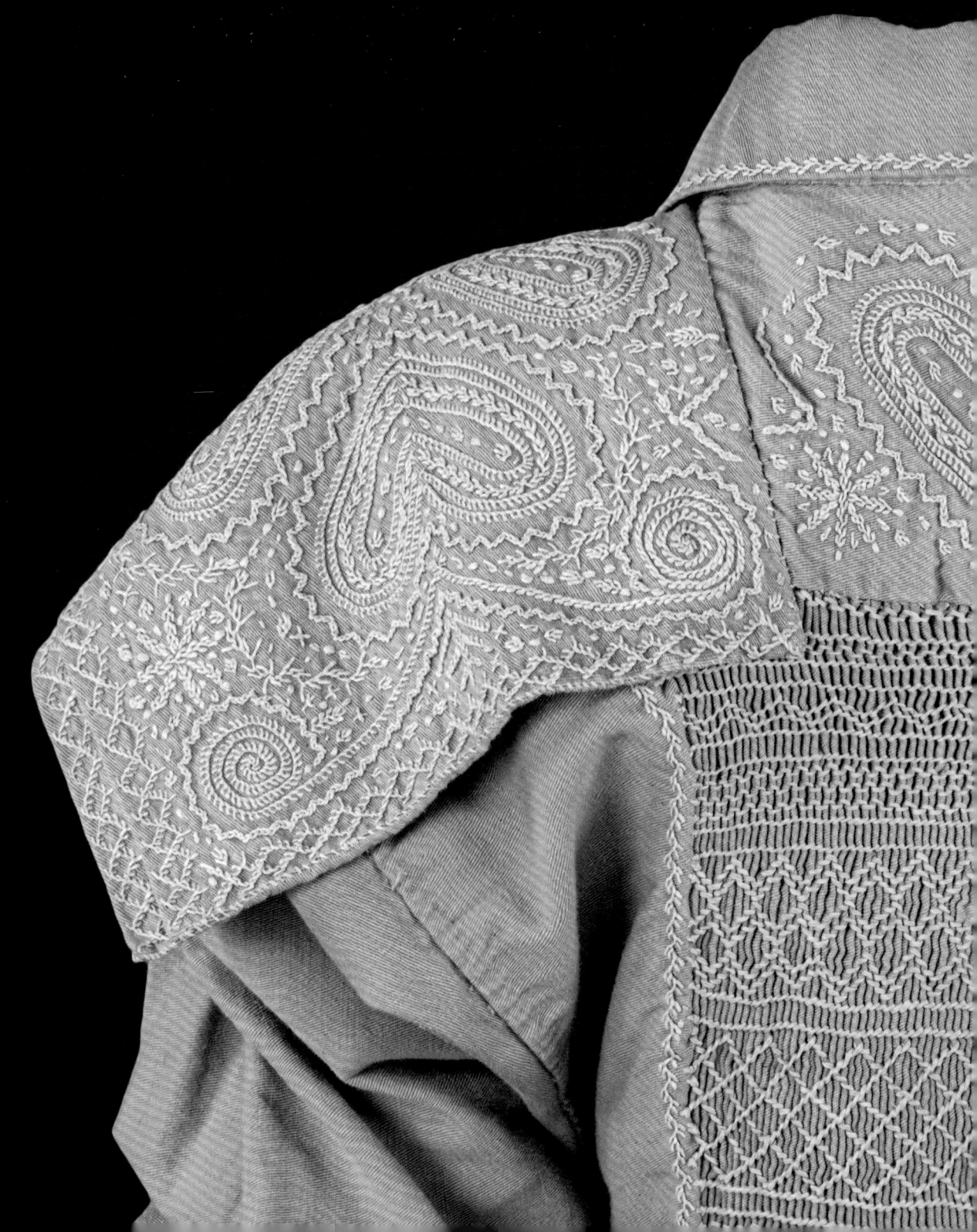

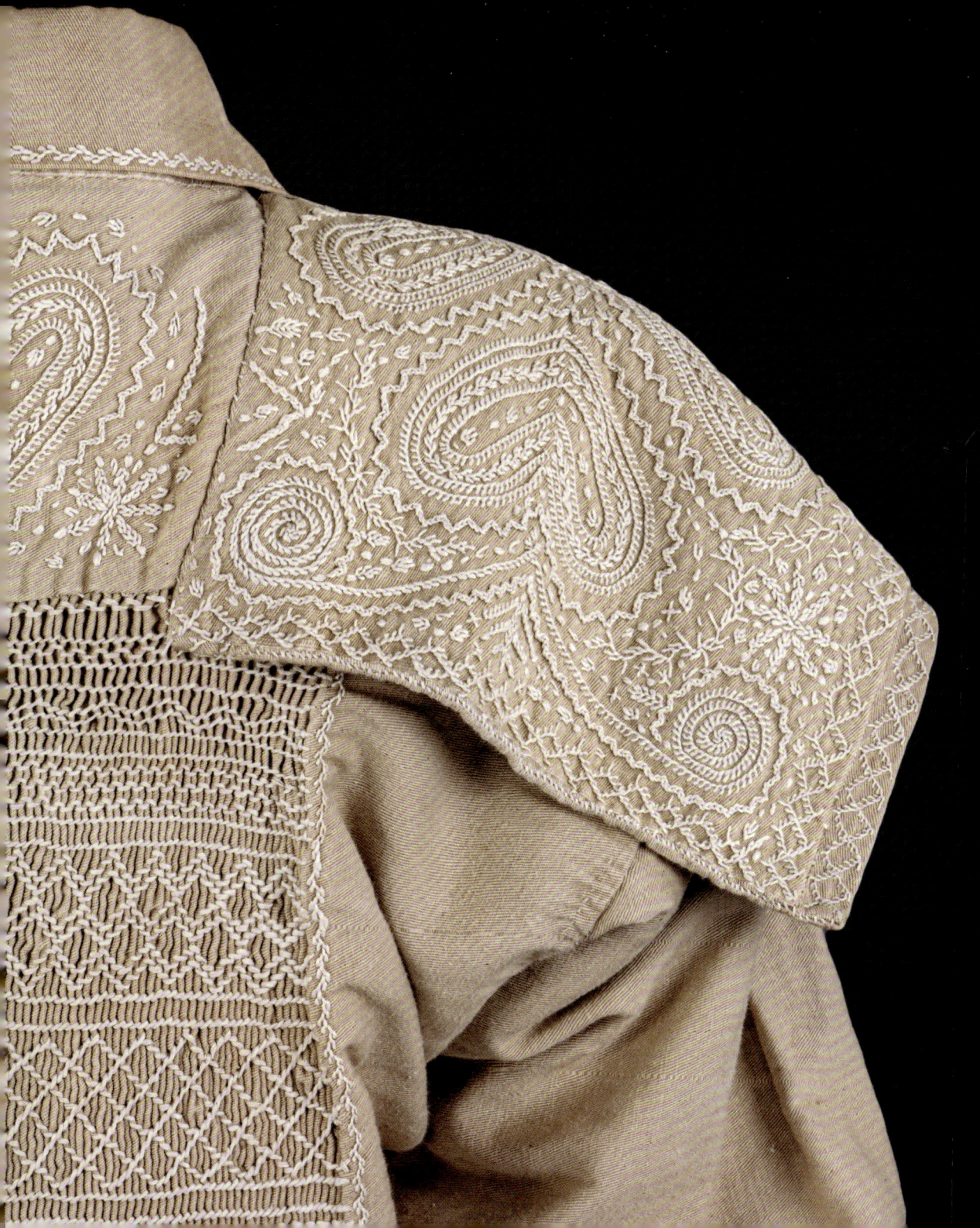

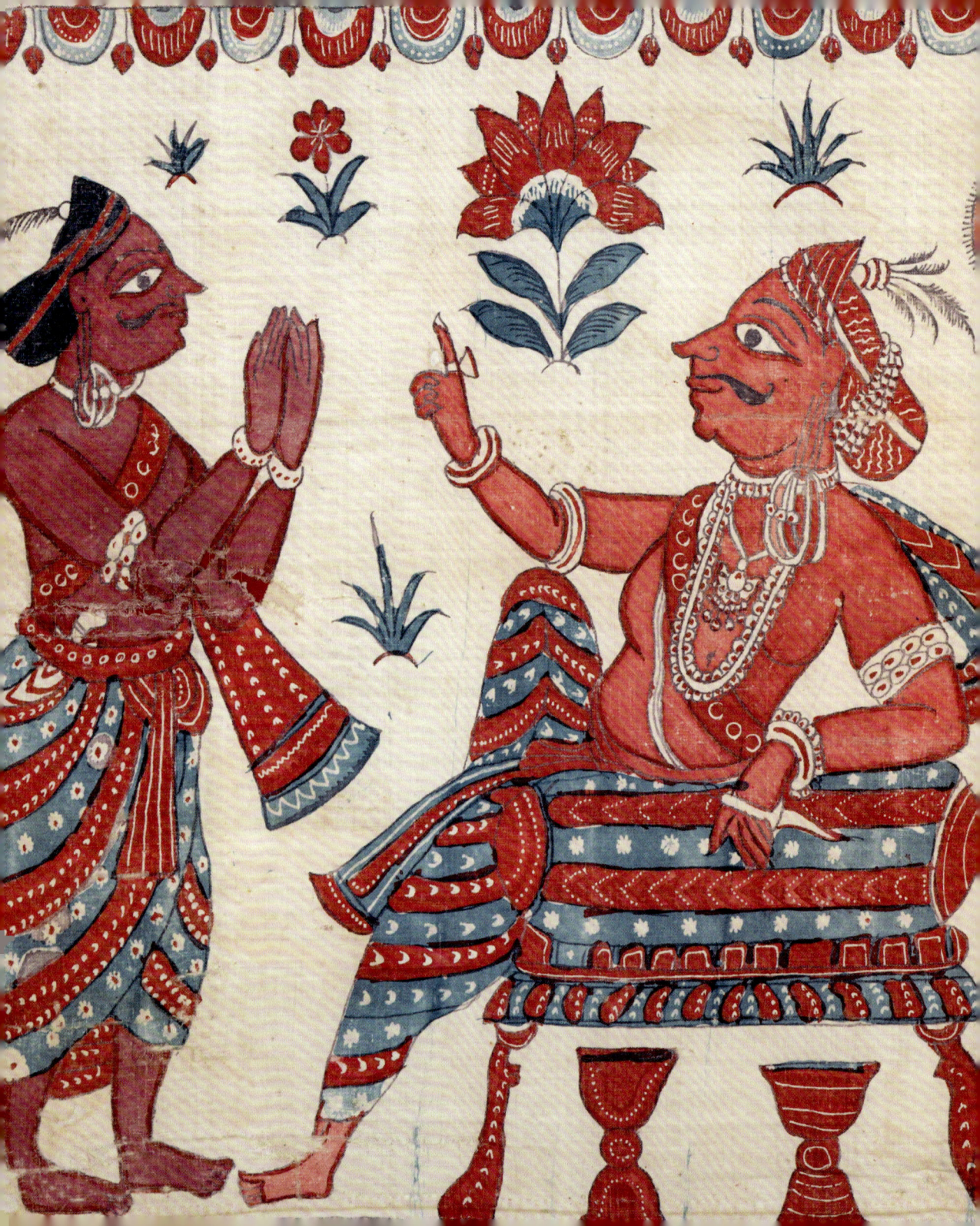

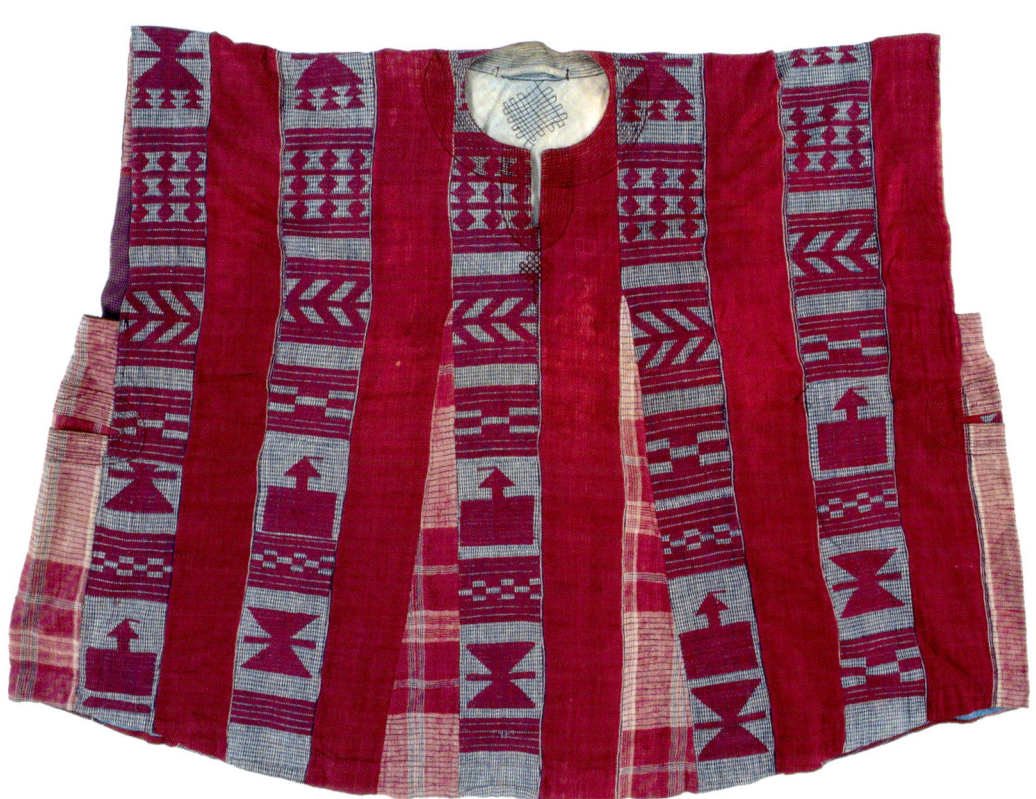

← **Status** *Court*
Chintz, India, mid-18th century. This detail shows two people wearing printed cottons, a standing figure and a seated princely one depicted with more elaborate jewellery

↑ **Status** *Court*
Hausa robe, Nigeria, 19th century. Made by Yoruba weavers using magenta silk traded from across the Sahara, this is an expensive cloth made into a robe for a community leader. The brilliant colour makes it easily identifiable as a luxurious fabric

"Clothes are shorthand for being human; they are an intimate, skin-close craft form."

↑ *Radical Fashion*, Claire Wilcox (2001)

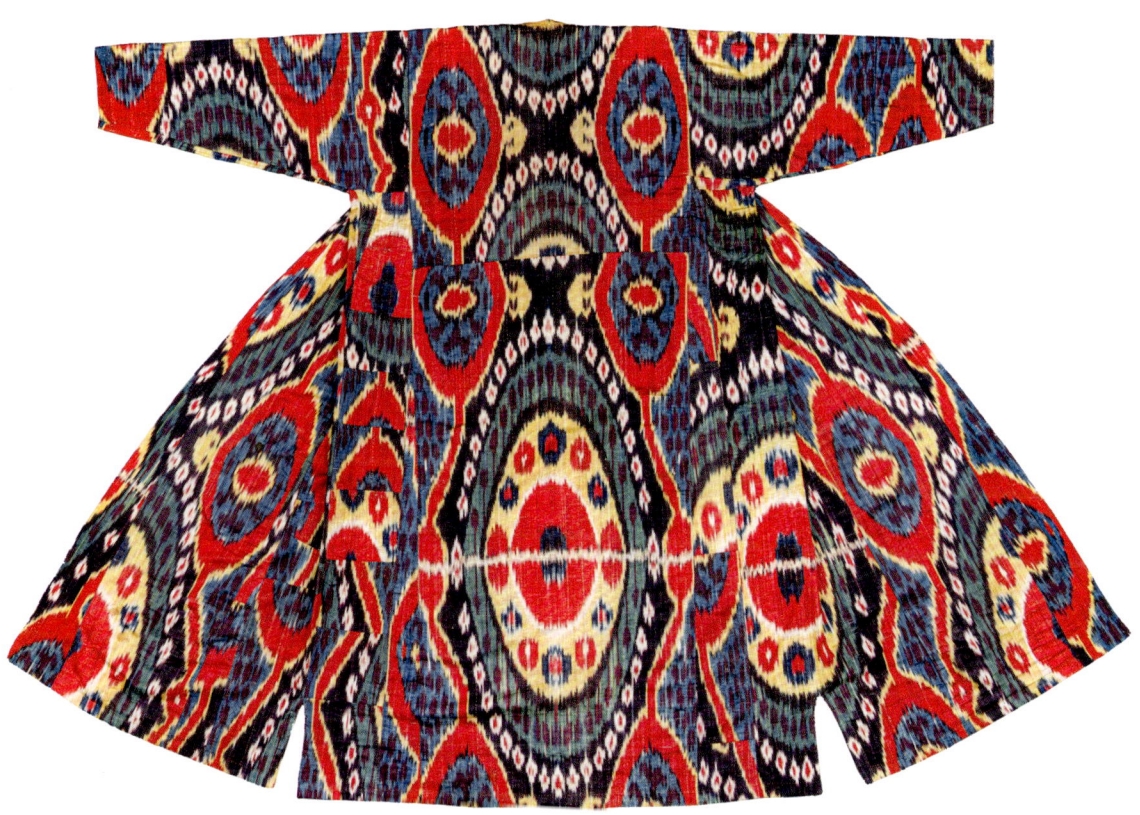

Robes of honour Although the materials and designs associated with clothes are often thought of as the prime conveyors of status, throughout history textiles have also been used as means of storing wealth, awarding position, rewarding achievements and conveying patronage from the royal court. There are numerous instances of rulers presenting subjects with robes of honour, which in turn reinforce elite taste, and reserve the best-quality textiles for restricted use.

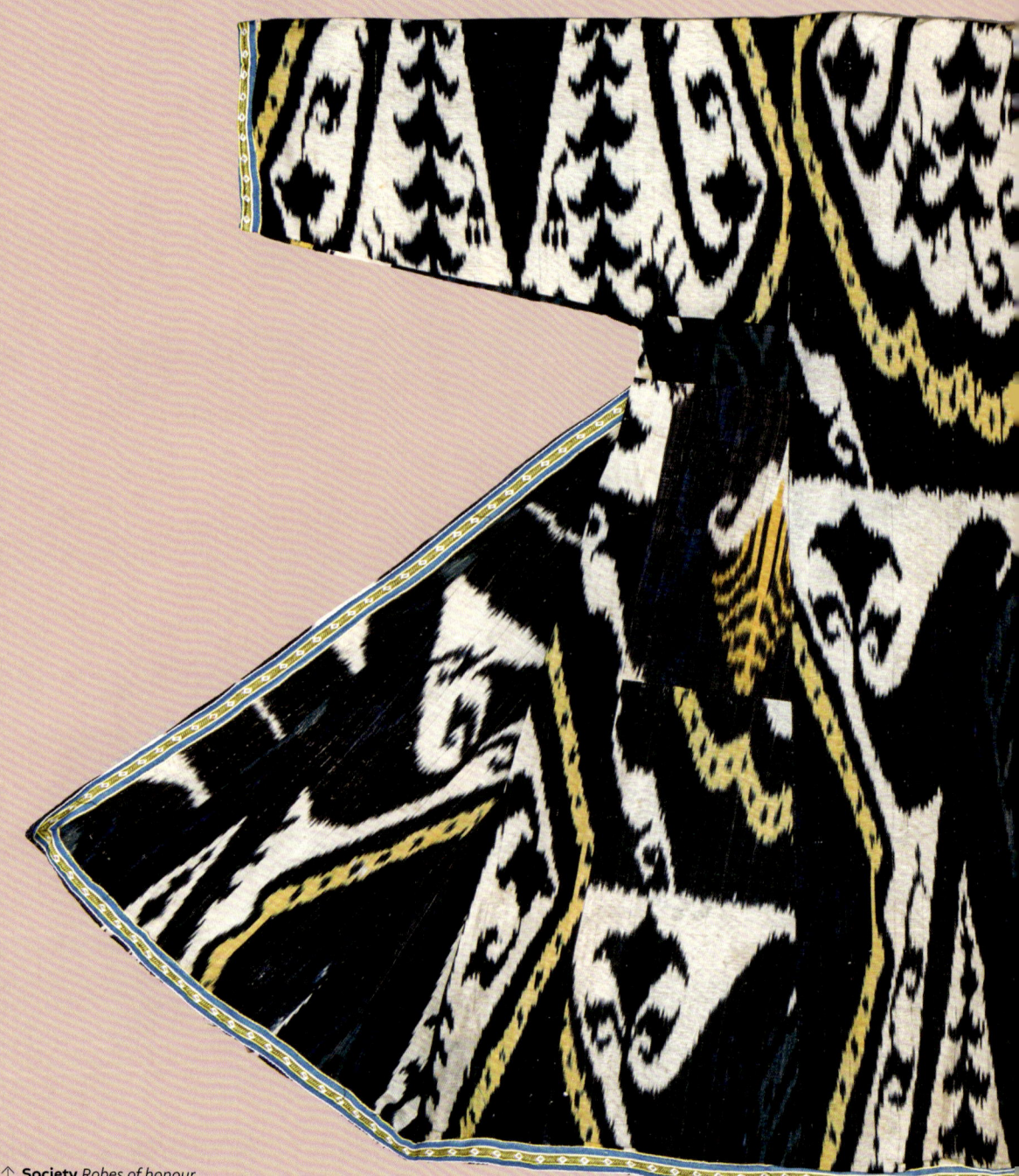

↑ Society *Robes of honour*
Chapan or robe, Uzbekistan, 19th century. The minimal colour palette here helps to demonstrate that in the tailoring of this chapan little regard was given to the matching or aligning of the pattern; it simply was not seen as important

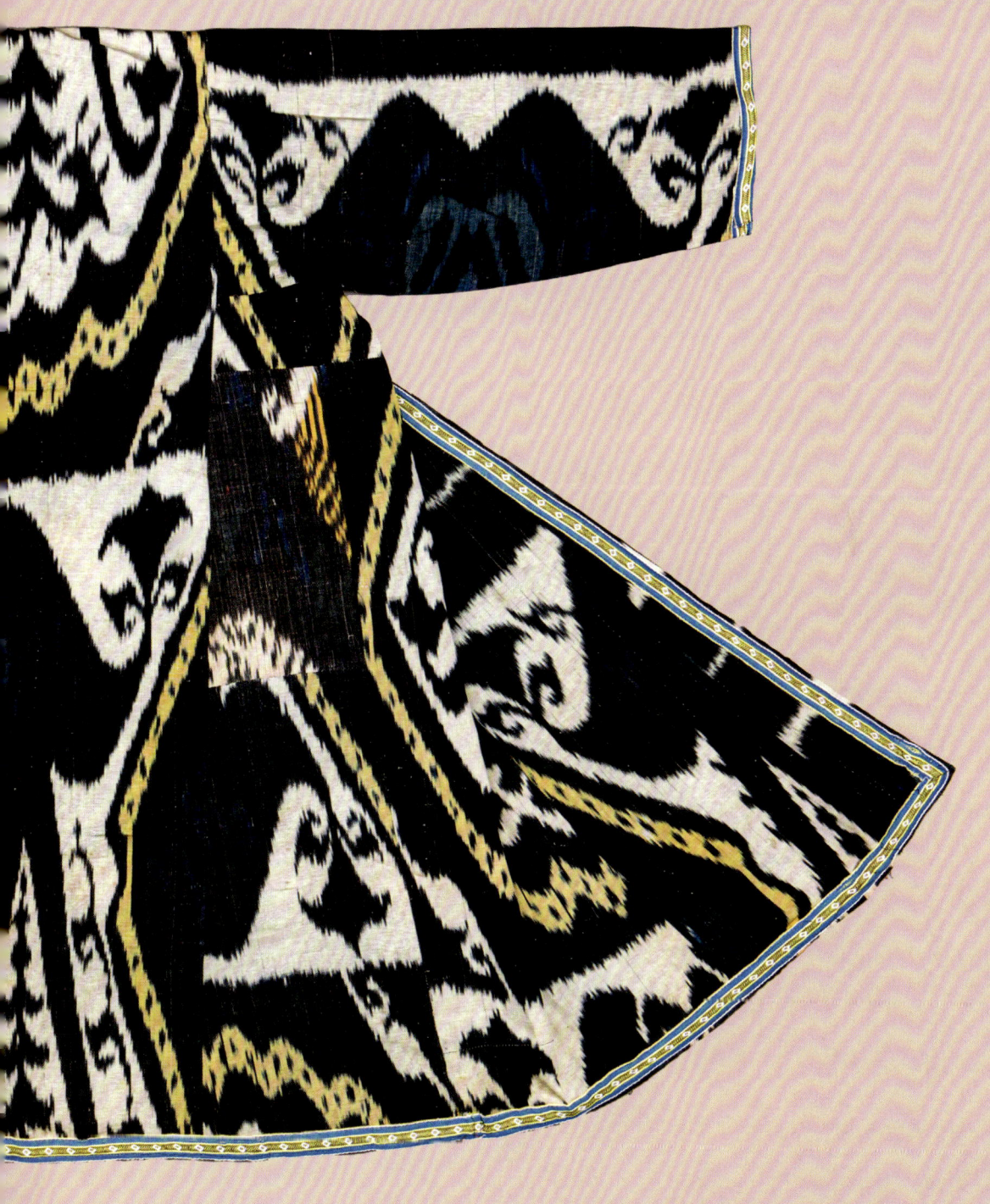

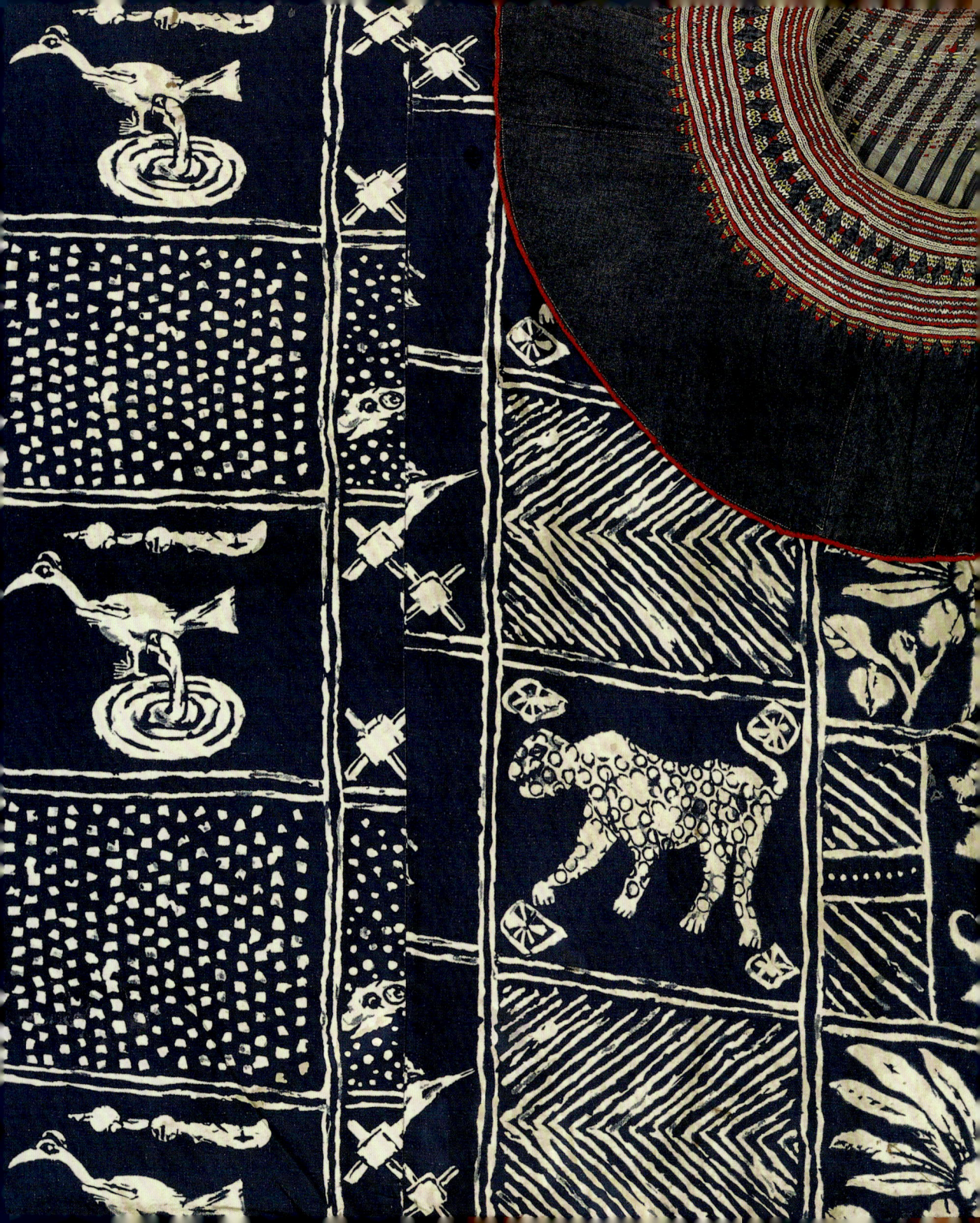

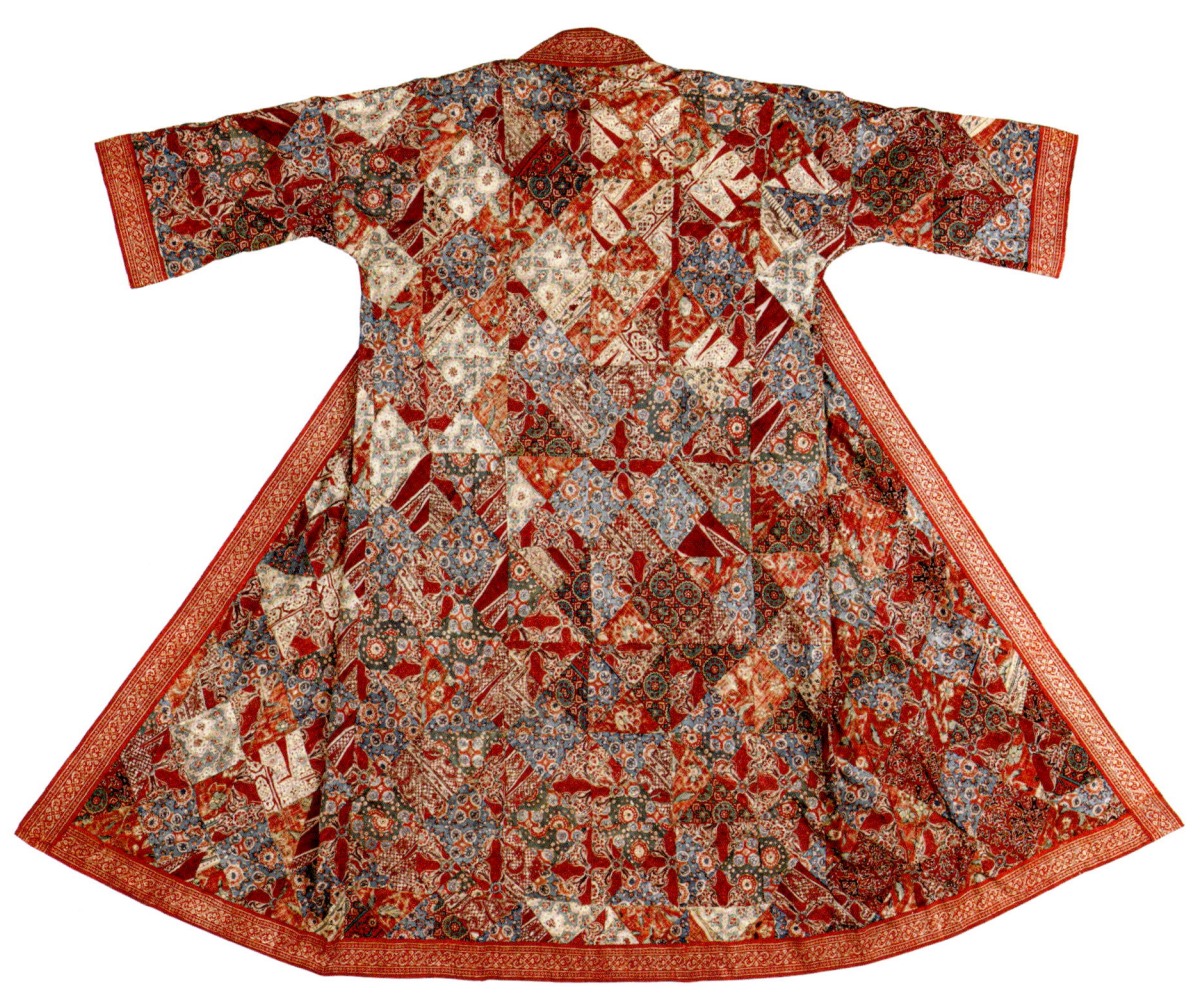

← **Society** *Class*
Chief's robe, Cameroon, late 19th century. This robe can be
viewed as an interesting example of cultural exchange since
the vestment uses European printed cotton depicting images
of several types of Ashanti gold weights

↑ **Society** *Class*
Robe, Indonesia, 19th century. Made in the 19th century from
small fragments of 18th- and 19th-century Indian chintz, this
robe – with its silk lining and brocade edgings – expresses the
great value that was ascribed to Indian cotton cloth

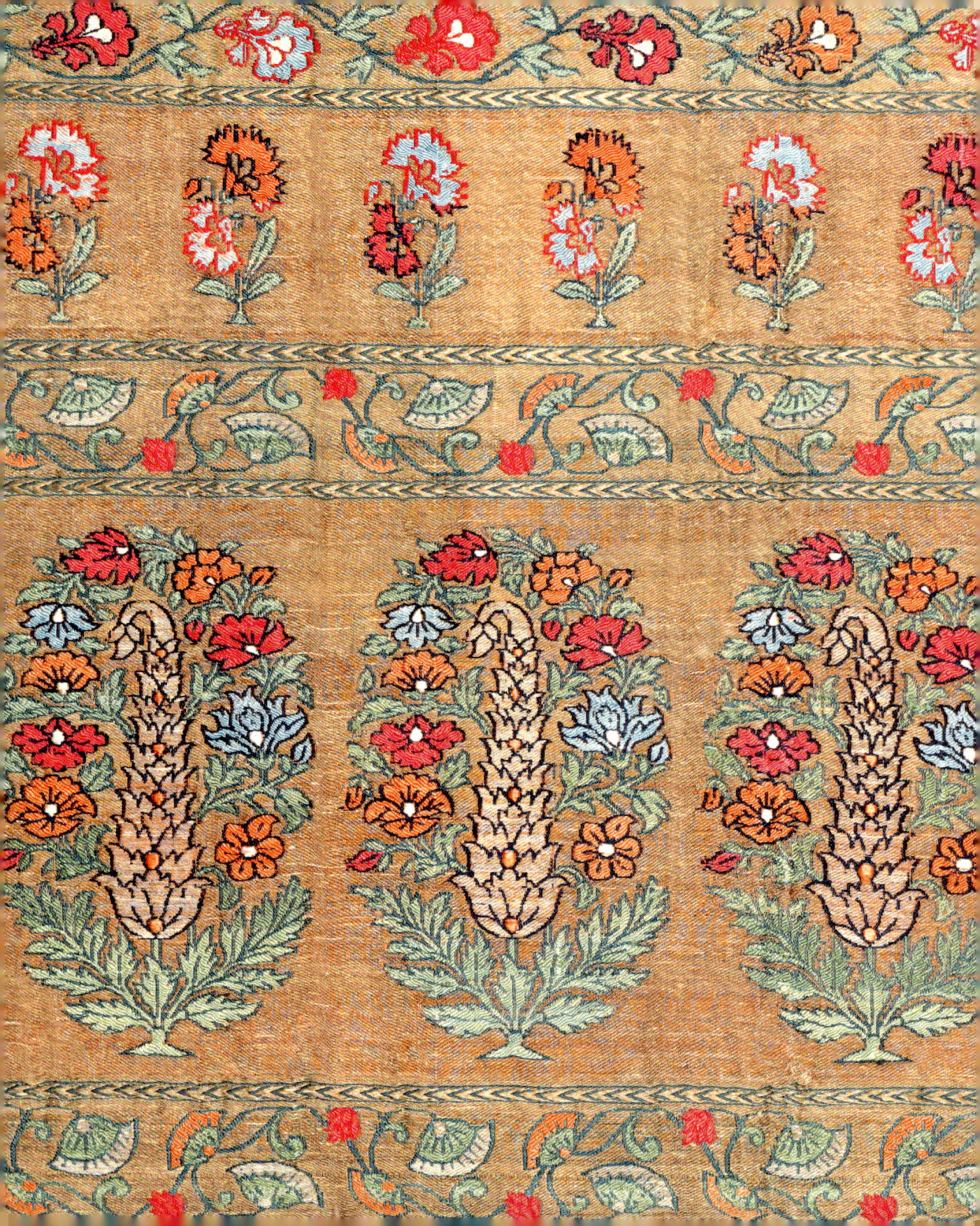

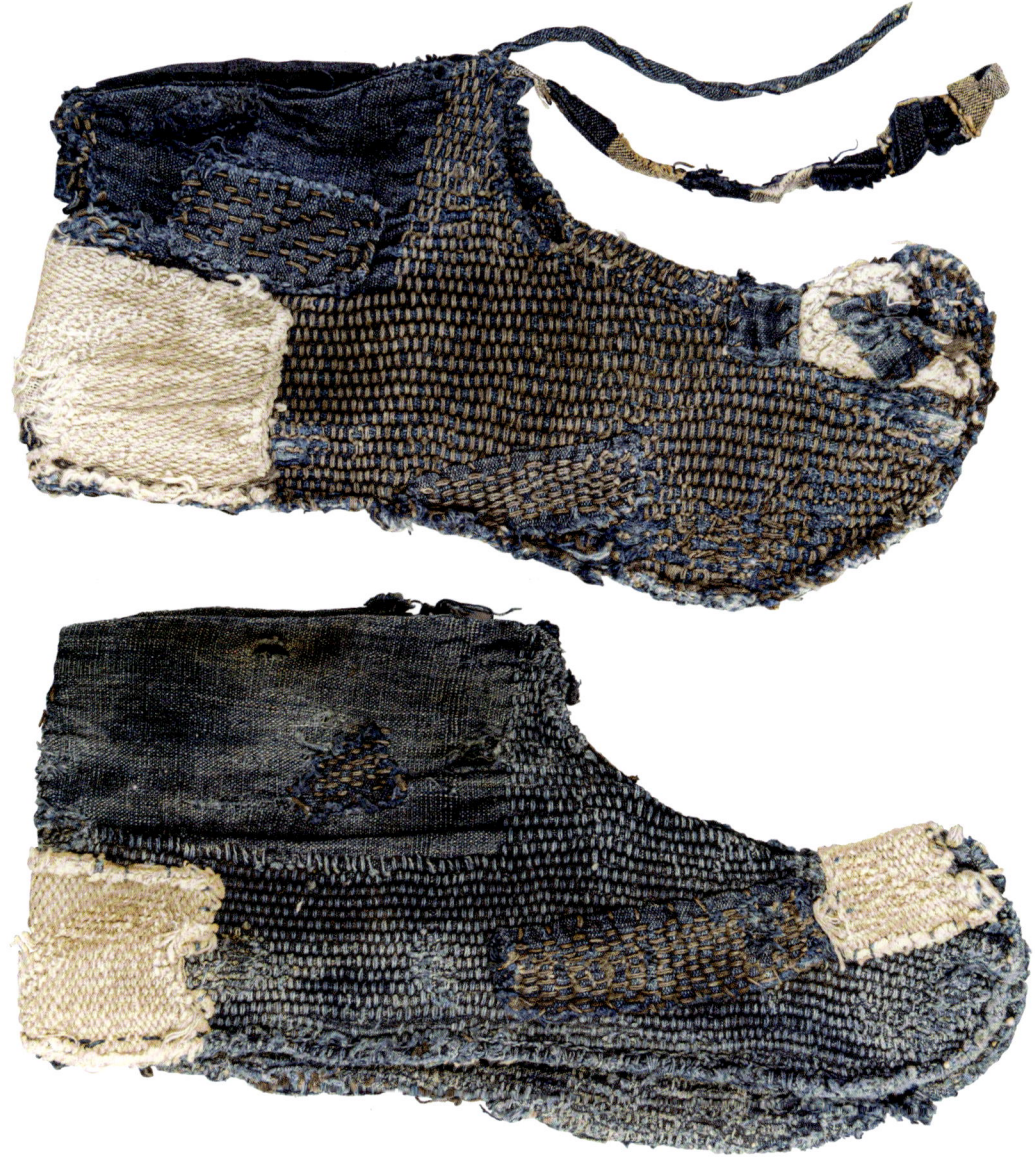

← **Society** *Wealth*
Cloth of gold, sari end, Ahmedabad, Gujarat, India, 19th century. The gilded silver is woven with silk to create a heavy dress panel. Stiff with material wealth, this garment sees an optimal display of its true value

↑ **Society** *Wealth*
Tabi or slippers, north Japan, 19th century. Made from scraps of indigo-dyed cotton that is then stitched and wadded for strength, these shoes would have been used by rural farmers, for whom they provided some dryness and warmth

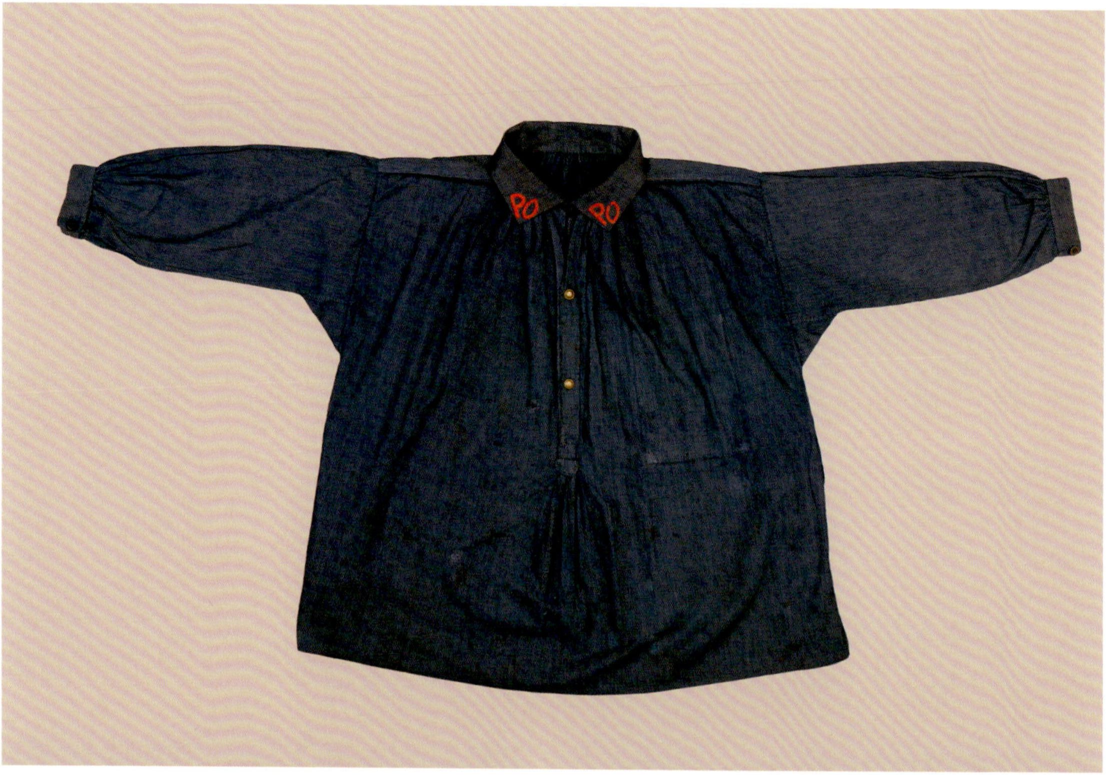

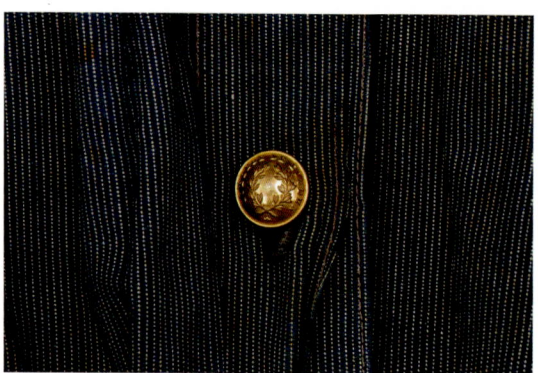

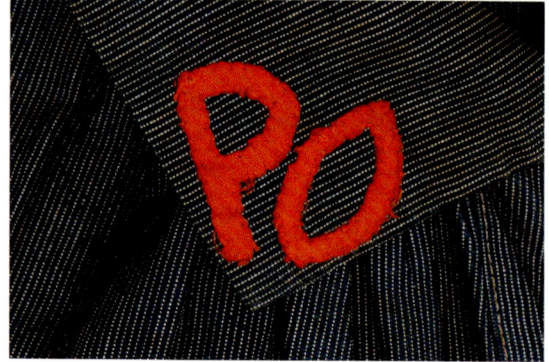

↑ **Society** *Wealth*
Jacket, France, 19th century. This workman's jacket or smock is in indigo-dyed cotton, the common medium for workwear in the region. The word denim comes from 'de Nîmes', the French town where it was first made

→ **Society** *Wealth*
Kimono, Japan, 19th century. Although simple, this would have been a prestigious garment in north Japan. It is made from handspun cotton using shibori or tie-dyeing, a technique of great variety and sophistication

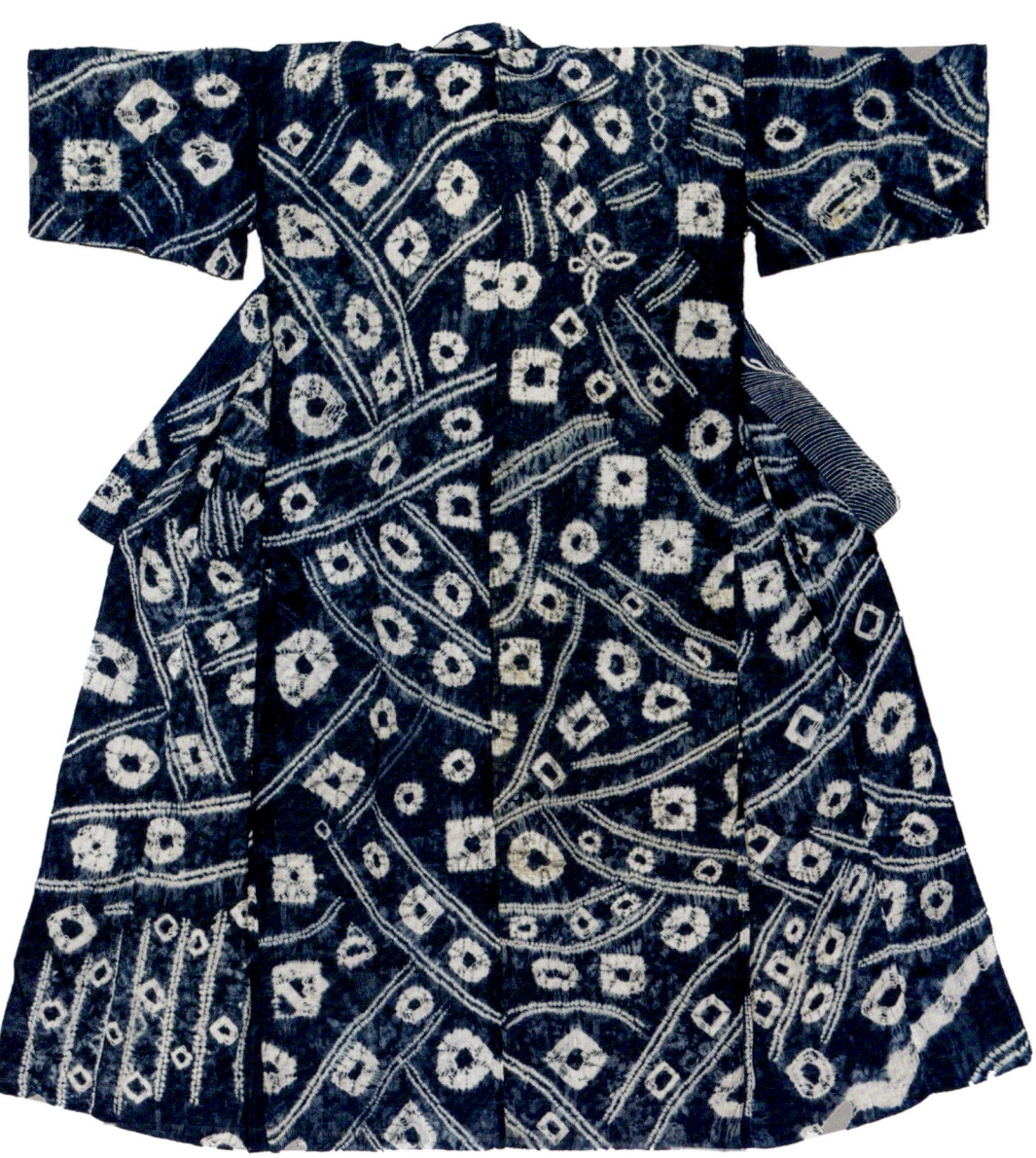

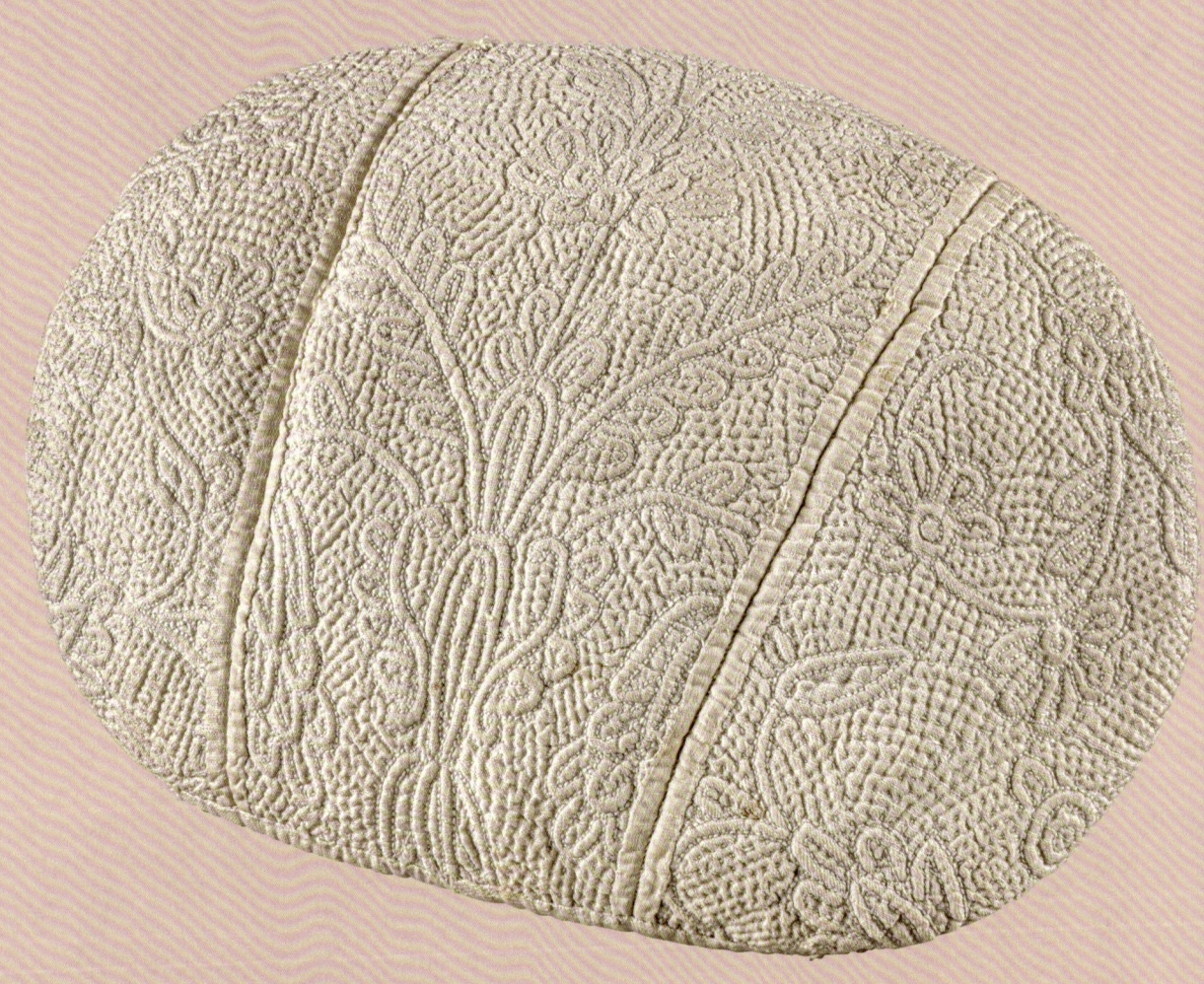

↑ **Society** *Hats*

Child's cap, England, circa 1800. This embroidered piece was
made through the complicated processes of cording and
quilting. The three panels form a bonnet that would have been
tied under an infant's chin

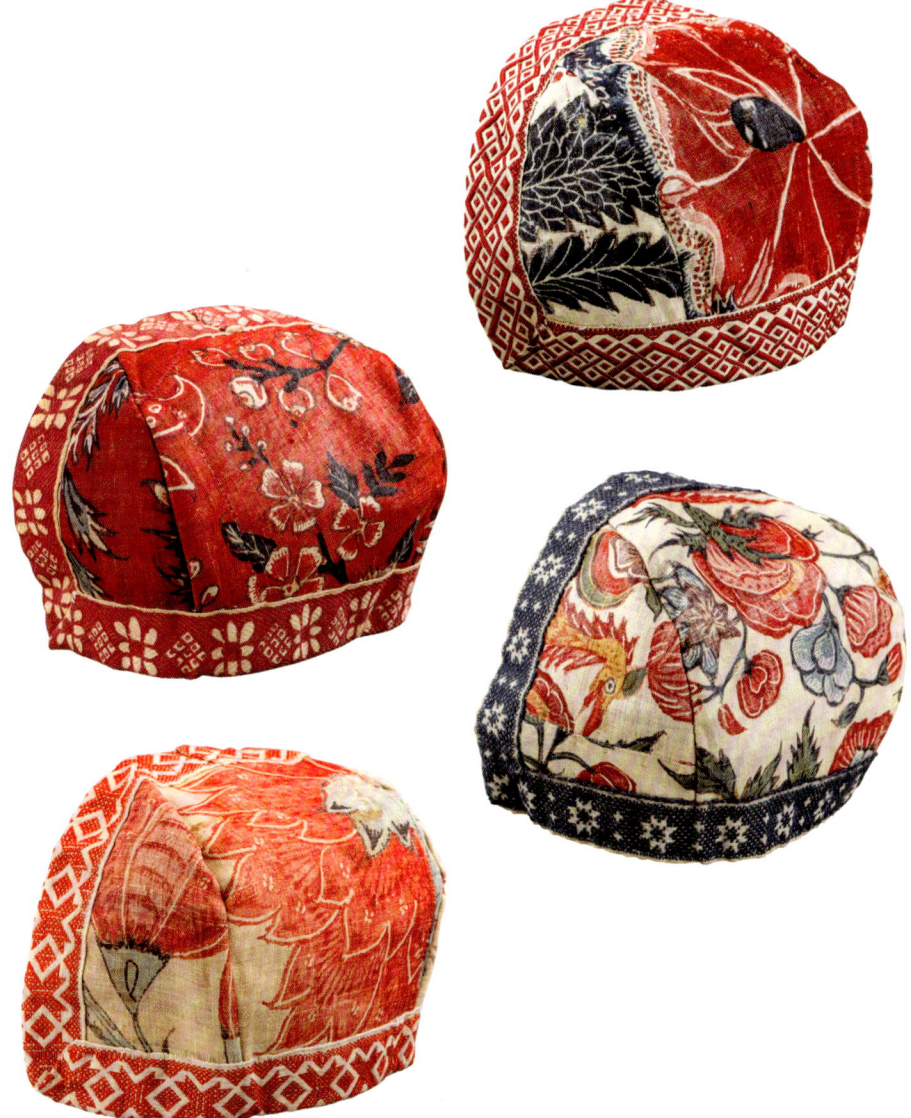

↑ **Society Huis**
Bonnets, Marken, the Netherlands, circa 1750s. Made for babies, these caps were crafted from fragments of expensive Indian chintz. Such a prestigious fabric was not to be wasted, and these tiny caps meant even the smallest of scraps could be used

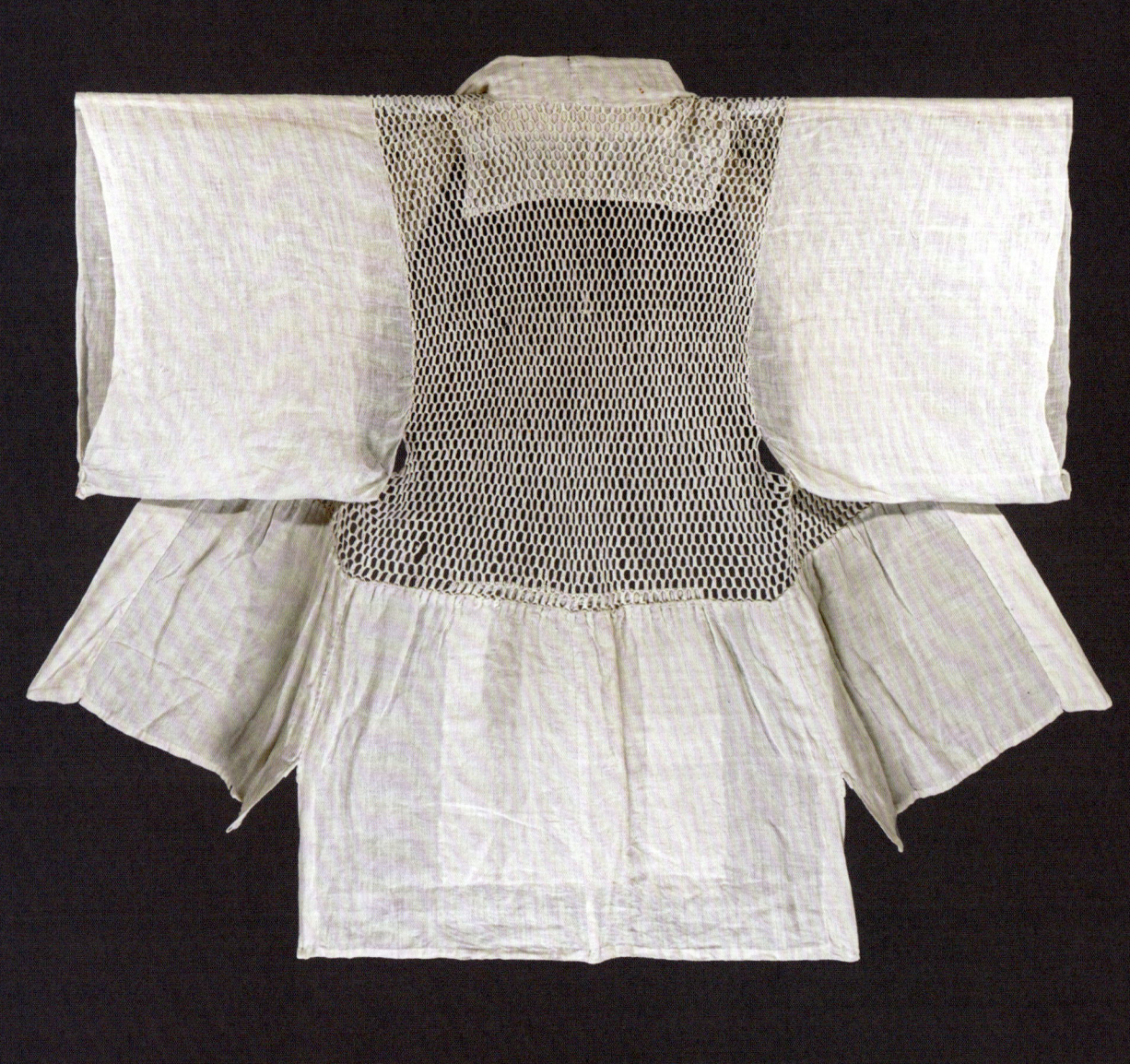

← **Society** *Wealth*
Undergarment (ase-hajiki), Japan, 20th century. Made from
washi (paper) and hemp, this was worn in summer to help
keep cool and to catch sweat. It was an expensive luxury
hidden from view.

↓ **Society** *Wealth*
Pashmina coat, Kashmir, India, 19th century. The silk
embroidery on this pashmina coat speaks of luxury and
bespoke tailoring

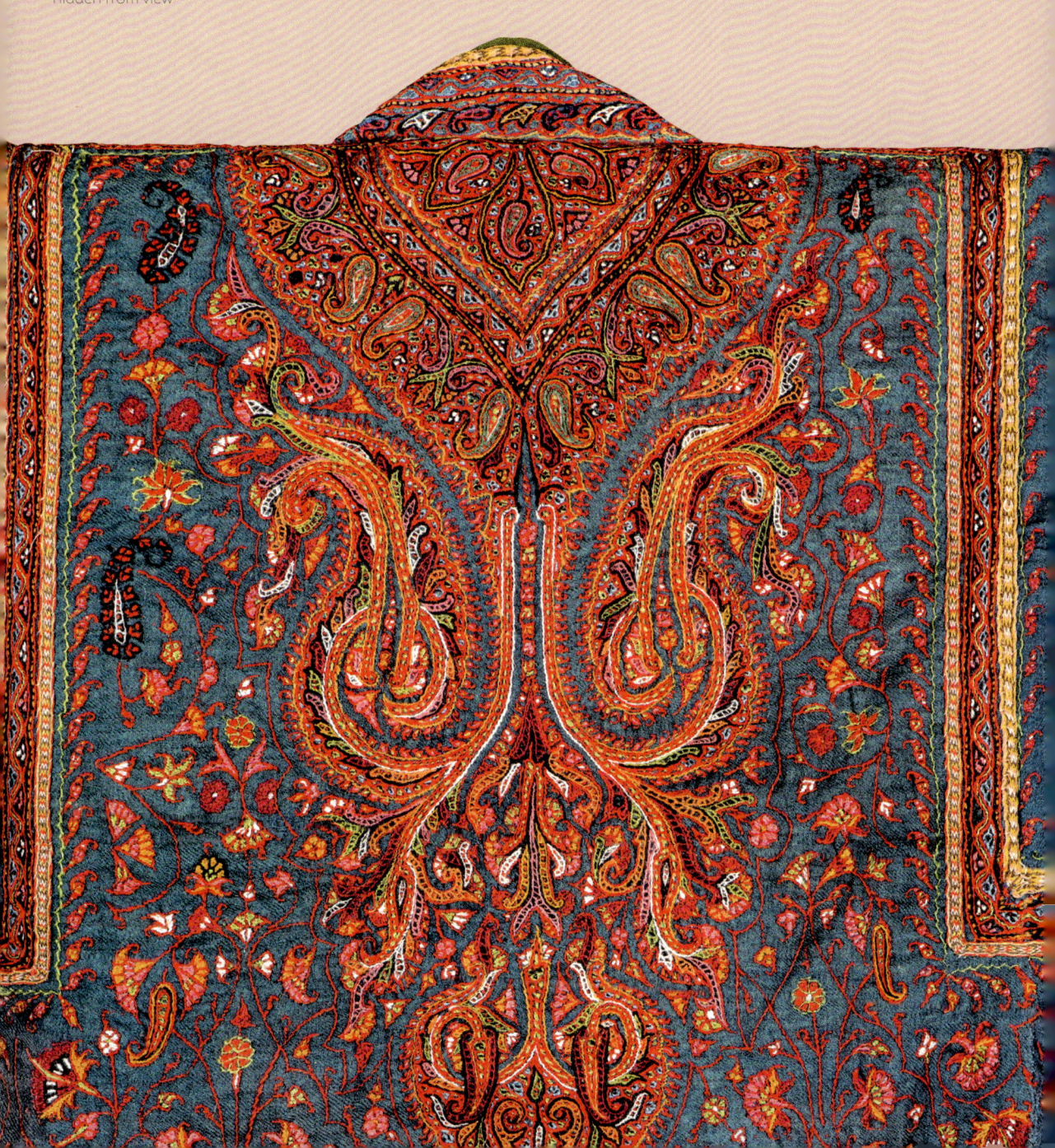

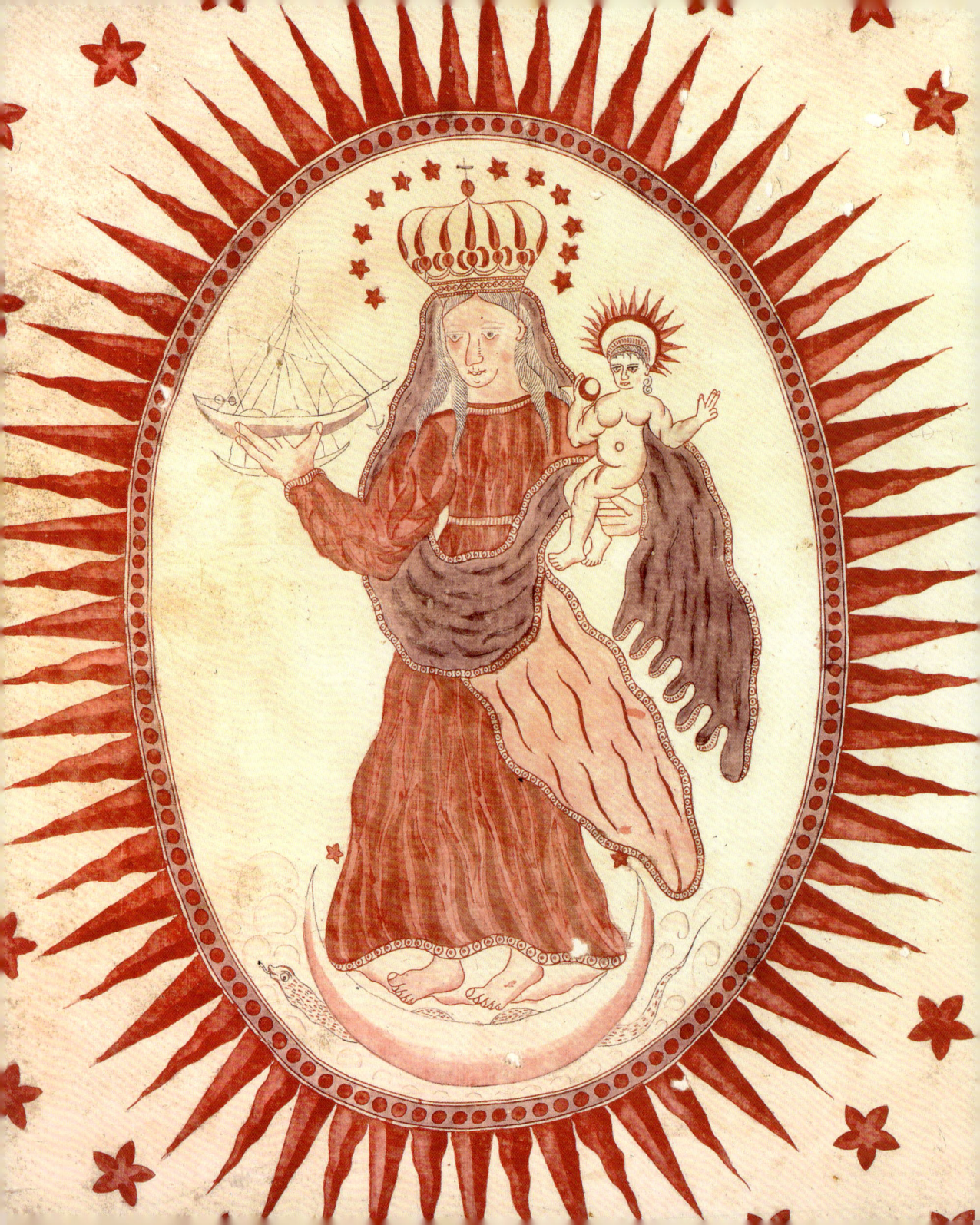

Belief, Myth & Magic

"The true mystery of the world is the visible, not the invisible."

← **Faith** *Celebrations*
Chintz hanging, Coromandel Coast, India, 18th century.
Portraying the crowned Virgin holding the Christ Child, this
textile would have been used as an altar cover, frontal or
curtain in a Sri Lankan Catholic church

↑ *The Picture of Dorian Gray*, Oscar Wilde (1891)

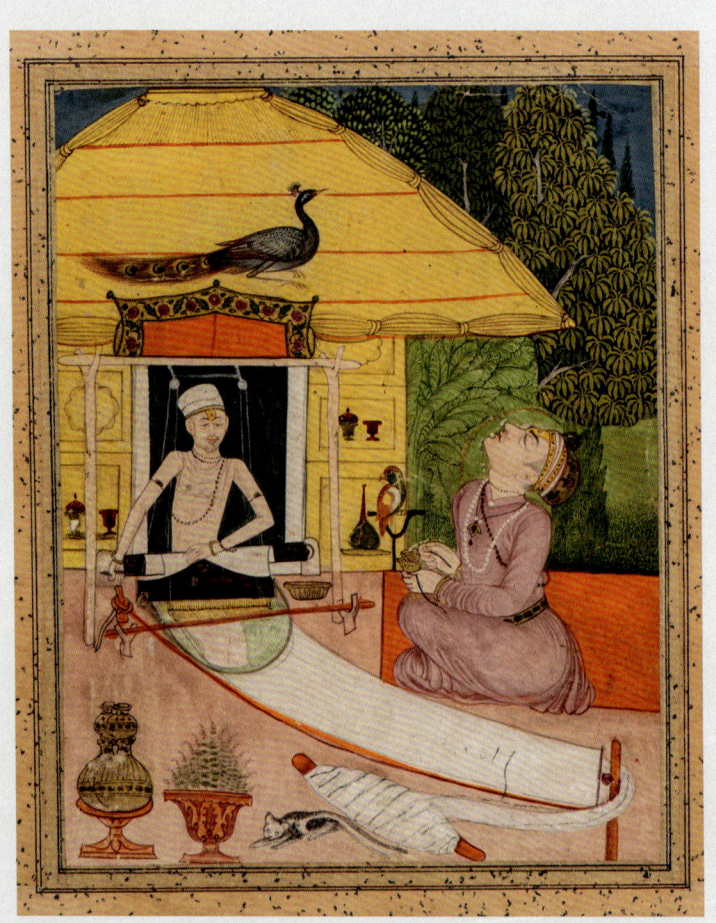

↑ **Illustration**
Kabir, The Weaving Poet. Miniature painting,
Rajasthan, circa 1800. A cotton cloth is
being woven on a horizontal ground loom

The often handmade and culturally idiosyncratic nature of textile production has meant that the product may well possess a spiritual power, imparting divine inspiration. Textiles can assist in birth, marriage, death, prayer and meditation. In burial services, they may be a key component, as in the Jewish tachrichim, or in the practice of mummification in ancient Egypt. England's 'Burying in Woollen Acts' of the late 17th century even sought to control the use of textiles in burials as a means of protecting national wool production.

Textiles are often among the objects that families pass down through generations; they have therefore long been treasured as heirlooms infused with collective memory. In many cultures, weavings can become talismanic, with spells embroidered upon clothing as a means of protecting the wearer.

Through ceremonial dress, communities communicate ancestry, lineage and belonging, as in the kente cloth of Ghana, in which different colours signify diverse meanings. Textiles have even been used as information systems, as in the Indian astrological chart included in this chapter.

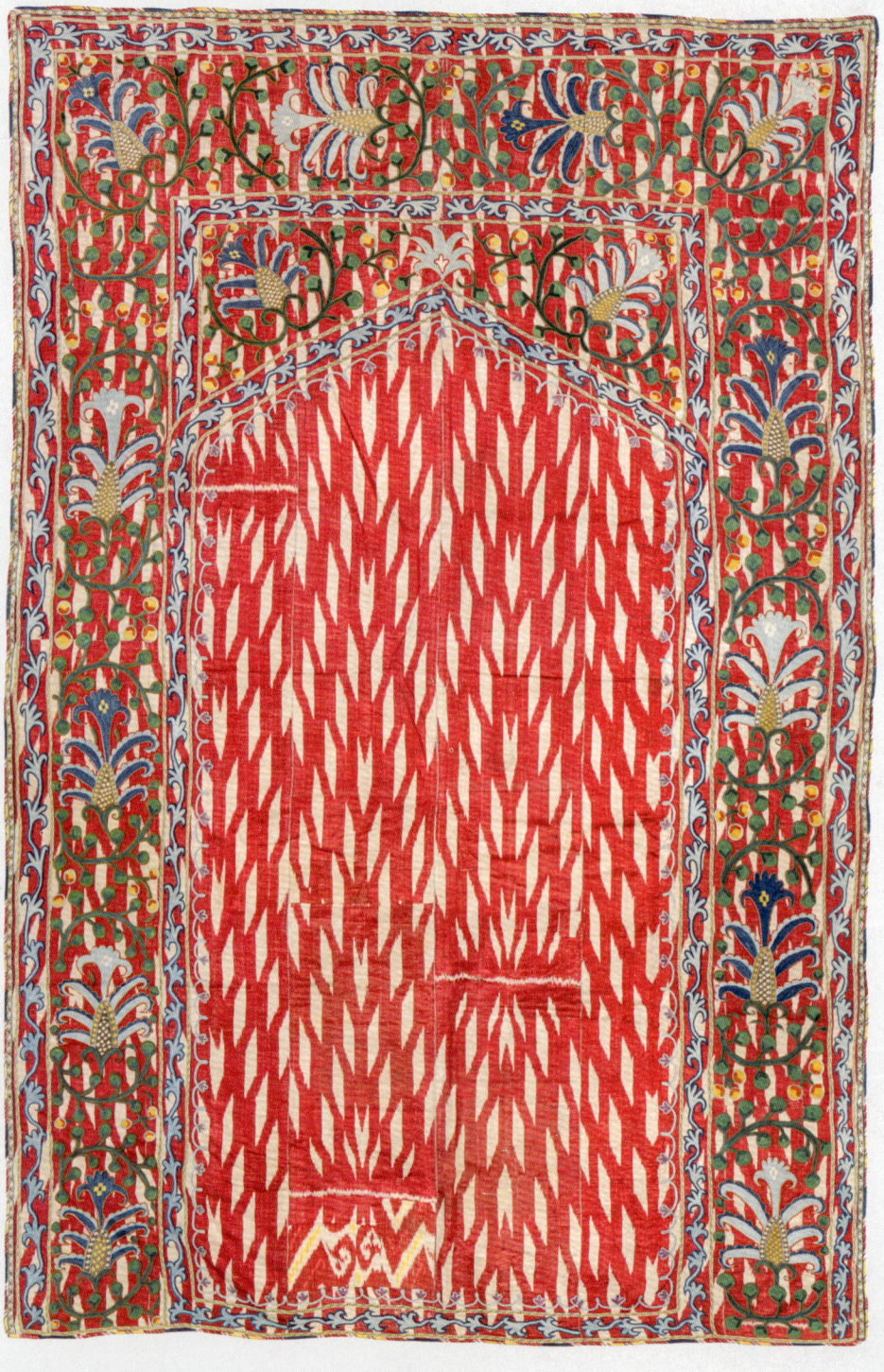

← **Faith** *Prayer*

Hanging, Uzbekistan, 19th century.
Embroidered in silk, this niche design panel
would have been used as the sheet for the
wedding bed of a newly married couple.
Often misunderstood as a prayer arch, the
niche conveys the blessing and sanctity of
marriage and is not totally divorced from
notions of faith and prayer

→ **Faith** *Prayer*

Jain religious hanging, Gujarat, India, 19th
century. Embroidered in silk, it depicts rooms
in the Heavenly Mansion that only the faithful
will occupy

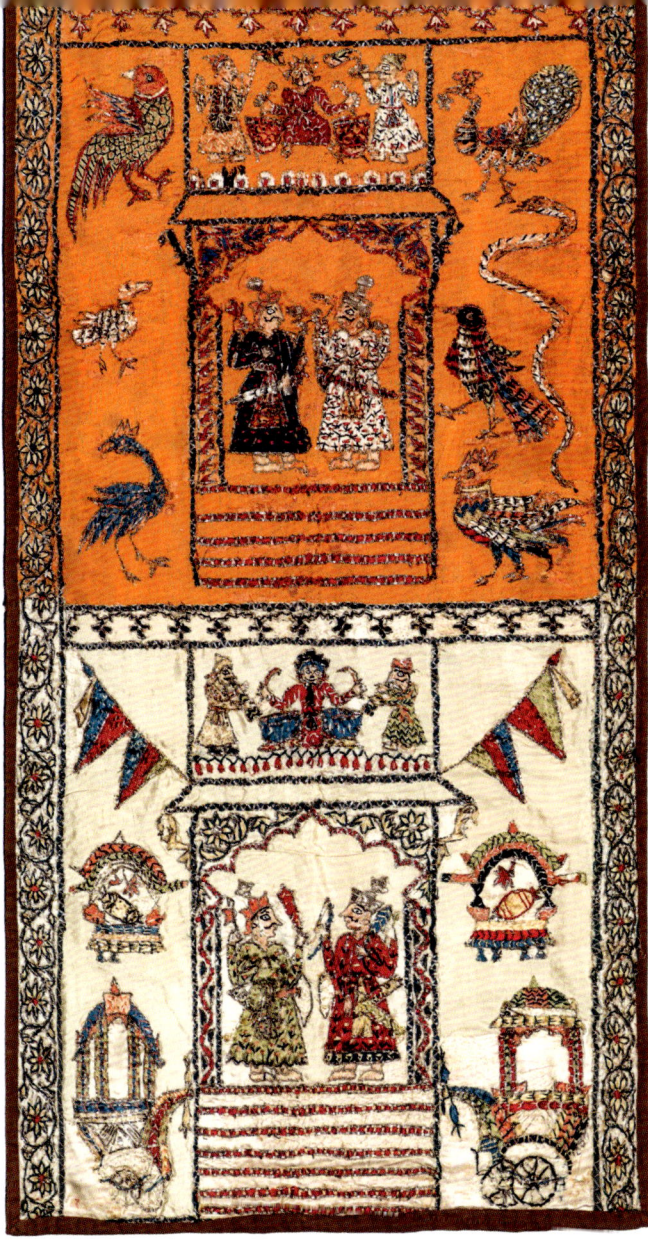

Faith Textiles are used in all religions as means of conveying faith and directing prayer; sometimes, when decorated with prayers or constituting wrappers for amulets, they are even employed as a form of protection. Textiles are deeply immersed in many belief systems. They can be found at ceremonies and places of worship, integrated within faith practices or used for storytelling and acts of reverence and remembrance.

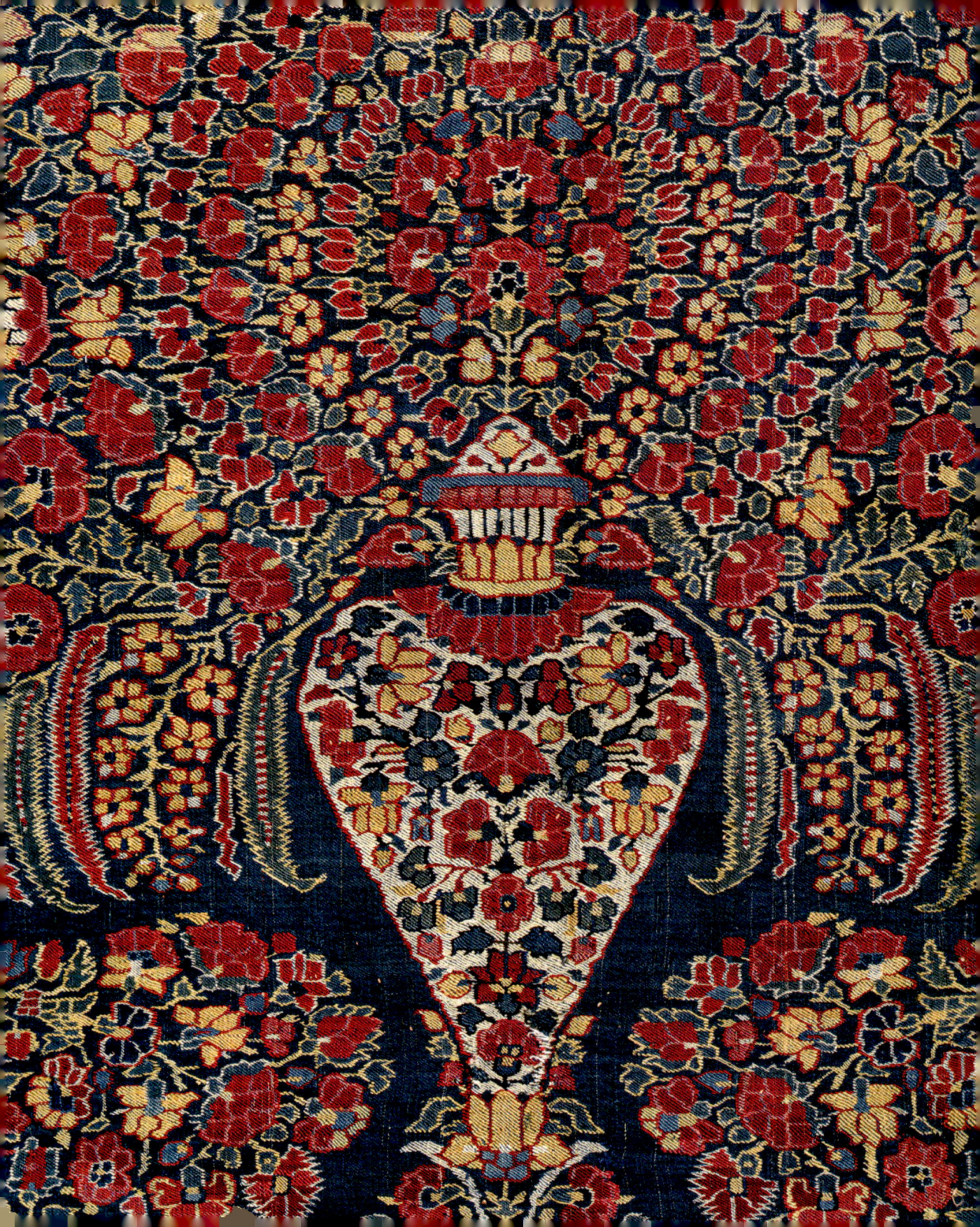

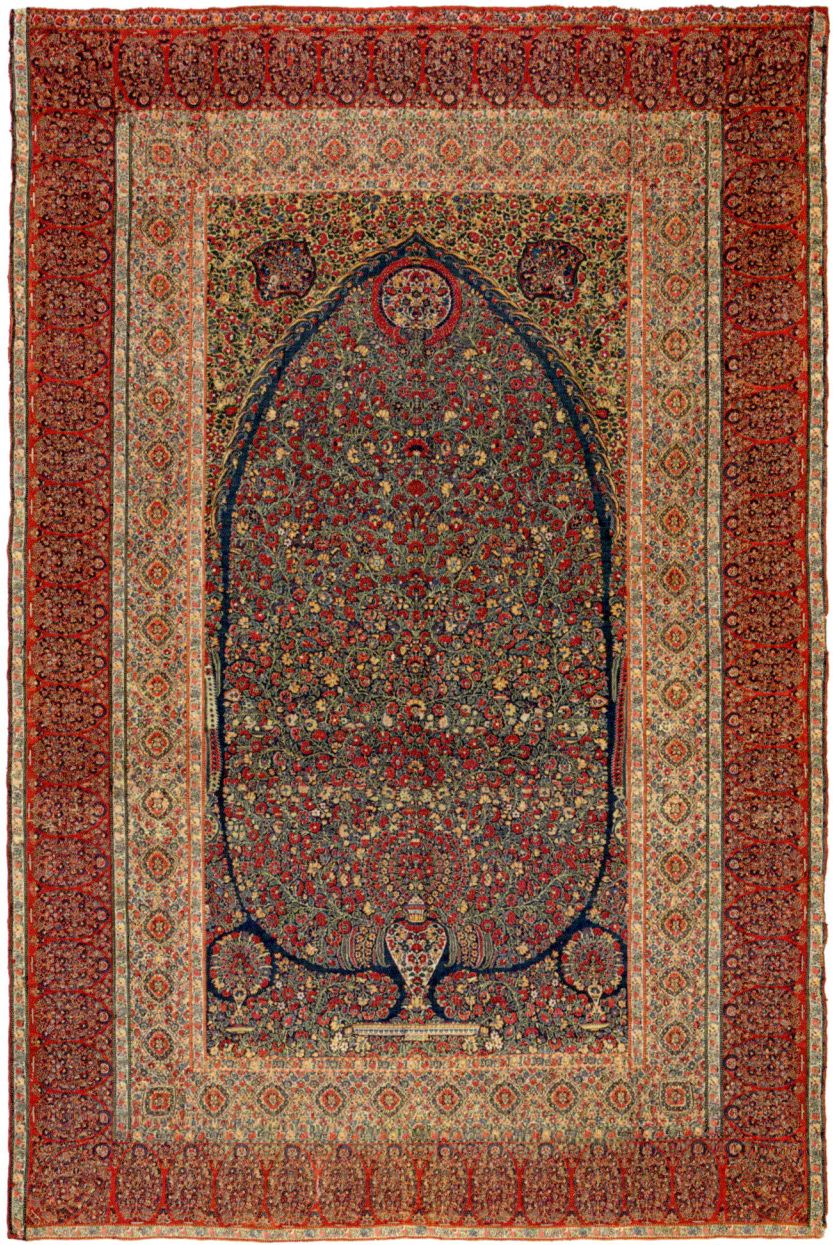

←↑ **Faith** *Prayer*
Kashmir millefleurs hanging, north India, 18th century.
Densely woven in a shawl technique with fine pashmina wool,
the niche-like format suggests possible devotional use

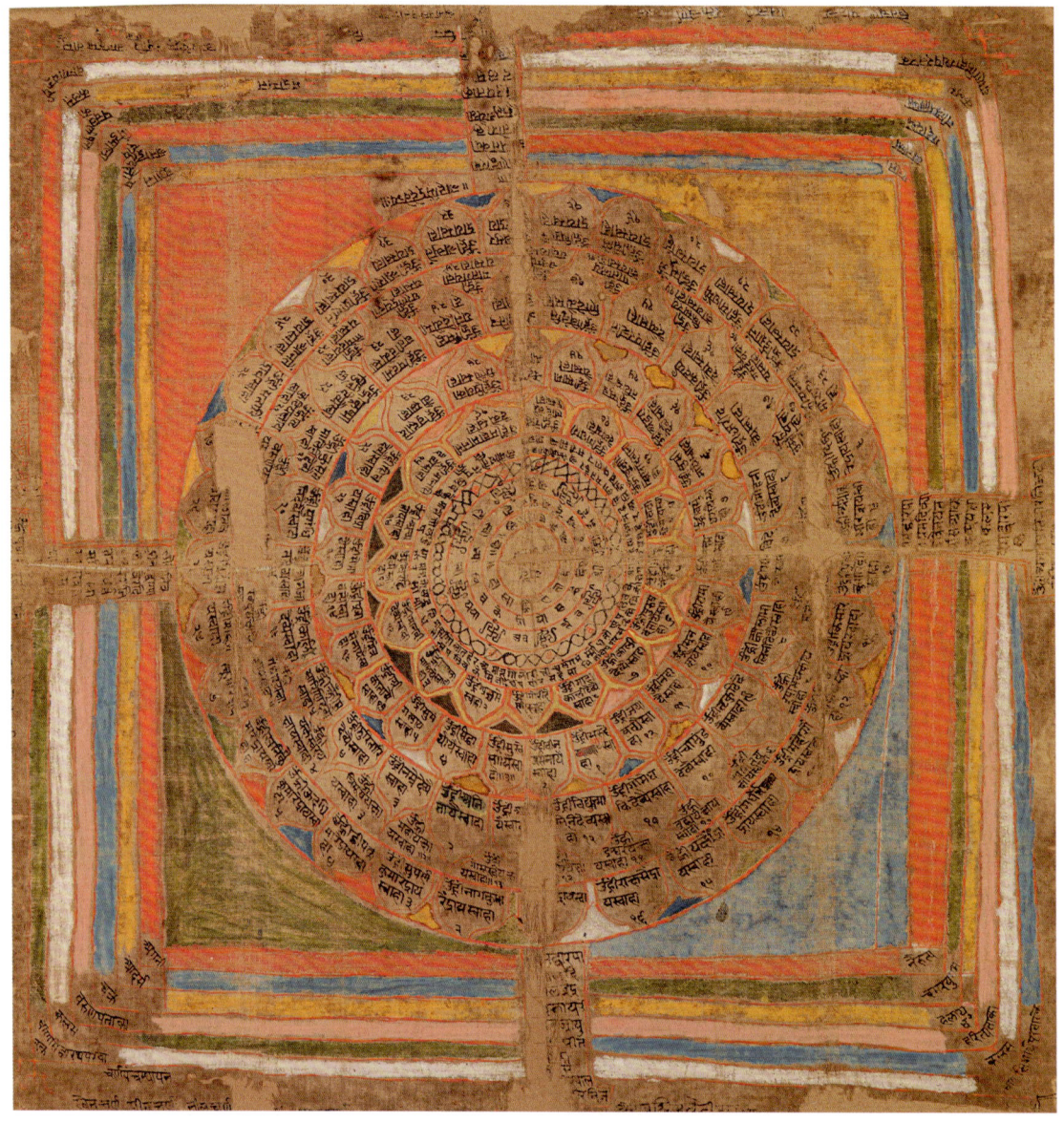

↑ **Faith** *Enlightenment*

Painting, India, 19th century. In Tantric religions, yantras such
as this combine mantras, shapes and images to aid the faith in
meditation and could have been used at home or in a temple

→ **Faith** *Enlightenment*

Buddhist chintz canopy or small stupa cover, Coromandel
Coast, India, circa 1700. Found in Sri Lanka, this cover depicts
the lotus from above, a symbol of knowledge and enlightenment

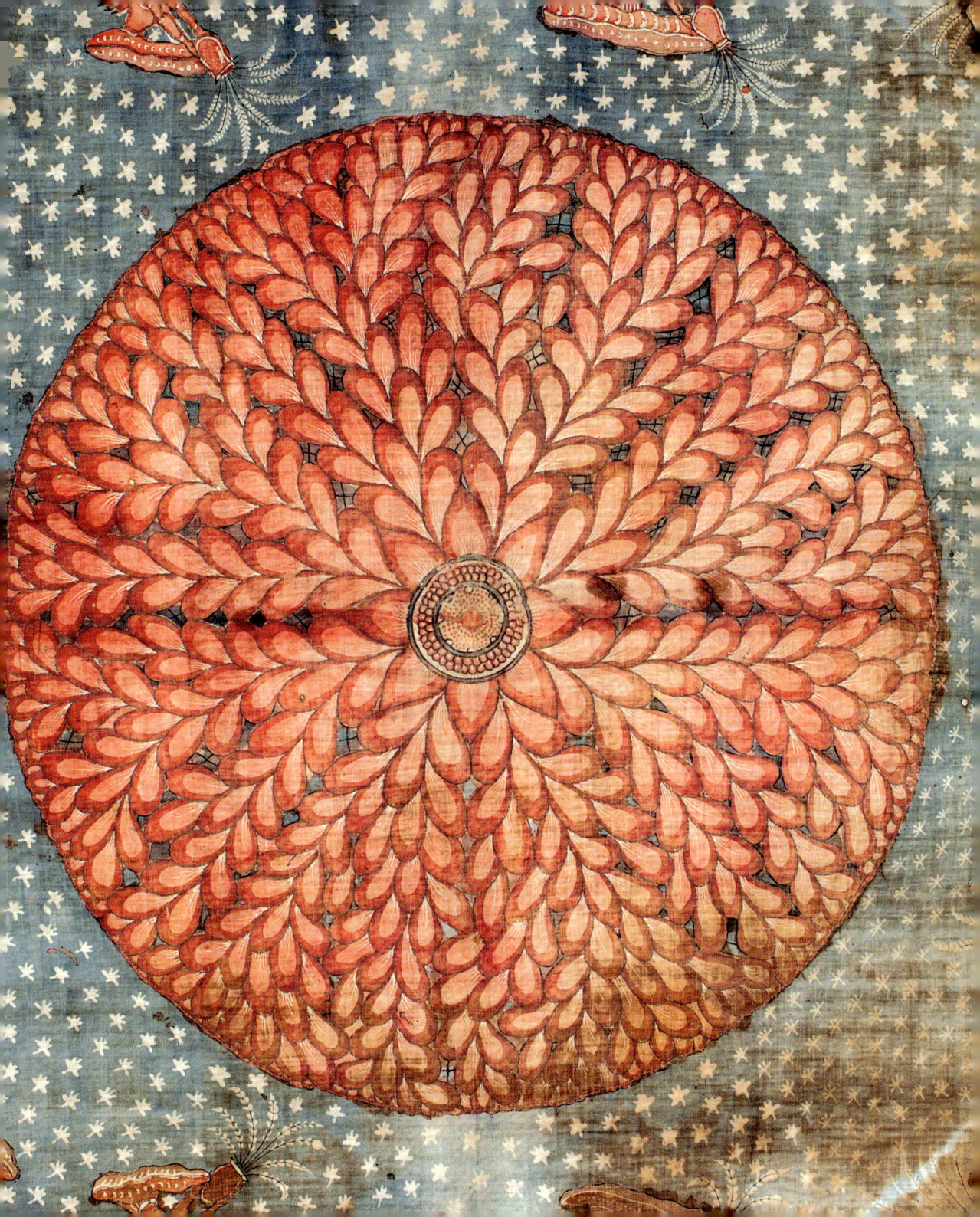

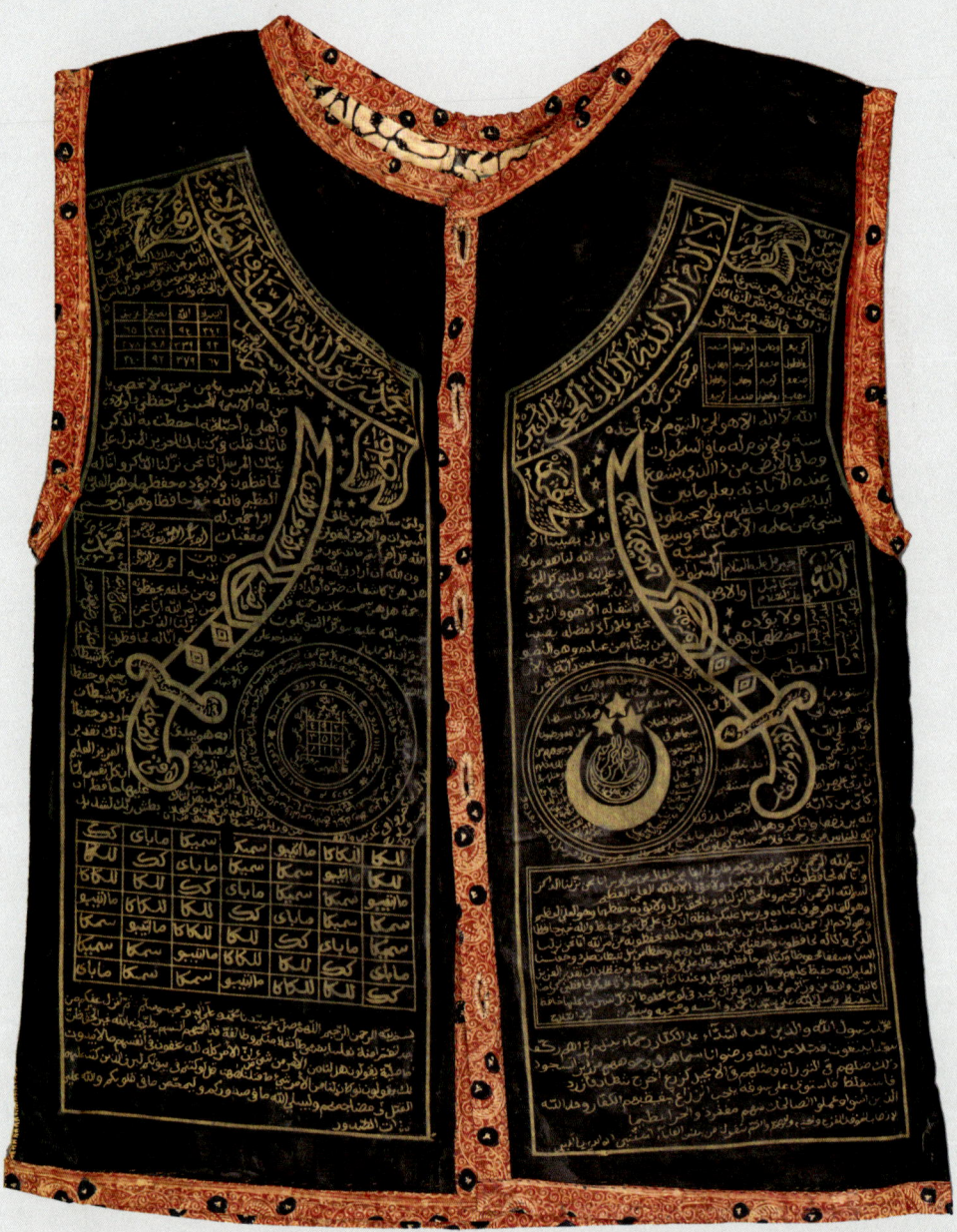

↑ Faith *Protection*

Warrior's batik jacket, Sumatra, Indonesia, 19th century. This talismanic vestment uses Islamic script to ward off the evil eye and protect the wearer. The sword and crescent design shows the close relationship fostered by trade between Indonesia and Ottoman Turkey, which directly influenced the style of a large group of Islamic calligraphic batiks

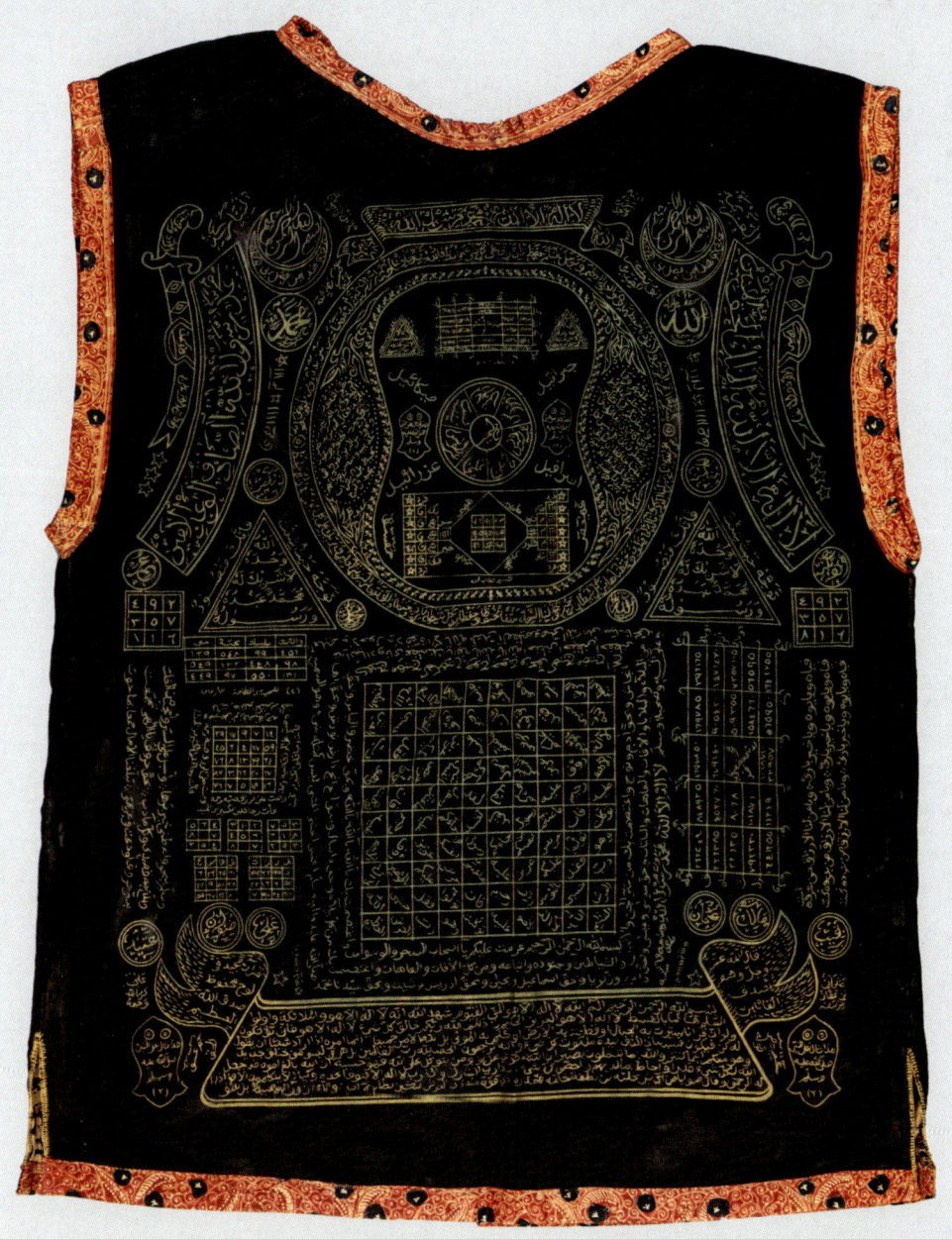

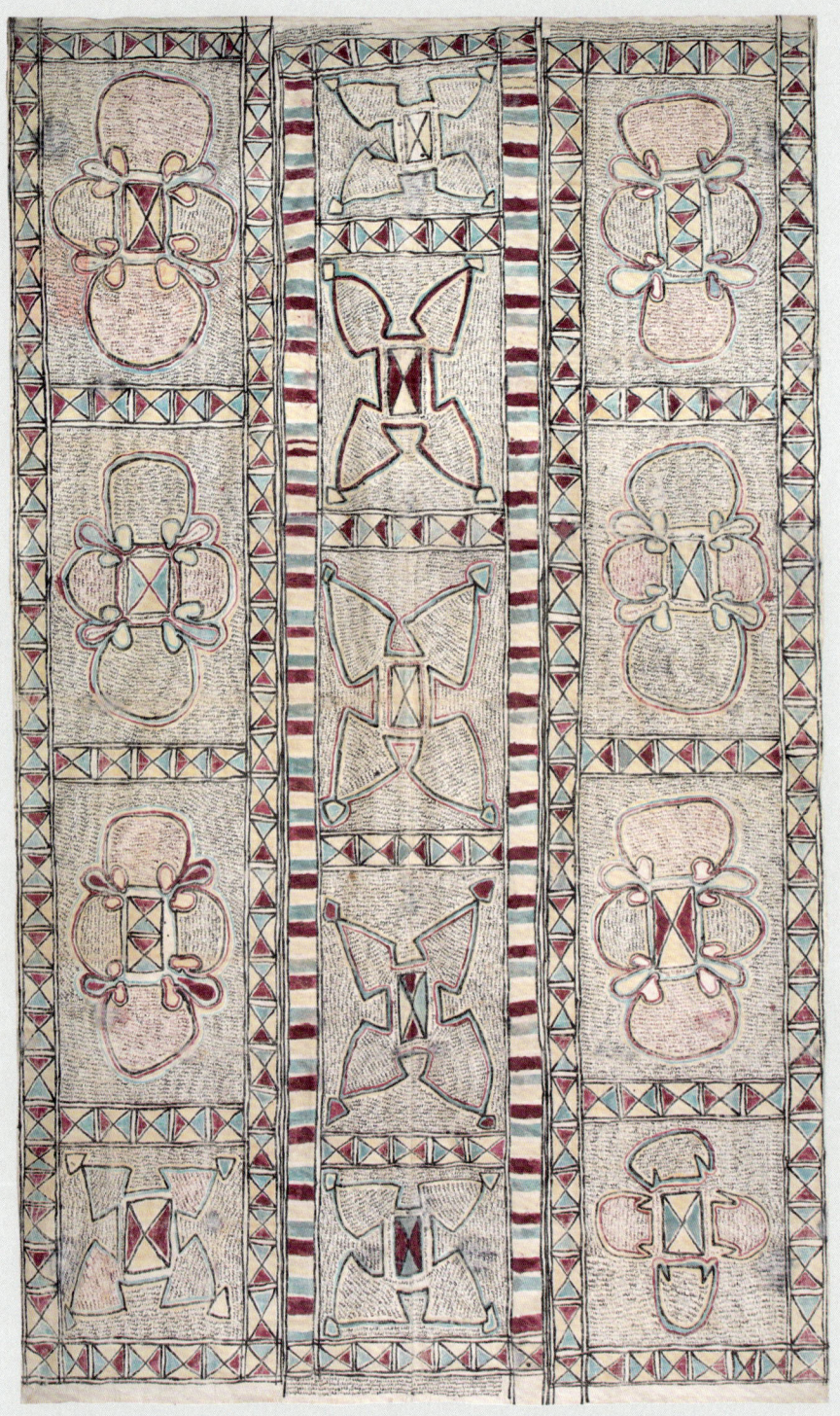

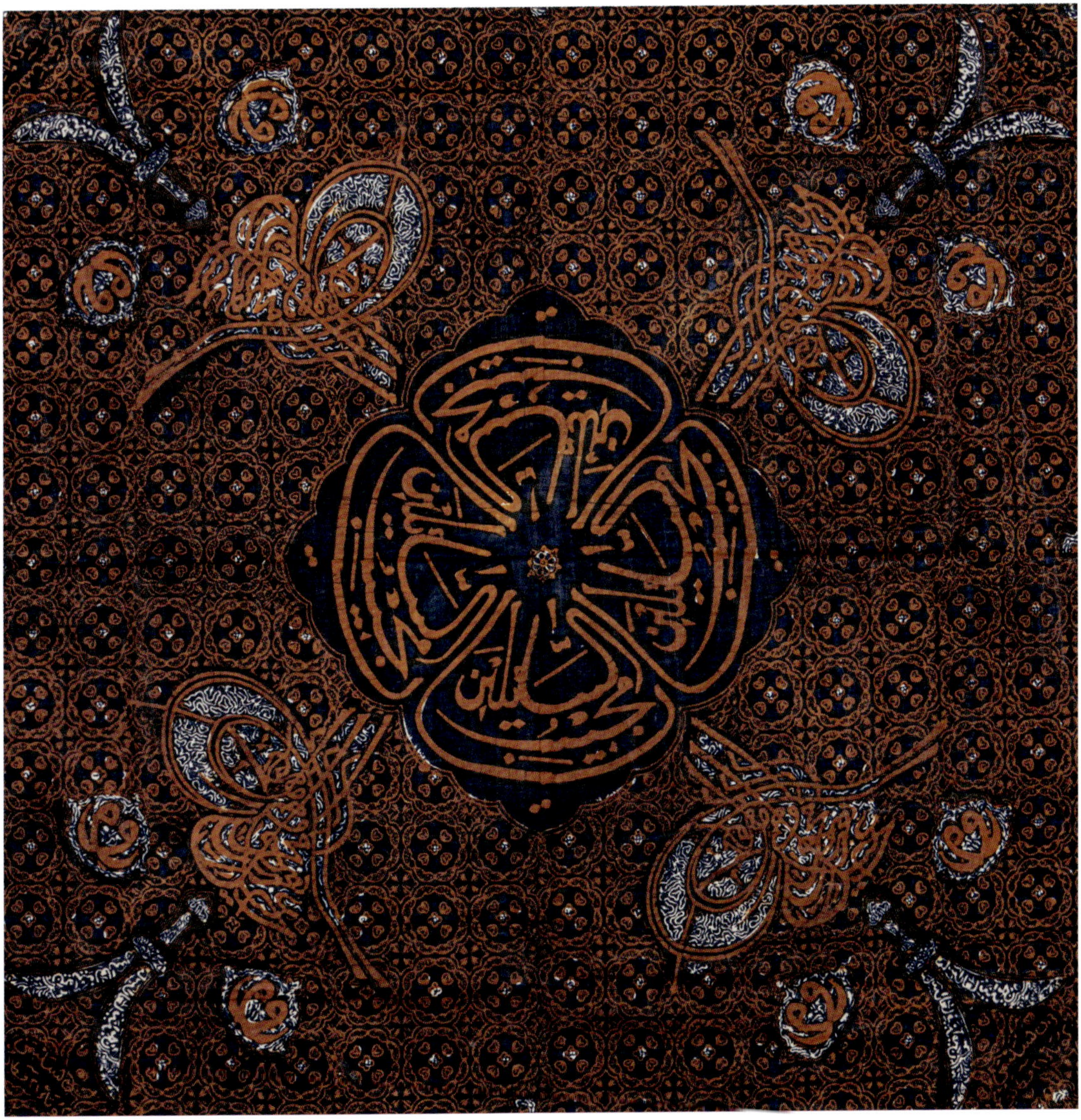

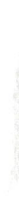

← **Faith** *Protection*
Man's wrap used by Ashanti royals, Ghana, 19th century.
Faux-Arabic script drawn by scholars but without any legible
meaning decorates this cloth, which also contains depictions of
talismanic objects

↑ **Faith** *Protection*
Batik turban cover, Sumatra, Indonesia, 20th century. The
dense floral design hides the tughra or signature of the Ottoman
sultan, thereby invoking both worldly and divine protection

↓ **Faith** *Pilgrimage*
Cotton pilgrim's jacket, Japan, 19th century. The numerous
stamps are collected from temples during a set pilgrimage,
concrete traces of devotion

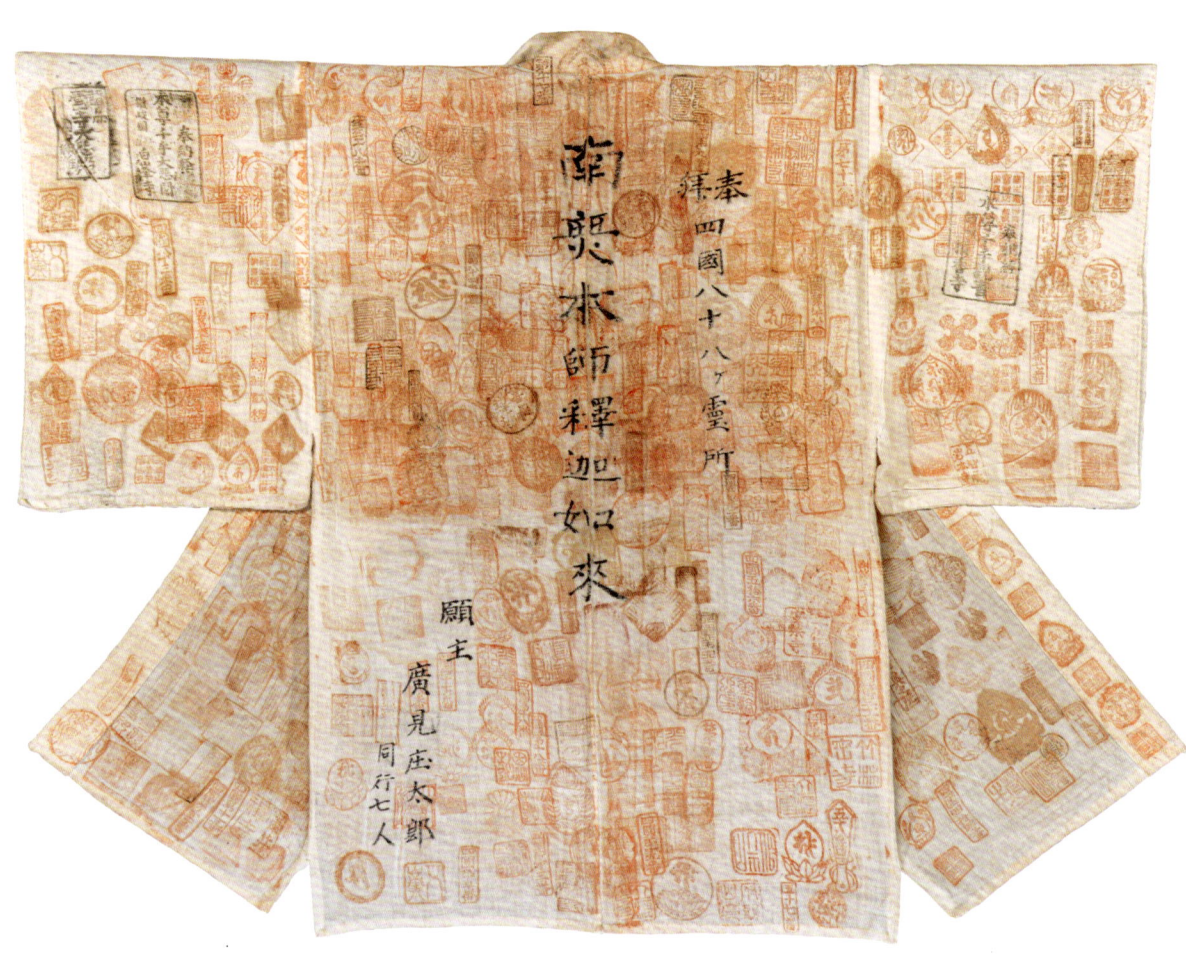

→ **Faith** *Pilgrimage*
Shrine hanging, Uttar Pradesh, India, 19th century. This appliqué
hanging was an offering to the shrine of an 11th-century Muslim
warrior saint, venerated by Muslims and Hindus alike, and uses
iconography that is meaningful across communities

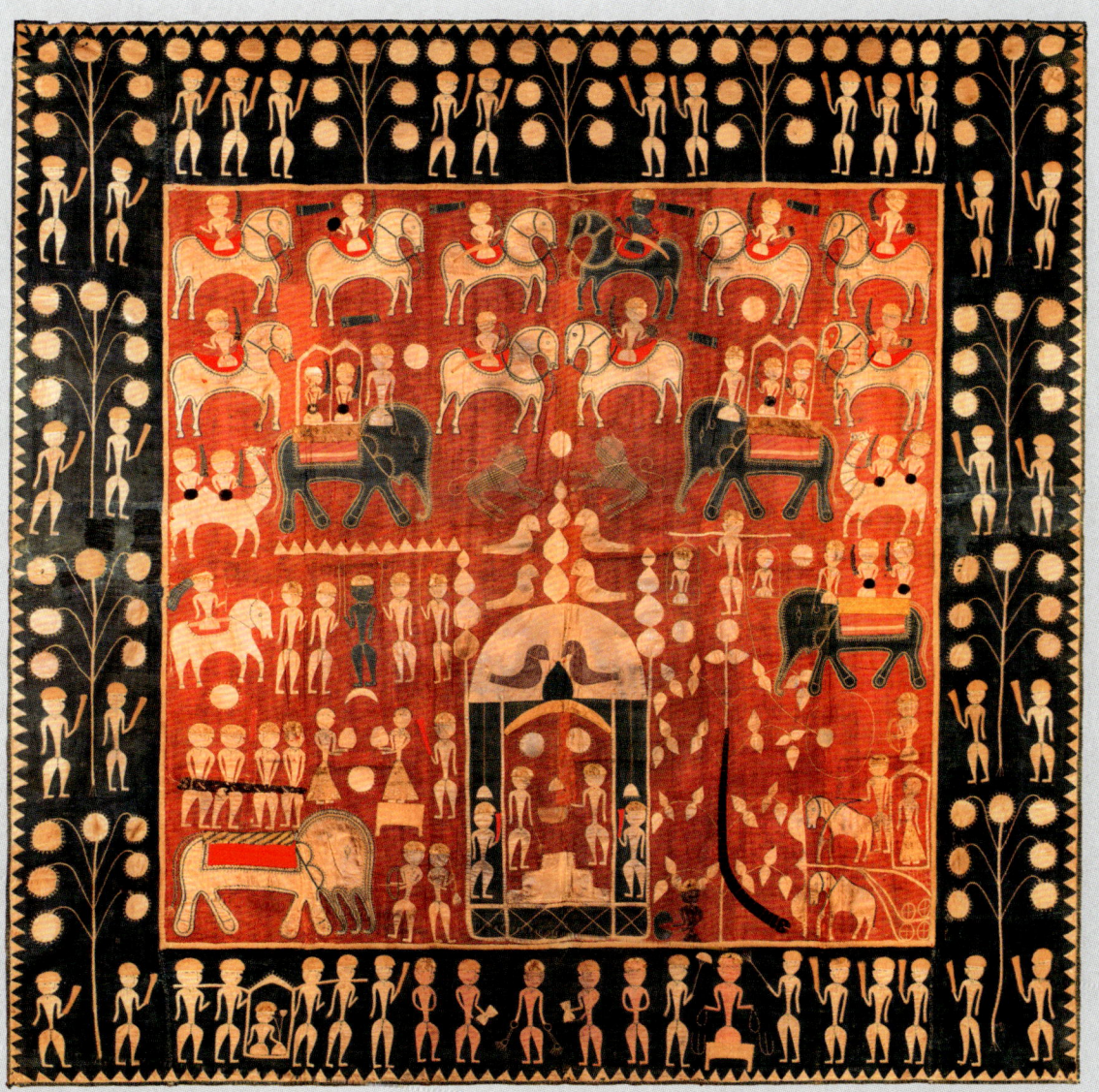

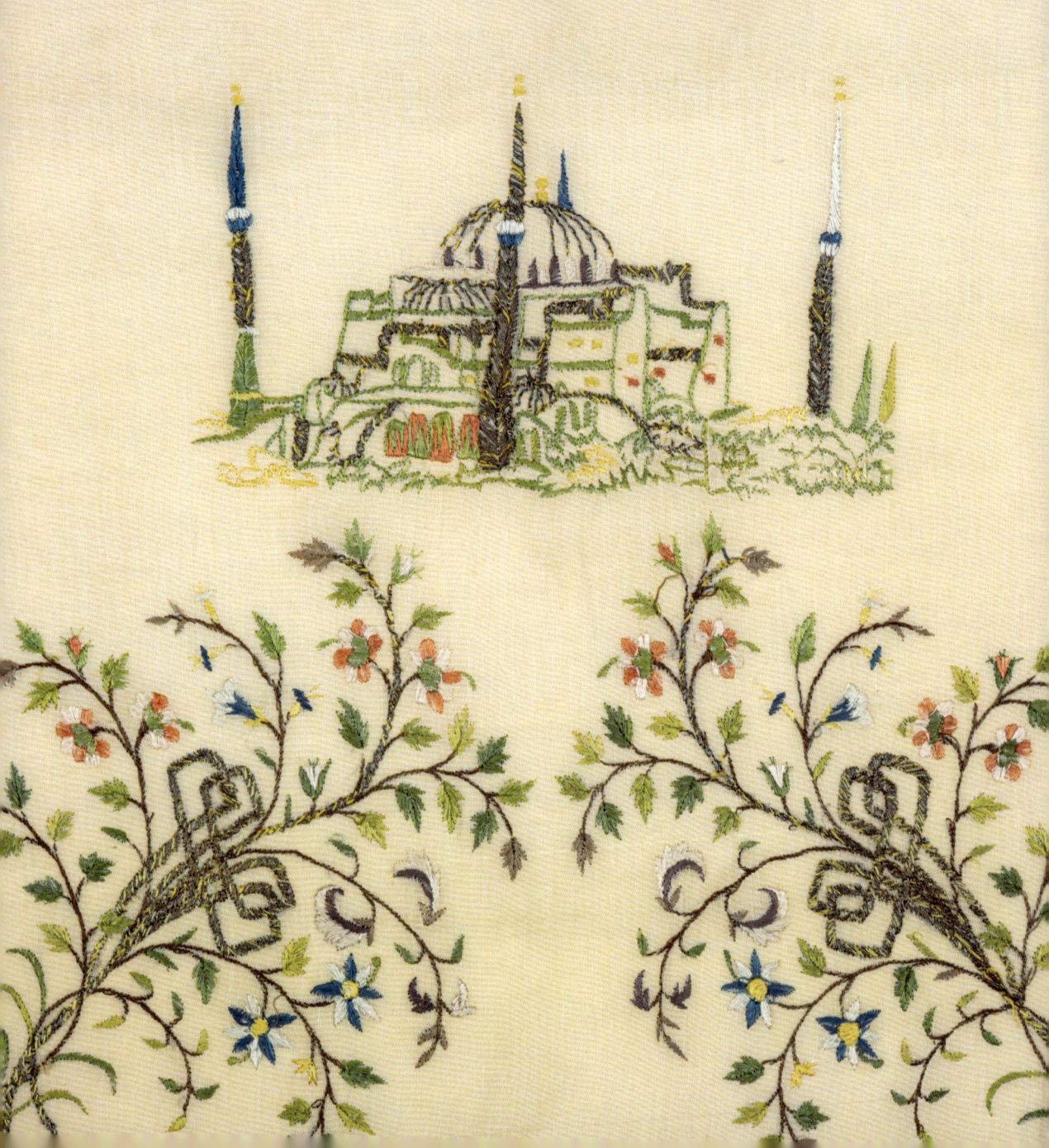

↓ **Ceremonial** *Devotion*
Embroidered cover, Ottoman Turkey, 19th century. The silk and
metal-thread embroidery shows the 6th-century Hagia Sophia
repurposed as a mosque with minarets and whirling dervishes

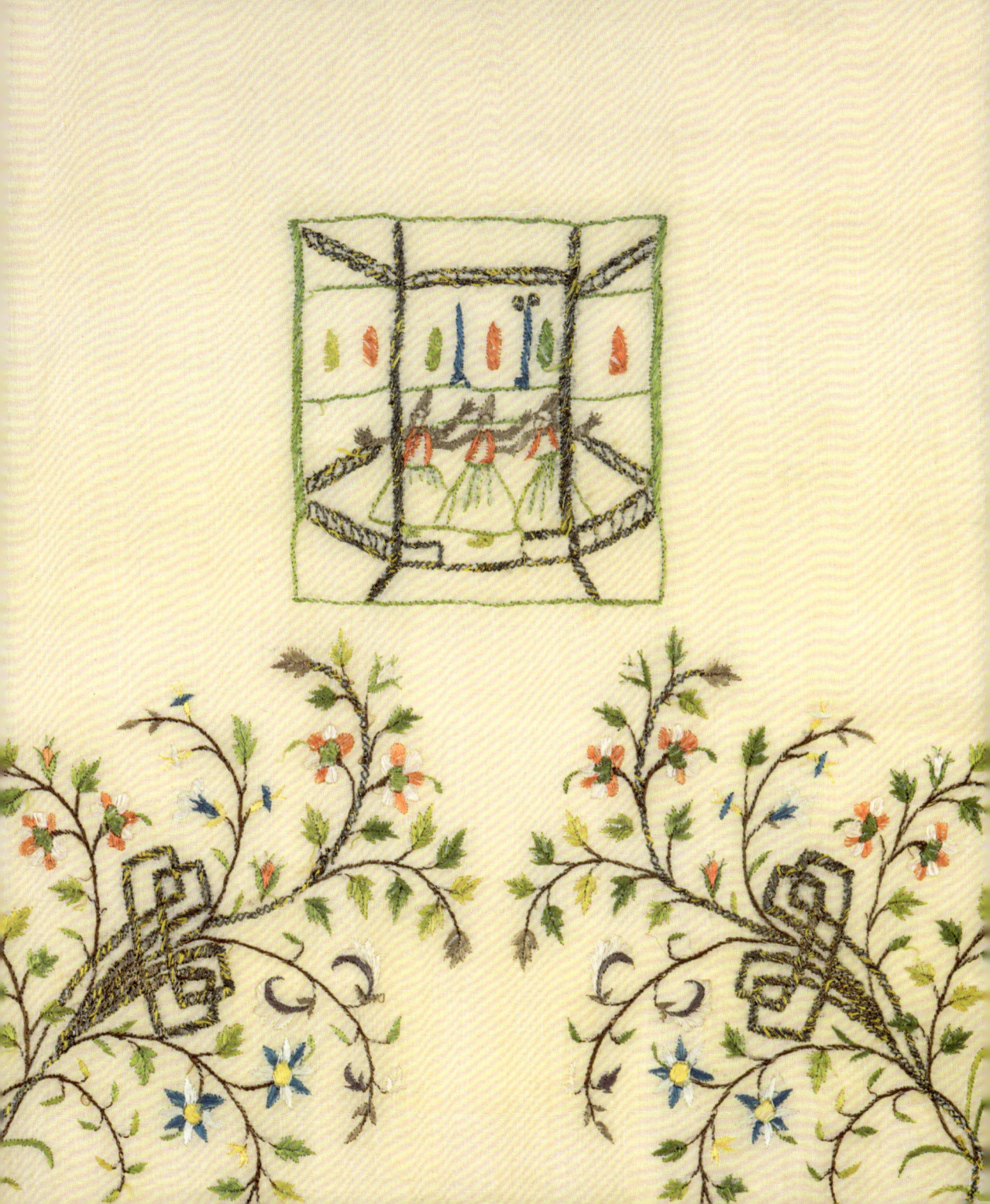

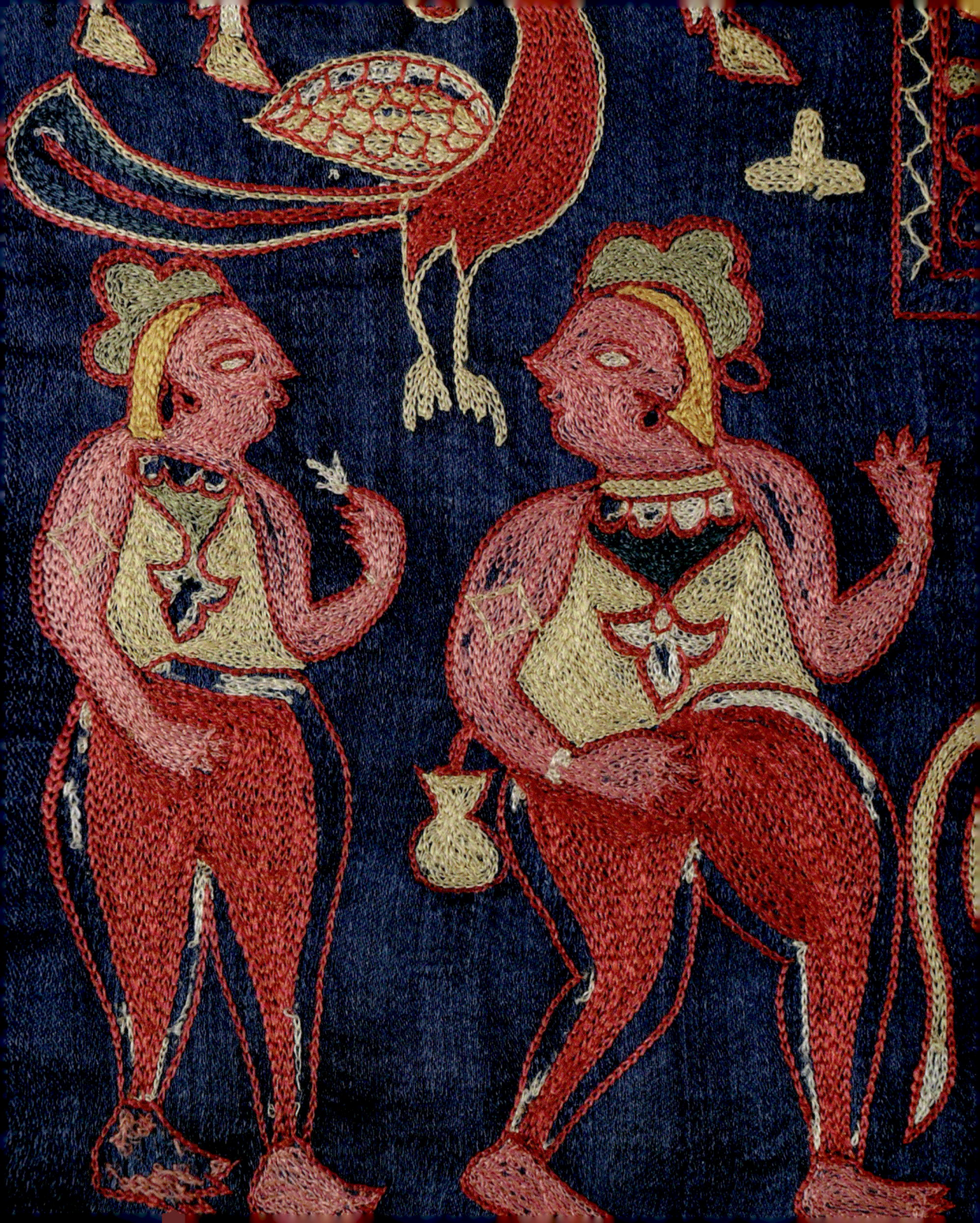

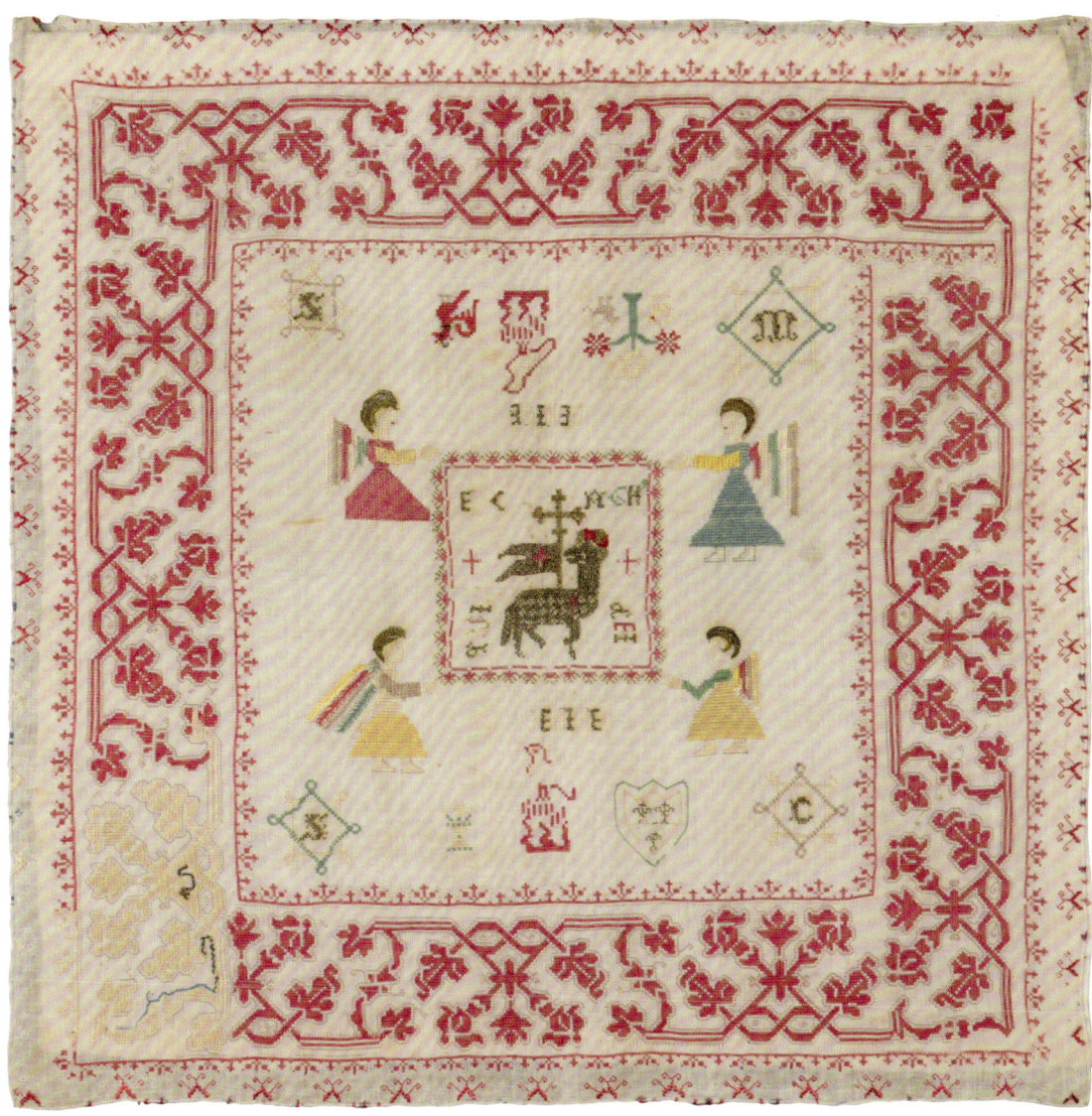

← **Ceremonial** *Devotion*
Pichwai, Gujarat, India, 19th century. This embroidered silk would have been used on the steps of the temple. The border detail shows Lord Krishna as a cowherd holding a pot of butter

↑ **Ceremonial** *Devotion*
Chalice cover, England, 17th century. Embroidered in silk, this would have been draped over the offering of wine with the angels pointing towards the congregation during communion

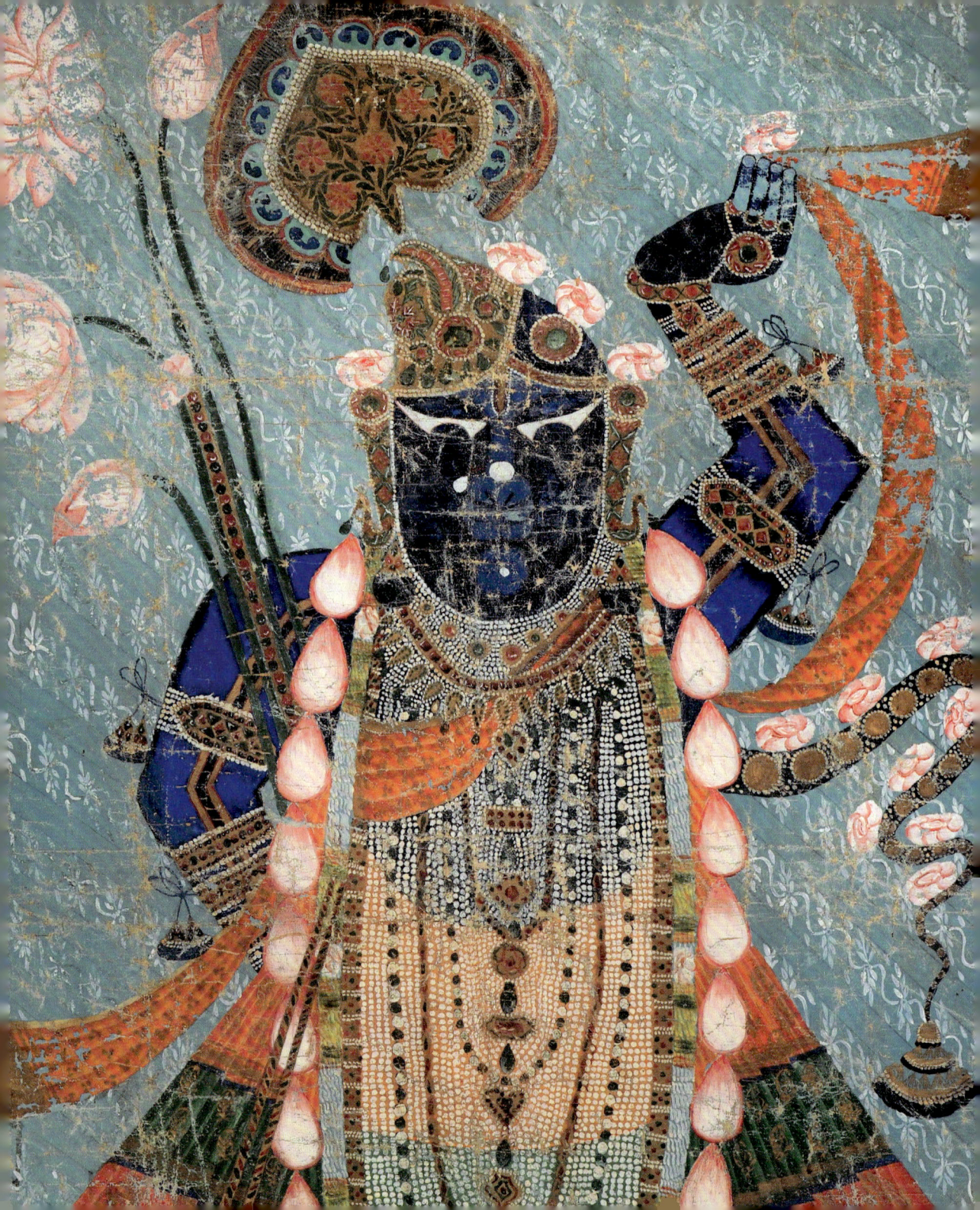

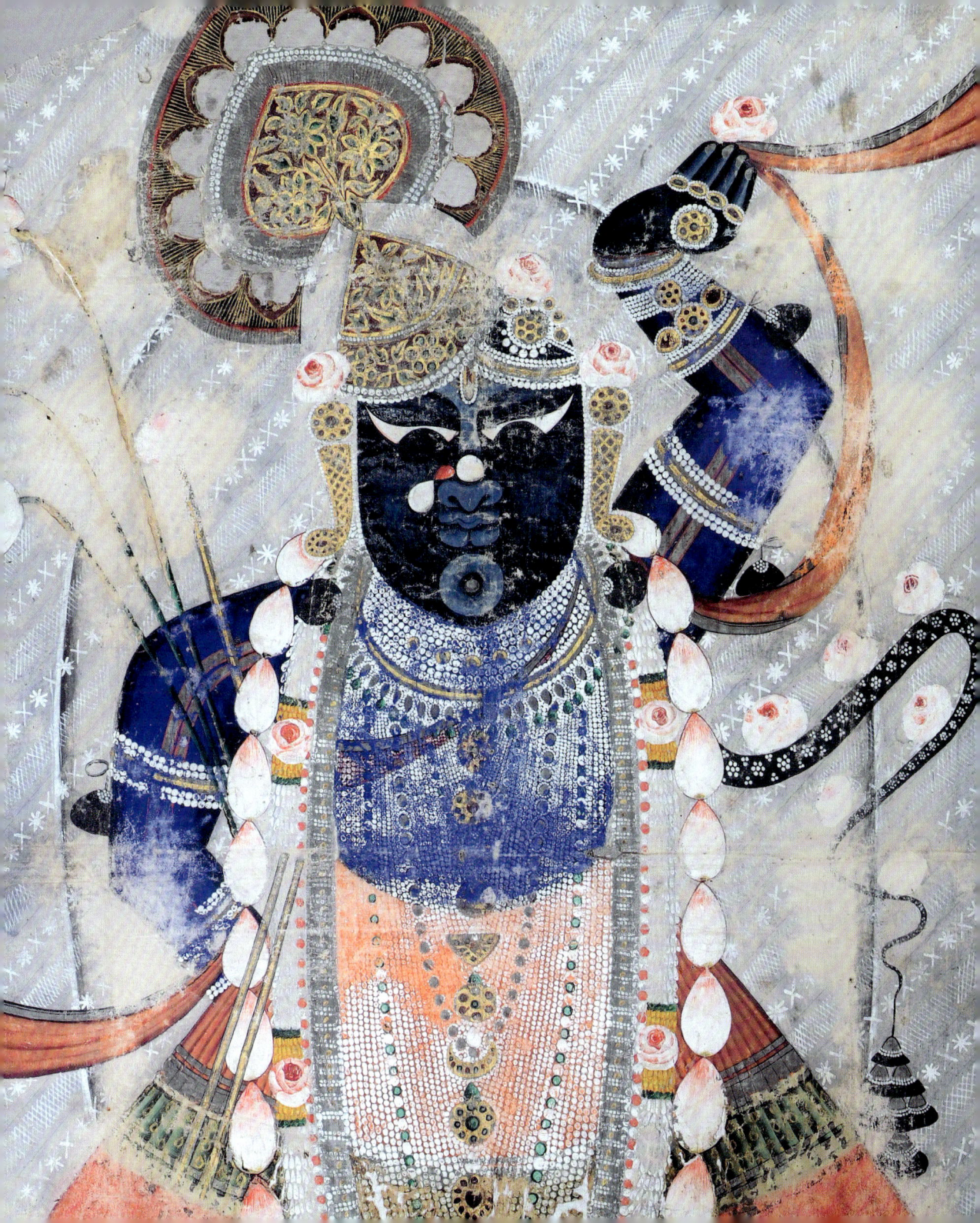

↑ ↑ **Ceremonial** *Devotion*
Pichwais, Gujarat, India, 19th century. Such temple hangings
are used exclusively in the Pushtimarg, in shrines devoted to
Krishna. Both these devotional images show Krishna in the
same pose, in front of the painted European net curtains that
were also popular

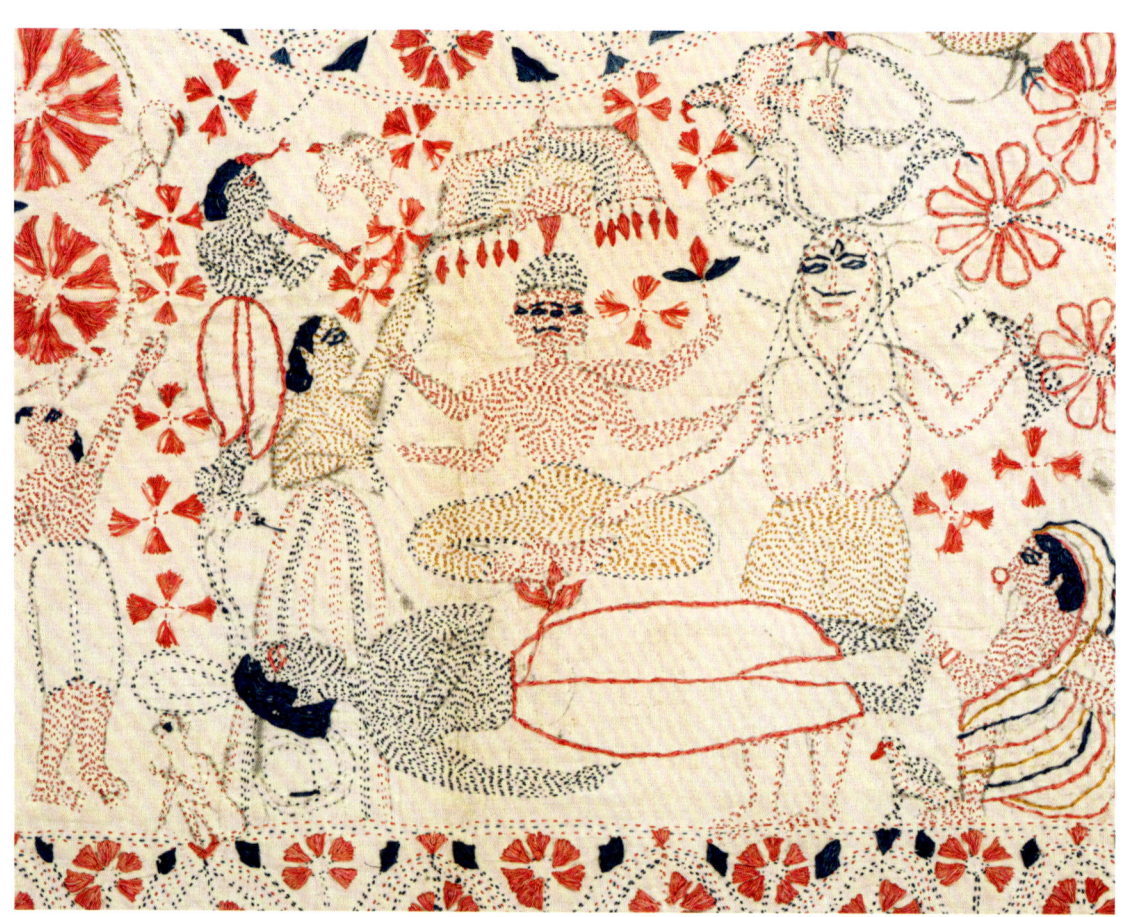

↑ **Ceremonial** *Devotion*
Kantha, undivided Bengal, late 19th century. This cotton
embroidery is unusual in that it shows four scenes from Hindu
texts that imply that it would have been intended for a religious
rite. These ubiquitous covers are seldom so clearly pictorial

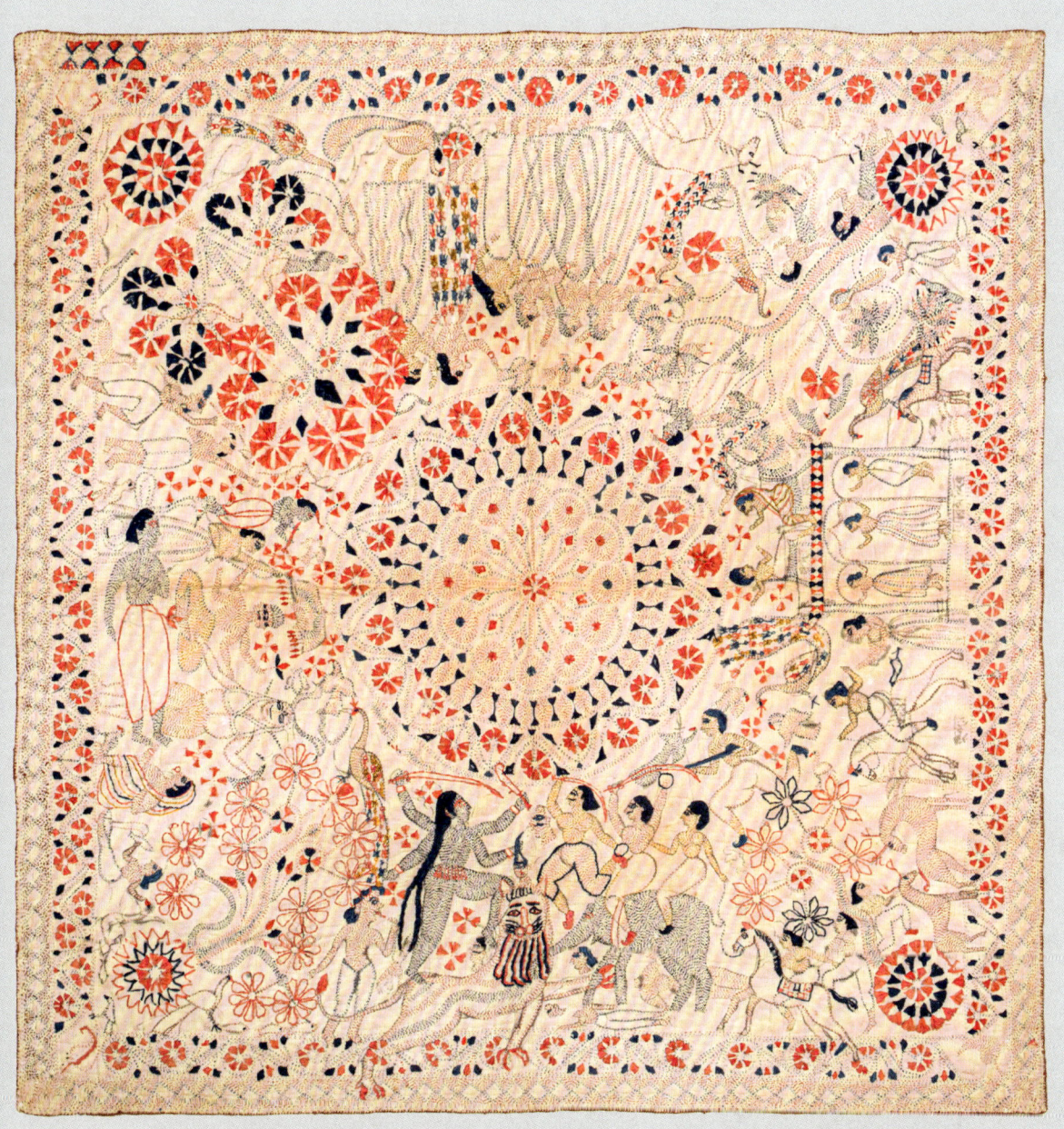

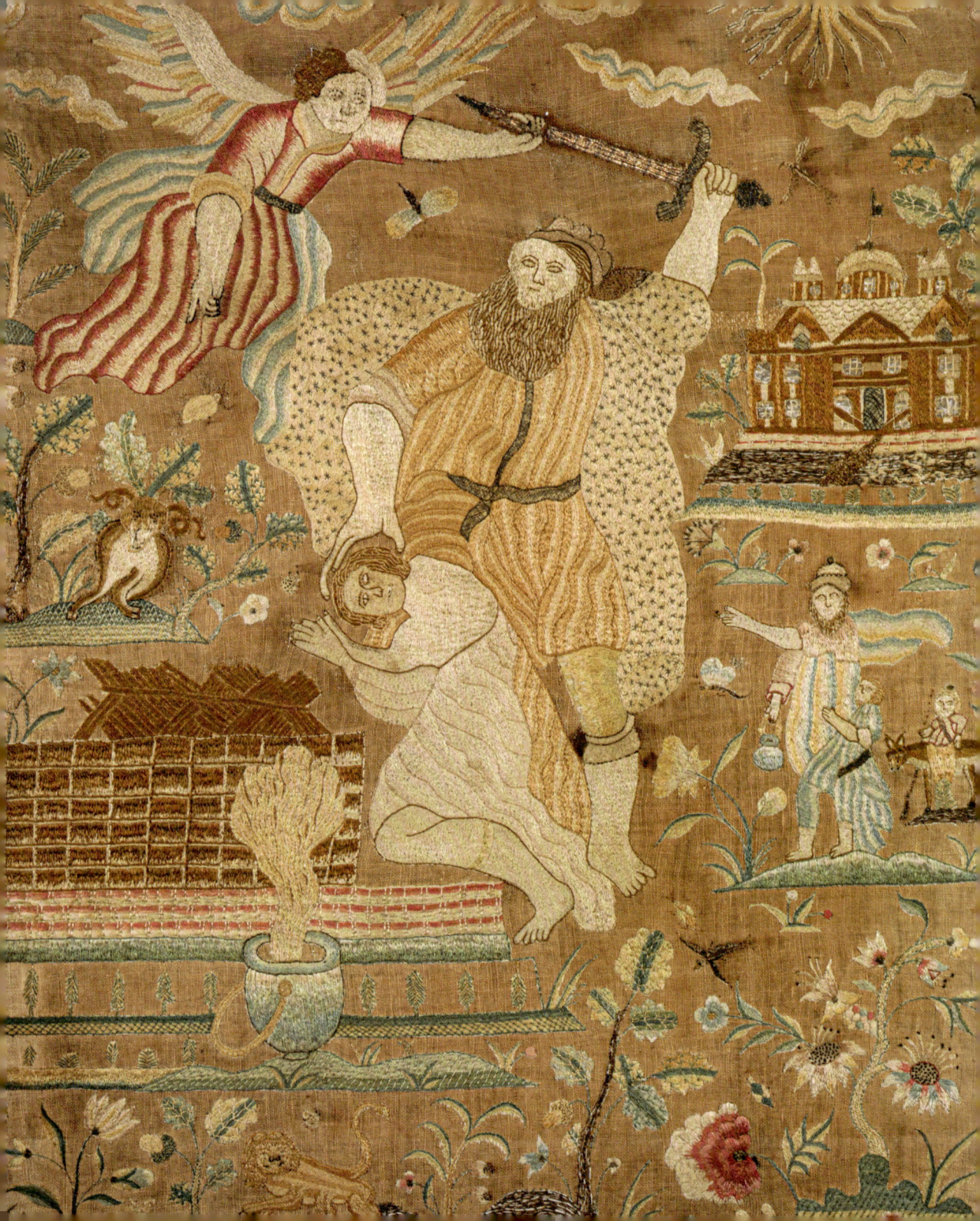

← **Ceremonial** *Devotion*

Silk embroidery, England, 18th century. In this Old Testament scene, Abraham obeys the word of the Lord and prepares to sacrifice his firstborn, Isaac

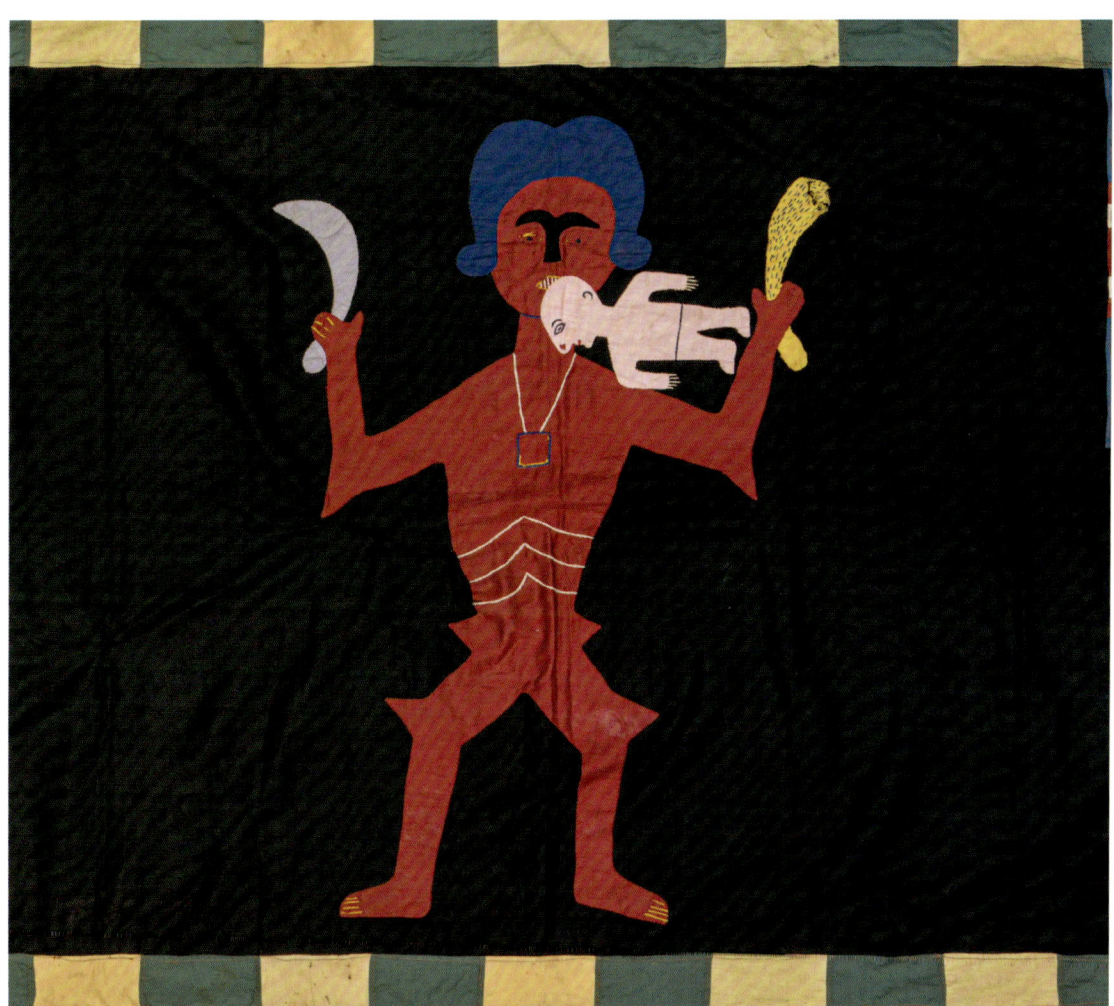

↑ **Ceremonial** *Devotion*

Asafo flag, Ghana, 19th century. The gruesome depiction of a person being devoured is a portent of the company's ability to invoke a devil or god and strike fear into the hearts of its rival companies

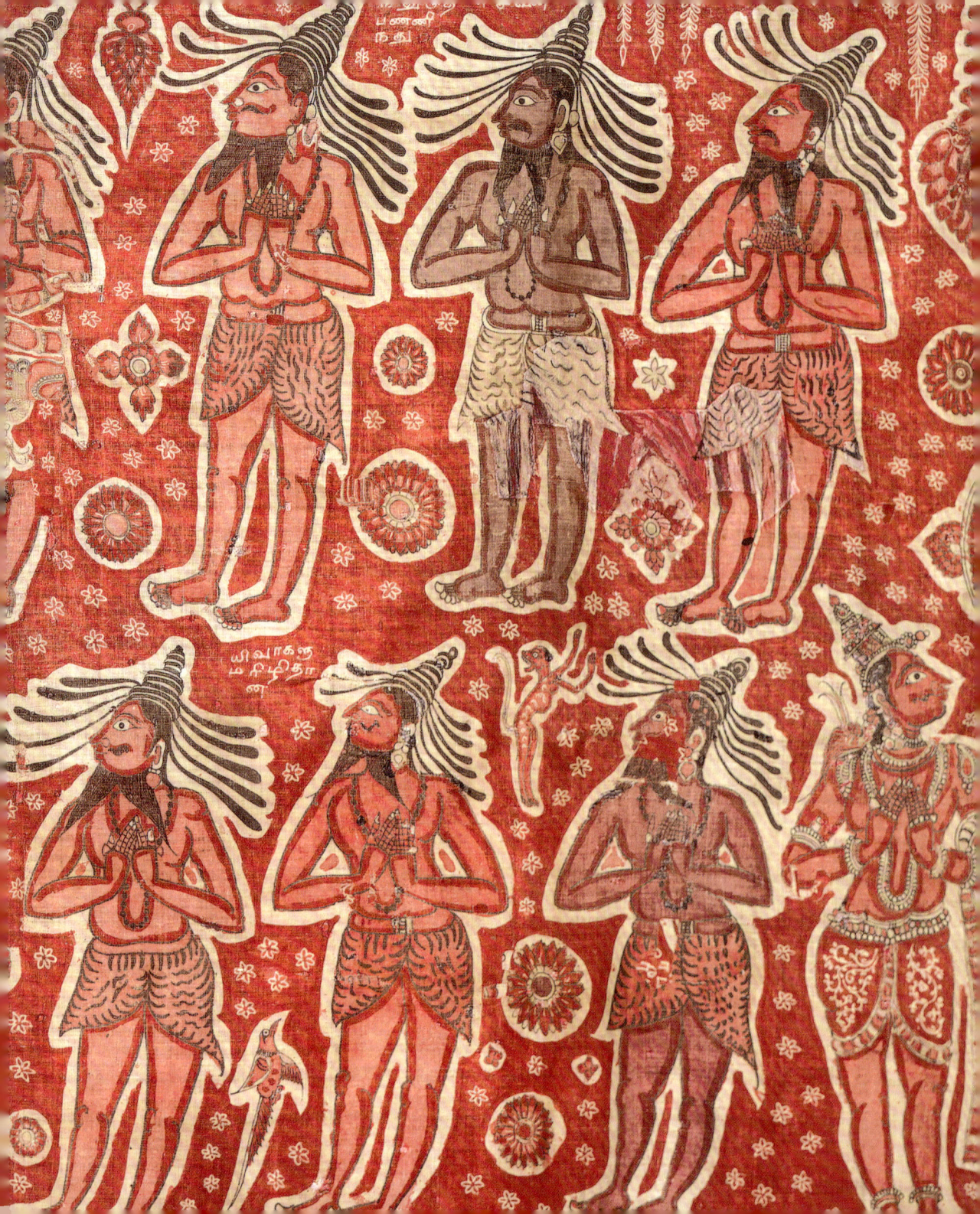

← **Ceremonial** *Devotion*
Temple hanging, south india, 18th century. Depicting the well-known story of the Coronation of Rama, it shows seven Hindu rishis or saints with their distinctive dreadlocks

↓ **Ceremonial** *Devotion*
The Herb Picker, chintz hanging, south India, 17th century. The herb picker's necklace shows that he is a devotee of Shiva, collecting leaves as an act of faith for use in a religious ceremony

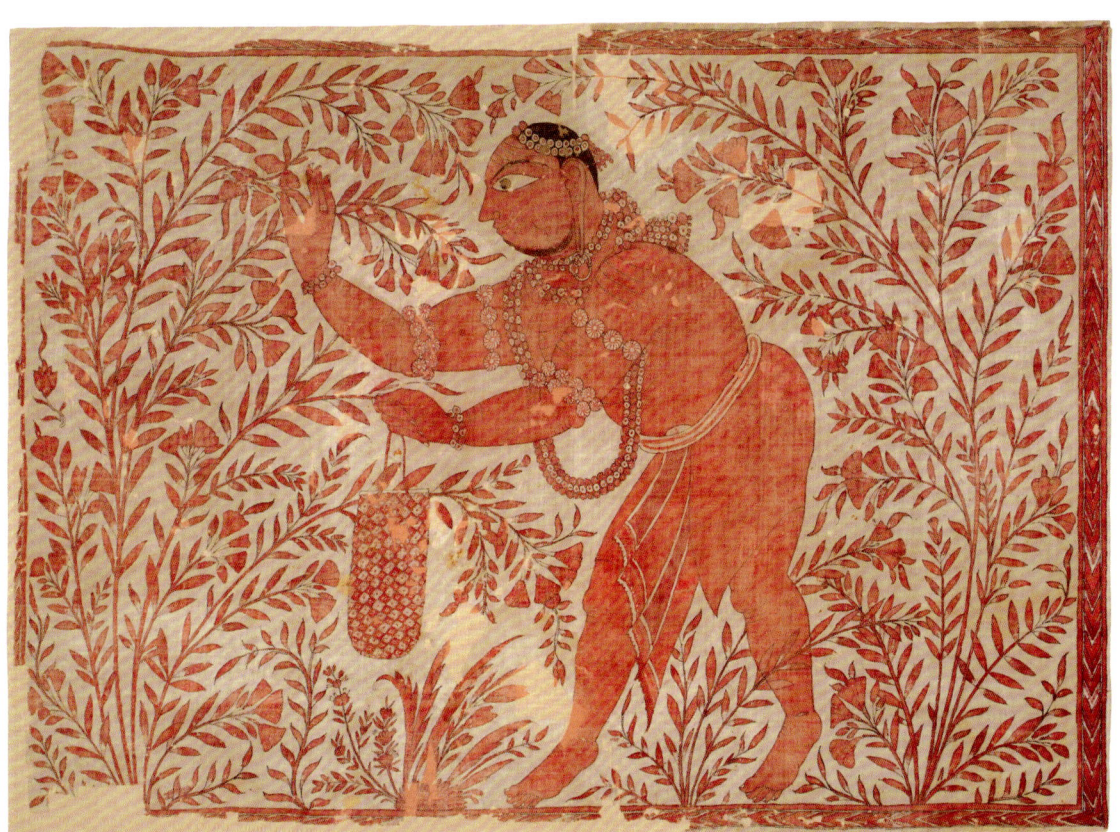

↓ ↓ **Ceremonial** *Devotion*
Temple hanging, Ghana, 20th century. Covered with faux-Arabic writing, this textile delineates places of worship and is more architectural than obviously talismanic in purpose

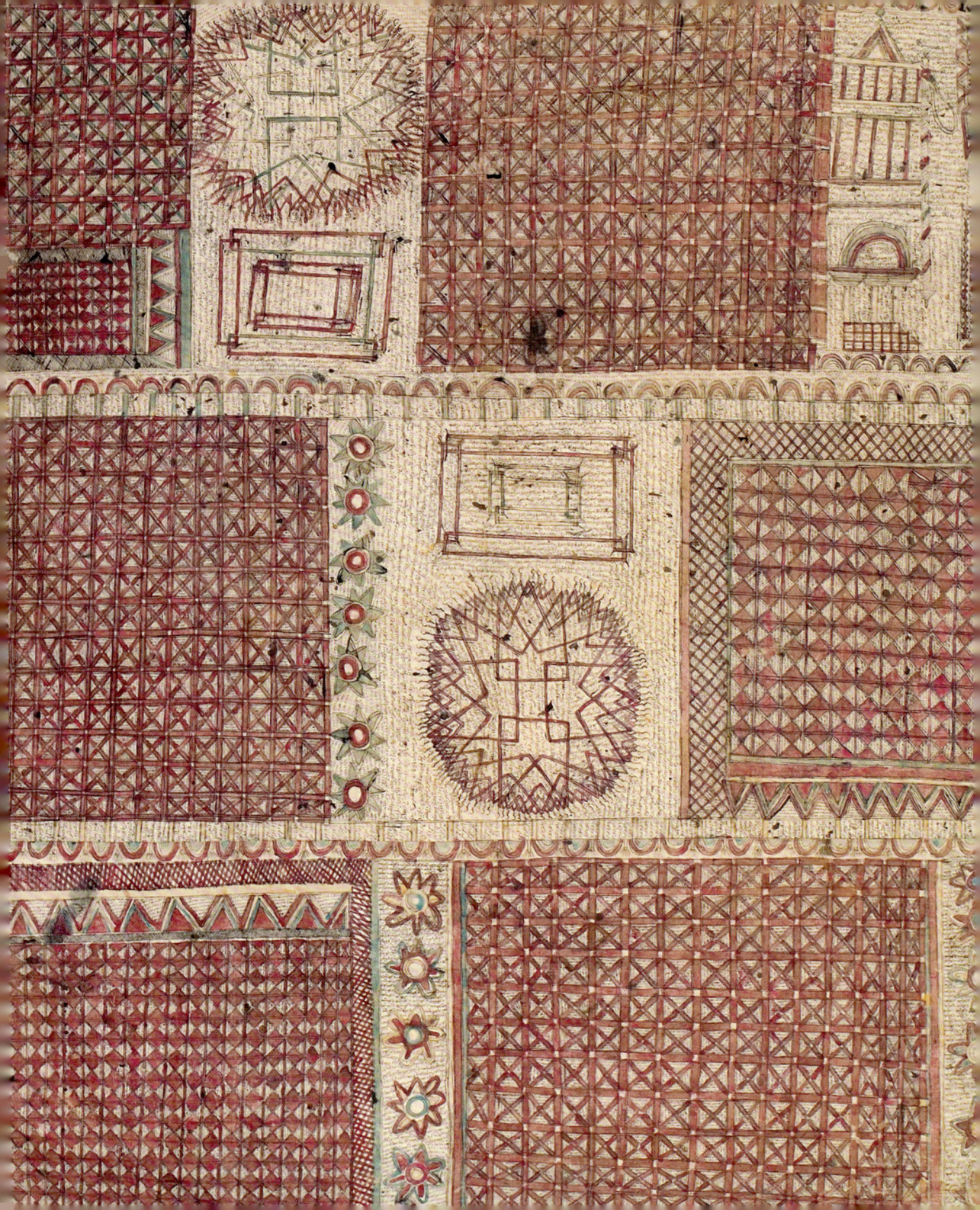

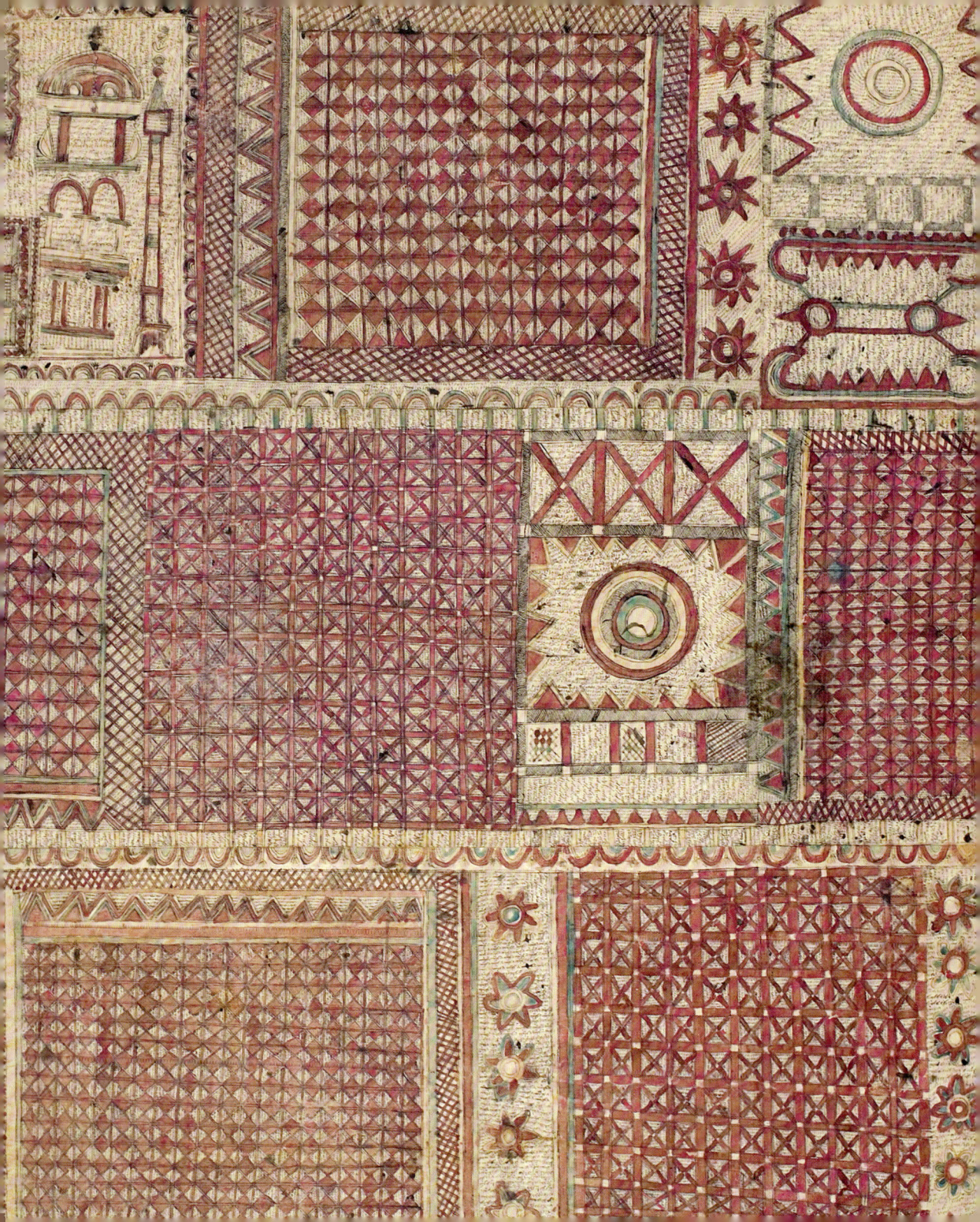

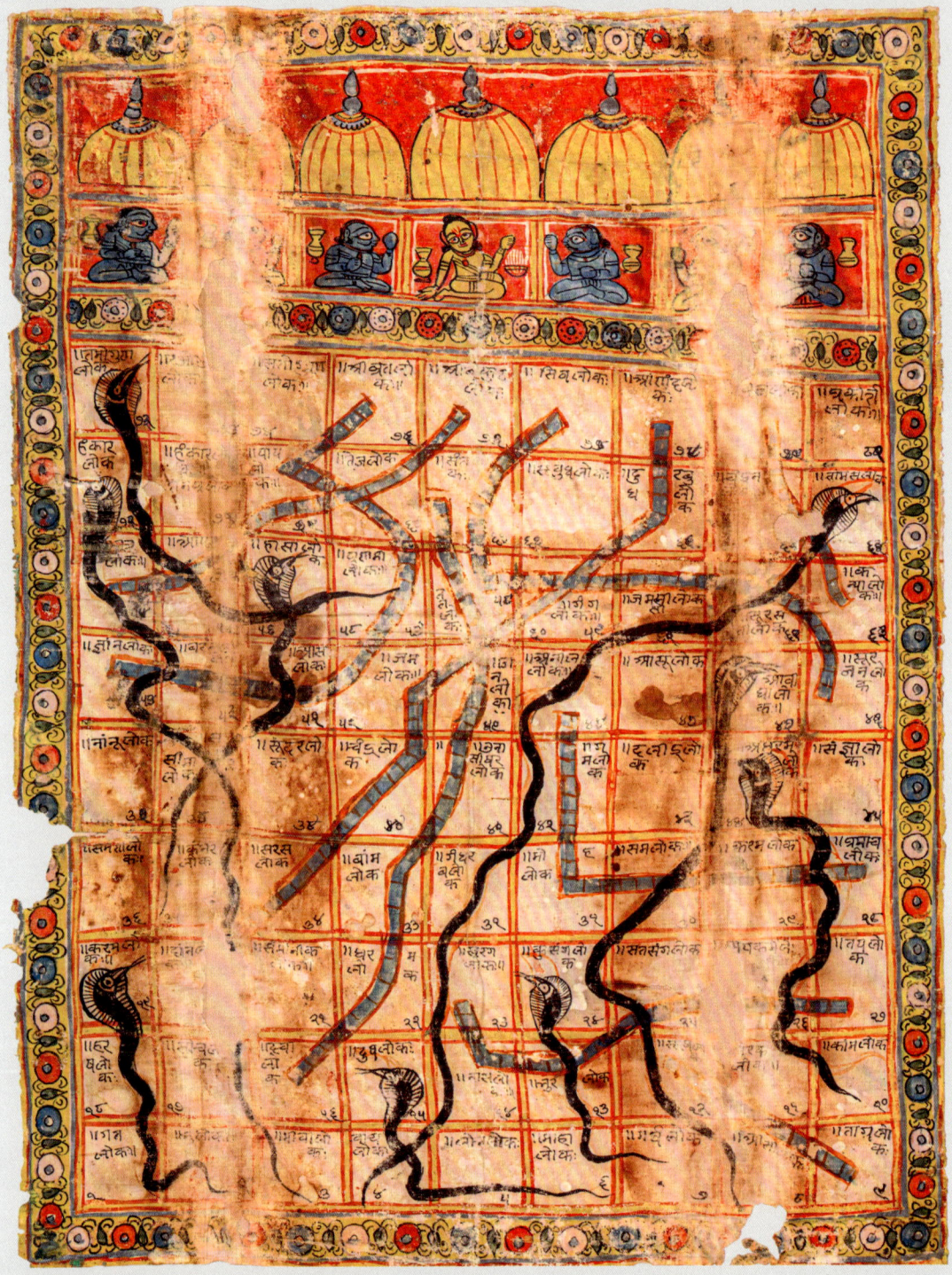

← **Ceremonial** *Devotion*

Jain cloth, Gujarat, India, 19th century. The game of snakes and ladders originated in medieval India, where it was seen as a representation of a person's upward course in religious life

↓ **Ceremonial** *Devotion*

Jain painting, Gujarat, India, 16th century. Used for worship and prayer in a Jain temple, this painting has a central figure representing one of the religion's 24 enlightened teachers

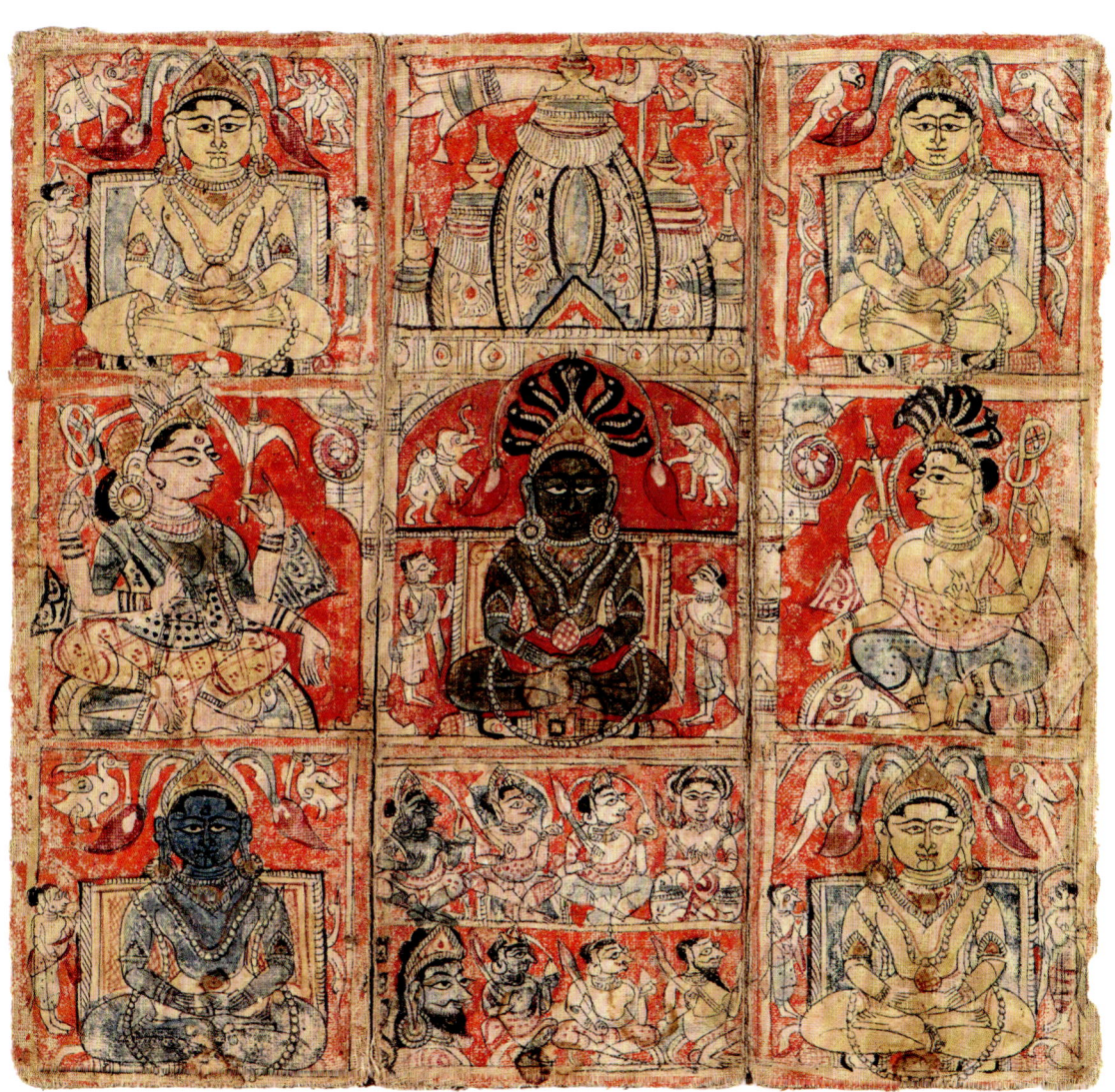

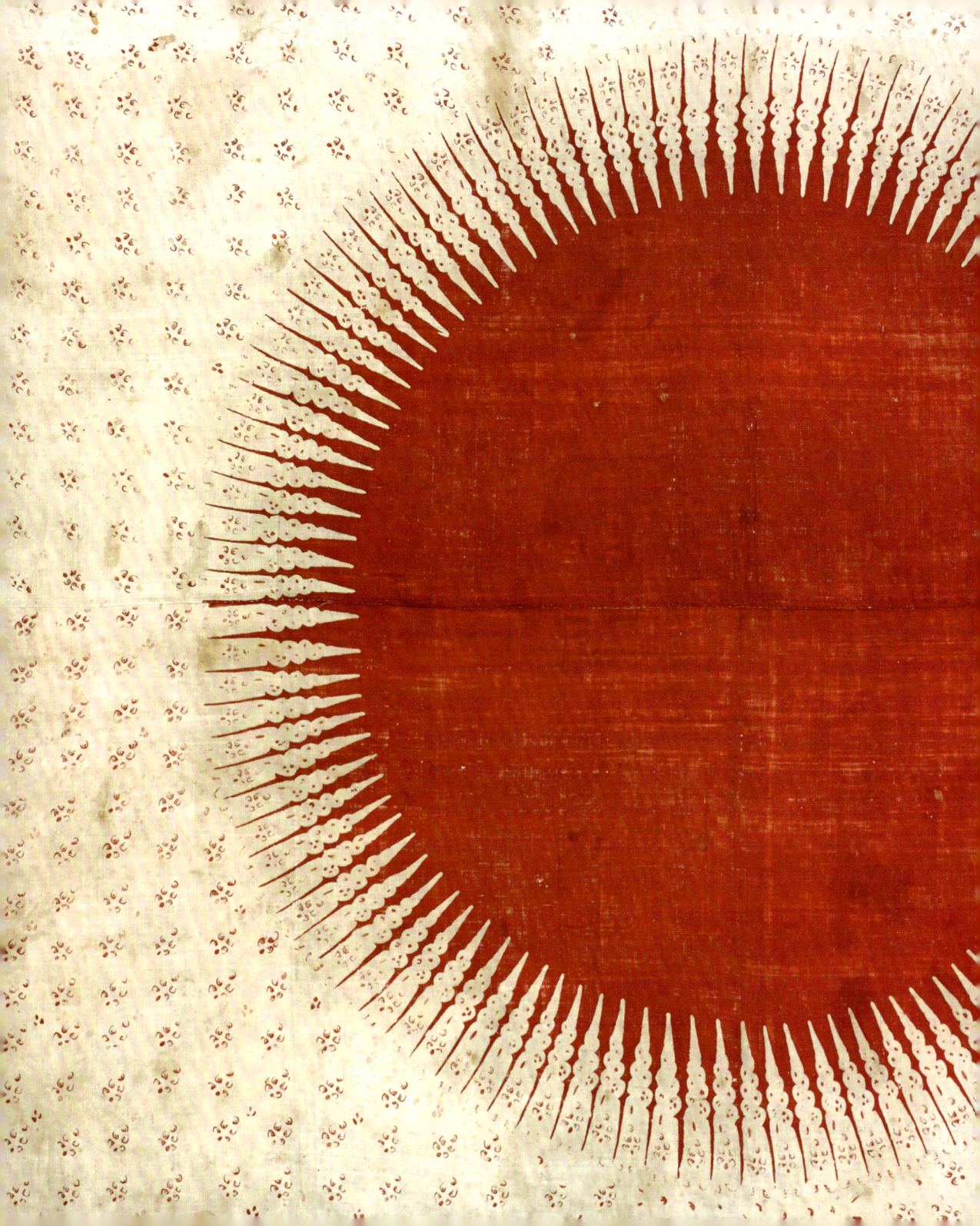

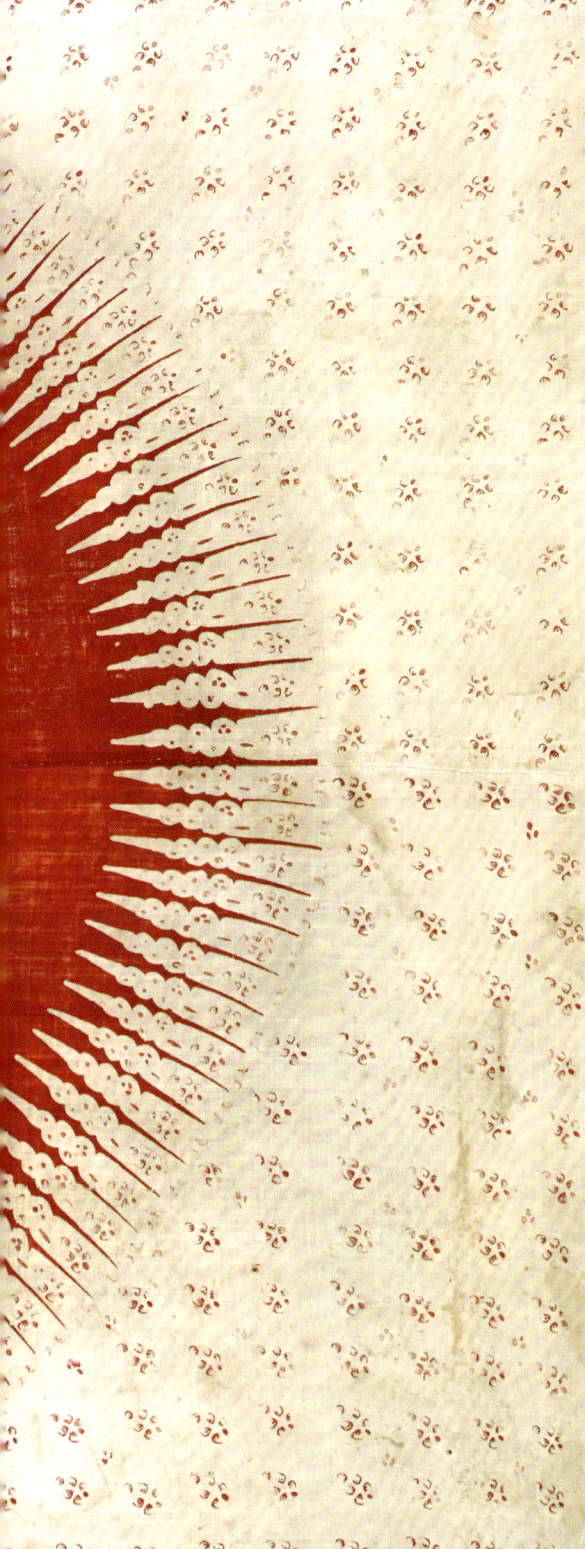

← **Ceremonial** *Devotion*
Ceremonial hanging, India for the Indonesian market, 18th century. Found in Sulawesi, where the pulsating sun design is called mata hari, meaning 'eye of the day', this prestige cloth would have been used in rites of passage ceremonies

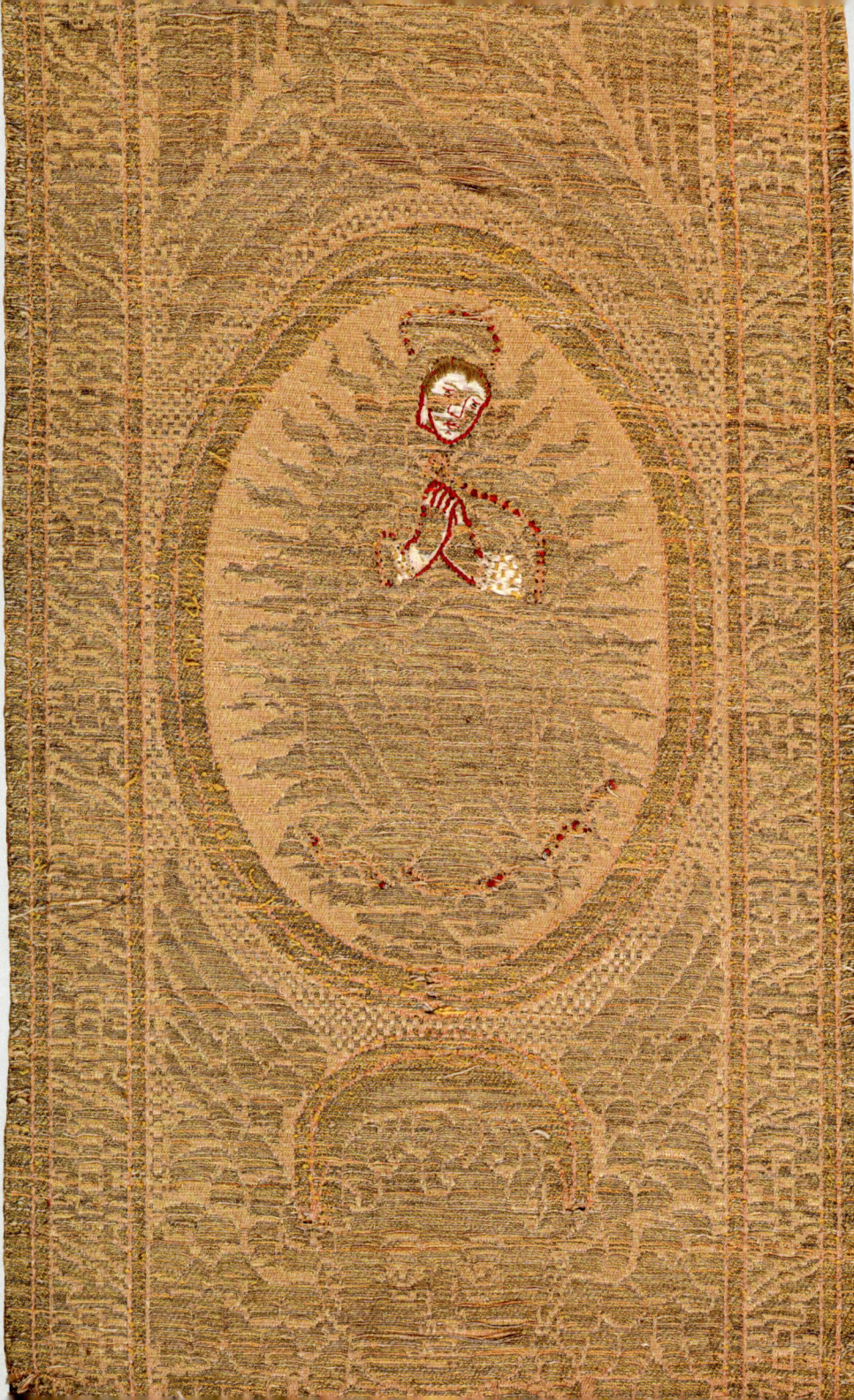

← **Ceremonial** *Devotion*
Orphrey fragment, Italy, 17th century. This silk and gold thread orphrey from the 1600s depicts a saint, perhaps the Virgin Mary, and is typical of the rich decoration of liturgical vestments

↓ **Ceremonial** *Devotion*
Sogdian samite fragment, Central Asia, 6th–8th century. This prestigious and precious silk was reportedly preserved inside the lining of a much younger religious vestment

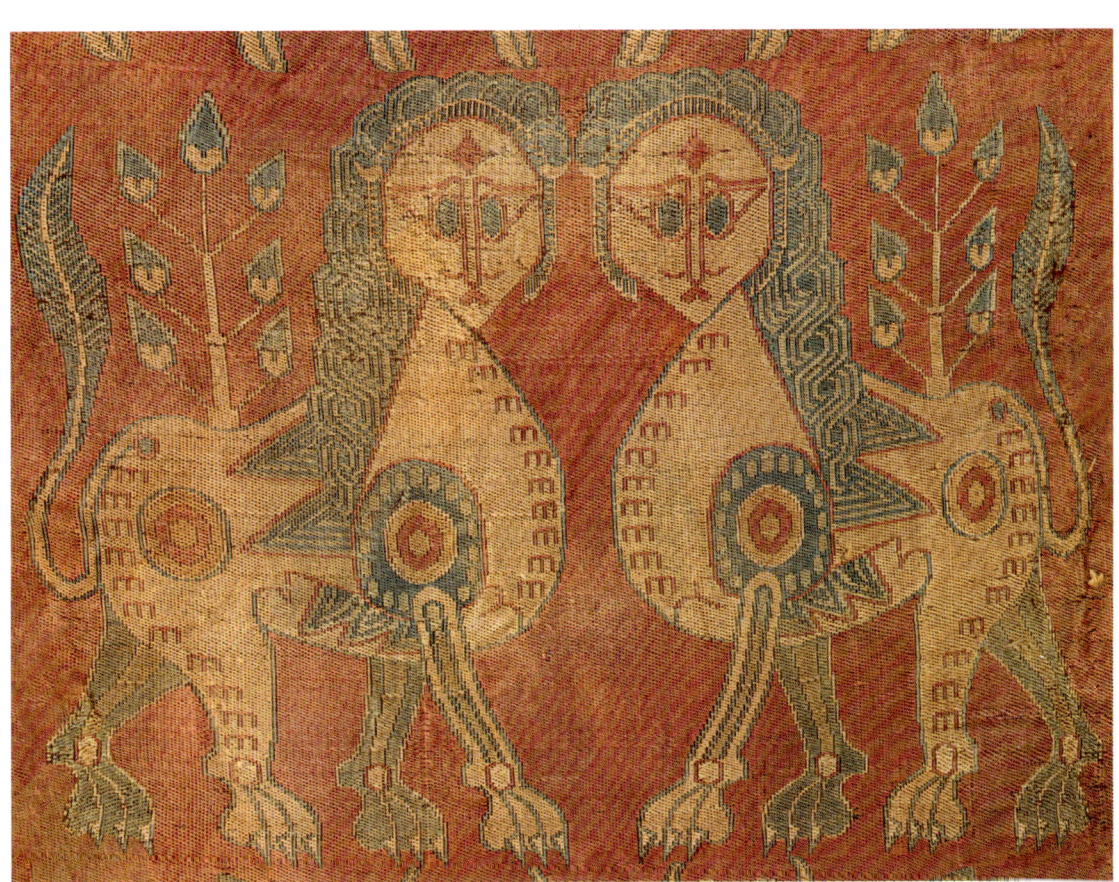

↓ ↓ **Ceremonial** *Devotion*
Pichwai, Gujarat, India, 19th century. This enigmatic temple cloth shows richly decorated cows with gilded horns looking up towards Lord Krishna, who is out of sight

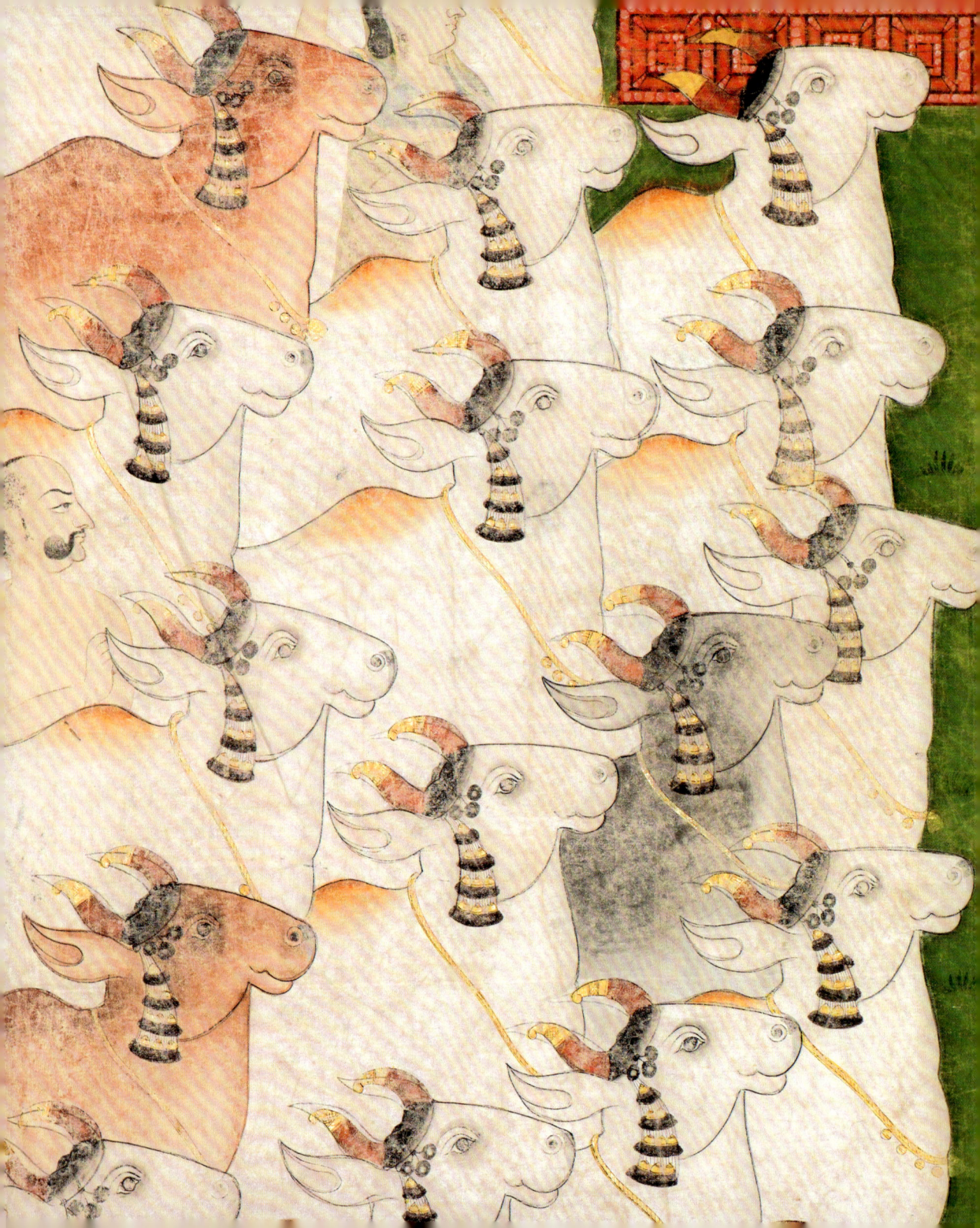

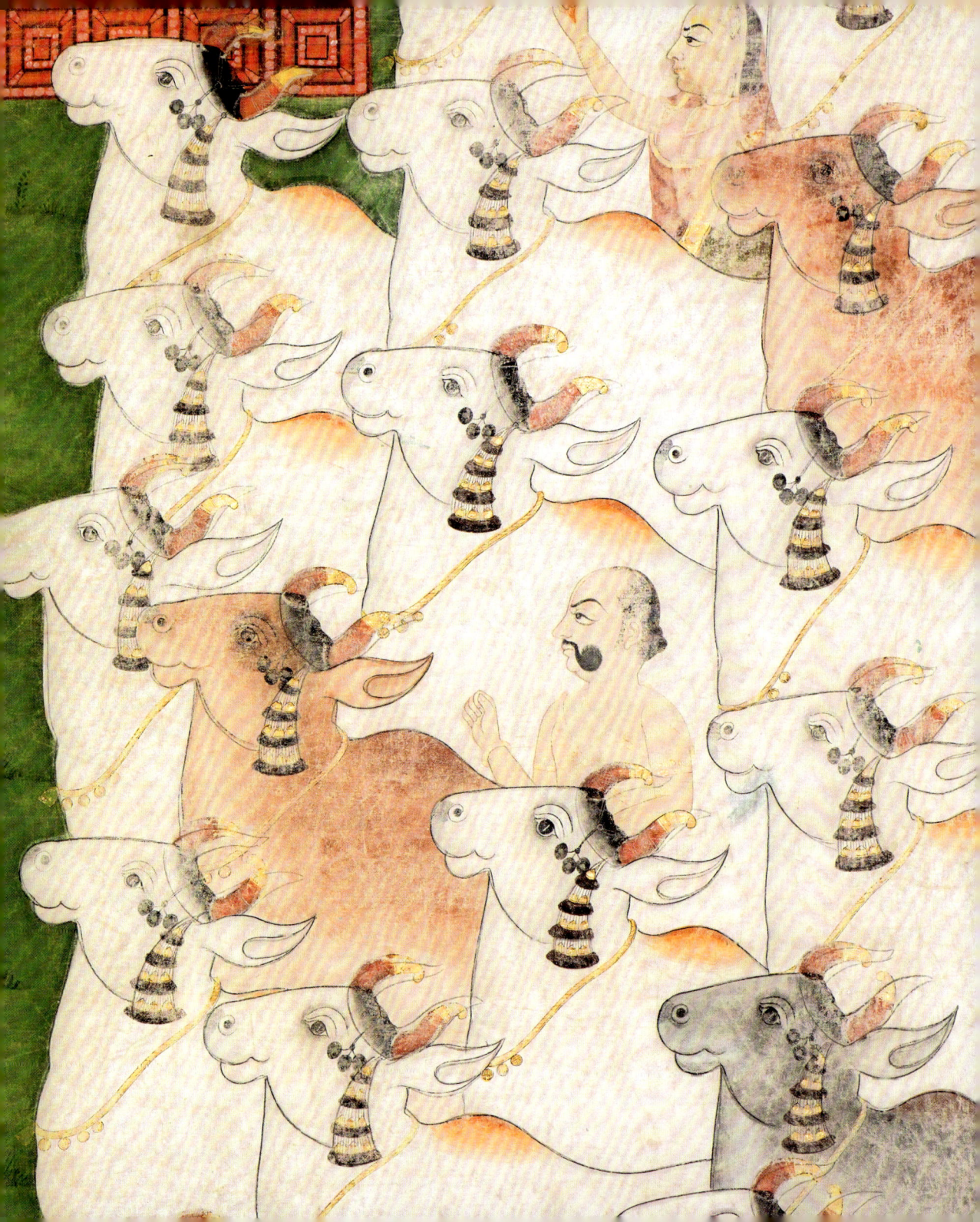

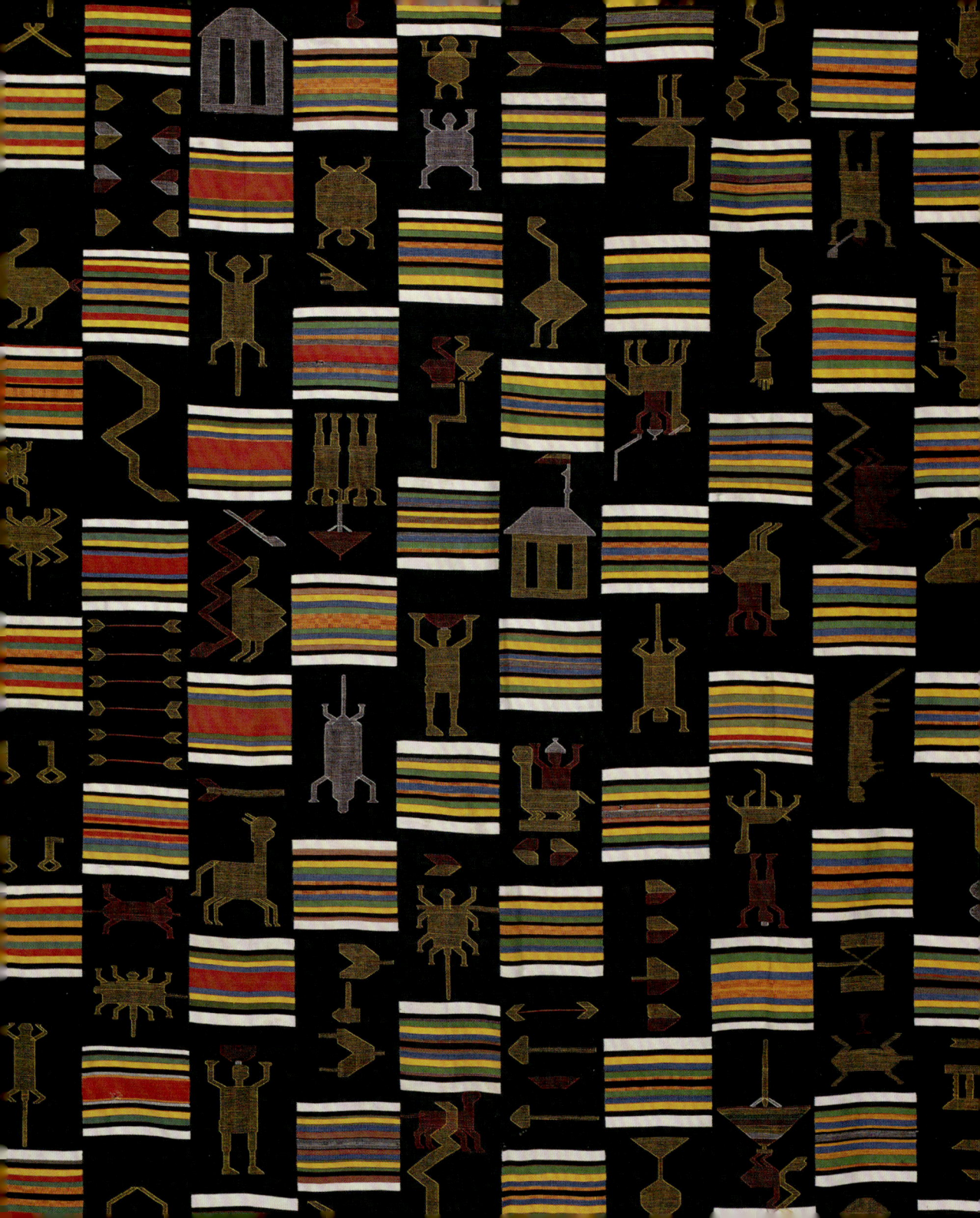

Patterns of Life

"Everyone sees the unseen in proportion to the clarity of his heart, and that depends upon how much he has polished it. Whoever has polished it more sees more — more unseen forms become manifest to him..."

← **Form** *Function*
Man's cloth, Ewe people, Togo, late 19th century. The size and variety of the figures and other designs are unique and the work of a master weaver

↑ Rumi, as quoted in *The Sufi Path of Love: The Spiritual Teachings of Rumi*, William C. Chittick (1983), p. 162

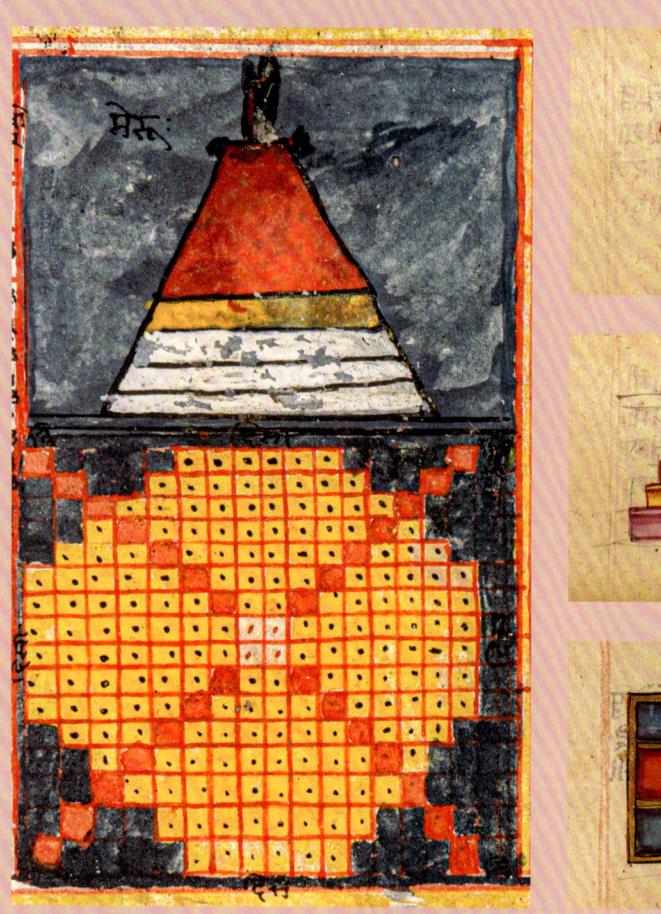

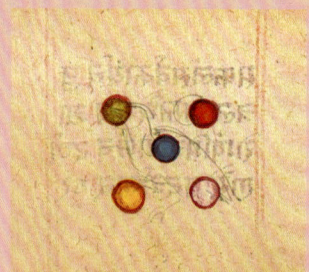

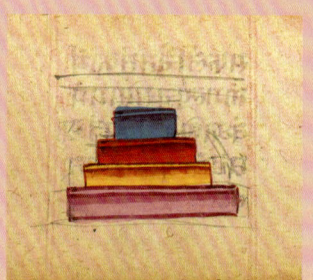

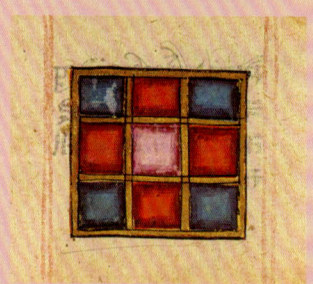

↑ **Illustration**
Paintings from Indian
manuscripts, 19th century

Through pattern and colour, textiles express something beyond their practical purpose. One can begin to view chintz, for example, not solely as a product of decorative ambition, but as artefacts to be read and interpreted. Beverly Lemire and Giorgio Riello take this approach towards 18th-century chintz, deeming it a form of print culture that had wide influence within and beyond India.

The form and function of a textile can define its design, as can the manner in which it is made. The movement of the loom and intersection of warp and weft can interlace colours in simple and subtle contrasts and transport modular patterns into modernist masterpieces. Through weaving, embroidery or even dye processes, textile artists place motifs within their work that can reflect both personal and cultural significance. Not only can textiles suggest meaning, but on a basic level they celebrate the enjoyment of creation and self-expression.

The way in which the minimal and geometric translate across time and traditions helps to make textiles seem simultaneously ancient and modern. The deep indigo-dyed cottons of Japan and Africa are firmly rooted in local traditions, yet seem to have a reflection in our obsession with blue denim, showing that there is nothing new in this world of textiles.

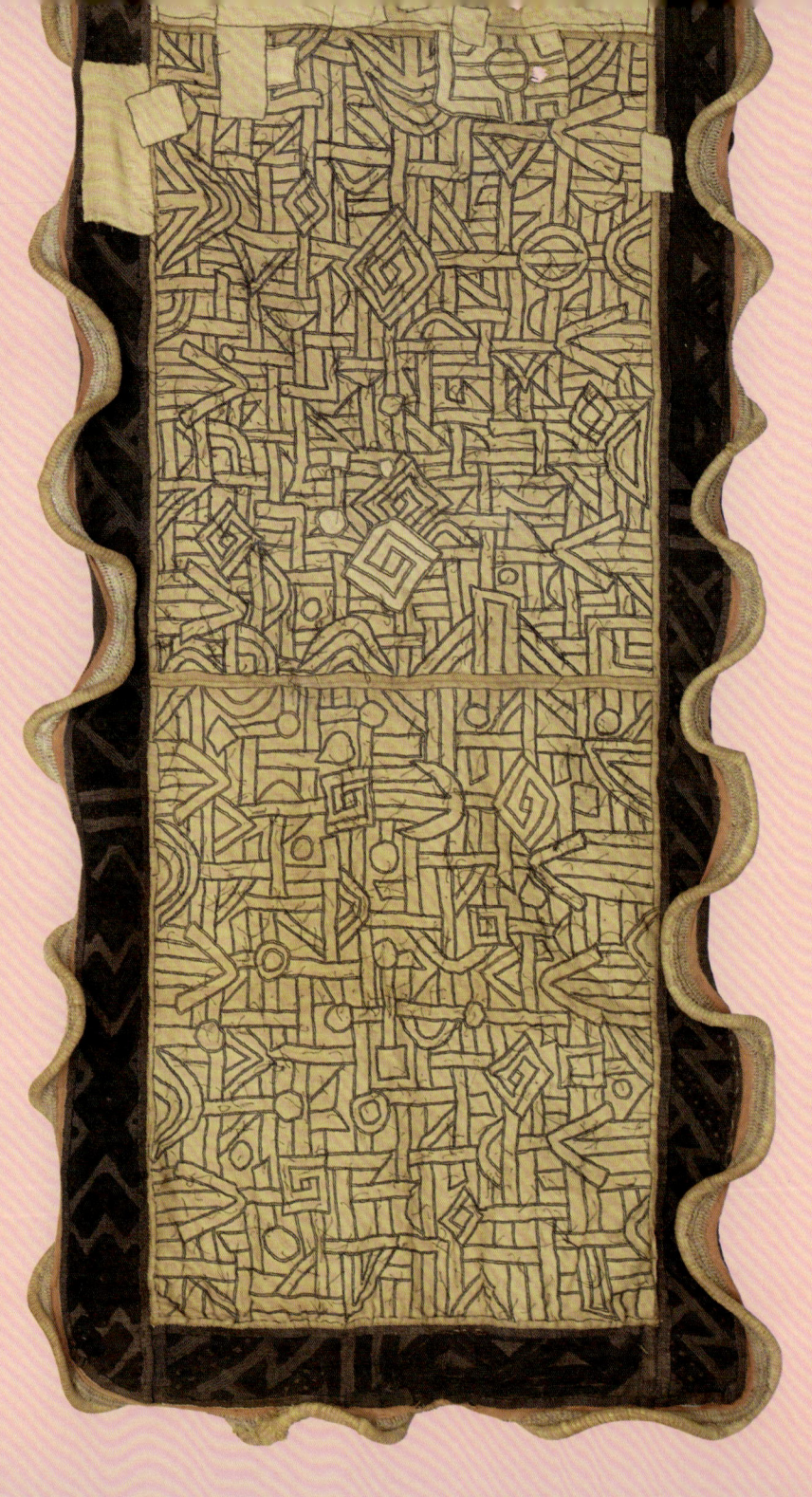

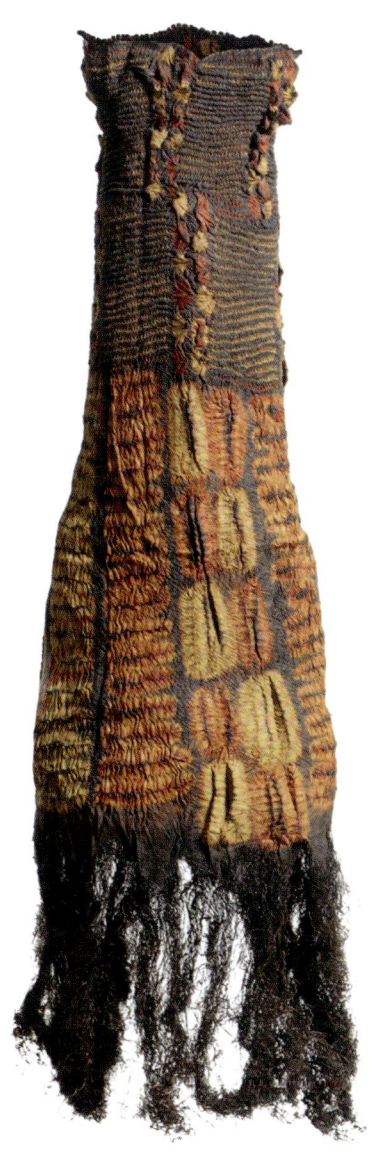

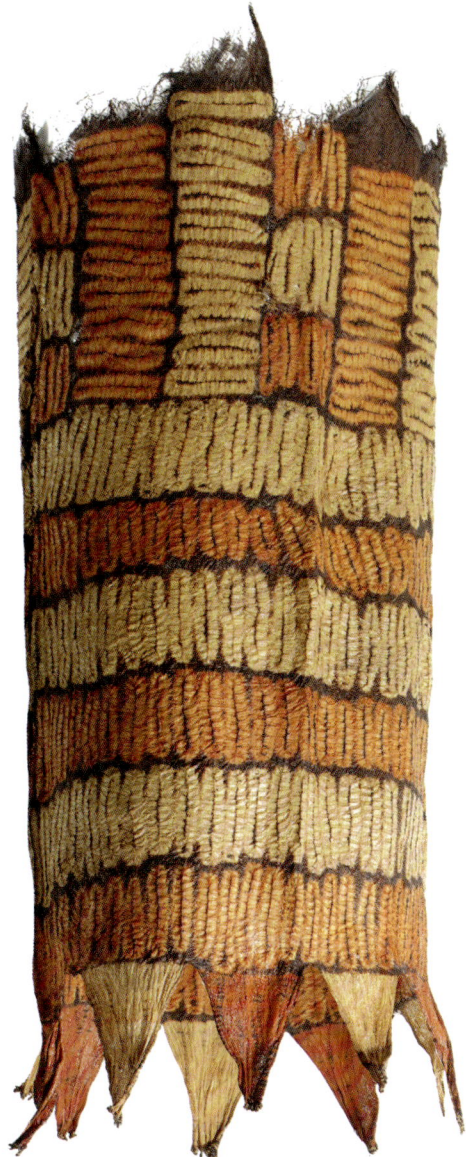

←**Form** *Function*
Raffia skirt, Central African Republic, 20th century. This long
and abstract design skirt is wrapped around the body several
times when worn

↑ **Form** *Function*
Raffia skirts, Dida, Ivory Coast, 20th century. These tube-
shaped skirts are tie-dyed and then opened up, with the natural
elasticity of the grass fibre acting like a modern stretch fabric

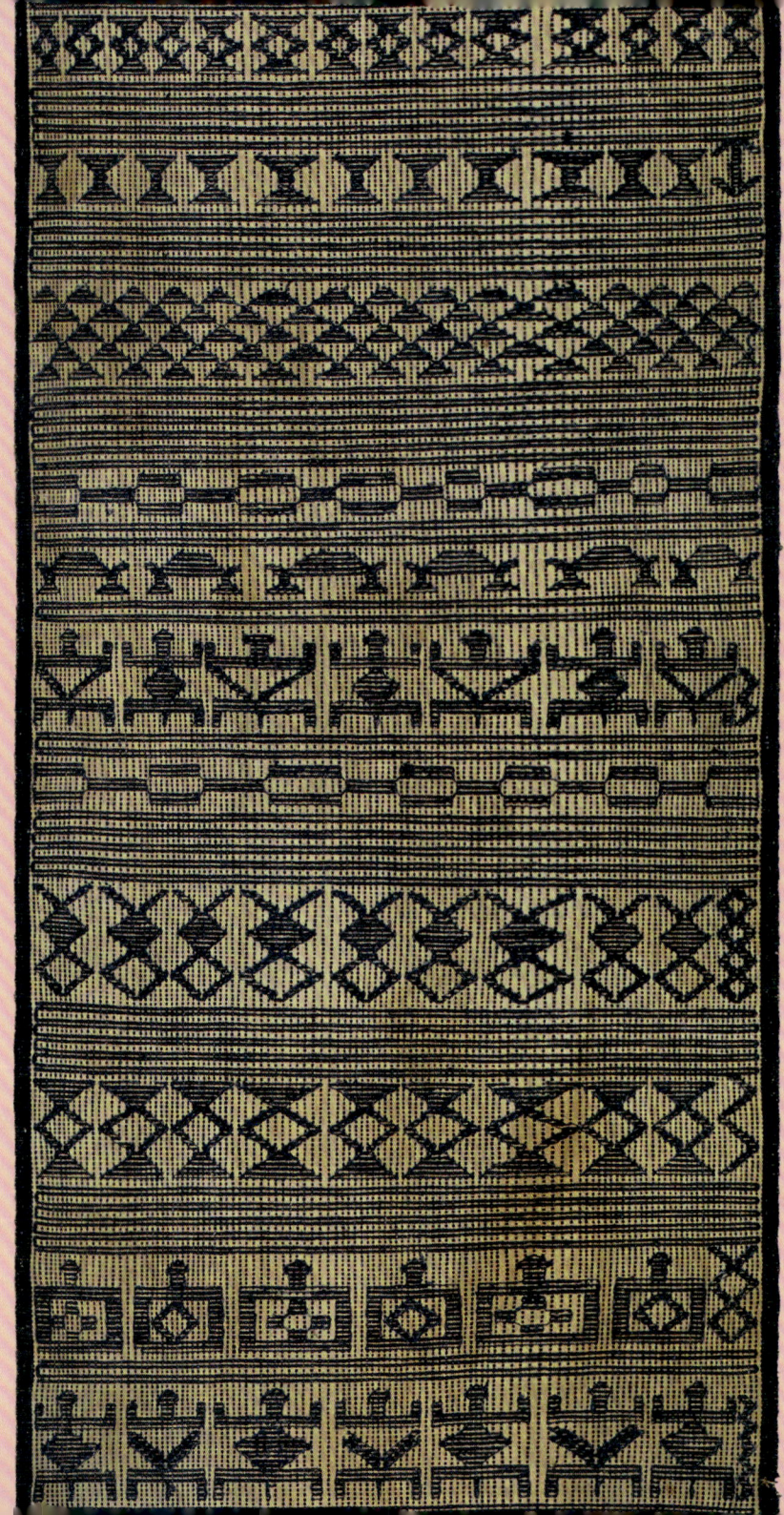

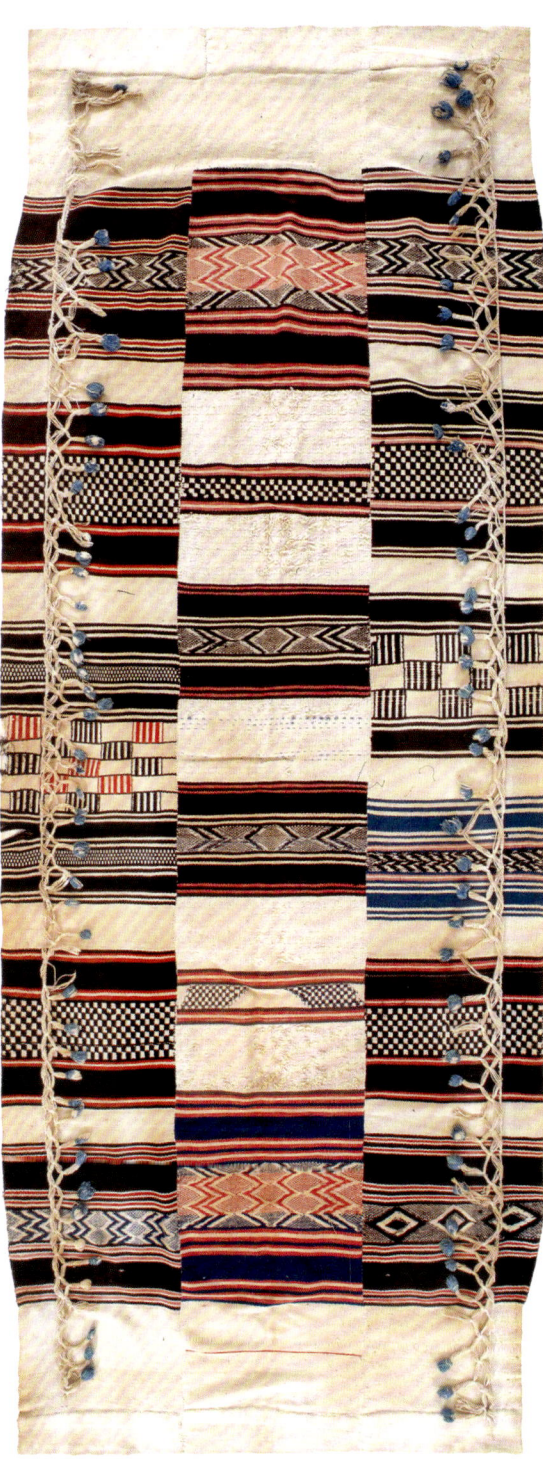

← **Form** *Function*
Baby-carrying cloth, Nigeria, early 20th century. A mother would wind this unique cloth around herself and secure it in the front – a timeless baby carrier

→ **Form** *Function*
Hammock, Sierra Leone, 19th century. Made from locally grown cotton, this hammock would have been used to carry a chief. The bearers would have also carried a canopy to shelter their leader from the sun

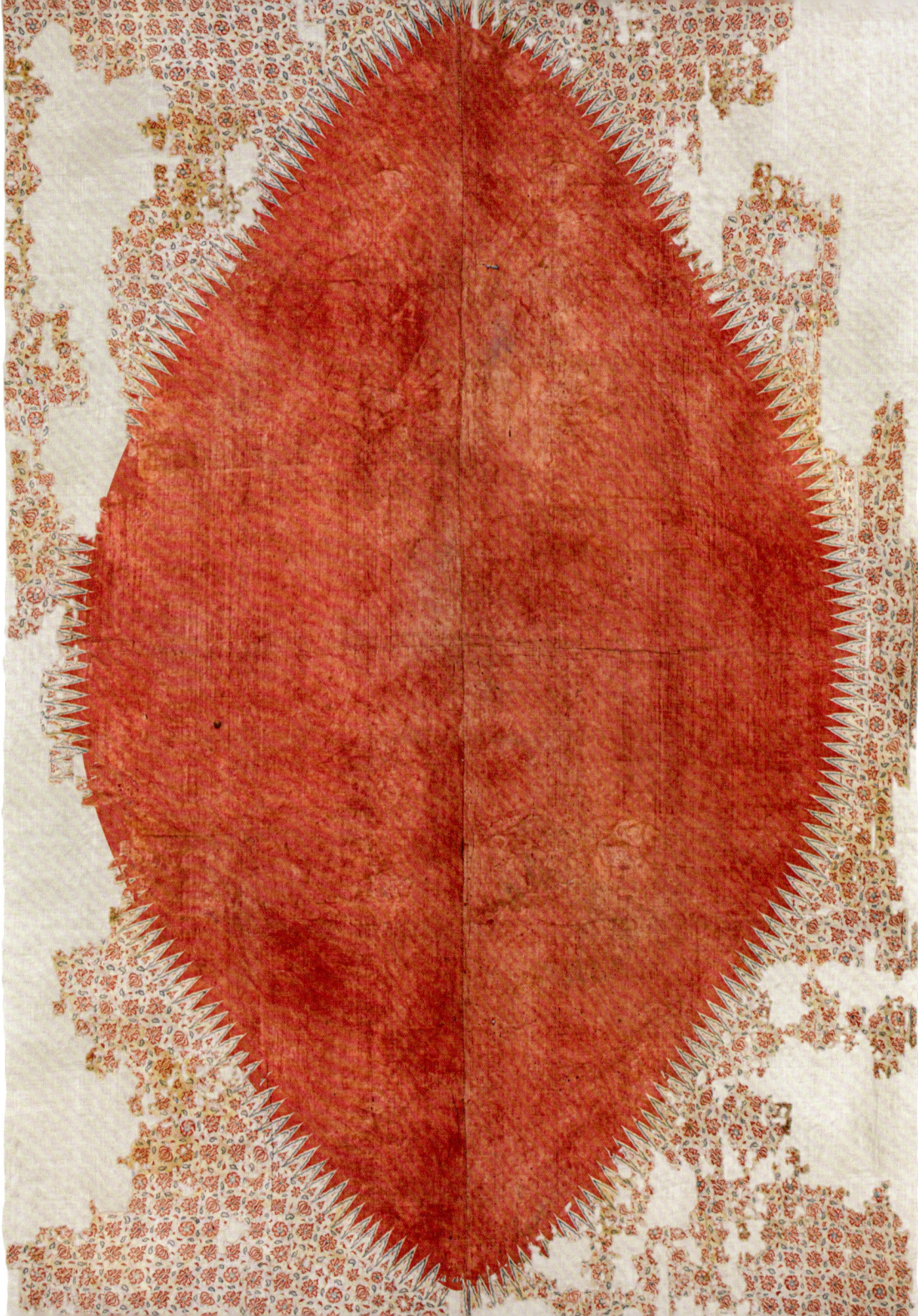

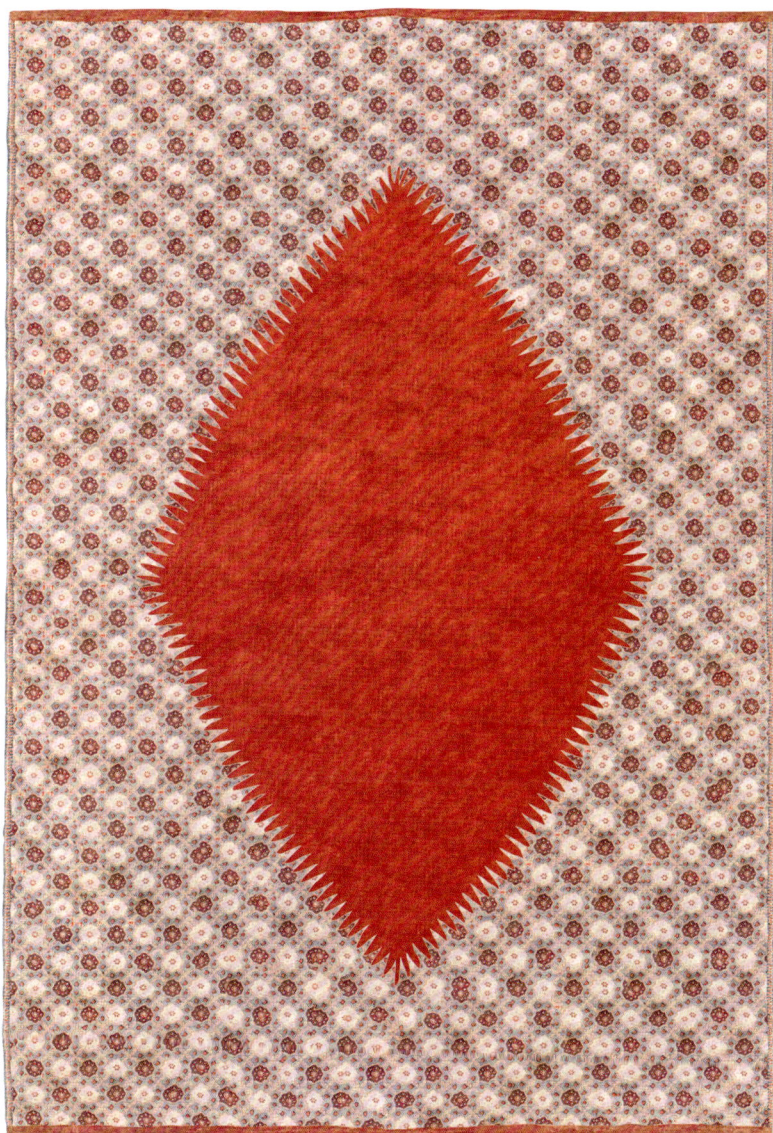

← **Form** *Function*
Ma'a or ceremonial textile, India, early 1700s. Made in India for
sale to Indonesia, this very large textile was found in Java. The
local name, ma'a, means sacred heirloom textile. These clothes
were preserved for generations in long houses

↖ **Form** *Function*
Ma'a or ceremonial textile, India, 18th century. The age of
these textiles was only discovered through carbon-14 dating
techniques in the last 30 years. Some of these Indian trade
textiles date from as far back as the 14th century

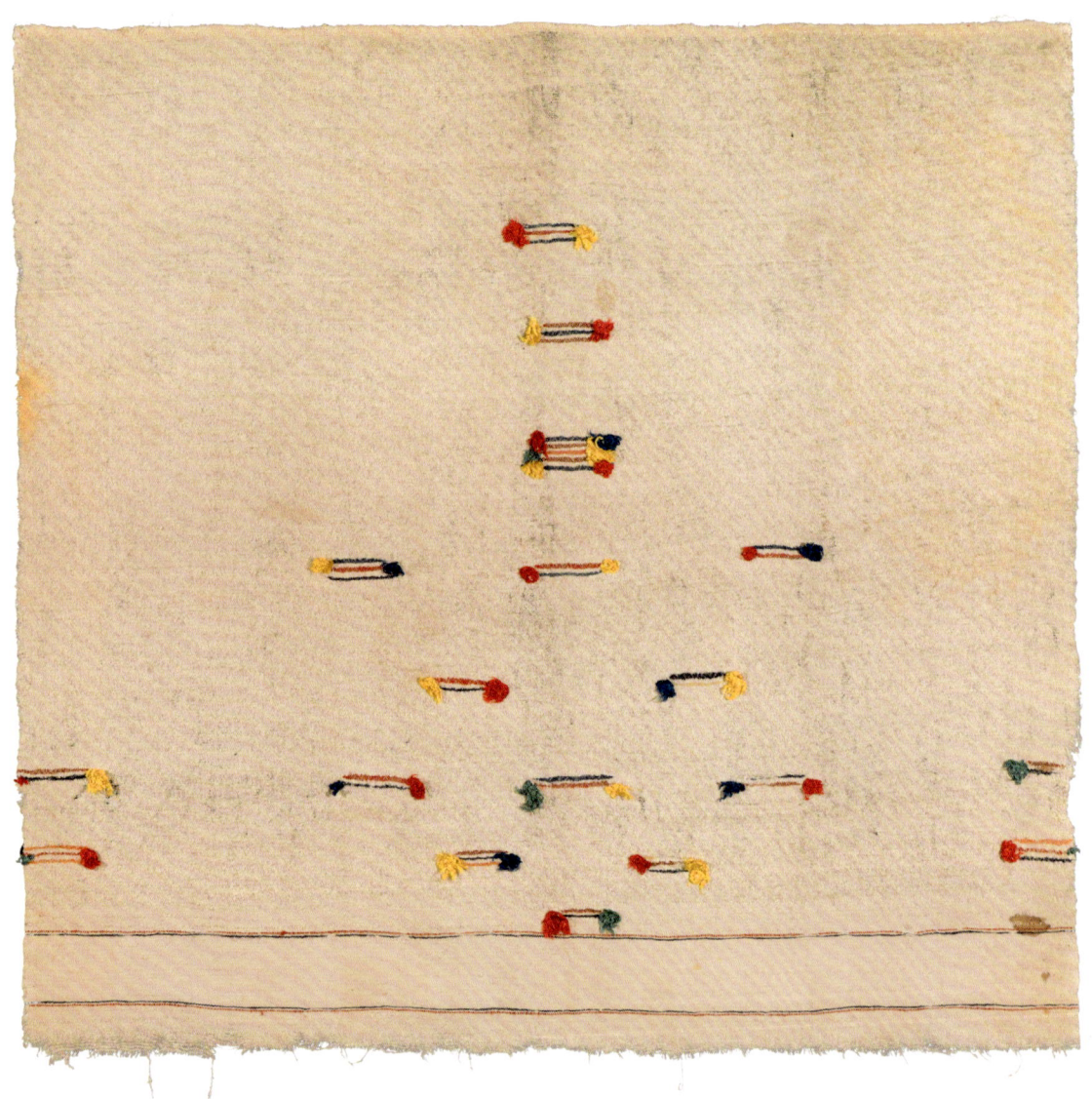

↑ **Form** *Function*
Head covering, High Atlas, Morocco, 19th century. The location
of the red, yellow and green silk motifs was carefully chosen.
These pops of colour would be clearly visible when the textile
was draped over the head and shoulders of the wearer

→ **Form** *Function*
Mantle, Tunisia, circa 1900. The embroidered corner
decoration and tie-dyed band would have been on show when
its owner donned this mantle on high days and holidays

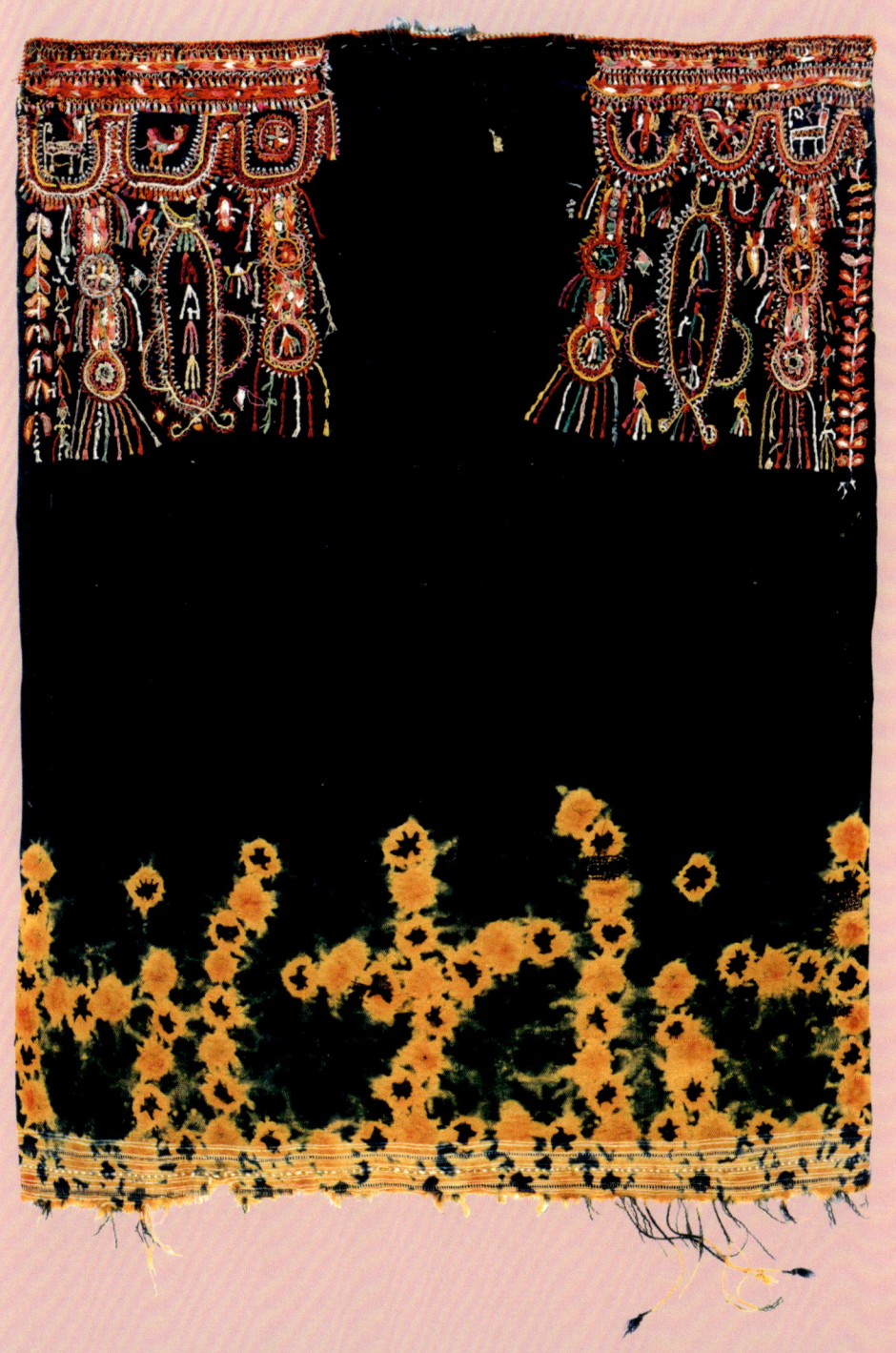

"The response to color... is emotional; thus there is no guarantee that what is produced in an intellectual manner will be pleasing to the emotions. Man responds to form with his intellect and to color with his emotions; he can be said to survive by form and to live by color."

← **Form** *Function*
Ewe kente cloth, Ghana, early 20th century. Only a few examples of such high-quality cloths as this were made. Among the animals and abstract motifs created by the weaver with supplementary wefts is a depiction of two figures stretching warp threads – textile making within a textile

↓ **Form** *Structure*
Boro, Japan, 20th century. This futon cover was made by the poorest members of the agricultural communities in north Japan to provide warmth. The material is indigo-dyed cotton rags bought from itinerant dealers or gathered locally

→ **Form** *Structure*
Ewe kente cloth, Ghana, 19th century. Seven narrow strips with eleven different patterns were woven separately by a master weaver and then joined together to construct this large prestige cloth intended for a male wearer

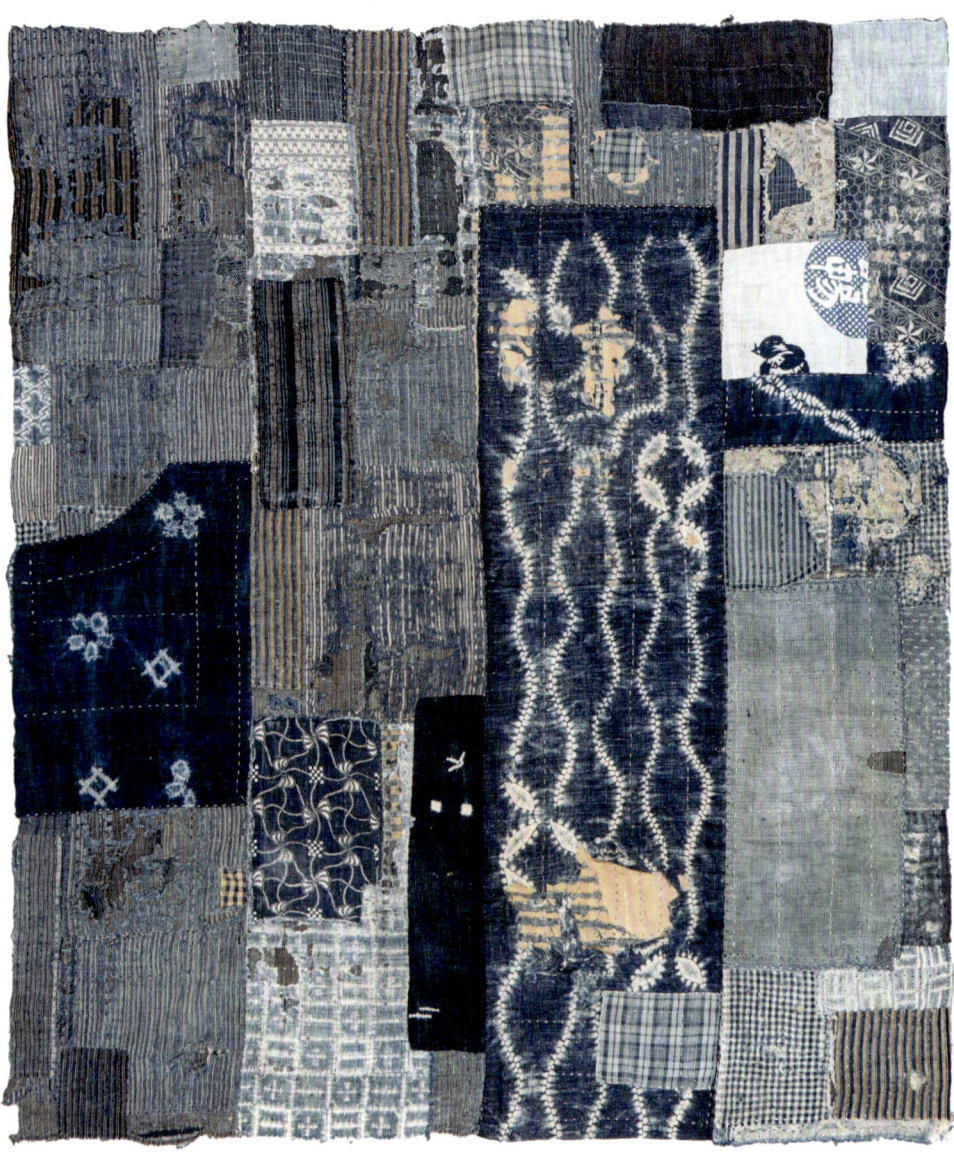

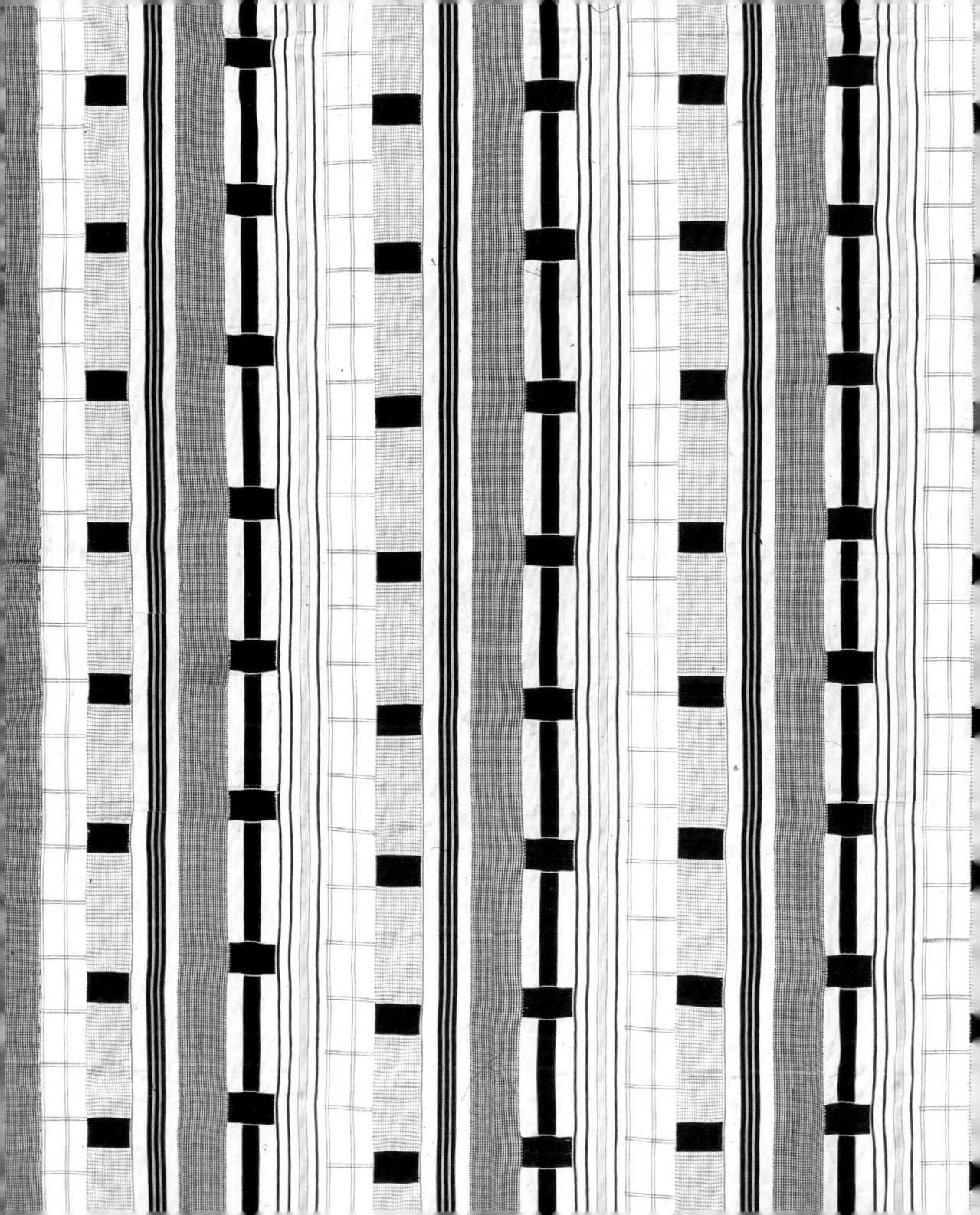

↓ **Form** *Structure*

Tekke Turkmen chyrpy, Central Asia, 19th century. Contrary to what we may initially think, this is a mantle worn over the head rather than a coat; the 'sleeves' are purely decorative. The colour and designs indicate that this garment was made for a woman of 60 years of age or over

→ **Form** *Structure*

Cloth, Ivory Coast, 19th century. This type of cloth is wrapped around the body like a toga. The central design falls in the front, while the white lines create an undulating rhythm. Rather than seeing this garment as a rectangle, we must try to picture it as it was intended to be seen: in three dimensions and in movement

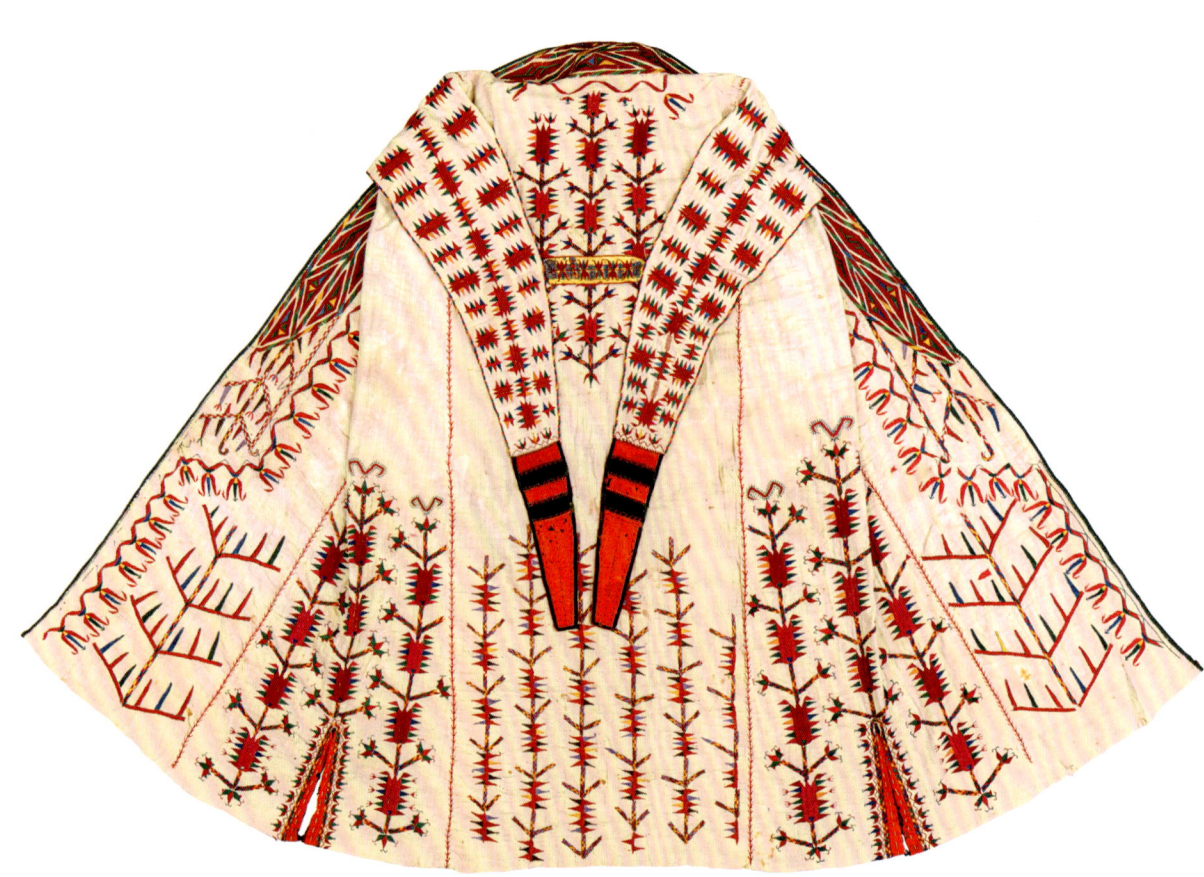

↓ ↓ **Form** *Structure*

Sampler, Turkey, early 19th century. Collected by the Embroiderers' Guild in the early 1900s for its variety of stitches and designs, this sampler has no obvious direction to it. With more than 130 different designs, it is a snapshot of the motifs and stitches in use in Ottoman Turkey at the start of the 19th century

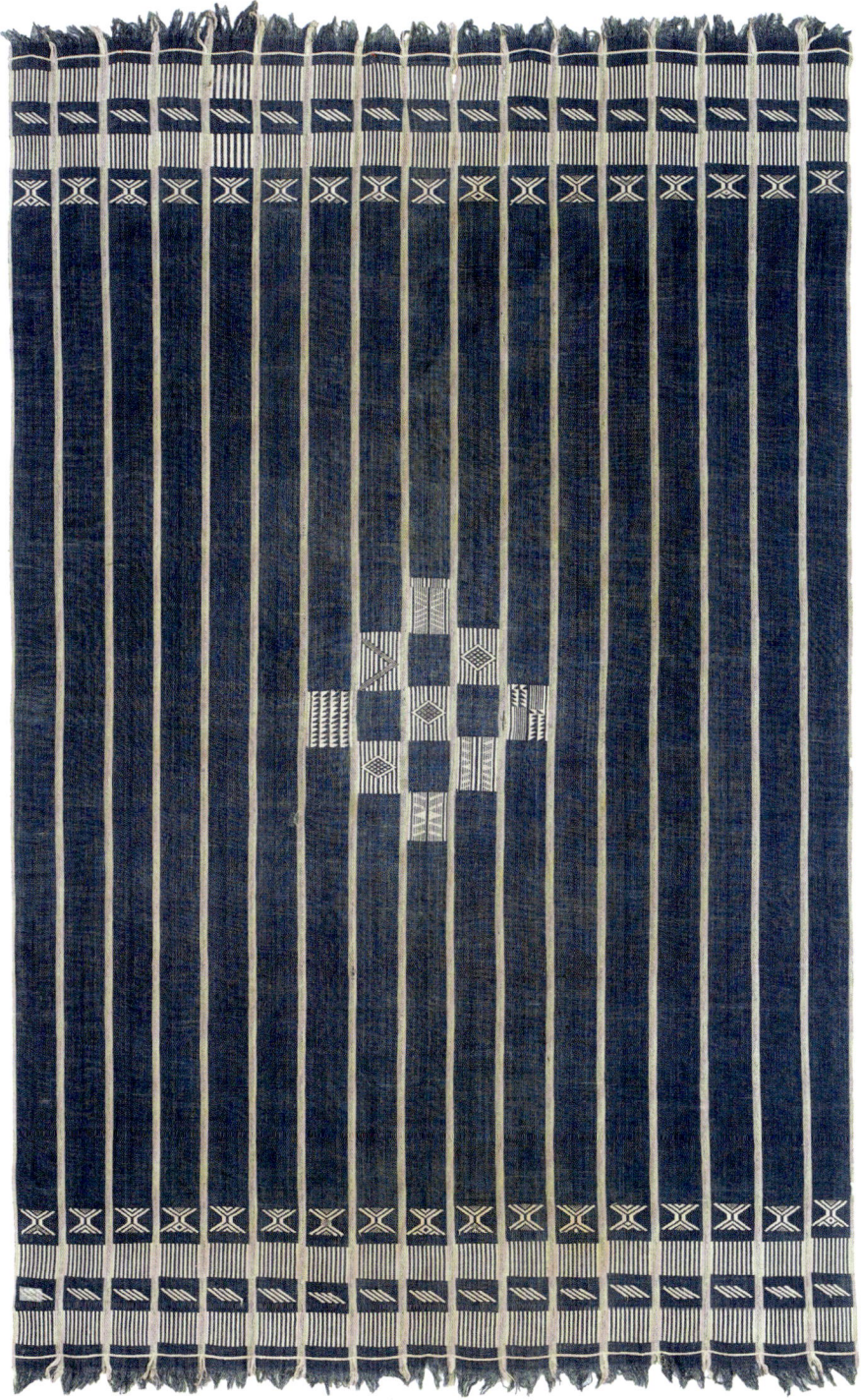

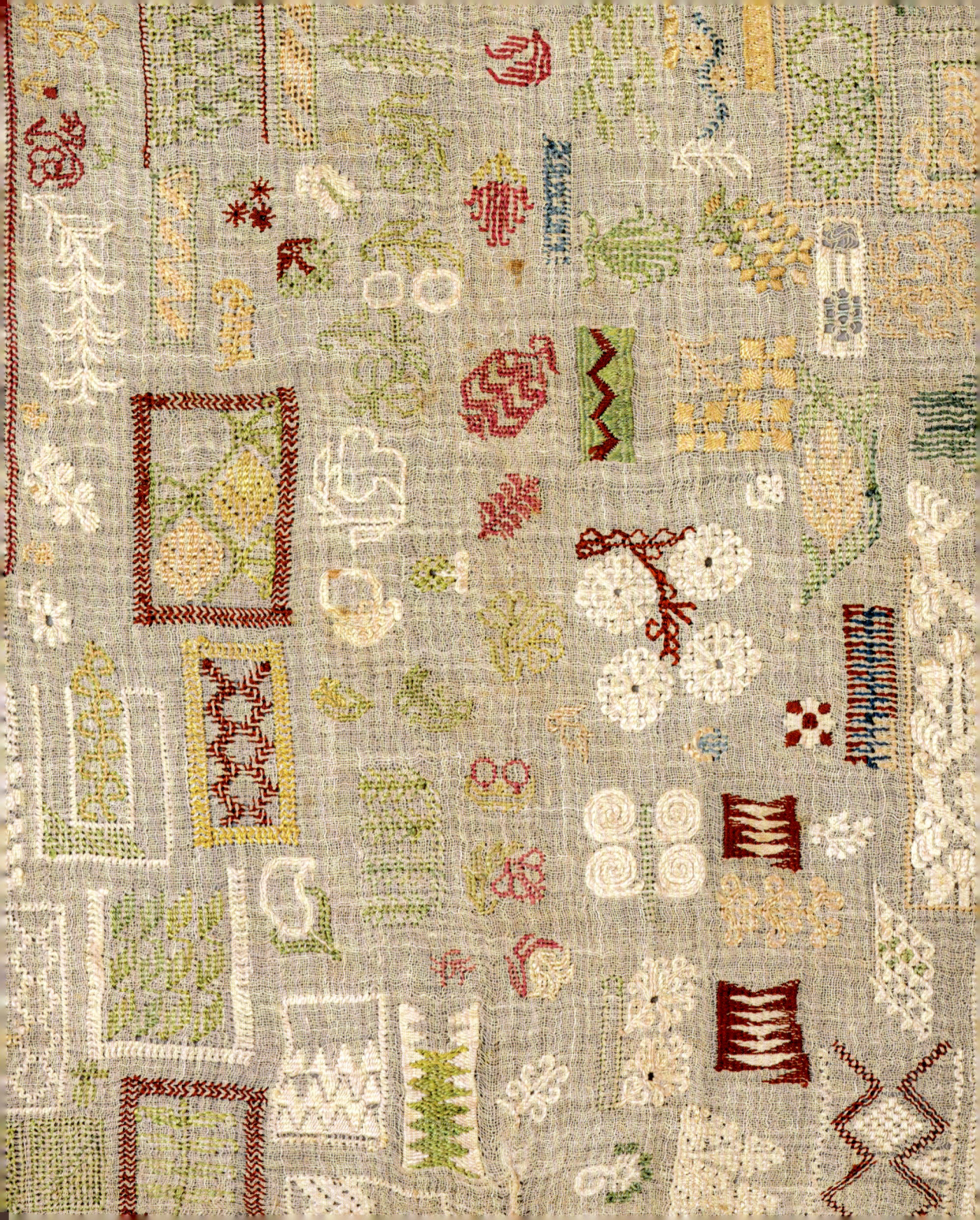

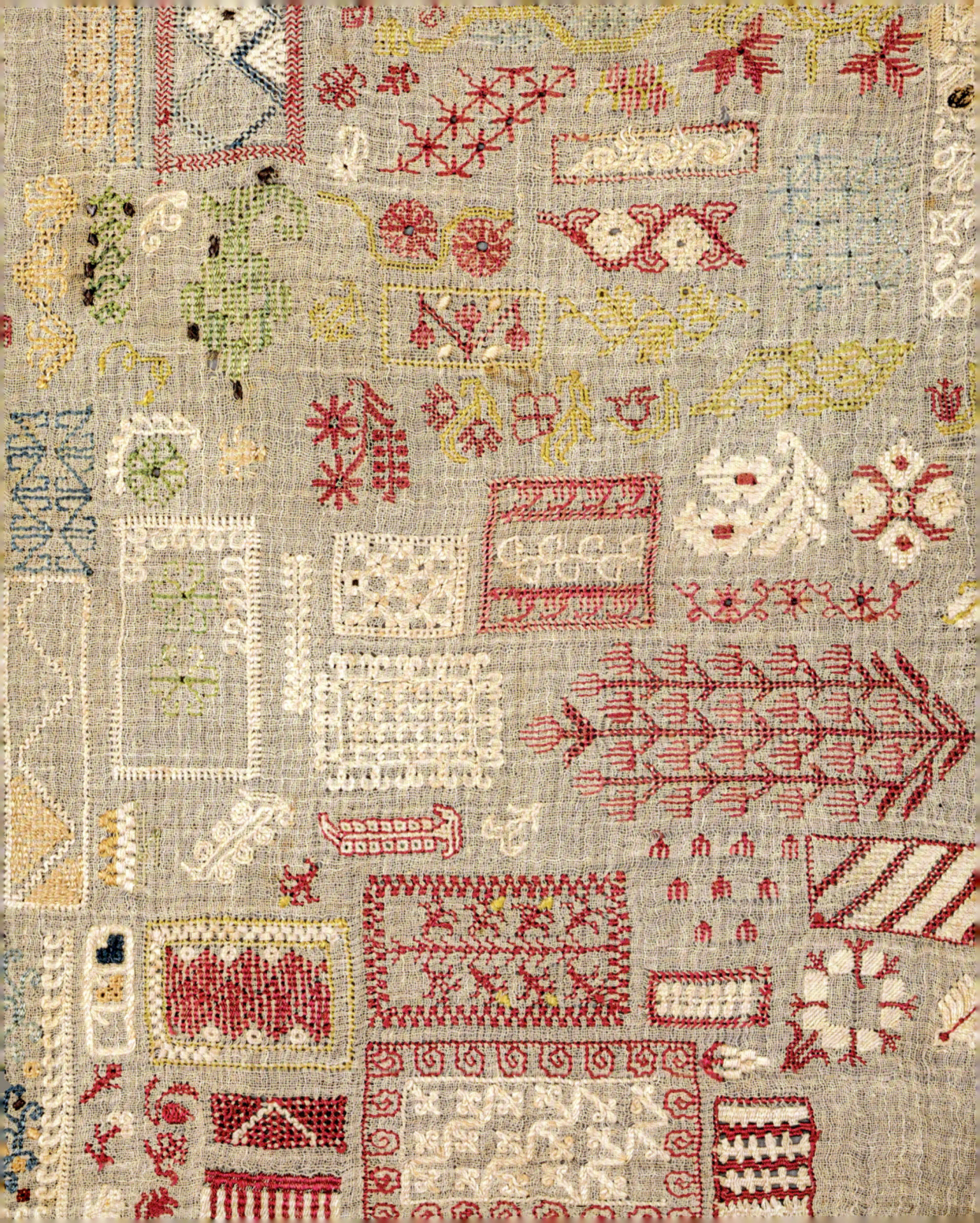

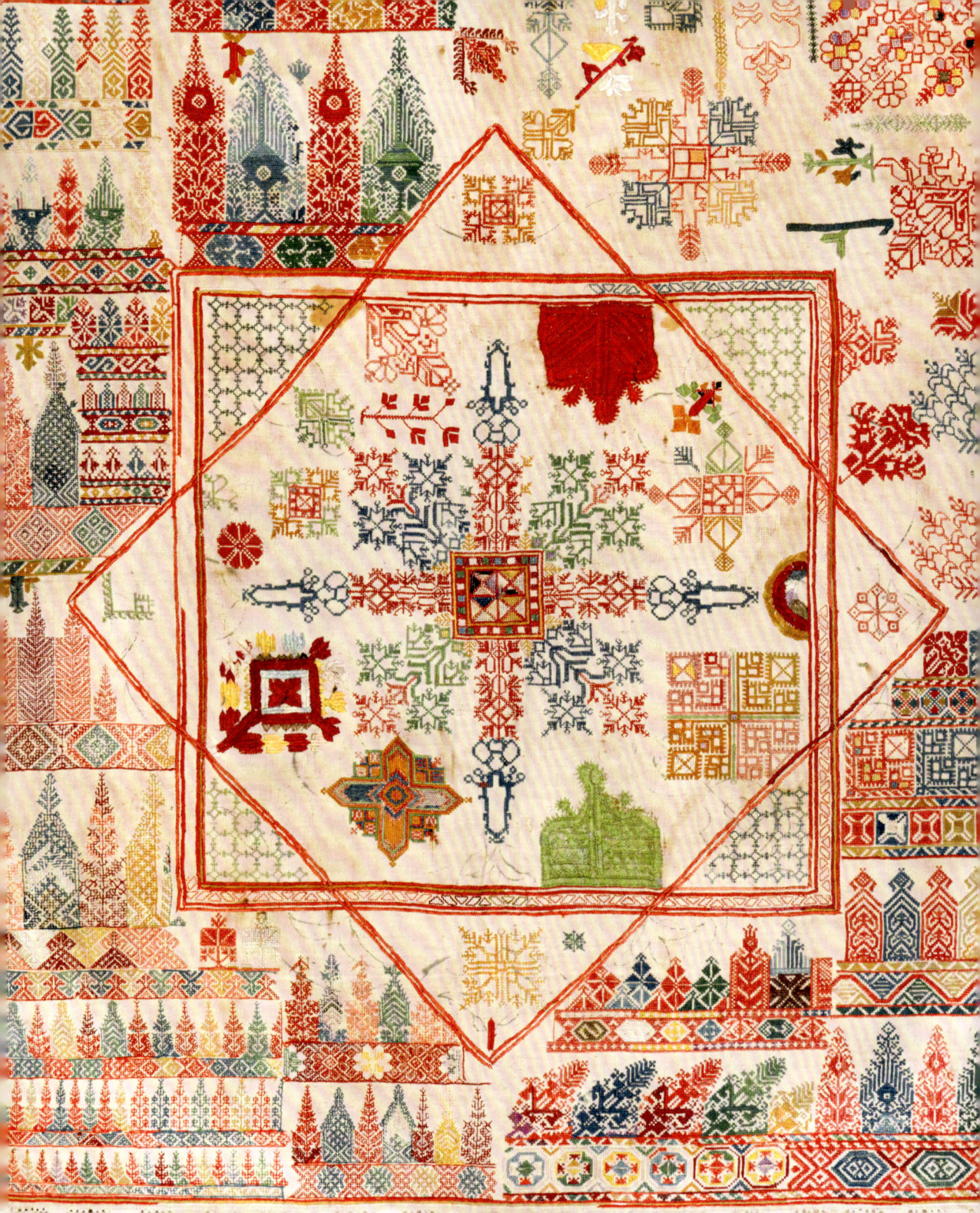

← **Form** *Geometry*

Sale sampler, Morocco, 18th century. This sampler shows not only the geometric designs used on embroideries in the period but has created them in a geometric composition to reinforce the form with an eight-pointed star at its centre

↓ **Form** *Geometry*

Fez seat cover, embroidery, Morocco, 19th century. This is a perfect representation of the symmetry achieved with embroidery. Many symbols from the sampler opposite are used but appear to be different because of the use of a single colour

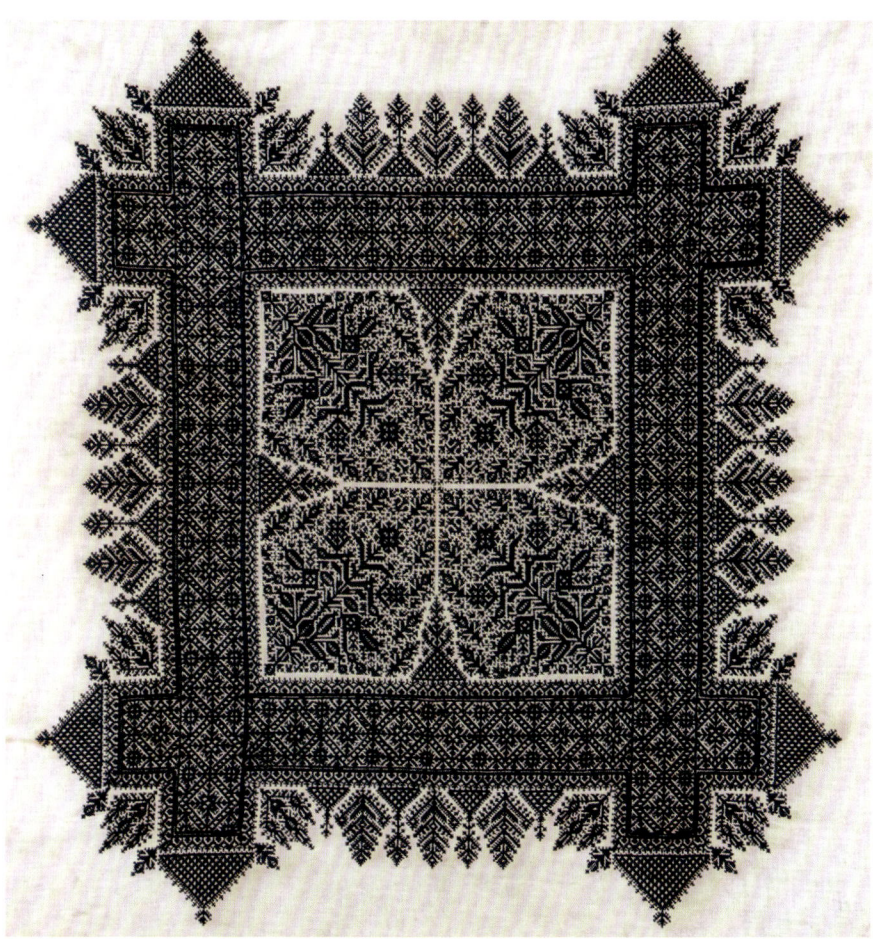

Geometric pattern finds its fullest expression in Islamic art. The almost mathematical approach to pattern building reflects not only a belief in the infinite nature of creation but also allows for representation of the interconnectedness of all things. This decoration based on circles, squares and triangles can be extended infinitely and is found in many media: from manuscript illumination to tilework on buildings through to textiles. Textiles are an ideal vehicle for this form of artistic expression since their very construction is usually based on a form of geometry, either through the combining of warp and weft or the application of individual embroidery stitches.

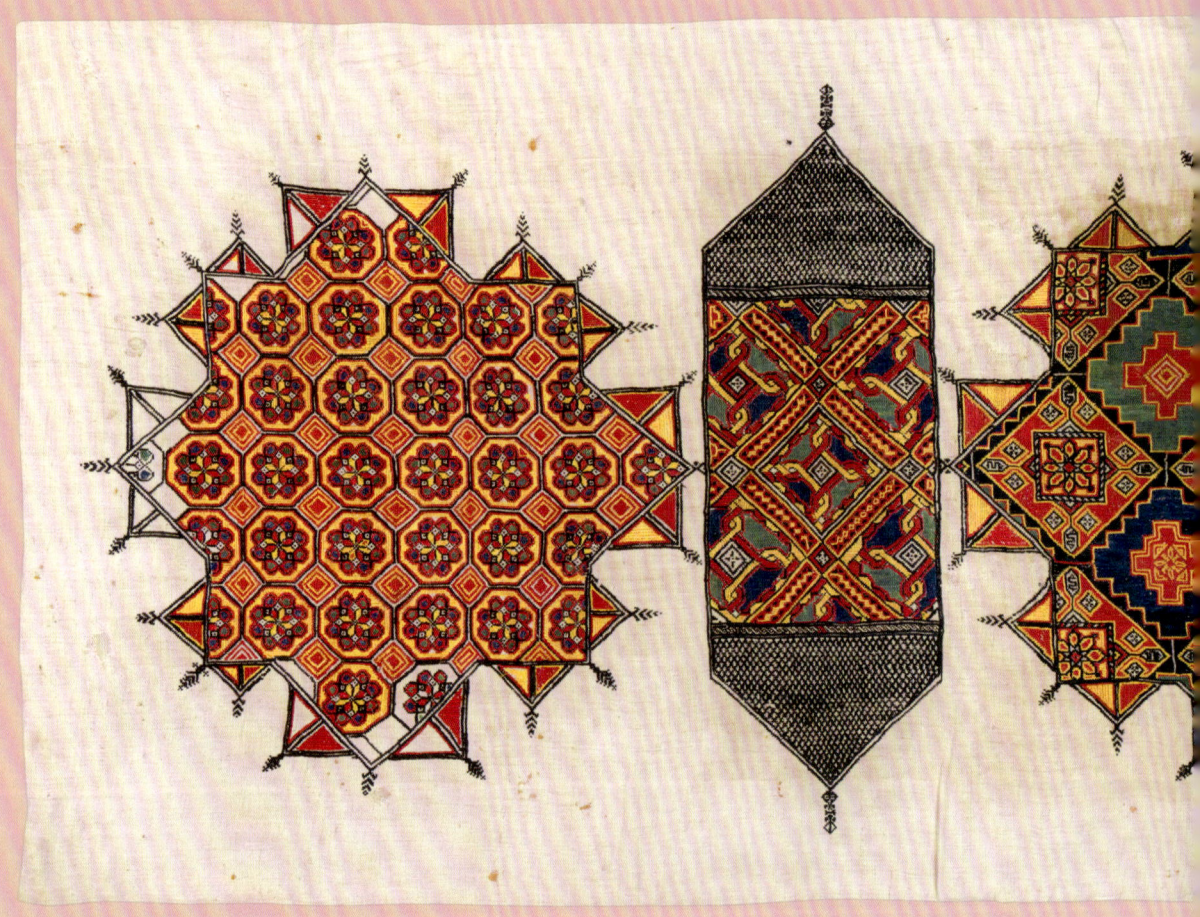

↑ **Form** *Geometry*
Chechaouen embroidery, Morocco, circa 1700. This fine silk
embroidery is called an arid, and is connected to medieval
Hispano-Moresque designs of Andalusia found on tilework
dating back to the 12th century. This textile art form is the
pinnacle of urban needlework traditions in Morocco. Arids were
originally used as hangings in the home

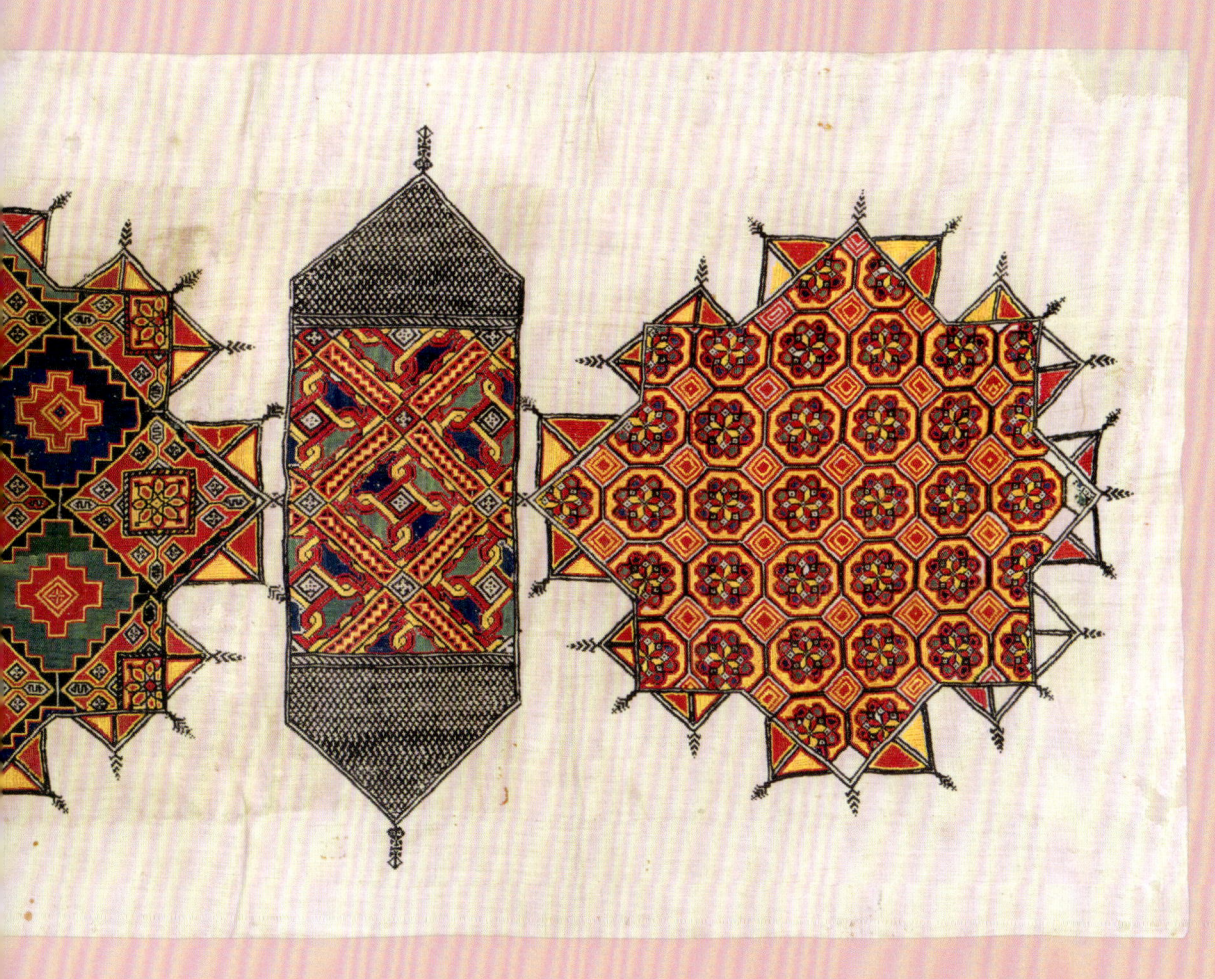

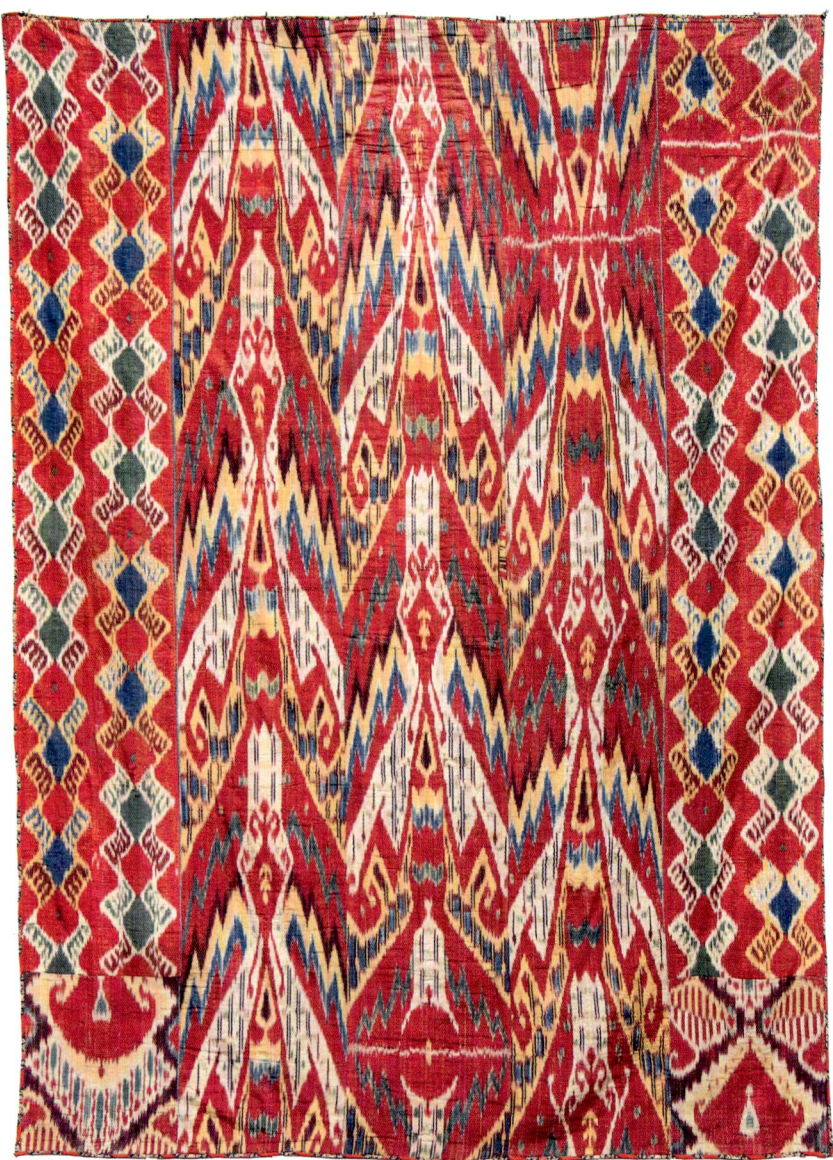

↑ **Colour** *Maximalism*
Ikat panel, Uzbekistan, 19th century. Three different designs
were used to make this panel; matching the pattern was not a
cultural or visual requirement

→ **Colour** *Maximalism*
Ikat panel, Uzbekistan, 19th century. The threads are dyed
before weaving, and here five colours are used to create a
virtuoso expressionist composition

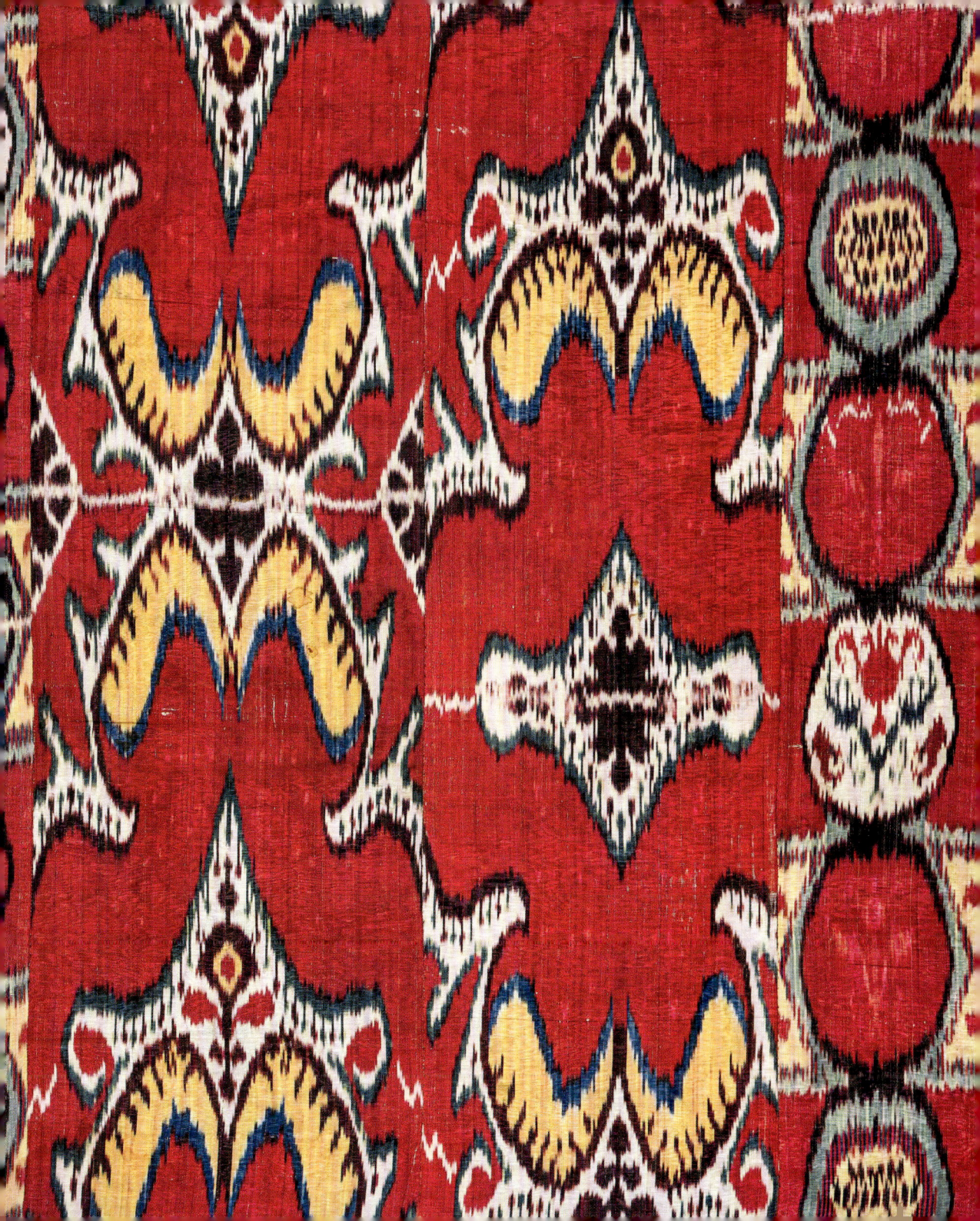

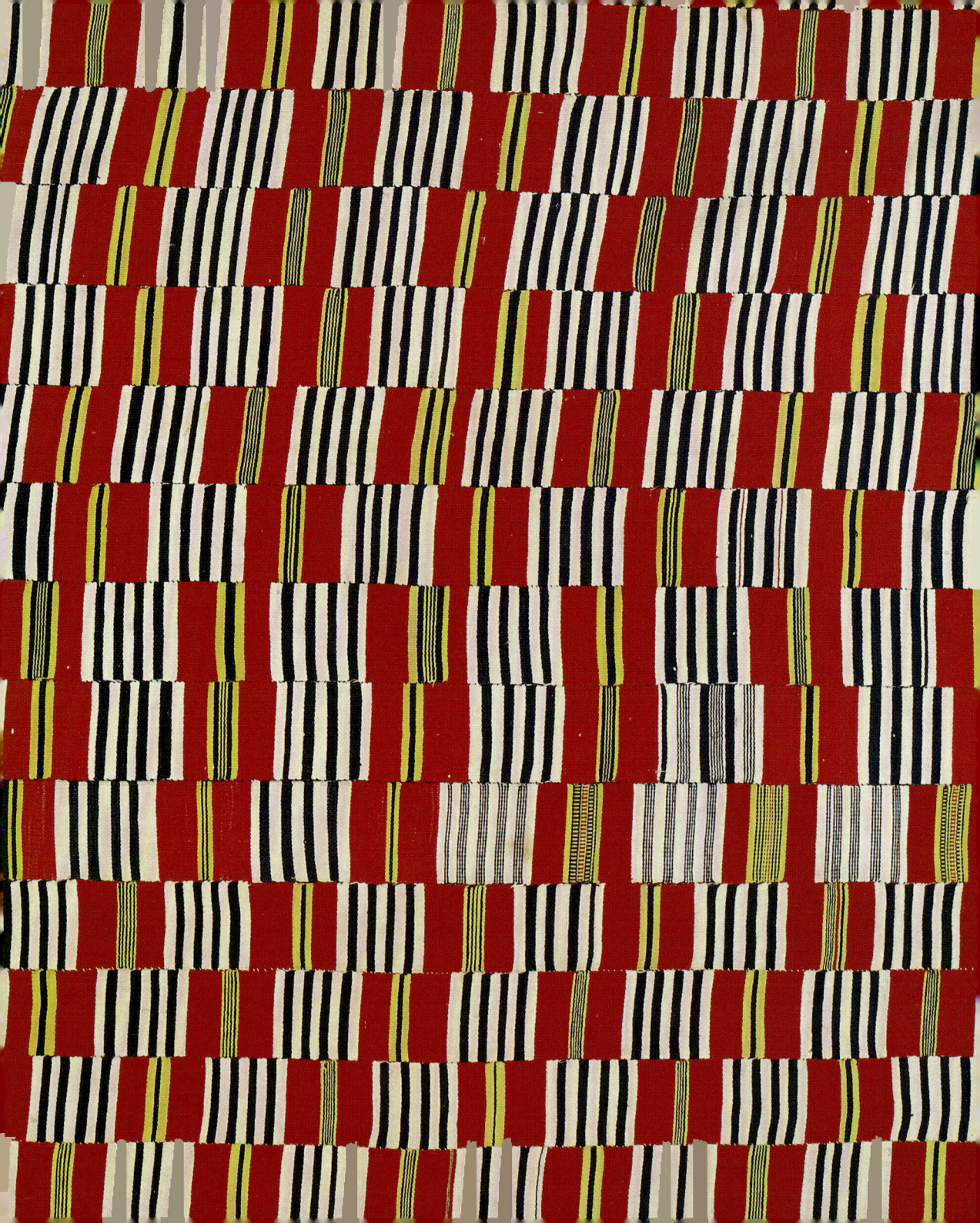

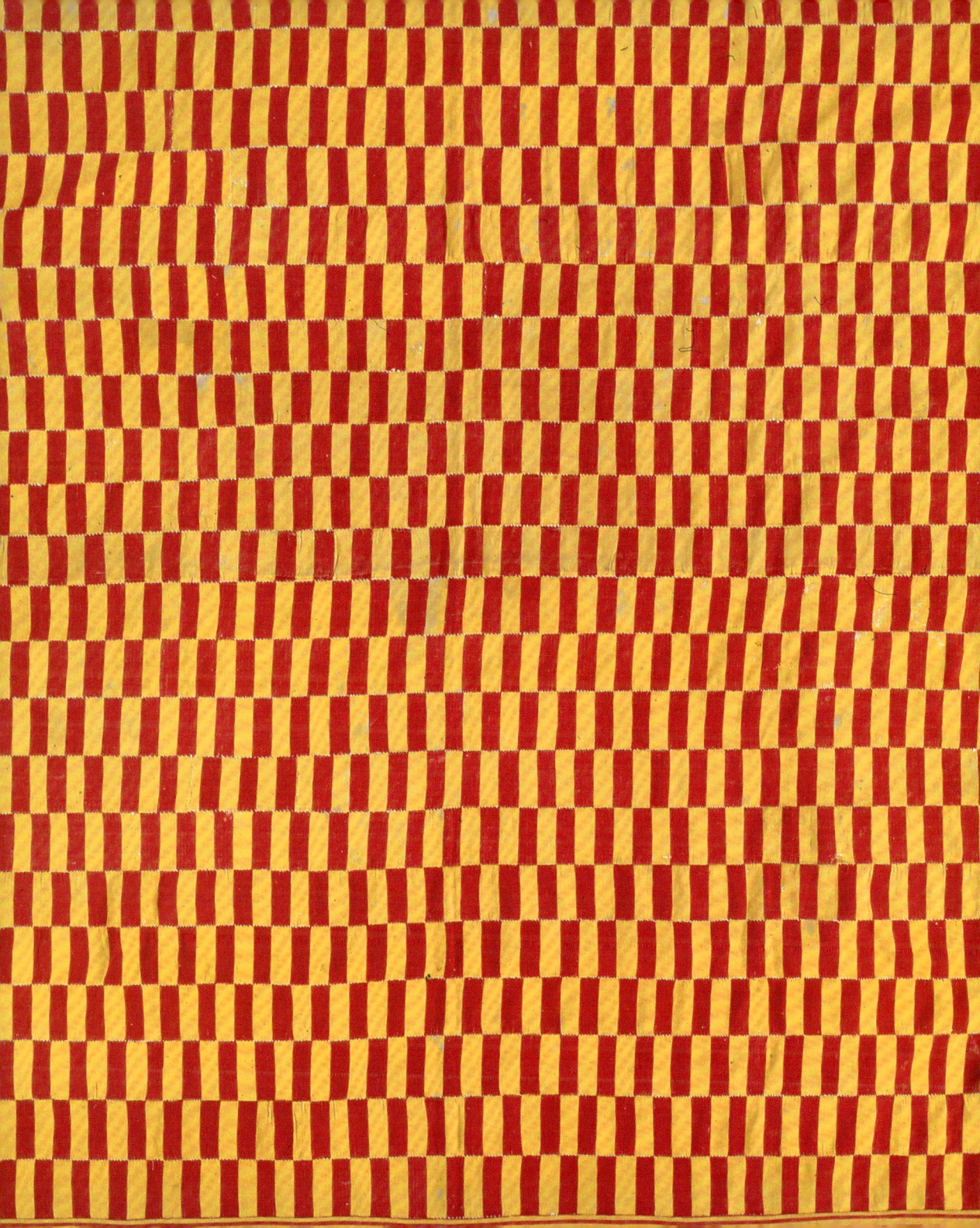

Ewe cloth, Ghana, early 20th century. This is a simple weave employing a limited palette, but the slight misalignment of the constituent woven strips completely changes the composition

Ewe cloth, east Ghana, circa 1900. Typically these wrapping cloths were woven in red and white. Here the yellow and red create a vibrant grid

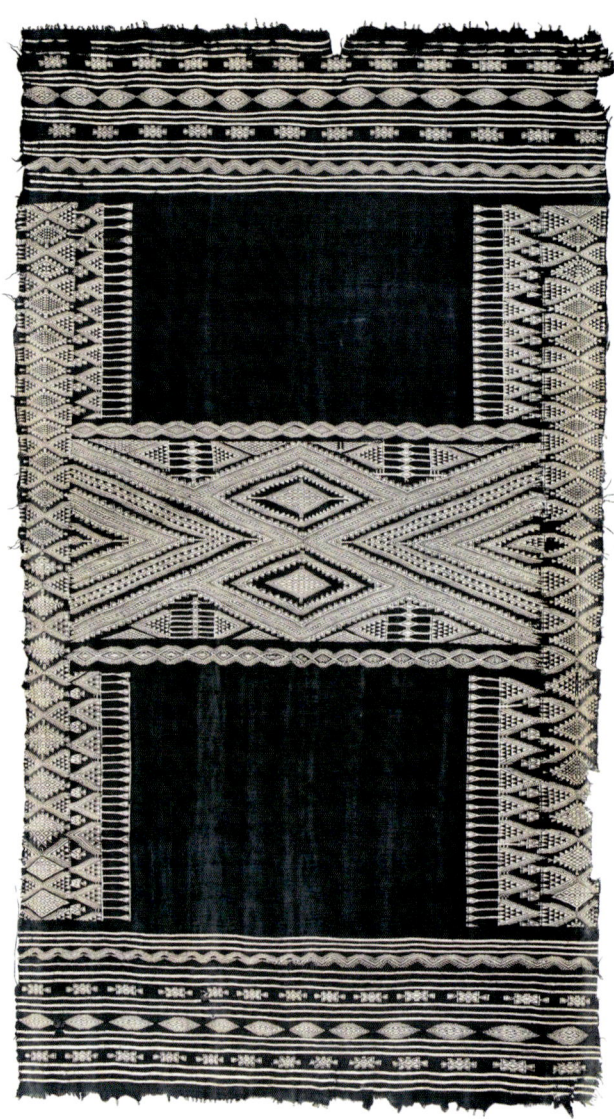

↑ **Colour** *Monochrome*
Bakhnug wedding shawl, Tunisia, 19th century. White cotton and midnight-blue wool make up this cloth. Indigo is a preservative for wool but does not easily adhere to cotton

→ **Colour** *Monochrome*
Pashai jacket, Afghanistan, 20th century. Much can be achieved with only two tones, as demonstrated by the fine black cotton embroidery on this jacket

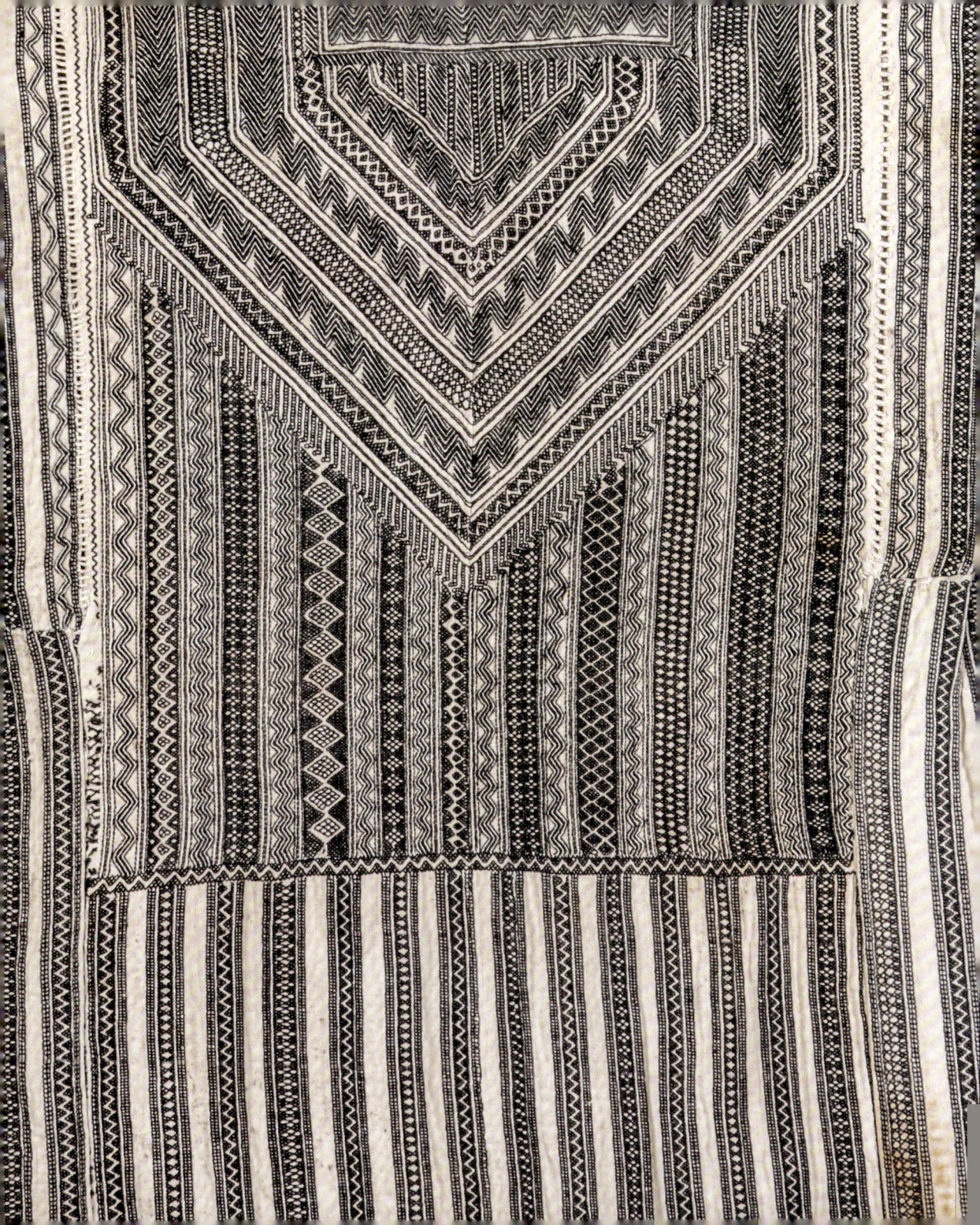

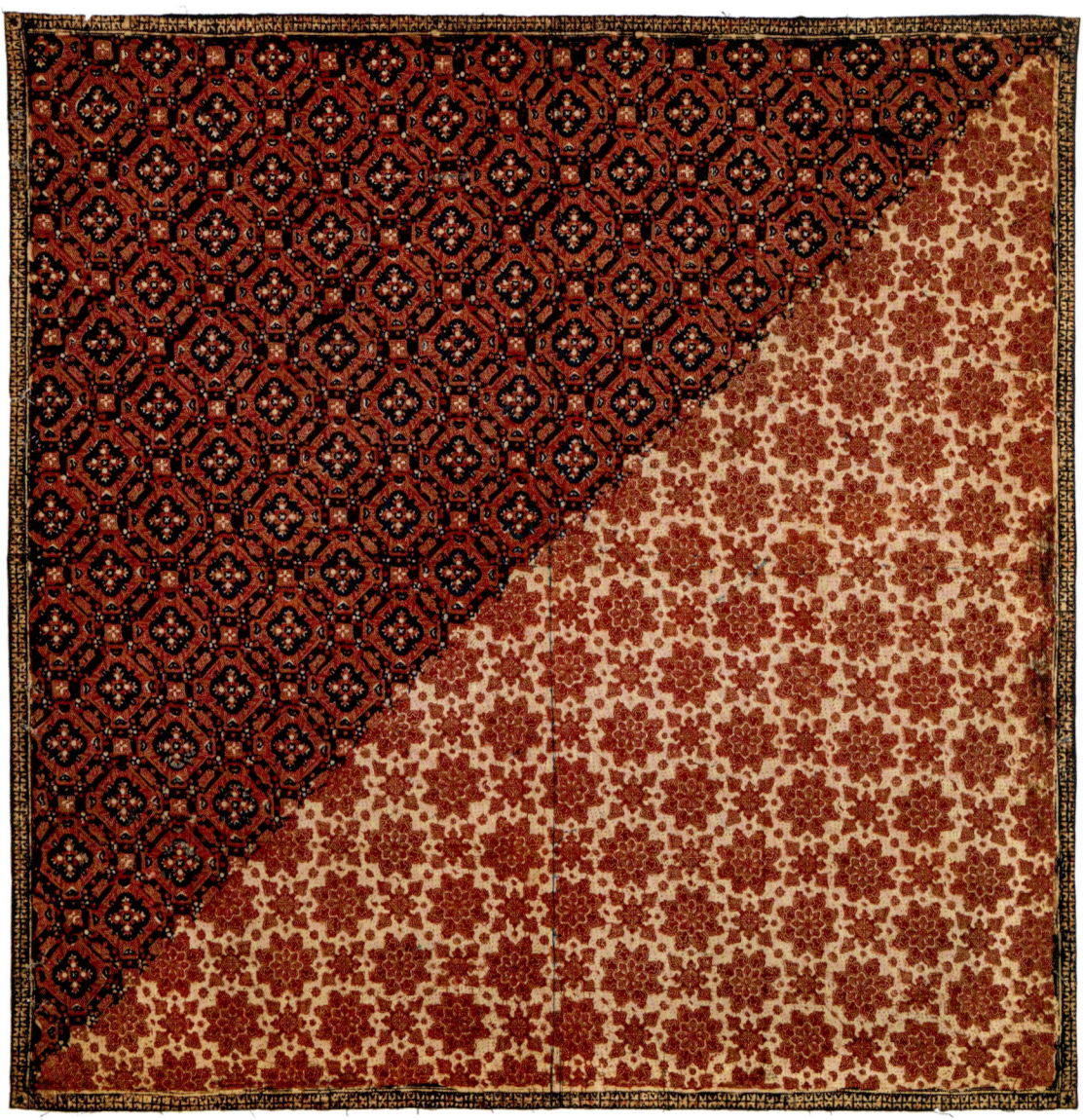

↑ **Colour** *Monochrome*
Batik head covering, Java, Indonesia, 20th century. The brown tones come from a dye from the bark of the soga tree. Dye recipes were handed down through generations of batik makers

→ **Colour** *Polychrome*
Chechaouen embroidery, Morocco, 18th century. The silk ground takes on yellow hues that are almost golden. It was replaced by actual gold thread in later examples

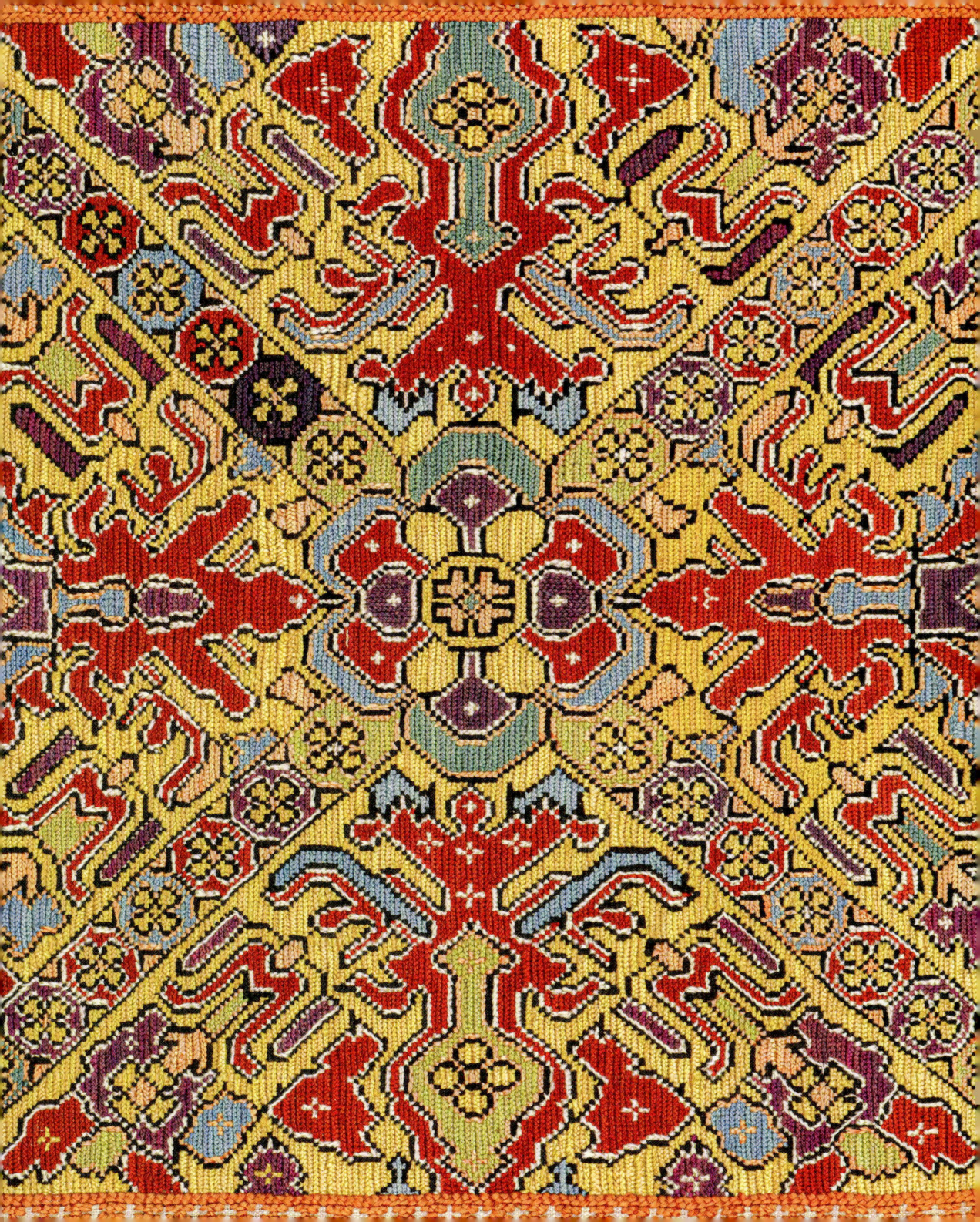

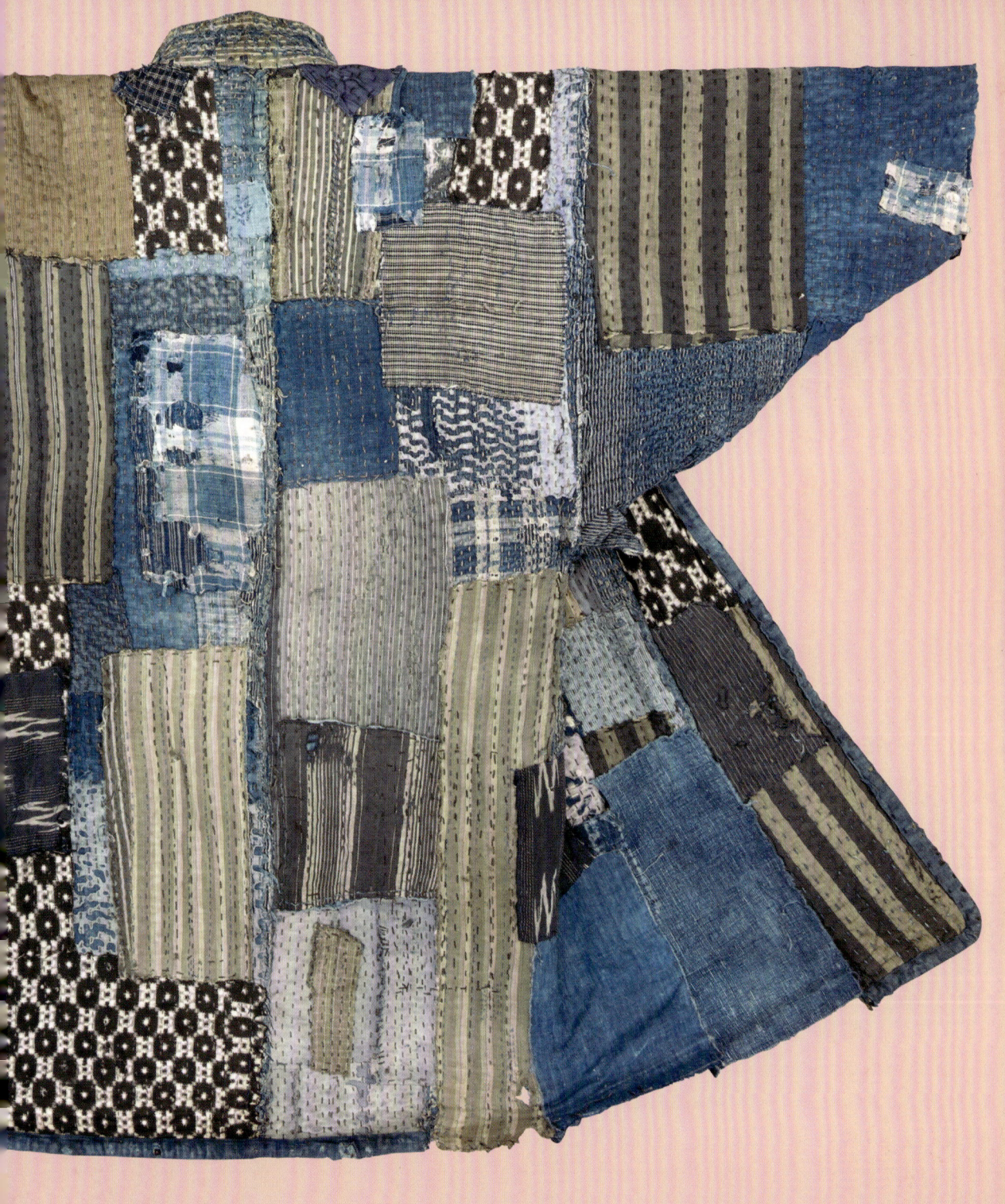

← **Composition** *Meaning*
Boro kimono, Japan, 19th century. The patched indigo cotton coat expresses a respect for materials borne out of limited resources. Cotton arrived relatively late in Japan, offering warmth and some waterproofing for farmers

↑ **Composition** *Meaning*
Shawl, southern Anti-Atlas, Morocco, 20th century. This shawl is dyed with indigo. Indigo is an imported dye, and several dye baths are needed to achieve this deep colour – making the shawl an expensive item

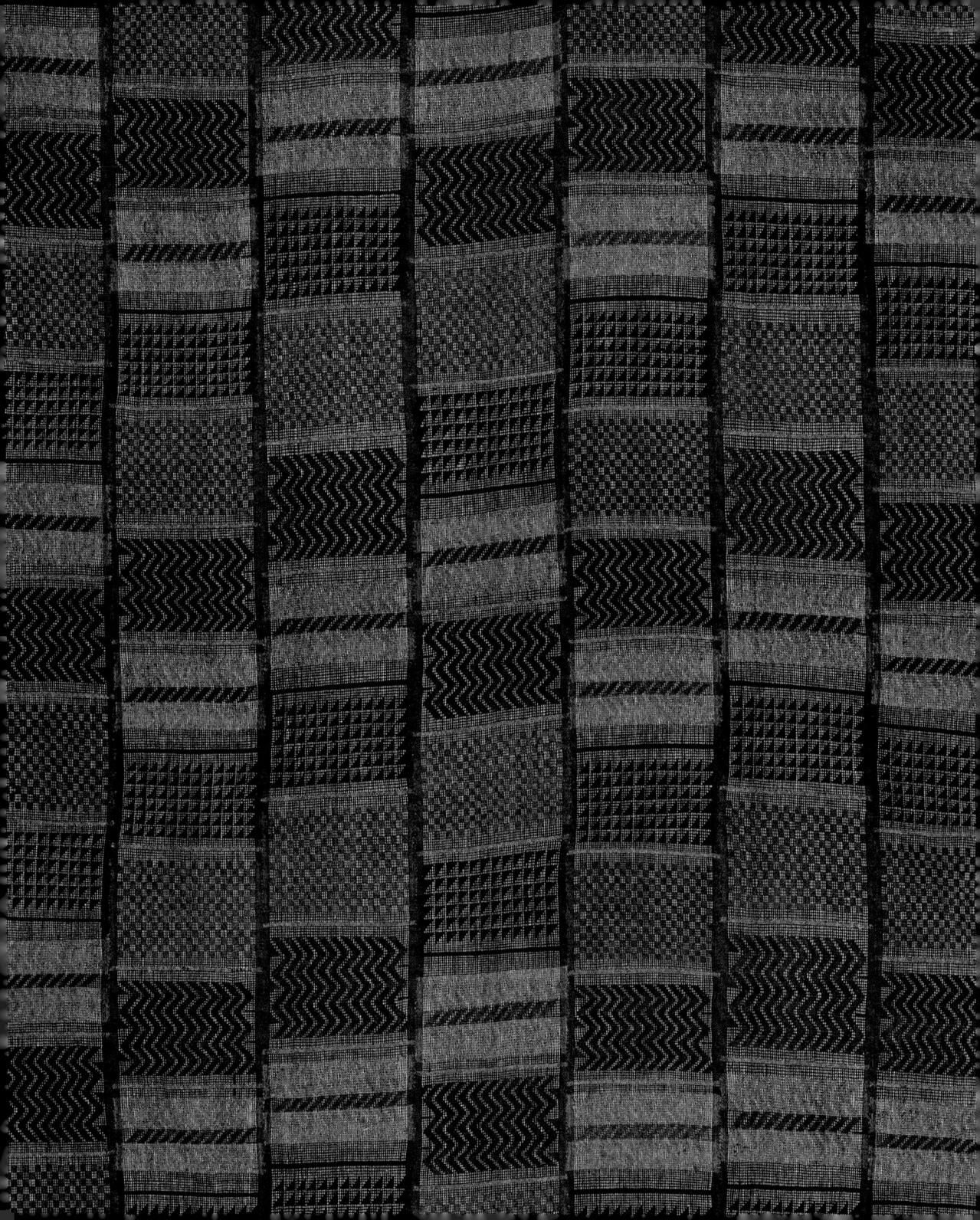

← Composition *Meaning*
Wearing cloth, Nigeria, 19th century. The unusual colour palette shows wealth: the handspun and locally dyed blue cotton is matched with imported green silk and a purple silk called alaari. Alaari was recycled from European silk weavings, overdyed to take on a purple colour and then traded across the Sahara to West Africa

→ Composition *Meaning*
Woman's shawl, southern Tunisia, 20th century. The red shawl is used for all social and religious occasions, with the colour symbolising the passage of a young girl to becoming a married woman. Such a shawl would be part of every bride's trousseau

↓ Composition *Meaning*
Bagh, Punjab, India, early 20th century. The ground of this head covering is golden with the addition of reds and blues and greens, rather than the two colours usually seen in earlier cloths. This is a sign of access to a wider variety of dyes in the villages of Punjab by this period. Although the front is almost completely covered with silk, the back has almost no trace; none was wasted in the unnecessary carrying of thread

↓↓ Composition *Meaning*
Kente cloth, Asante, Ghana, 19th century. This part of Africa was known as the Gold Coast, and the yellow ground of this all-silk cloth is locally called 'gold dust', a reference to the gold dust that was used as currency in the region in the period before the arrival of the colonial powers

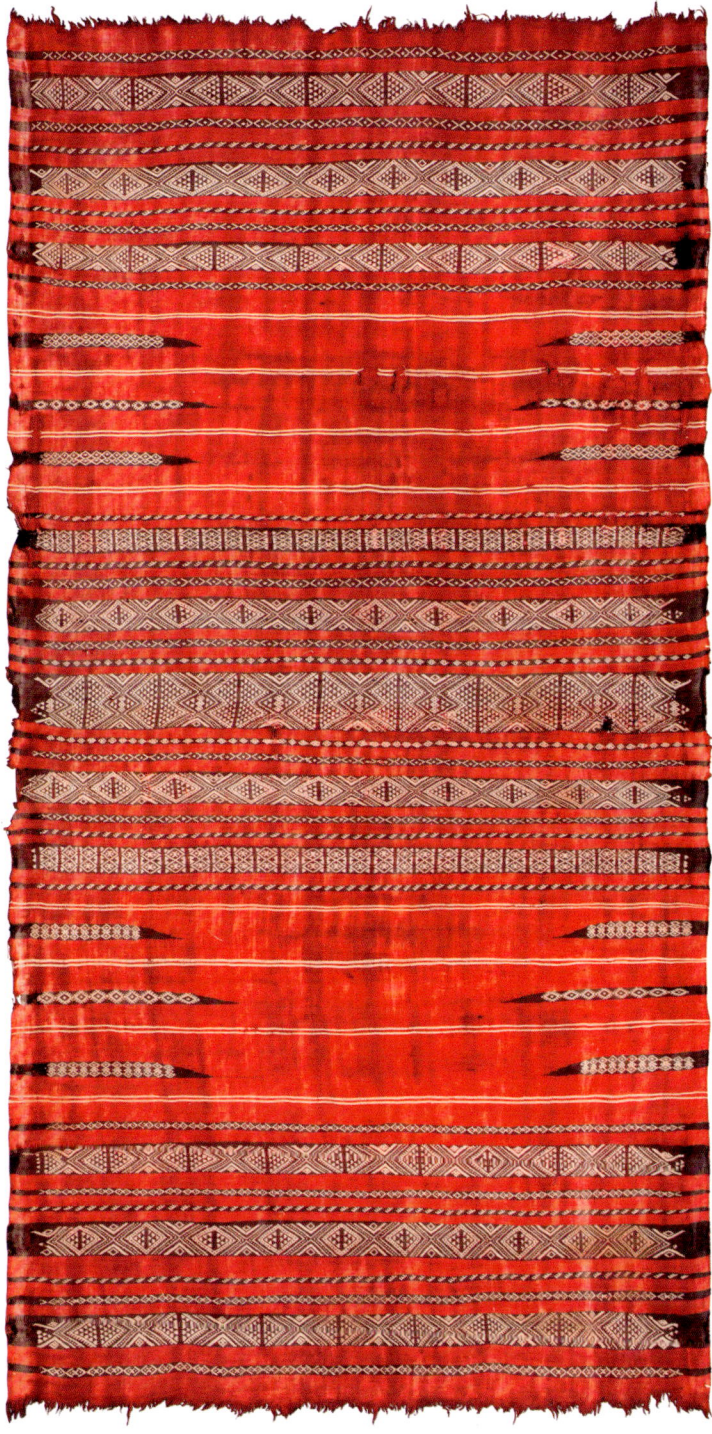

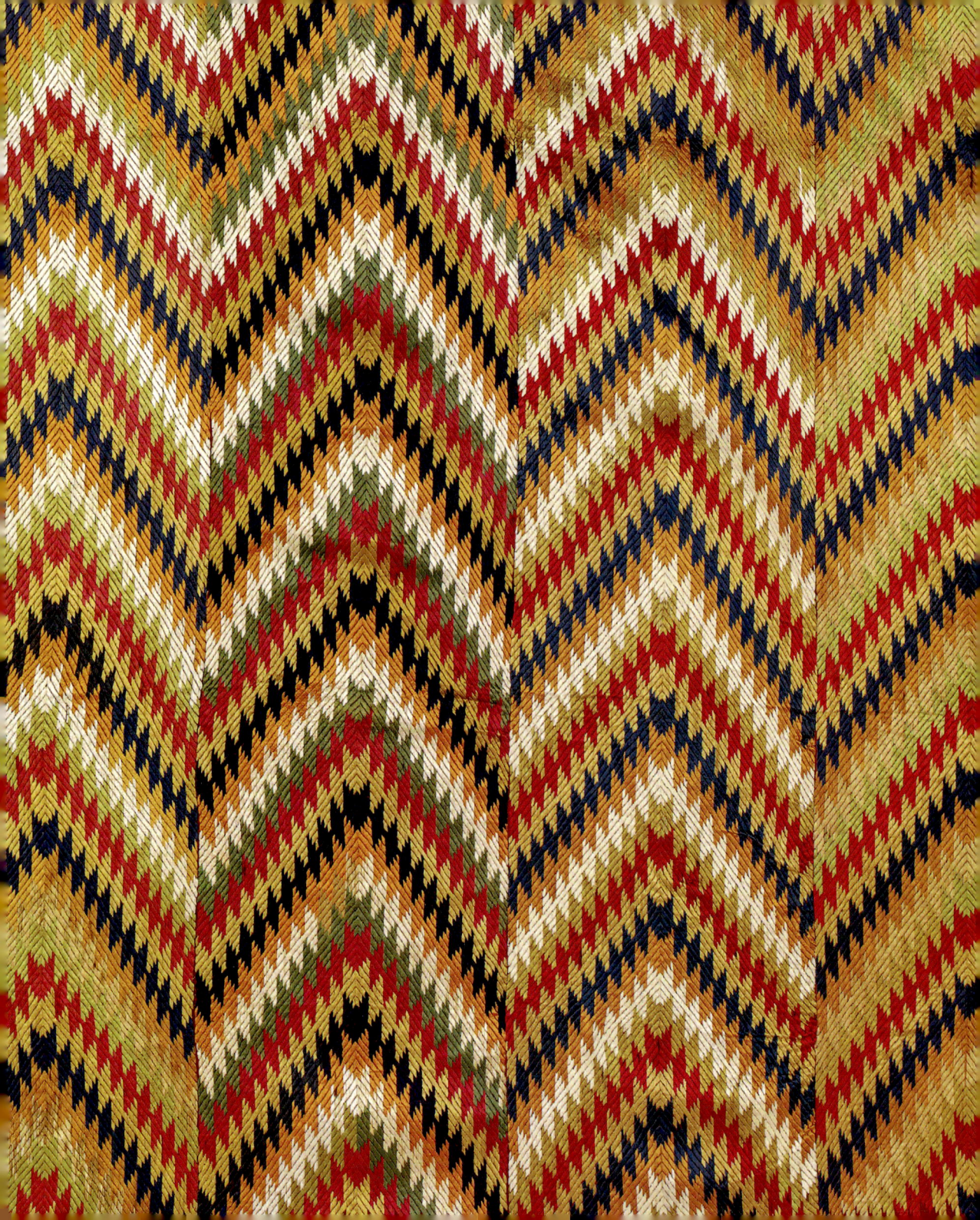

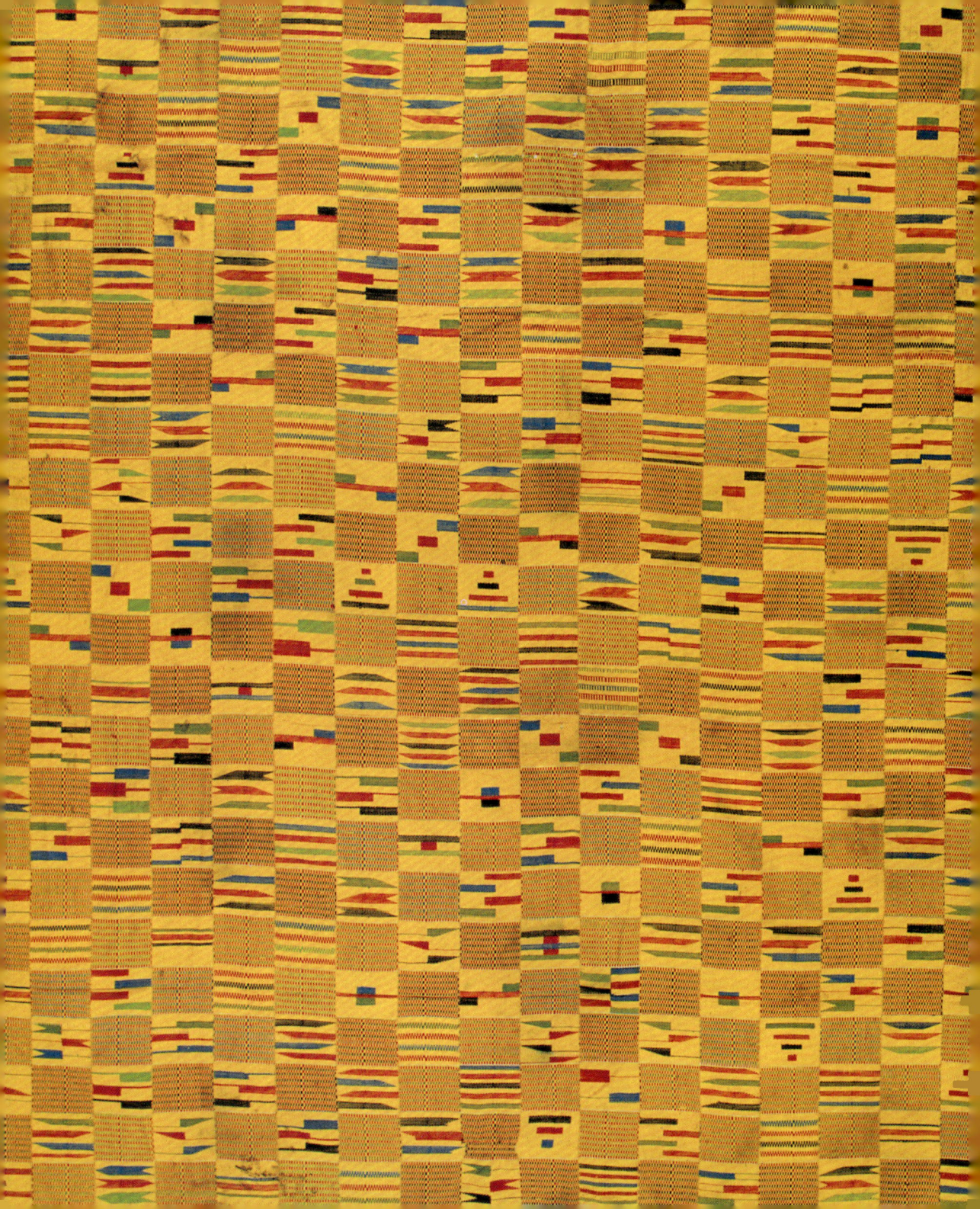

↓ **Composition** *Mark making*
Sampler, the Netherlands, 18th century. Young girls would learn to stitch in a variety of techniques by creating these samplers. In this example, there seems to be an attempt to create a pleasing composition, reflecting the intention for this to be a display item as well as a learning tool

→ **Composition** *Mark making*
Sampler, the Netherlands, 18th century. From this sampler, we get a taste of how clothes would be mended in Holland in the 1780s. Clothing was expensive and therefore carefully looked after – a far cry from the fast fashion that is widespread today

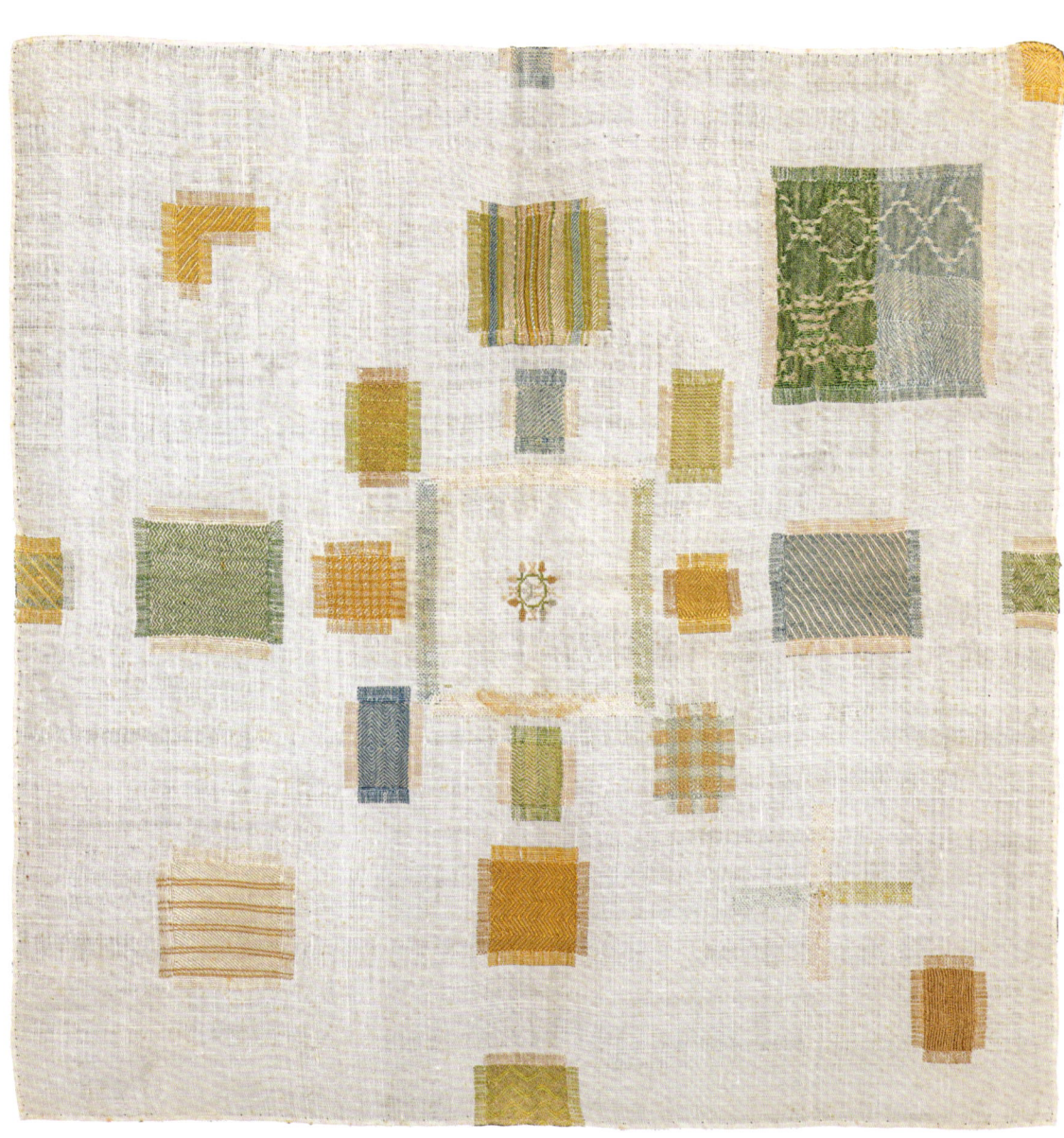

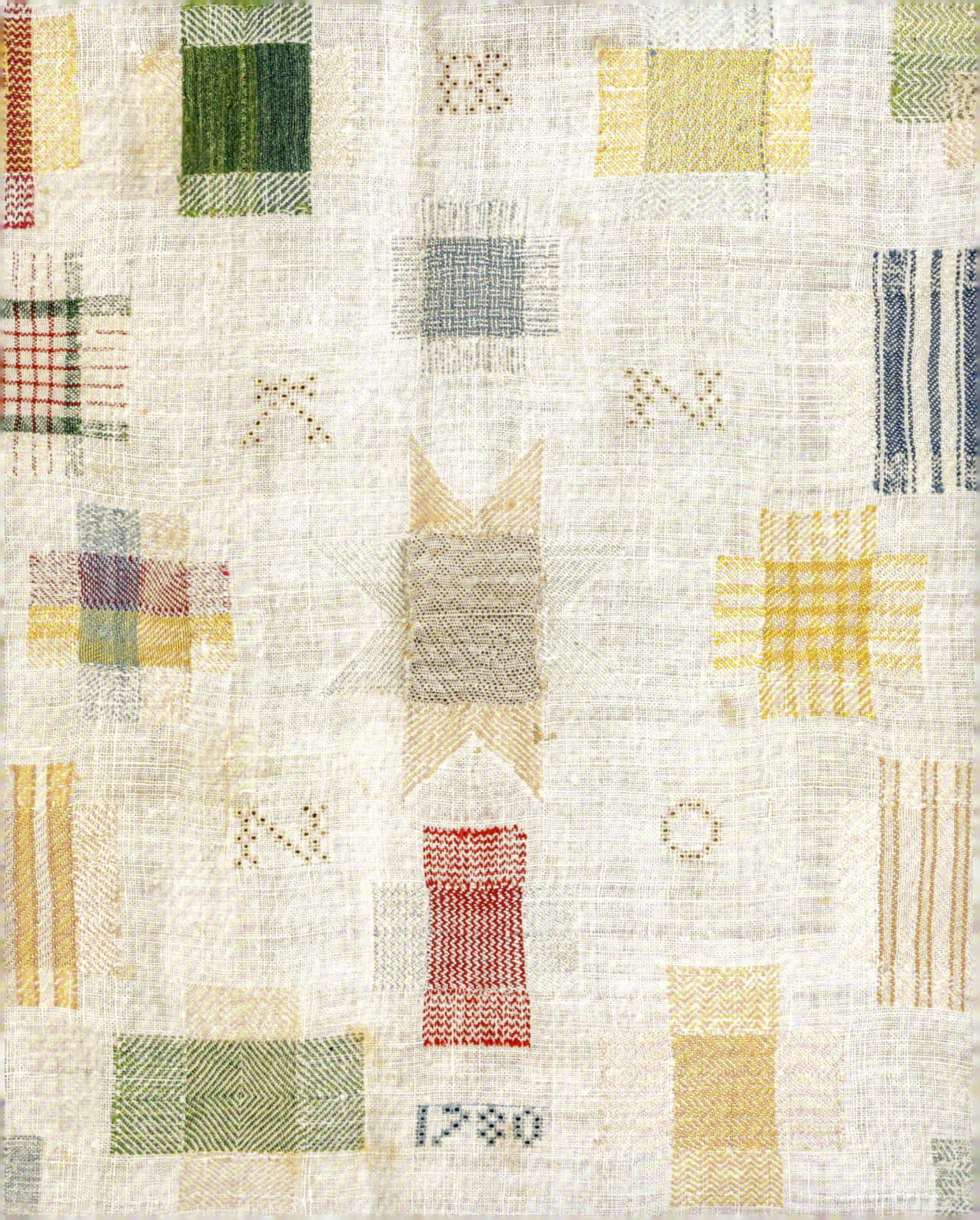

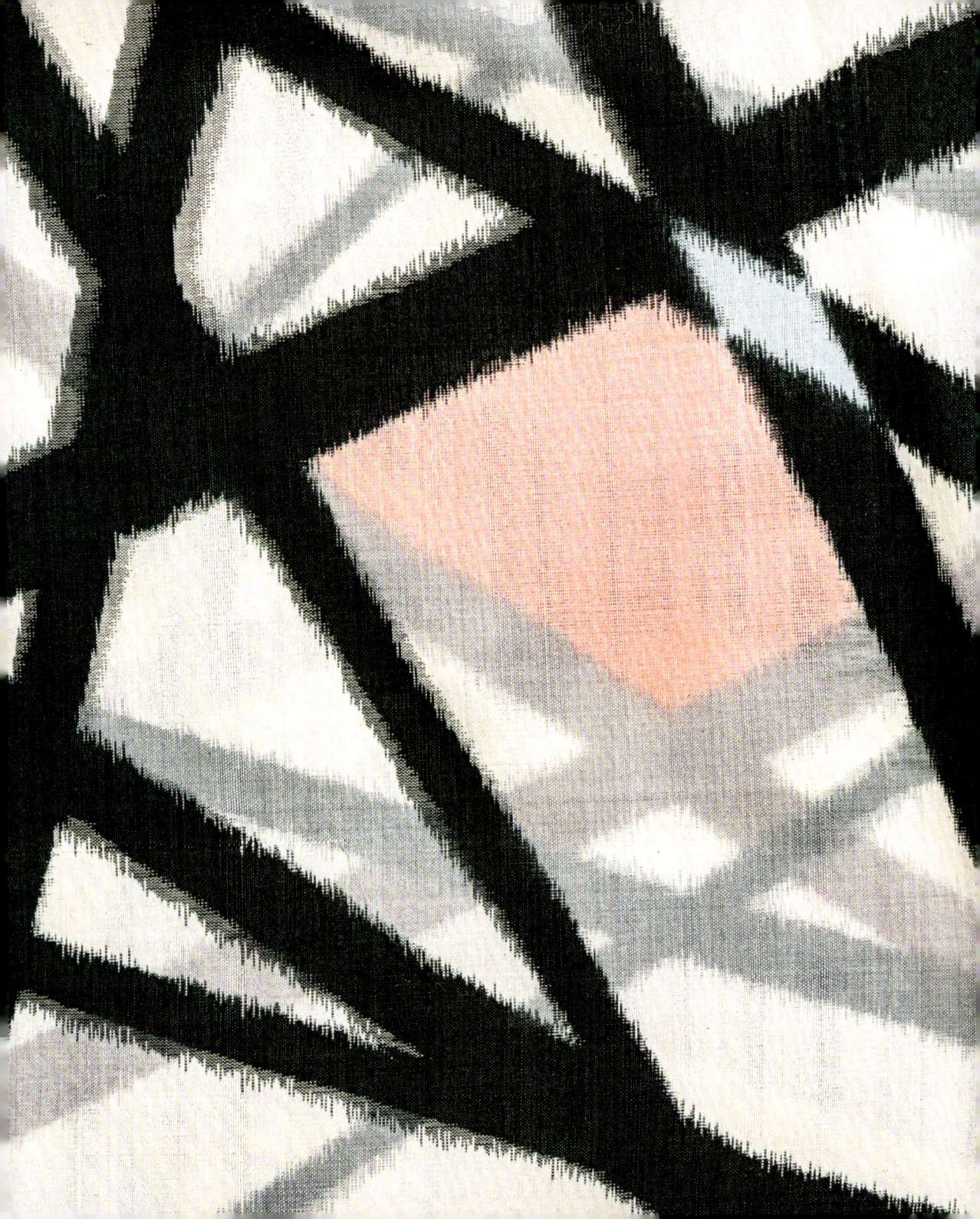

↑↑ **Composition** *Mark making*
Cape, Pashtun, Afghanistan, 20th century. The scale of the
embroidery and its intensity of hue makes it vibrate against the
black ground. The stitches are bold and confident

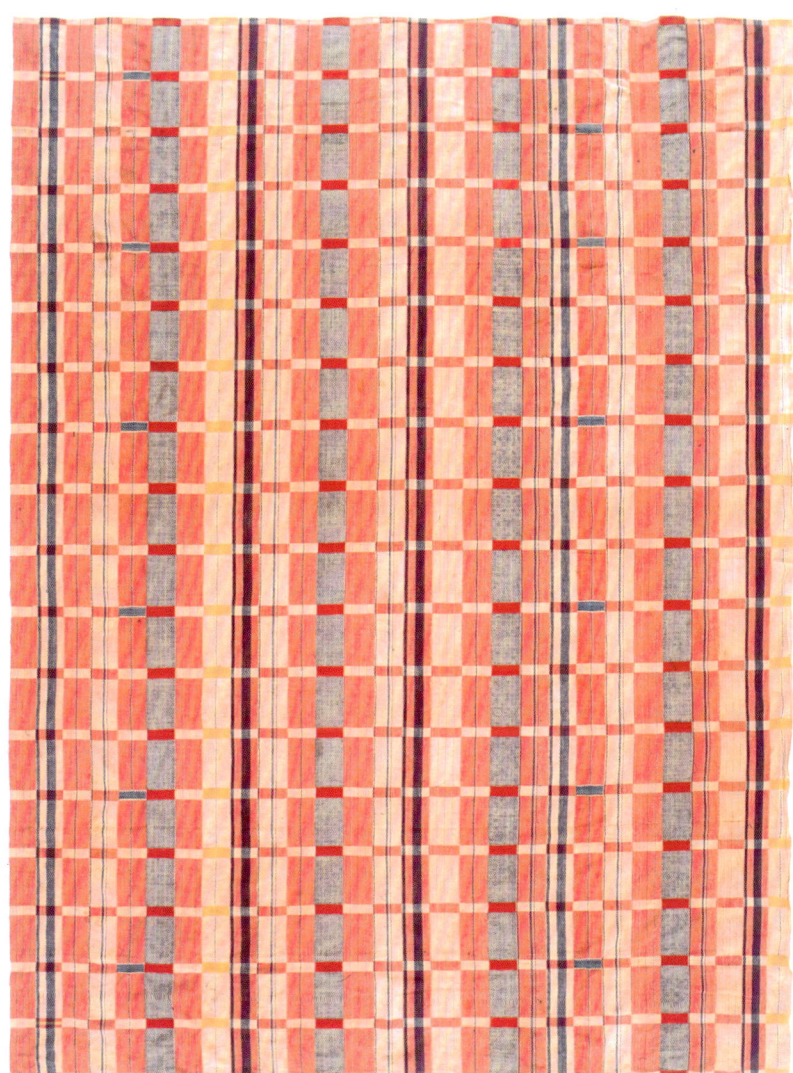

← **Composition** *Modernism*
Meisen kimono, Japan, 20th century. This robe is inspired by early
20th-century art. In this period Japan was modernising and
moving away from traditional conservative taste. Through these
kimonos, middle-class women showed their outward-looking
modern taste

↑ **Composition** *Modernism*
Ewe wearing cloth, east Ghana, 19th century. This looks like a
modernist textile, but is in fact a traditional cloth made from 28
vertical strips. Each strip was woven separately and then joined
to its peers, a process requiring the weaver to carefully plan the
design sitting down at the loom

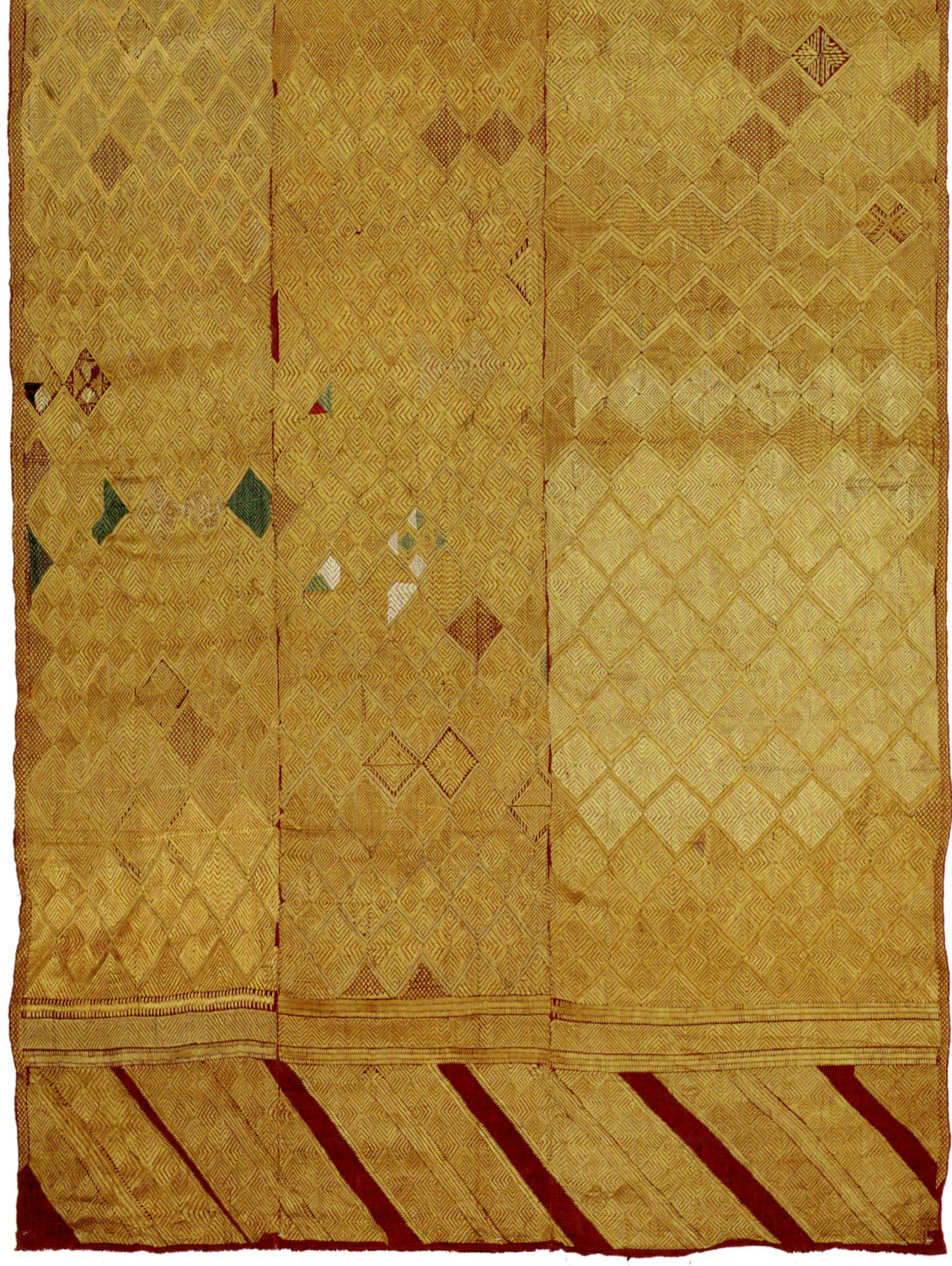

← **Composition** *Colour field*
Bagh, Punjab, India, late 19th century. This shawl is fully
embroidered in gold-coloured floss silk on a red ground,
which can be glimpsed through the gold field. Carefully laid
stitches create rhythm and depth in a textile that relies on very
few colours; the embroidery is carefully executed so that the
shimmering silk reflects light at different angles across the field

↑ **Composition** *Colour field*
Headscarf, Anti-Atlas, Morocco, 20th century. Half of this textile
is resist dyed with henna – a fairly straightforward process that
produces an astonishing result. This remarkable colour field
composition, for all of its contemporary appeal, is part of a
design heritage going back centuries. Textiles are special in the
way they combine the artistic with utilitarian

↓ **Composition** *Colour field*

Asafo flag, Ghana, 19th century. This unique flag has no pictorial element or visual allusion to a proverb, the normal components of an Asafo flag. It is unusual in its purely aesthetic approach and use of patchwork. Four colours is all it takes to create this memorable design

→ **Composition** *Colour field*

Woman's apron, East Asia, 20th century. The astonishingly bright colours of this apron are made using natural dyes. The intensity is achieved by submerging the yarns multiple times in the dye vat. The colours are then carefully arranged into gradated bands, making this a textile colour field composition

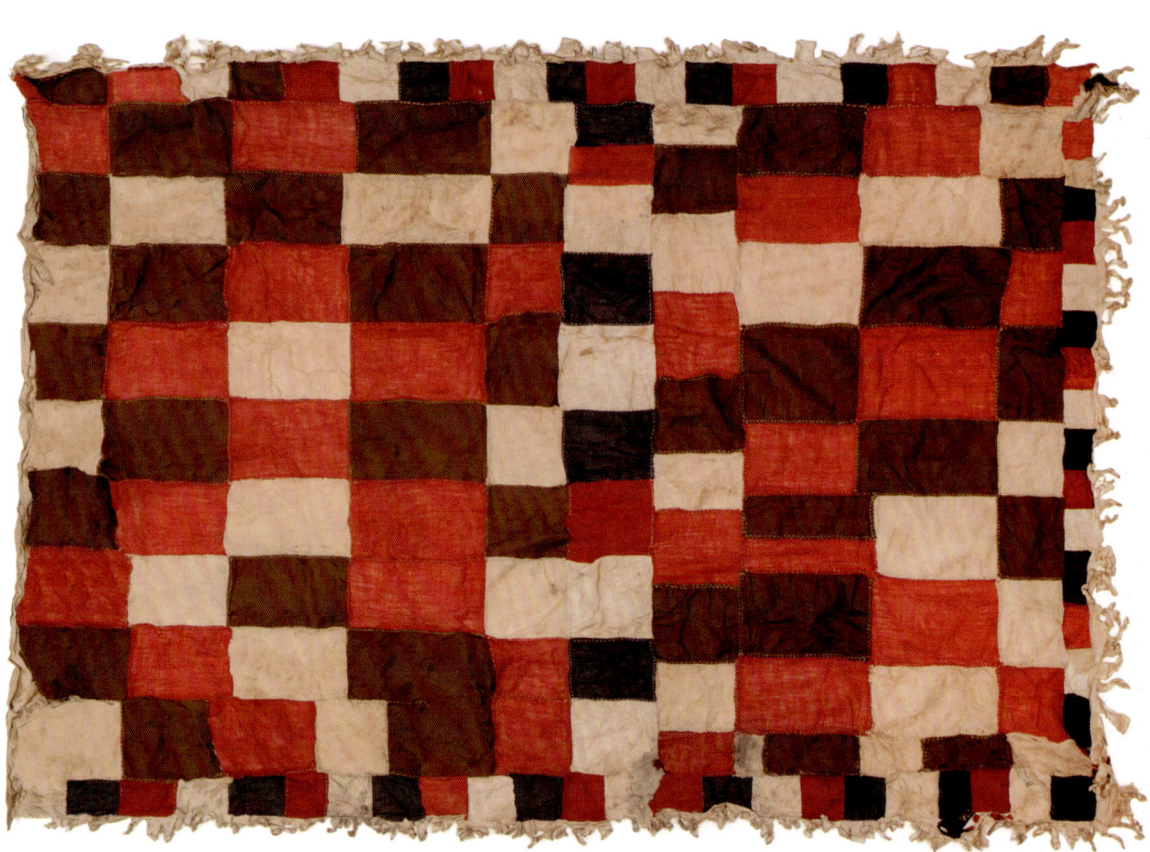

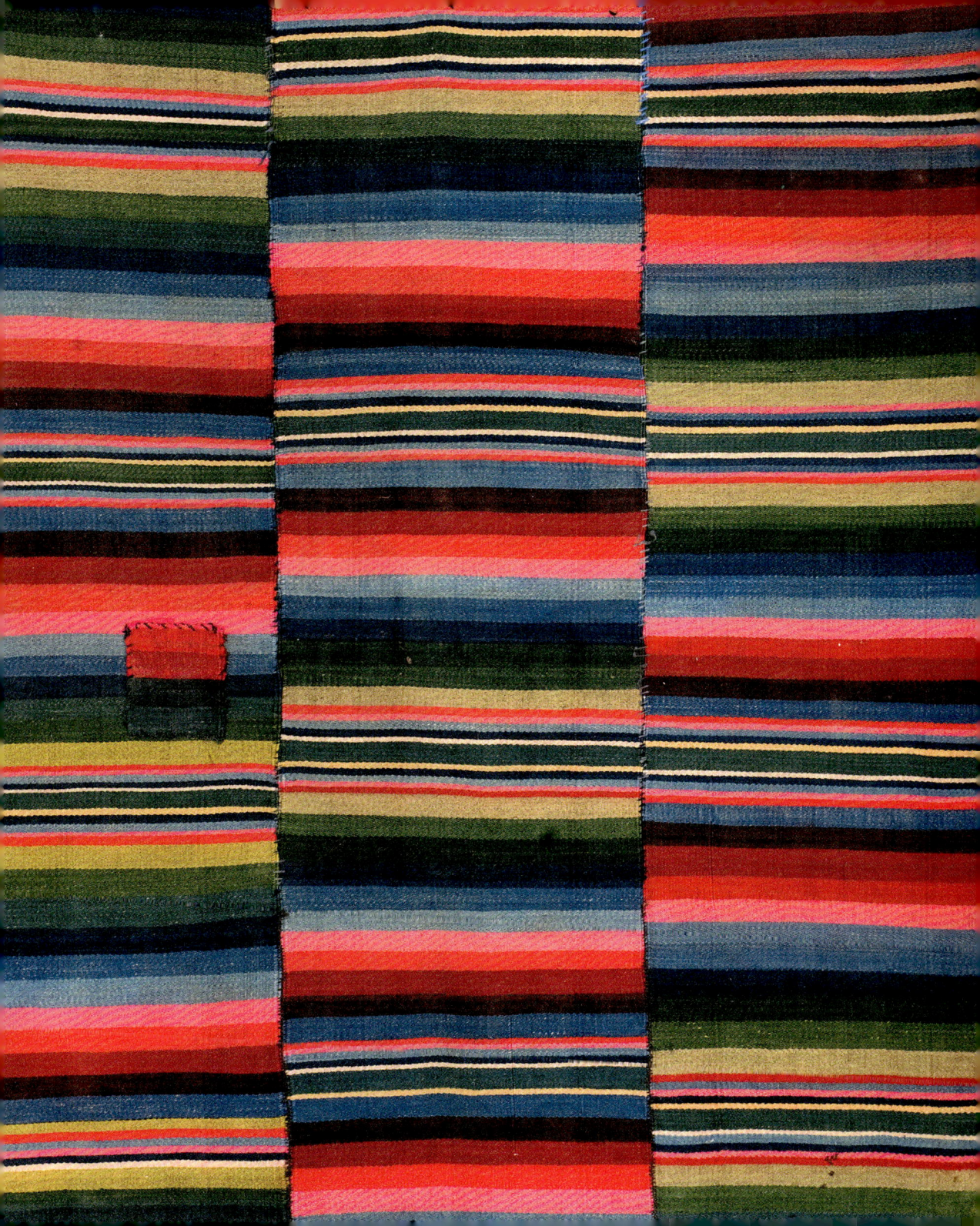

↓ Composition *Circles*

Meisen kimono, Japan, 20th century. It is clear from first glance that this kimono is woven in sections. An effort has been made to join together the yellow and red circles across the hems

→ Composition *Circles*

Shawl, Rajasthan, India, 20th century. These overlaid and interconnecting circles are made using a tie-dye technique. Small seeds are tied into the cotton, protecting small areas from the dye, leaving them white or ready to be dyed in a different shade

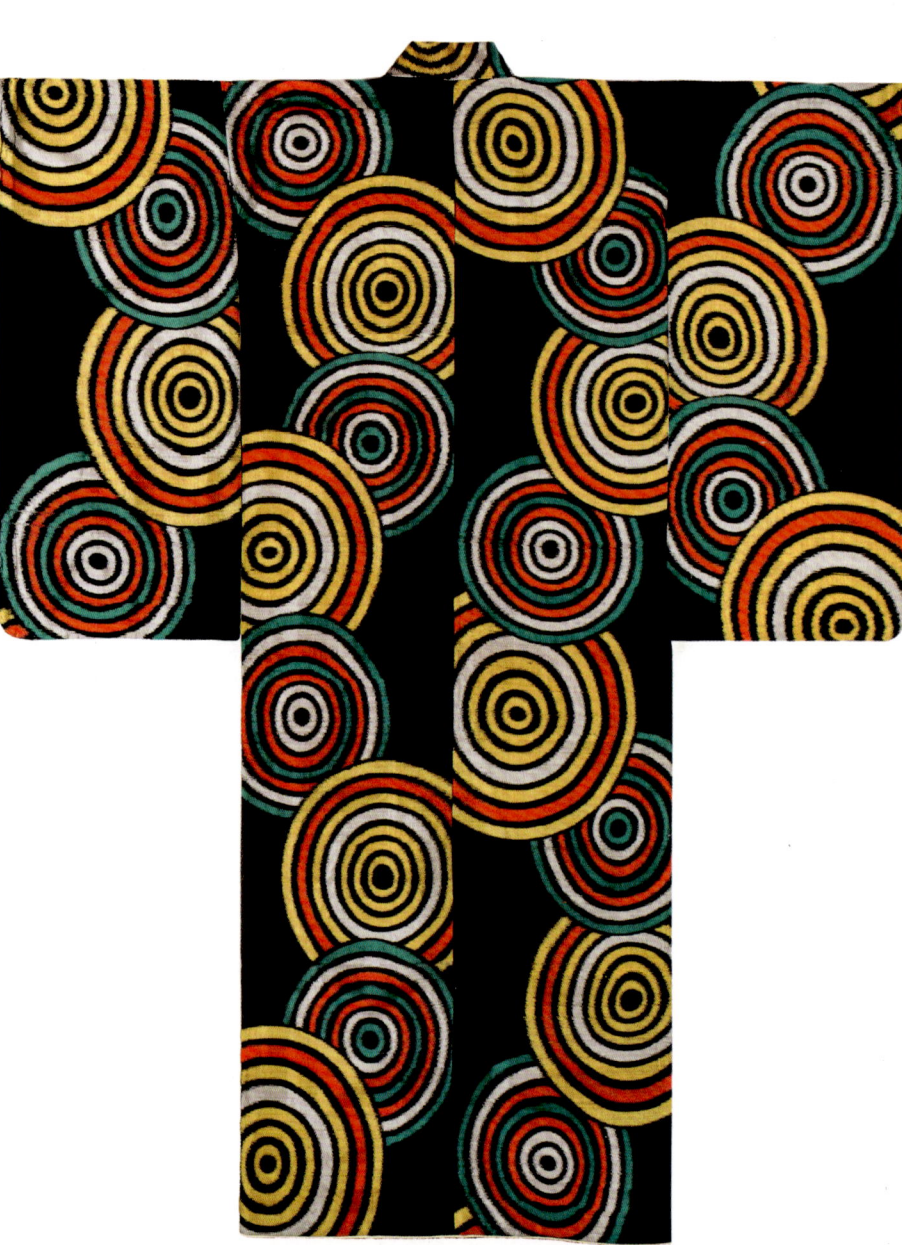

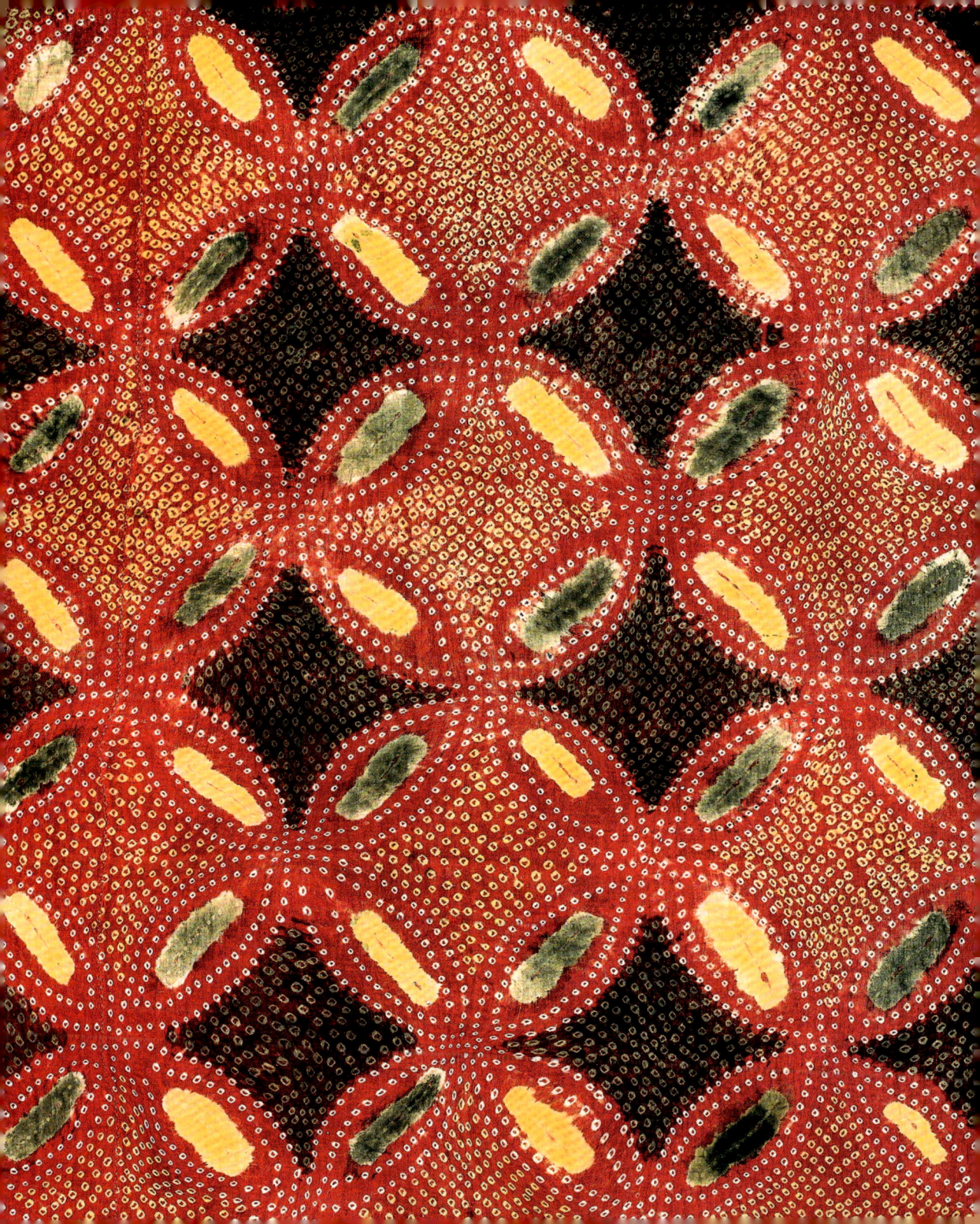

↓ **Composition** *Abstract*
Sampler, the Netherlands, dated 1824. This needlework
sampler reads more like an abstract picture than an
instructional tool. The overlaying and combining of the
stitches is particularly pleasing, creating new patterns

→ **Composition** *Abstract*
Prestige display cloth, Mende, Sierra Leone, 19th century. Here
the patterns are made by inserting extra black wefts. The comb
motifs in the centre probably represent amulets, and may have
a protective function

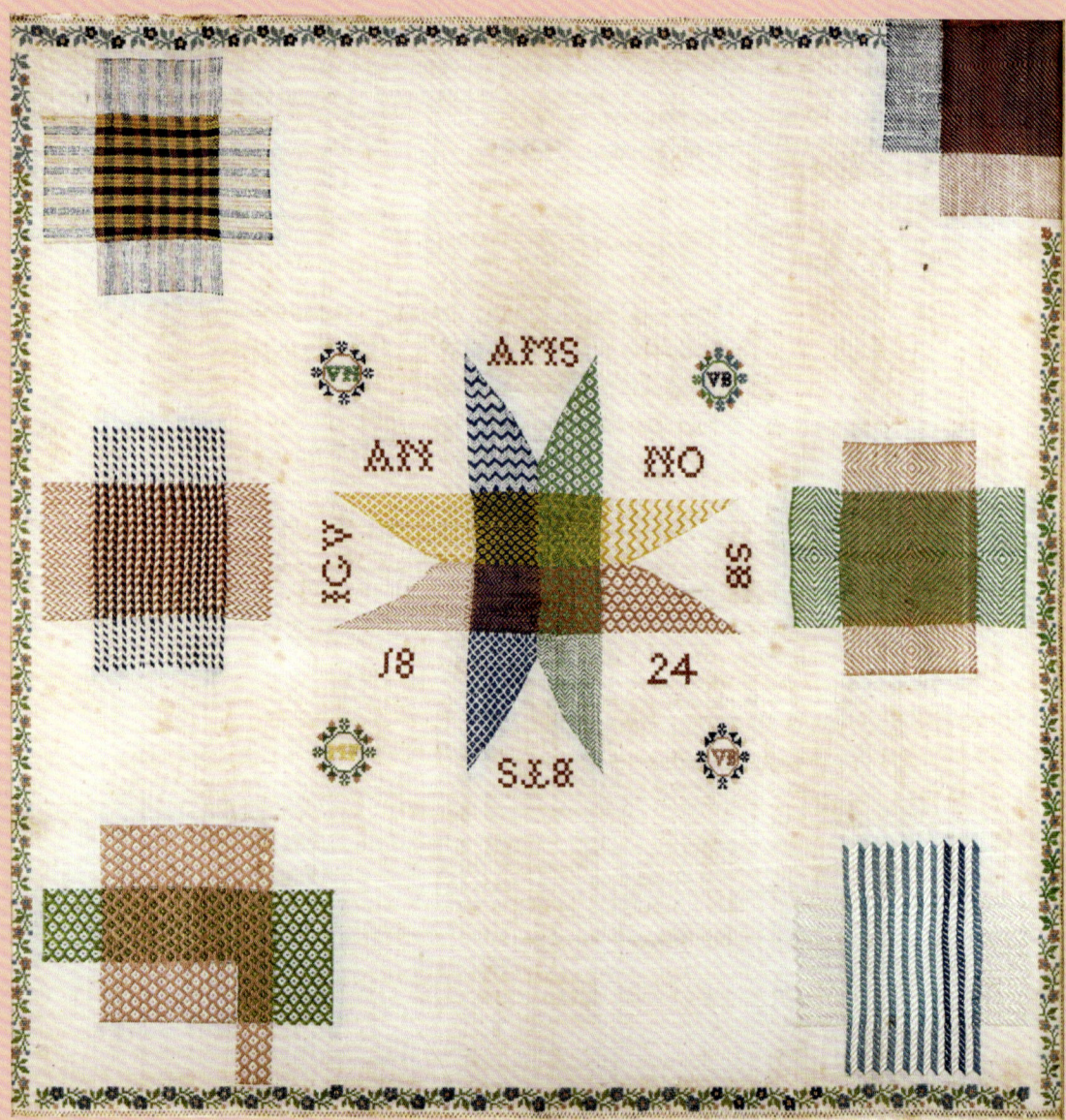

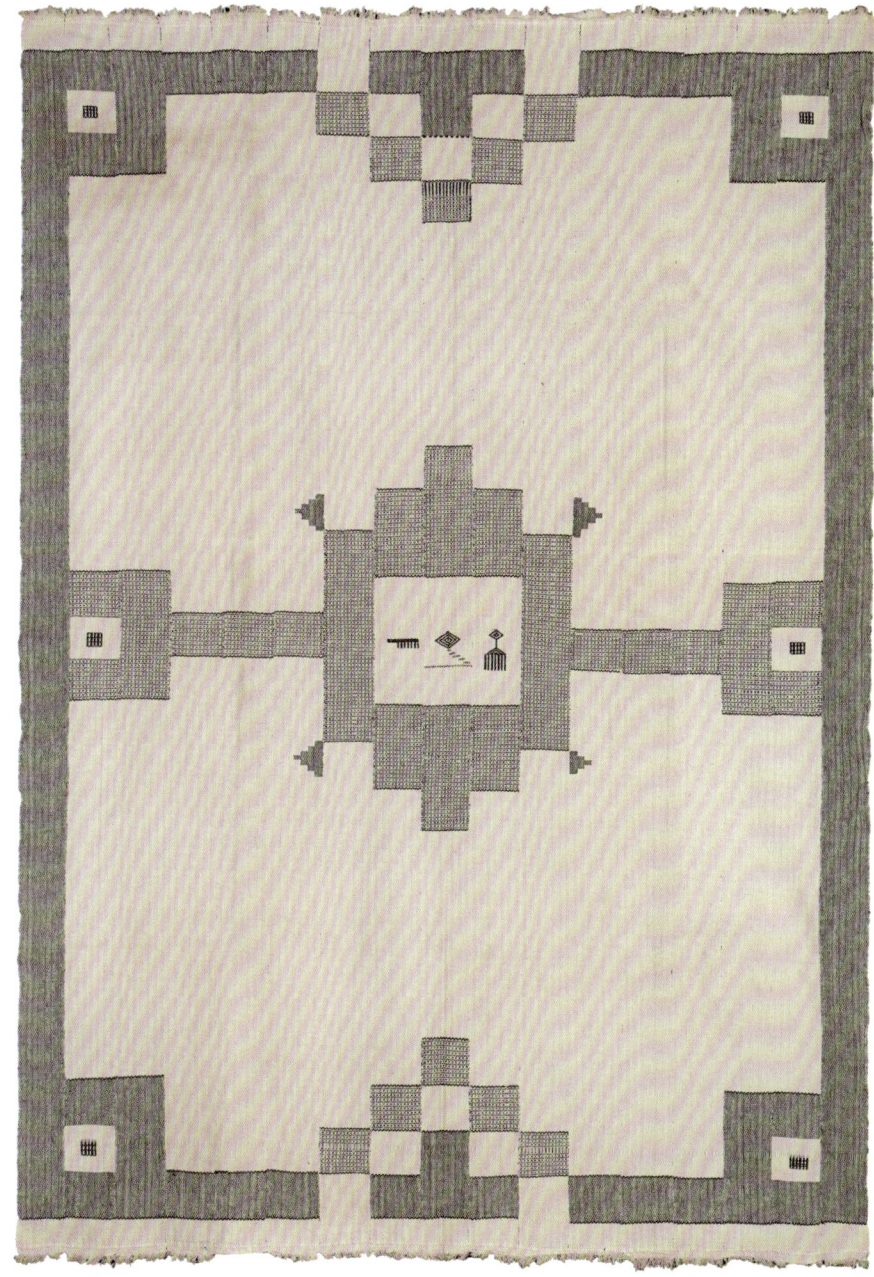

↓ **Composition** *Maximalism*
Ceremonial cloth, Gujarat, India, 13th–14th century. The resist-dyed and block-printed pattern consists of huge leaves. The effect is reminiscent of moving through dense jungle

↓↓ **Composition** *Maximalism*
Shawl, Kashmir, India, 19th century. The fractal-like paisley design of this shawl radiates from a central circle. It is no wonder this groovy pattern had a revival in the 1960s

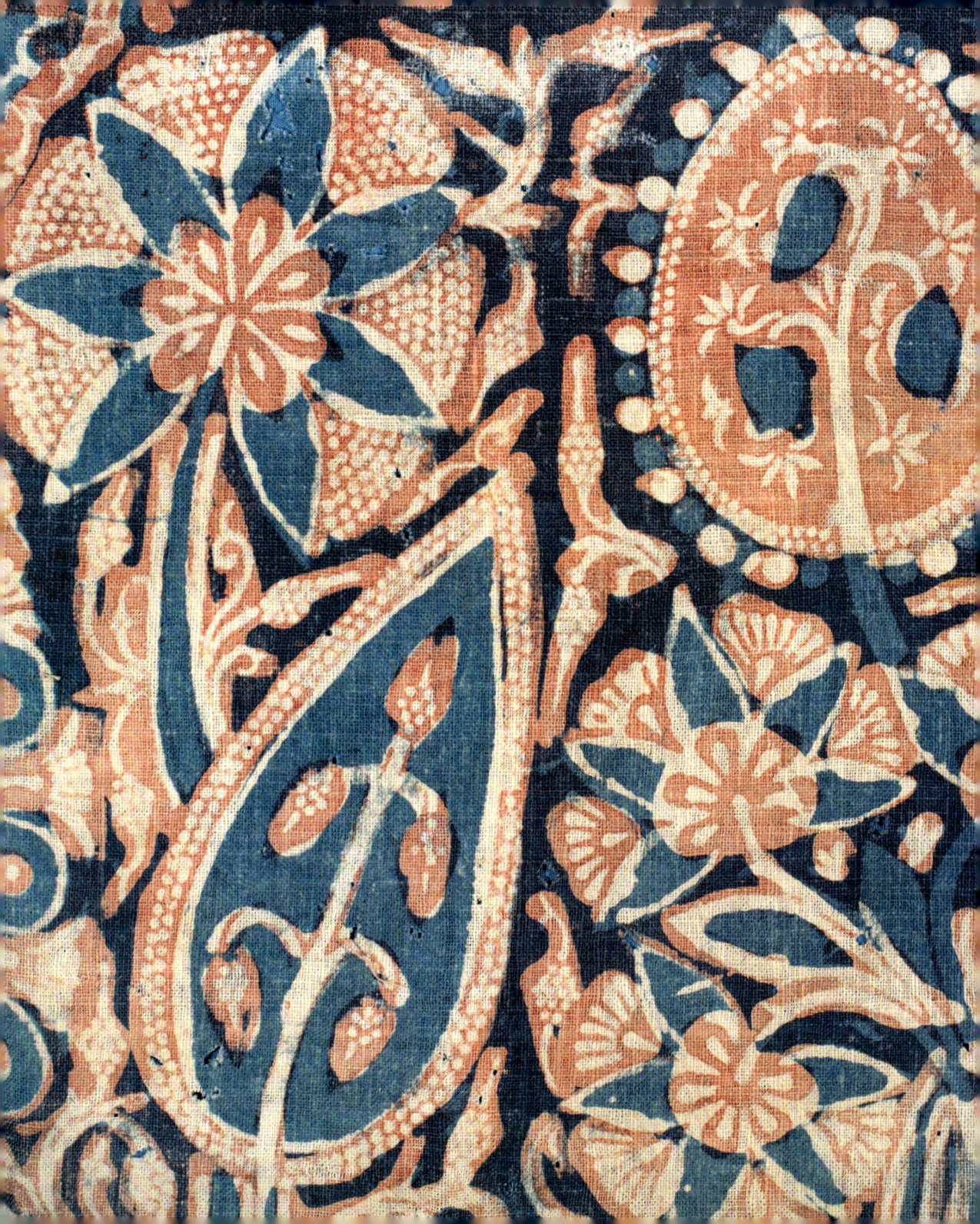